Accountability
IN AMERICAN EDUCATION

Frank J. Sciara

Richard K. Jantz

Ball State University

ALLYN AND BACON, INC., BOSTON

Library of Congress Catalog Card Number: 74–188225

Contributing Authors

Robert F. Alioto, Superintendent of Schools, Pearl River, New York; Dwight H. Allen, Dean, School of Education, University of Massachusetts; George A. Baker III, Program Associates, RELCV Junior College Division; Terrel H. Bell, Deputy Commissioner for School Systems, U.S. Office of Education; Kuno E. Beller, Department of Psychology, Temple University; C. A. Bowers, Department of Educational Foundations, University of Oregon; Conrad Briner, Professor and Chairman, Faculty of Education, Claremont Graduate School; Richard L. Brownell, Program Associates, RELCV Junior College Division; Robert Buser, Associate Professor of Secondary Education, Southern Illinois University; Robert L. Crowson, Bureau of Higher Education, Michigan Department of Education; Arthur L. Costa, Associate Professor of Education, Sacramento State College; Luvern L. Cunningham, Dean, College of Education, The Ohio State University; D. D. Darland, Associate Executive Secretary, National Commission on Teacher Education and Professional Standards; Don Davies, Deputy Commissioner for Development, U.S. Office of Education; Henry S. Dyer, Vice President, Educational Testing Service; Joe Ellis, Professor of Secondary Education, Northern Illinois University; Mario Fantini, Dean of Education, State University College, New Paltz, New York; Rudolph J. Fobert, Superintendent of Schools, Lexington, Massachusetts; Edith Green, U.S. Representative, Third Congressional District, Oregon; Lloyd Hendrickson, Minot State College; Girard D. Hottleman, Director of Educational Services, Massachusetts Teachers Association; Peter A. Janssen, Station WETA-TV, Washington, D.C.; Christopher Jencks, School of Education, Harvard University; David L. Jesser, Associate Director, Improving State Leadership in Education, Denver; J. A. Jungherr, Assistant Superintendent for Business, Pearl River, New York; Roger A. Kaufman, Professor of Human Behavior, Graduate School of Human Behavior, U.S. International University; Robert E. Kraner, President, EPIC Diversified Systems Corporation; Burton W. Kreitlow, Professor of Adult Education, The University of Wisconsin; W. Stanley Kruger, Chief, Program Development Staff, Division of Plane and Supplementary Centers, U.S. Office of Education; Leon M. Lessinger, Professor of Education, Georgia State University; Felix M. Lopez, President, IMPART, Inc.; Teresa MacNeil, Department of Adult Education, St. Francis Xavier University, Nova Scotia; Alfred J. Mannebach, Research Coordination Unit, University of Kentucky; Reed Martin, Education Turnkey Systems, Washington, D.C.; Albert V. Mayrhofer, Vice President for Research and Development, Learning Foundations, School Services, Inc.; T. R. McConnell, Center for Research and Development in Higher Education, University of California; Floyd L. McKinney, Research Coordination Unit, University of Kentucky; Edward J. Meade, Jr., Program Officer-In-Charge, Public Education Program; James Mecklenburger, EPOA Fellow, Instructional Systems Technology, Indiana University; William A. Mehrens, Department of Counseling, Personnel Services and Educational Psychology, Michigan State University; John D. Millett, Ohio Board of Regents, Columbus; William G. Milliken, Governor of Michigan; Edgar L. Morphet, Director, Improving State Leadership in Education, Denver; John E. Morris, Assistant Professor of Professional Laboratory Experiences, Georgia Southern College; Robert J. Nash, Assistant Professor of Education, University of Vermont; Samuel Nash, New Haven, Connecticut, Public Schools; Russell W. Peterson, Governor of Delaware; John W. Polley, Assistant Commissioner, New York State Department of Education; David Rice, President, Evansville Campus, Indiana State University; John E. Rouché, Director of RELCV Junior College Division; Ronald Schwartz, McGraw-Hill World News Bureau, Washington, D.C.; Ralph W. Tyler, Science Research Associates, Inc., Chicago; Harold V. Webb, Publisher, American School Board Journal; Robert L. Whitt, Professor, Drake University; Thomas P. Wilbur, Michigan Department of Education; Aaron Wildavsky, Graduate School of Public Affairs, University of California; Amos A. Wilder, Motown Records, Detroit; Charles H. Wilson, Chancellor, North Orange County Community College District; John Wilson, EPDA Fellow, Instructional Systems Technology, Indiana University

Contents

Preface

One of the most rapidly growing and widespread movements in education today is educational accountability. Fed by federal funds and foundation grants and nurtured by the vested interests of various groups, private learning corporations, concerned taxpayers, alarmed administrators, and school board members, the concept of accountability manifests itself in a variety of forms. The profound impact the accountability concept is making on thought and practice in schools is important to all serious students of American education.

The purpose of this book is to provide critically selected articles which trace the development, problems, potential forms, and current practices in educational accountability. Articles were selected in an attempt to include many philosophical as well as practical viewpoints from authors representative of the groups concerned about public education in general and accountability in particular.

Part I traces the development of the accountability concept, examines the philosophical bases of various interest groups, and probes the roles of school personnel and institutions from a variety of perspectives.

In Part II, a number of approaches for realizing educational accountability are scrutinized. These approaches range from the most talked about to those that are little known but also offer promise. Reports of accountability projects already attempted are also to be found in this section.

Each Part is followed by a bibliography of corollary references of benefit to readers desiring additional information.

It is our hope that this book provides a deeper understanding as well as definitive direction for educational accountability. This book may be used profitably in several ways: as a supplement to such courses as school administration, supervision, educational foundations, or trends and issues in education; as a source book for practitioners and advanced students concerned with examining important views, trends, and issues in educational accountability; or as a reference for anyone wishing to gain insight into the developing role of educational accountability in American schools.

The editors wish to express sincere appreciation to the authors, editors, and publishers who gave permission to reprint their material in this book.

Part I

The Call to Accountability

The age of accountability is dawning in American education and could well become one of the most important educational movements in the decade of the 1970s. Beginning as a flickering spark in the twilight of the 60s, and fanned into flame by the federal government, politicians, taxpayers, unhappy parents, as well as private learning corporations, accountability has been transformed from a theoretical notion to a formidable force in American education.

Although the term is so new a precise definition has yet to emerge, its general meaning and thrust are quite clear: "the condition of being accountable, liable, or responsible" (*Webster's New World Dictionary*). Basically, accountability means that public schools must prove that students at various levels meet some reasonable standard of achievement. The concept further implies that schools must show they use funds wisely—that expenditures justify educational outcomes.

School personnel are being pushed to explain the efficacy of their programs. A new definition of the adequate school is being forged on the anvil of public opinion. Public opinion polls over the past few years have consistently recorded substantial majorities favoring teacher accountability. No longer are the majority of taxpayers satisfied with the old triad of the past—qualified teachers, the latest equipment and methods, and modern school plants—as indicators of effective schools.

Because our society is so complex, major influences that brought the accountability concept to the forefront of thinking regarding America's schools are not easily distinguishable. Some give credit to the report of the Commission on Equal Educational Opportunity (Coleman Report), which concluded that input into a school (such as reduced class size, new buildings, modern equipment) is not a reliable measure of how good the school is. Others cite the effect of the U.S. Office of Education when in late 1969 it began requiring program audits for Title VII (bilingual) and Title VIII (dropout prevention) programs. Whereas programs funded through the USOE formerly required only fiscal audits, this new requirement audited the program through previously established student performance goals. And President Nixon emphasized the concept of accountability when he stated in his address on educational reform in early 1970, "We have, as a nation, too long avoided thinking of the productivity of schools."

The National Assessment Program has been another influence on the movement towards educational accountability. Attempting to establish a qualitative measure of American educational efforts, the program concentrates on determining what youngsters know and can use in problem solving. A sample of the body of knowledge which persons of a certain age group can reasonably be expected to command is utilized to make such an assessment. Without doubt, the philosophy underlying the entire national assessment movement has cast its shadow over local school districts. Findings reported through the National Assessment Program will undoubtedly exert some influence on local schools and indicate new directions for them to take.

As educational budgets continue to spiral upward, there has been greater pressure by taxpayers and parents for school accountability. With the largest portion of educational budgets allocated to salaries, a more sophisticated audience is questioning the relationship between school costs and student performance. The issue has not become a question of whether to have accountability, but an attempt to determine what kind of accountability is to prevail. Allied with this issue is the question of who is accountable: board members, administrators, or teachers? The growing public demand for a system of accountability that will improve student performance must be met.

Should teachers be held accountable? An opinion poll of a national sample of school administrators, conducted by *Nation's Schools*[1] in late 1970, revealed that 72 percent favored teacher accountability. It is significant, however, that a mere 23 percent favored the use of internal incentives with teachers.

David Wagoner, a school board member, writes:[2]

> The ills of public education will be cured, say the education watchers, if only school boards are made accountable. Hold the feet of boardmen to the fire of accountability is the current cry.

Wagoner, however, disavows this responsibility as one to which board members should answer. It's the teacher, he says, because of collective bargaining power and declaration of teacher rights, who should be held accountable. He further states:[3]

> In the negotiations process this means that school boards must bargain to establish and maintain their own rights—the right to expect that teachers will improve the performance of their students, the right to hold teachers accountable for their pupils' failures and to reward them for their successes in the classrooms.

Obviously, this school board member, unlike school administrators, favors the use of salary differentials along with teacher accountability.

Several writers have adopted the stand that good teachers stand to gain from the accountability concept. One such writer is Arthur H. Rice:[4]

> Public education is not our special birthright. Rather, it is a tax-supported service in which teachers participate. Public education belongs to all the people, and all the people have the right to seek its improvement, to determine its purposes, and to evaluate its outcomes.

Ripples on the sea of accountability are being generated by the positions taken by the teachers' professional and union organizations. Helen Bain, president of the National Education Association in 1970, reflects the position that, "To make the easy assumption that teachers are primarily responsible for the quality of education today is absurdly naive."[5] Furthermore, she states, "The classroom teacher has either too little control or no control over the factors which might render accountability either feasible or fair."[6]

A major NEA priority for the 1970s is achievement of teacher self-governance, which would allow teachers control of their own profession. Then, says the NEA, teacher accountability can be expected.

Elements of conflict are apparent in public pressure on school boards and administrators for teacher accountability in the face of declared opposition by the nation's most powerful teacher organization, NEA. The manner of resolution of this problem remains to be seen. Meanwhile, various forms of accountability are being tested. The California State Board of Education has adopted a new regulation, effective with the 1971–1972 school year, which requires every candidate for high school graduation to demonstrate at least eighth-grade proficiency in math and reading. Forms of accountability presently include performance contracting, merit salaries, voucher plans, planning-programming-budgeting (PPBS), and National Assessment. A common thread in the fabric is the attempt to measure educational outcomes through quantifiable scores.

As the application of the accountability concept becomes more widespread, a change—or perhaps a renewed declaration of educational purpose—will be one of the outcomes. What shall be the educational priorities for which teachers are to be held accountable? The effort of Americans to determine the purposes of their schools has been little more than an exercise in frustration. Writings such as, "Which knowledge is of the most worth?" (Spencer), "Knowledge for what?" (Lynd), as well as declarations of purpose by learned educational societies, have failed to produce a unity of purpose. As Goodlad has stated:[7]

> Few state departments of education and even fewer school districts have seriously tried to determine the precise purpose of their schools and the objectives to be achieved. And yet Americans cling stubbornly to the idea of local control of education while permitting, through sheer neglect, many of the most important decisions to be made by remote curriculum planners. To develop an increased awareness of what these decisions are and to whom we are leaving the responsibility for making them is a curricular debate for tomorrow.

At the present time, the accountability thrust seems to be directed primarily in the areas of improving pupils' reading and arithmetic scores. A debate is sure to rise over school priorities. Shall the cognitive goals of literacy take precedence over the affective goals of humanity? While mention is made of accountability in Georgia in 1819, an historical frame of reference on this topic can be readily found of the accountability efforts in Ontario, Canada, from 1876 to 1882. During those years, payments to high schools were largely dependent on the number of students who passed an intermediate exam after a year or two of attendance. This resulted in deliberate coaching for exams, with concentration of teaching efforts upon the average and slightly below-average. The bright and the dull students were neglected, because the former could pass the exam without any help and the latter couldn't pass it anyway. Although standards were raised according to the adopted criterion, this practice was abandoned in 1883 after a protest against the sacrifice of all other educational values for the attainment of this goal. Is history doomed to repeat itself?

Articles included in Part I, The Call to Accountability, are selected with the express purpose of examining viewpoints of the forces which have influenced growth of the accountability movement, as well as those educational groups affected by establishment of the accountability concept. An attempt is made to answer such questions as:

Why is accountability necessary?

How can the accountability concept be applied to educational institutions at various levels?

What shall be the responsibility of school personnel as accountability
  is applied?
For which ends shall school personnel be held accountable?
How is accountability viewed by school boards, administrators, and
  teachers as new roles are identified?

A variety of articles from different areas presents a wide range of views
and positions.

For the reader desiring additional references, a bibliography is
found at the end of Part I.

REFERENCES

1. "Large Majority Favors Teacher Accountability," Opinion Poll, *Nation's Schools,* 86:33, December 1970.

2. David E. Wagoner, "Do You Know Anything at All About How Well or How Much Your Teachers Teach?" *American School Board Journal,* 158:21, August 1970.

3. *Ibid.,* p. 22.

4. Arthur H. Rice, "Good Teachers Stand To Benefit from Accountability Plans," *Nation's Schools,* 86:16, December 1970.

5. Helen Bain, "Self-Governance Must Come First, Then Accountability," *Phi Delta Kappan,* 51:413, April 1970.

6. *Ibid.*

7. John I. Goodlad, *The Changing School Curriculum* (New York: The Fund for the Advancement of Education, 1966), p. 17.

CHAPTER 1.
DEMANDS OF TAXPAYERS AND GOVERNMENT FOR ACCOUNTABILITY

Implications of Accountability for Educational Program Evaluation

W. STANLEY KRUGER

*Kruger proposes a particular type of accountability for education: pro-
gram accountability. This concept is based on an effective program and
the responsibility of schools to produce optimum results with the resources allocated to that particular program. Other forms of accountability, such as fiscal or instructional, are incorporated into this concept. The author lists twelve critical factors: community involvement,
technical assistance, needs assessment, change strategies, management
systems, performance objectives, performance or program budgeting,
performance contracting, staff development, comprehensive evaluation,
cost effectiveness, and program auditing. Kruger states that accountability is important and worth the expenditures of effort required, but
it should not be promoted as a panacea for the many complex problems
of American education.*

The concept of accountability in education, from our point of view,
has two primary concerns: the responsibility of the Educational Enterprise to provide programs which will effectively develop the human
potential of a wide variety of client groups within a diversity of service
communities; and, the responsibility of the Enterprise to efficiently
utilize the various resources entrusted to it by the supporting society.
The concept emphasizes optimal attainment of objectives in both
these areas of concern, and maximization of the desired relationship
between them.

W. Stanley Kruger, "Implications of Accountability for Educational Program
Evaluation." Paper presented at the Invitational Conference on Measurements in
Education, University of Chicago, April 1970, ERIC Document ED-043-665. Re-
printed by permission.
Mr. Kruger is Technical Assistance Coordinator, Division of Plans and Supple-
mentary Centers, Bureau of Elementary and Secondary Education, U.S. Office of
Education.

An "Impossible Dream?" We think not; although some dreaming is involved, because some planning is involved. Because some planning is involved, some evaluation is involved—and it must be evaluation with a mission.

As the complexities of modern society generate new demands upon education, they also generate new demands upon other social services, increasing the competition for resources in the public sector. Thus, events transpiring in the real world and attitudes of the public mind combine to stress greater attention to the necessity and value of public education, and a parallel attention to the necessity for increased implementation of principles of accountability in the conduct of educational programs.

It is not sufficient merely to take notice of a need for accountability, or to exhort its virtues. Deliberate, systematic, and consistent procedures for development, implementation, evaluation, and refinement must be vigorously pursued. The tenets of the concept permit nothing less from those who would embrace it.

Most federal programs in education support projects which are intended to ameliorate and resolve critical problems in the field. If this undertaking is to be realized, the design, operation, and management of these projects must incorporate specific policies and procedures directed toward the attainment of accountability objectives; not only for the direct effect on critical-problem solution, but also for the indirect effect of generation of support for continued efforts in critical-problem areas. In the process, we need also to demonstrate techniques with high potential for the renovation and renewal of traditional program areas, and facilitating systems. Nowhere is this need greater than in the major urban complexes of our Nation.

With the passage of the 1967 amendments to the Elementary and Secondary Education Act of 1965, two new federal programs were established: to support projects in the areas of Bilingual Education (Title VII) and Dropout Prevention (Title VIII, Section 807). At the time that basic program regulations, manuals, and related materials were being prepared, it was decided that these programs provided an appropriate vehicle for a concerted effort to establish accountability principles in the administration of federally-supported projects in elementary and secondary education, through a focus upon specific aspects of project design and management. The new programs would permit Office of Education staff members to apply, from the beginning, many lessons learned in the administration of other federal programs; particularly from the experience of Title III (Supplementary Centers and Services). This component of the Elementary and Secondary Education Act, despite its great potential, has been unable to effectively demonstrate its accomplishments to the degree necessary to sustain continuing financial support at growth levels.

Although accountability in federal education programs is still very much in the developmental stage, the intensity of interest and effort is accelerating. The Commissioner of Education's operational objectives for Fiscal Year 1971 call for accountability concepts to be installed in ten discretionary-fund programs and five state-plan programs by June 30, 1971. Plans are now being implemented which will augment the efforts of what has heretofore been an extremely small staff effort devoted to theory-building, policy-and-procedure formulation, materials development, and staff training. Proposals are now being solicited, preparatory to contracts being let, which will assist in the refinement of conceptual elements and the production of program and instructional materials for use by headquarters, regional office, state-agency, and local-educational-agency personnel in disseminating and installing accountability concepts in identified programs.

It should be clear that we are considering a particular type of educational accountability—program accountability. That is, the responsibility of program personnel, whether in a small grant project, a local-school-system curriculum area, an entire local school system, a state school system, a federal program, the U.S. Office of Education, or the entire federal educational effort—to produce an optimum level of results with the resources available to them. Subsumed in this consideration of program accountability are other accountability considerations current in the educational literature, such as "research accountability," "instructional accountability," and "fiscal accountability," each of which has particular implications for certain critical factors in program accountability. The focus we would hope to realize, however, is upon the performance of specific, rather complex, organizations with specific, rather complex, responsibilities.

It is incumbent upon us, of course, to move beyond concept definition, statement of purpose, and justification of need. What are the critical factors of program design, operation, and management which must receive particular attention if greater dimensions of accountability are to materialize? We have identified twelve: community involvement, technical assistance, needs assessment, change strategies, management systems, performance objectives, performance or program budgeting, performance contracting, staff development, comprehensive evaluation, cost effectiveness, and program auditing. Of these twelve factors, at least ten are significant in their implications for educational program evaluators. Let us quickly review these ten factors:

First, community involvement. A minimum base of community support must be ascertained before the commencement of any significant program activities. Beyond this, program personnel should explore every possibility to involve members of appropriate concerned community groups in program planning, operation, and evaluation. This involvement should include participation in policy determination and in such procedural activities as technical-skill levels may warrant. A commitment to accountability, then, requires early involvement of program evaluators, to assess initial and continuing degrees of community-support and to assess community-personnel capabilities in relation to program skill-requirements. The latter activity, in fact, becomes, on a broader scale, an essential element of another accountability factor, that of:

Technical assistance. Early in the planning of program activities, the planning staff should undertake a "capability survey." This survey consists of setting down the major program objectives, activities, and functions and assessing existing system capabilities to accomplish them. Where capabilities do not exist, they must be acquired, either as permanent system additions or on a technical-assistance, consultant, or performance-contract basis. Program evaluators' skills are needed in the assessment of existing capabilities in a number of task areas, most particularly to assess the existing capability to undertake and complete the assessment and comprehensive evaluation necessary to determine program objectives, the extent of program-objectives realization, and the levels of performance efficiency.

In *needs assessment,* assuming that basic assessment capability has been determined or acquired, early planning activities will include a basic assessment of target-group (client) and situational factors, leading to the establishment of task objectives and strategy goals designed to meet needs in the respective areas. This activity takes place, of course, in a climate of existing value systems and policies which may also require review in the total needs-assessment process. The acquisition of basic decision-making data in this phase of program planning is extremely critical, and will demand the skill and resourcefulness of able evaluation personnel.

Next we determine appropriate *management systems.* A variety of program design and management techniques have been developed in business and industry which are now being adapted for use in the educational field. These techniques include Program Evaluation and Review Techniques (PERT), Critical Path Method (CPM), Program Planning and Budgeting Systems (PPBS), Management By Objectives (MBO), etc. Most deal with resource allocation of time, personnel, and funds, in relation to specified elements of the primary tasks to be accomplished through program activities. The decision to employ any of these systems dictates certain functions, arrangements, and resource requirements for program evaluation and, thus, involvement for program evaluators. Within the schema of the selected management systems, program planning proceeds to the specification of:

Performance objectives. The keystone of program accountability is the statement of program objectives in performance terms, to include the nature of performance expected, the direction or level of performance accomplishment expected, the units of performance measurement and means of accomplishing the measurement, and the primary conditions under which performance is expected to be conducted. Objectives must be specified for each program component, activity, or function; by target-group (client) ; and in immediate to long-range classification. Assistance to program staff in framing performance objectives in measurable terms is a primary program evaluator function.

Now, *performance contracting.* Where the decision has been made to add program capability by other than permanent system additions (the most desirable procedure, where feasible) for continuing program activities or functions, the addition should be through performance contracting. The emphasis in performance contracting is not on traditional *input* factors (i.e., dollars to be spent, man-hours to be committed, supplies and equipment to be consumed) , but, instead, on *output* factors—the product element obtained upon realization of performance objectives set forth and accepted by the contractor as the condition for compensation. The skills of the evaluator, again, are needed to assist in the structuring of performance specifications, to assure that they are, in fact, stated in significant, valid, measurable terms. Beyond this, the evaluator will be called upon to provide the data necessary to determine the potential of proposed services, in relation to the potentials of alternative services which might accomplish the defined objectives, including the potential of existing or traditional services being utilized by the system. Finally, the program evaluator must determine if and when performance specifications have been met, so that compensation can be made.

A standard but important factor in accountability is that of *staff development.* Increased staff competency is essential to progress toward the achievement of objectives. Staff development which should involve program evaluators may be conducted in a wide variety of areas: the standards for writing performance objectives, the techniques for gathering data, the bases for interpreting evaluation reports, to cite a few.

Next we examine in more detail the accountability factor of *comprehensive evaluation.* This is, of course, the accountability factor of primary concern to program evaluators, and a primary concern for many of us who work in the administration of federal programs. The 1967 Miller report on the first-year Title III proposals found evaluation to be the weakest element in the proposals. The 1968 report of the Second National Study of PACE found, in a review of 94 planning projects, that "only 30 . . . were judged as having adequate evaluation procedures in the project design . . . contrasted to 31 projects which gave *no evidence whatsoever* of evaluation procedures." Of 43 operational projects, "a little over eight percent of the projects had made plans and promised to be adequate for evaluation of their projects; about 70 percent . . . had done a little, and about 13 percent had not bothered with evaluation at all."

From our own work with federal programs, we can only conclude that the *typical* federally-supported project has an evaluation process that is unplanned, partial, incompetent, uncoordinated, remote, terminal, narrow in perspective, and underfunded. Project evaluation has largely been an intuitive process conducted by key project staff on an expediency basis. While this may have sufficed, in many instances, to maintain project operations at the minimum level necessary to assure continued receipt of federal funding, it provided little of the substance needed for: (1) accomplishing analyses of program effectiveness or impact, cost-benefit relationships, or cost-effectiveness comparisons; (2) creating an impetus for systemic change; or (3) disseminating and otherwise promoting the adoption of innovative practices.

Who is responsible for the status quo, which someone has defined as "the mess we're in?" Many share the blame. Ultimately, for federally-supported projects, the responsibility rests with the federal program administrators who permit the funding of poorly-designed projects, or who permit them to continue under conditions of indeterminate effectiveness. We are the ones who have produced the program manuals which, at worst, have made no mention of evaluation at all, or which, at best, call for applicants to:

A. Where applicable, describe the methods, techniques and procedures which wil be used to determine the degree to which the objectives of the proposed program are achieved.
B. Describe the instruments to be used to conduct the evaluation.
C. Provide a separate estimate of costs for evaluation purposes. This amount should be included in the proposed budget summary.

Instructions like the ones just quoted provide little guidance for the development of an adequate evaluation plan. Then we have compounded the problem in its initial states, in some instances, by permitting proposal evaluation-plan review, project negotiation, and project monitoring to become the sole responsibility of staff who have extreme difficulty in distinguishing validity from reliability, and who may associate a "Bell curve" with the styling of a Princess telephone.

If our own concern for accountability is legitimate, then what is being done to improve what has been a situation of extreme delinquency?

First, we are emphasizing the necessity for completion of an evaluation plan prior to the commencement of project operations. The plan is to have *adequate scope,* to be based upon the specification of performance objectives for all basic program activities. For these performance objectives, the plan is to indicate key factors and responsibilities associated with measurement techniques and instruments, data collection, data analysis, reporting, and dissemination. Key evaluation-process events are to be posted to an evaluation plan "time-line" preparatory to inclusion in an overall project work-activity schedule. This "time-line" provides a ready assessment as to whether or not the evaluation process is planned as a *continuous* activity rather than a terminal one.

The evaluation plan is to provide for evaluation of objectives-accomplishment at both the *operational* and at the *management* levels and, within these levels, for attention to evaluation of both *product* and *process.*

It can readily be seen that we expect the program evaluator, or better, the program-evaluator team, to possess skills in both of the broad areas of "educational evaluation" and "management-operations analysis." The capability survey discussed previously should give careful consideration to the competency of existing system resources to perform effectively in *both* areas of a comprehensive evaluation process. The survey should also explore all possibilities for close *coordination* between the project evaluation process and the more general evaluation activities of the school system, so as to maximize the effectiveness of both. Written commitments establishing this interrelationship should be secured.

It should be apparent by now that we envision evaluation as a fundamental management function, and the evaluator team as an integral part of the project management team. We understand program evaluation as a functional skill, rather than as a program phase. Our approach is intended to be a systems approach, with the evaluation process continuously gathering and analyzing data for reporting through "feedback" or "looping" arrangements to the planning process. No longer is "objectivity" a primary characteristic of the evaluation process (although consistency with reality is much admired). We cannot ask program evaluators to develop the schizophrenia that would be required if they were to be "integral" and "objective" simultaneously. Nor do we want to promote the procrastination, aloofness, ignorance, disinterest, and superficiality that has too often resulted from undue concern for objectivity. Objectivity *is* a desirable quality in the assessment of program operations; we believe it can more effectively be acquired through an additional program-management activity.

This design may seem to present a large order. It should be pointed out, however, that we have been citing *essential characteristics* or elements of an adequate evaluation design, not the *detail* required for each element. Detail requirements, and the resources to meet them, are a necessary but *separate* consideration, calling for priority and feasibility "trade-offs" within resource constraints. Program evaluation, in the minds of too many evaluation specialists, is synonymous with controlled variables, matched groups, normal distributions, equidistant-interval measures, inferential statistics, and .01 levels of significance. Unable to attempt the ideal in an area, they often attempt nothing; or deliver after the hour of need has passed. As a result, the project director frequently has no basis for decision-making when, perhaps, it would have been of tremendous value for him to have had some simple "exist–not exist" information.

Let us now move on to *cost-effectiveness*. We have chosen to separate cost-effectiveness analysis from comprehensive evaluation for special emphasis, as we did for needs assessment. It logically follows, of course, that indicators of unit objectives-achievement, when coupled with indicators of unit costs, provide us with the basis for cost-effectiveness analysis. We are quick to admit our awareness of the difficulties involved in attributing performance gains to specific project activities or in allocating general costs to those activities. We are approaching this problem through stages of "successive approximation." This year, for example, we are attempting to determine an achievement profile for the cluster of objectives specified for a project component or activity area and to relate this benefit to the full-time-equivalent participant cost associated with total component or activity costs—a relationship of "black boxes," if you will. However, since some of our projects within a given program have similar component/activity objectives, we have a basis for rudimentary comparisons of cost-benefit profiles for different program approaches within comparable environments. In this movement toward definitive cost-effectiveness analyses, the program-evaluator team has a prominent role; in determining the cost-benefit relationships for the project of immediate concern, and in the development of feasible techniques for valid cost-effectiveness analyses in larger-system applications.

Finally, the *program audit*. To more effectively monitor the activities of the program-evaluator team and, thus, to act as a performance quality control on the evaluation process, we have developed the concept of the program auditor. The program auditor is expected to bring three major qualities to program operations: *objectivity, expertise,* and *perspective.* The ultimate purpose of the program audit is the improvement of program operations through the improvement of program evaluation. More specifically, the program auditor, through a planned, pre-determined series of activities, highly dependent upon sampling techniques, is to determine the appropriateness of evaluation procedures, in design and in operation, and to verify the results of the evaluation process, thus giving the results an additional measure of credibility. The latter aim is, again, a matter of considerable value to the beleaguered school system in the modern urban complex.

I have briefly discussed several accountability factors with substantial implications for the program-evaluator team. A given factor cannot be considered independent of the others; nor are the factors discrete. They are ordered in what is to us a logical relationship, approximating the sequence in which project planners need give the factors attention. Other arrangements may be more logically organized and, thus, more meaningful to others. We do anticipate changes and refinements in the constitutent elements comprising our accountability model. We do feel, however, that the present model has already demonstrated its effectiveness in bringing into focus those aspects of program design, operation, and management upon which we must all diligently work if we are to achieve greater performance in educational programs accompanied by a better use of valuable resources.

We have had our share of problems in our efforts *re* accountability. In fact, we have encountered most of the problems associated with attempts to bring about systemic change; with our own staff as well as with state and local-school-system personnel.

The inertia of rest is a powerful force. A systematic approach to educational program operations, even if its ultimate benefits are visible, requires a persistent effort in *advance-planning, precision,* and *thoroughness* far beyond that heretofore found in most educational programs. Many who undertake the challenge grow weary enroute, and find contentment in pasting new labels on old practices. Many of our Golden Helmets of Mambrino are really shaving basins!

To continue with Don Quixote for a few more moments, I would have to say that many of us have been sent forth by our Lords, in quest of accountability, without a horse or a suit of armor. It is far too easy for upper echelon administrators, in the view from the castle tower, to fix upon the prize and to be oblivious to the resources and support necessary for its attainment. We have recognized this to some extent in our relationship with local educational agencies and now provide developmental grants for projects selected from preliminary-proposal applications, so that necessary technical assistance and supporting services can be available for the development of defensible plans of operation. We have also established budgetary allocations for evaluation in operational grants at the level of 10 percent of total budget, with an additional 2 percent for program auditing.

We have not, however, made equivalent resource provisions in our own operations. As a consequence, we have program materials available on some accountability factors, nothing on others—leading to an uneven emphasis and implementation of the model to date. In many areas, our public relations efforts have outstripped our program development efforts. Forthcoming developmental contracts will assist in correcting this imbalance.

Accountability is not without its critics—hence the need for a suit of armor. Antagonism toward "thinking through" a new approach to program and project administration is prevalent, as the possibility of change brings a perceived threat to established securities. Often project and program personnel have interests only in general matters of project design or in a narrowly-defined curriculum field, and cannot be "bothered" with those aspects of project management, however vital, for which they have little personal concern. Others have vested interests which may be endangered by a more open, more coordinated, more interdependent approach to management. Others have legitimate concerns which they are unable to intellectually reconcile with the methodology of accountability—the "there's trouble in the affective domain" syndrome. All of these groups may find it to their advantage, from time to time, to hurl "New Cult of Efficiency" barbs at the proponents of accountability.

The challenge before us is that of demonstrating that accountability *can* contribute to the fulfillment of all legitimate concerns, that it *should* expose illegitimate concerns, that it *is* worth the expenditures of effort required, and that it need *not* be devoid of humanism. Meanwhile, we dare not promote accountability as a panacea for the many complex problems of American education. These problems will not be solved by a single-minded approach. Accountability is important, of course, and always has been, although, perhaps, its principles have not fully developed under other designations, e.g., "quality" or "effectiveness." If a new designation will bring strength to needed emphasis, we should welcome a new designation. At the same time, we should not discard, in moments of hysteria occasioned by our anxiety to be rid of public charges of malfeasance as a profession, other valuable concepts, including "innovation," "comprehensiveness," "individualization," "relevance," and "liberation"—else we do a great disservice to our commitment to all that is truly meant by "Education."

Accountability: Watchword for the 70's

JOHN E. MORRIS

The success of education has often been determined by the performance of its end products. John E. Morris states that the concept of accountability is not new, but that its form has varied from time to time. He identifies seven reasons for the current accountability on a public basis. The most serious questions center around accountability and the affective domain. Will accountability become the most interesting, challenging, disruptive, and in the end most productive issue of the 1970s?

To think about education in terms of decades seems to be the "in" thing. Great emphases have been placed on *Schools for the Sixties* and *Schools for the Seventies* and in each decade much ado is made about educational problems and reforms. Most of the sixties were devoted to curriculum reforms resulting in a proliferation of NEWS—new math, new social studies, new English, new science—which were to contribute to the solution of many problems relating to student achievement. If the sentiment of certain educators, government, business, and lay leaders is an indication of what this decade holds, it is certainly the dawning of the age of accountability wrapped in the self-governance package of the educational profession and bound by performance contracts.

As yet, there seems to be no definition which can be considered an accurate index into the scope and meaning of accountability. Yet, the focus is certainly upon the achievement or lack of achievement of students who enter our public schools in relation to constantly increasing school budgets. The crux of the issue, in greatly simplified form, seems to be that if teachers cannot teach pupils to read; solve mathematical problems; speak and write correctly; memorize principles, laws, and formulas in science; and regurgitate names of people, places, things, and dates found in social studies texts; then some business concern will guarantee to do so at a predetermined level of performance and cost.

Accountability is not new to teachers and schools (although the use of the term in connection with teacher performance did not appear in the *Education Index* until June, 1970), for we have always been accountable to some one or some constituted authority. One of the

John E. Morris, "Accountability: Watchword for the 70's," *The Clearing House,* 45:323–327, February 1971. Reprinted by permission.

most revered teachers, Socrates, was accountable unto death for his teaching. The sophists were accountable to their students, for herein lay their means of livelihood. The first universities were, to a great extent, accountable to the student body and the local community. Today, the classroom teacher is legally accountable to the local school board and morally accountable to self, profession, community, and nation.

The form of accountability has varied from time-to-time, but the end product—performance—has remained relatively constant. Since the family was the first educational institution, parents were accountable for the instruction of their children in the form of skills necessary for survival. With the development of clans, tribes, and states, the functions of education became more formalized and the fortunes of the clans, tribes, and states were more or less determined by the performance of the educational system. In western education accountability has often taken the form of examinations administered at prescribed levels of the educational ladder. It was not uncommon for teachers to be retained, dismissed, or promoted on the basis of pupil performance on these examinations. A school whose students did not consistently score high on examinations might cease to attract sufficient students to make possible its continued existence. Merit pay, compensation of students for scholastic achievement as in the Martin Luther King Junior High School in Portland, Oregon,[1] and other "third factors" are means proposed or applied in an effort to insure accountability. The current emphasis for accountability has grown out of the movement for national assessment of education and President Nixon's "Message on Higher Education" which stressed the *wrongs* in education and the necessity for accountability.

In any country at any given time there exist critics, both in and outside the profession, who complain about declining standards, failure of students to learn basic fundamentals, teacher incompetencies, parental unconcern, over-permissiveness of administrators, decline of student morals, excessive expenditure of public funds, and a host of other real or imagined shortcomings. This was particularly characteristic of the immediate post-sputnik period when Russian education was considered by some, especially Rickover, to be superior to ours. It would indeed be interesting to know what public reaction would have been had the United States launched the first satellite. One can only assume that the opposite reaction would have been the rule. Now that our astronauts have walked on the moon on more than one occasion, it seems as though our schools are producing students who are capable of not only maintaining but advancing the technological and scientific progress so necessary to our well-being. If one reads "The Schools Behind Masters of the Moon,"[2] Polley's "What's Right with American

Education,"[3] and Rickover's "A Comparison: European Vs. American Secondary Schools."[4] one is confronted with the contradictions which are so characteristic of American society. It may be that the current emphasis on accountability is another such contradiction.

Reasons for Accountability Movement

There are several interesting generalizations which can be made about the reasons for the current emphasis on accountability. First, criticism and reform movements seem to wax and wane in relation to the current social milieu. The "roaring twenties" resulted in rapid changes in economic, societal, and personal values. Then came the depression and the frantic search for explanations as to the causes for such upheavals. The criticisms of this era are reflected by Professor Thomas H. Briggs when he stated that education should be a

> . . . long-term investment by the state to make itself a better place in which to live and in which to make a living, to perpetuate itself, and promote its own interests . . . . authorities have made no serious efforts to formulate for secondary schools a curriculum which promises maximum good to the supporting state . . . . there has been no respectable achievement, even in the subjects offered in secondary school curricula . . . . no effort has been made sufficient to establish in students appreciation of the values of the subjects in the curricula such as to insure continued study either in higher schools or independently after compulsory classes . . . . a state's attorney might conceivably present against an educational authority an indictment for malfeasance in office and misappropriation of public funds.[5]

The thirties witnessed rapid expansion of the progressive education movement aimed at eliminating many of these deficiencies.

Second, criticism and reform movements follow a shocking event in which we tend to come out second best. This is illustrated in the writings of Rickover, Bestor, and Conant in the post-sputnik era.

Third, since the schools are considered to be second only to the family in terms of safeguarding and extending traditional values, they are especially susceptible to attacks during times when these values are disappearing and new values to fill the vacuum have not been born. Such periods are characterized by mounting uncertainties, confusion, contradictions, and search, especially by youth, for identity. Jan Smithers, one of 775 youth included in a nationwide opinion poll, seems to express these conditions when she said: "Sometimes when I'm sitting in my room I just feel like screaming and pounding my pillow.

I'm so confused about this whole world and everything that's happening."[6]

Fourth, schools are supposed to prepare leaders who are able to solve many of the pressing social, political, and economic problems which confront a nation. Today the magnitude and hopelessness of the military entanglements in Indo-China and the Middle East, poverty, race relations, the drug problem, and violence on our campuses and in our streets is, to a very great extent, directed toward the educational institutions and accountability is the battle cry.

Fifth, the general state of the economy, coupled with the social factors already mentioned, is a major cause of the current emphasis on accountability. There is widespread and increasing militance on the part of voters toward inflation and tax increases. A record defeat rate of school bond issues and millage increases does not necessarily mean that voters are anti-education. Instead, there is resistance to all tax increases and it so happens that those involving school finance are about the only increases voters directly control. This resentment has certainly increased as a result of action taken by various militant groups, violence on the campuses of junior highs, high schools and colleges, and by creation of unitary school districts in the South and massive busing of students in some areas outside the South.

Sixth, there is widespread agreement that something is basically wrong with public education. Too many students cannot read, are deficient in basic communication skills, quit before completing the twelfth grade, and seem to be unpatriotic.

Seventh, today more parents are better educated because they have attended high school and college. They judge the progress of their children on the basis of their experiences and the widely publicized advancements in educational technology. They see the realities of the educational dilemma and are becoming more critical of and less willing to believe educational authorities. They are demanding that administrators and teachers be more accountable for the progress of students.

What Will Accountability Require?

It is too early to envision all that will be required in terms of knowledge, skills, attitudes, personnel, money, and technology to put public education on an accountability basis as envisioned, for example, by Lessinger.[7] However, a number of requirements are already evident.

First, Davies states that accountability will require ". . . changing people . . . and changing the institutions that control education."[8] Lessinger believes that ". . . educational accountability can be implemented successfully only if educational objectives are clearly stated before the instruction starts."[9] Since accountability implies predetermined levels of performance by students, an educational performance contract[10] would have to be initiated prior to the beginning of a prescribed program of instruction.

Second, accountability will most certainly require application of principles involved in differentiated staffing similar to those advocated by Olivero[11] and Barbee.[12] Perhaps a more fundamental requirement, and one which may be more difficult to secure, is self-determination of the teaching profession. Bain states that self-governance will have to become a reality before accountability is possible.[13]

Third, there must be more involvement of the community and teachers in determining policies, programs, performance levels, and incentive criteria.

Fourth, teacher education programs which are highly individualized, predicated on the basis of performance criteria, and providing more contact with the "real world" of teaching throughout the entire program instead of the limited experiences of present programs, will have to be inaugurated.

Fifth, there must be far more extensive and sophisticated use of educational technology than teacher education programs and public schools have been willing and/or able to use.

Sixth, a financial base to replace our present outdated and inequitable system of financing public education will have to be initiated.

Seventh, education must become, not only in theory but in fact, child centered. We will be forced to write programs for each child based on extensive results of highly sophisticated diagnostic instruments.

Eighth, the efficiency and effectiveness of the organization and administration of schools must be improved. The self-contained classrooms and principals who spend much of their time collecting lunch money and filling vending machines will have to go.

Ninth, instruments which are more reliable, individualized, and valid for measuring ability and performance in the cognitive and affective domains must be developed. Lessinger conceives of ". . . a process designed to ensure that any individual can determine for himself if the schools are producing the results promised. The most public aspect of accountability would be independent accomplishment audits that report educational results in factual, understandable, and meaningful terms."[14]

Tenth, new teacher-student roles and responsibilities will have to be defined and implemented. It is not certain what these would be, but the present ones of dispenser and container would either disappear or become more widespread.

Some Vital Questions

Accountability has already raised vital questions which must be considered before and *if* this concept advances beyond the experimental stages. The most serious questions center around accountability and the affective domain. We have long been aware of the vital role of such factors as attitudes, values, creativity, and self-concept, but have never come to grips with them. We, as teachers and parents, have long observed that it is not always the "most intelligent" student who is "successful." *Who* is to determine what values, attitudes, creative abilities, etc., are to be taught? *Who* will write the performance contract? *Who* will perform the "independent accomplishments audits?" *Who* will determine what influences education is to have on the shaping of American democracy and the quality of life of the American people and *how* will these influences be measured? In short, how can we ". . . gauge behavior modifications that schooling is supposed to effect."[15] Similar, although not as controversial, questions are in order for the knowledge and skills for which we are to be accountable.

Accountability also raises the issue of further dehumanization of education. There is already much discontent with the dehumanizing effects of teaching machines; computer assisted instruction; the "do not fold, staple, or mutilate" system of identification, scheduling, and reporting; the lack of a humanizing curriculum; and the bureaucratic, impersonal school organization.

Would accountability virtually force teachers to "teach the test?" There is evidence that this has already happened in the Texarkana project.[16] The same practice has occurred in the United States and other countries when educational performance, teacher retention, and school finances were, to a greater or lesser degree, determined by examination scores.

Further questions are asked by Davies:

> How do we move from a mass approach to teaching and learning to a highly individualized approach?
>
> How do we go about the "simple" task of treating each child as an individual human being?
>
> How do we substitute a vigorous, enjoyable classroom atmosphere for one that has too often been marked by competition, pain, fear, and failure?
>
> . . . how do we build into ourselves the capacity for continuing self-renewal, for meeting increasing demands for adapting to new roles?[17]

Future Prospects

It would be presumptuous to try to assess the possible impact of accountability on public education at this time. There are few certainties in those areas involving human beings. But one thing is certain—Pandora's Box has been opened and education will never be the same.

Approximately 200 school districts in various parts of the nation are trying accountability in some form. In Gary, Indiana, an elementary school has been completely turned over to Behavioral Research Laboratories for a three-year period. Dr. Alfonso Holliday II, president of the Gary school board, is quoted as saying: "With education costs rising 15 to 20 percent a year, we didn't feel we could keep asking for more money when our children were learning below their grade levels. . . . We are at rock bottom and must try new approaches. . . . We must be willing to be pioneers, and no longer say our children lack ability to learn."[18] John Gardner is quoted as saying that Accountability offers ". . . a well-tested way out of the dizzying atmosphere of talk and emotion . . ."[19] and Martin Filogamo of the Texarkana project believes that: "If it succeeds, it could well lead the way to the direct involvement of private industry in the education of the nation's school children."[20] The 70's promise to be interesting and challenging years in education, and *accountability* may be the most interesting, challenging, disruptive, and, in the end, productive issue of all.

FOOTNOTES

1. *Phi Delta Kappan*, June, 1970, p. 510.
2. "The Schools Behind Masters of the Moon," *Phi Delta Kappan*, September, 1969, pp. 2–7.
3. Ira Polley, "What's Right with American Education," *Phi Delta Kappan*, September, 1969, pp. 13–15.
4. H. G. Rickover, "A Comparison: European Vs. American Secondary Schools," *Phi Delta Kappan*, November, 1958, pp. 60–64.
5. Ellwood P. Cubberley, *Readings in Public Education in the United States* (Boston: The Riverside Press, 1934), p. 468.
6. "The Teenager," *Newsweek*, March 21, 1966, p. 66.
7. Leon Lessinger, "Accountability in Public Education," *Today's Education*, May, 1970, pp. 52–53.
8. Don Davies, "The Relevance of Accountability," *Journal of Teacher Education*, Spring, 1970, p. 128.
9. Lessinger, *op. cit.*, p. 52.
10. *Ibid.*
11. James L. Olivero, "The Meaning and Application of Differentiated Staffing in Teaching," *Phi Delta Kappan*, September, 1970, pp. 36–40.
12. Don Barbee, "Differentiated Staffing: Expectations and Pitfalls," *TEPS Write-in Paper No. 1 on Flexible Staffing Patterns*. Washington, D.C.: National Commission on Teacher Education and Professional Standards, March, 1969.
13. Helen Bain, "Self-Governance Must Come First, Then Accountability," *Phi Delta Kappan*, April, 1970, p. 413.
14. Lessinger, *op. cit.*, p. 52.
15. C. Grieder, "Educators Should Welcome Pressure for Accountability," *Nations Schools*, May, 1970, p. 14.
16. Stan Elam, "The Chameleon's Dish," *Phi Delta Kappan*, September, 1970, pp. 71–72.

17. Davies, *op. cit.*, p. 129.

18. "Where Private Firm Runs Public School," *U.S. News and World Report,* October 12, 1970, p. 41.

19. Lessinger, *op. cit.*, p. 52.

20. Martin J. Filogamo, "New Angle on Accountability," *Today's Education,* May, 1970, p. 53.

Accountability from a Humanist Point of View

C. A. BOWERS

Before one can talk about accountability, the purposes of education must be clarified. C. A. Bowers believes the purpose of education is an important philosophical question and should not be treated lightly. Accountability is a highly abstract concept which, if applied, would tend to politicize the educational process. Teacher accountability is incompatible with academic freedom, and does not reflect the needs of students. Are accountability and humanism mutually exclusive terms, or is there some place for the human element in the technological aspects of education?

There is increasing reference in the literature and public speeches to the importance of accountability in education. President Nixon, in his Education Message (March 3, 1970), stated that teachers and administrators should be held accountable for their performance. The Superintendent of Public Instruction in Oregon, Dale Parnell, has a commission working on the task of developing a master plan for the public schools that incorporates the principles of teacher accountability and management by objectives. A writer, commenting on the Texarkana experiment, suggested that perhaps the most far-reaching implication of performance accountability is its potential use in regular classrooms. "In the future," he wrote, "teachers might be required to show measurable evidence that their students are learning at a prescribed level in a prescribed amount of time."[1] At one level of analysis I find myself in general agreement with the concerns which underlie this emphasis on greater accountability in education. I can even see where accountability and management by objectives might have value in upgrading the teaching of such basic skills as reading and arithmetic.

C. A. Bowers, "Accountability from a Humanist Point of View," *The Educational Forum*, 35:479–486, May 1971. Reprinted by permission of Kappa Delta Pi, An Honor Society in Education, owners of the copyright.

But at the risk of seeming to oppose what is becoming another folk value, I would like to argue that when people extend the idea of accountability to all areas of learning in the schools, as is done in the three examples I cited earlier, they are obscuring fundamental questions that are vital to the performance of the competent teacher and to what I conceive to be the purpose of education.

If one examines the literature on accountability in education, he will find that the term is generally used in a highly abstract manner that suggests a hidden political purpose. When the advocates attempt to be specific about what they mean by accountability they invariably identify the quantitative aspects of education: rate of learning, finding the ratio between "inputs" and "outputs," and the unit cost. Later, I shall say more about reducing educational issues to quantitative terms. For now, I would like to analyze the consequences that would result for the student and teacher, if the idea of accountability were actually to be applied in concrete situations.

That the idea of accountability is used in a highly abstract manner can be seen in the fact that the "public" is always identified as the entity to whom the educator is to be held accountable. For example, Leon Lessinger, a former Associate Commissioner in the U.S. Office of Education and a leading advocate of accountability in education, asserts that the "public expects greater relevance in what we teach."[2] Who is this public? Does it have a common point of view, value system, and set of expectations so that everybody represented by the term "public" would agree on what is meant by "relevant education"? Lessinger, like other advocates of accountability, makes the mistake of treating the public as a unitary entity that shares a common set of values and expectations. This is surprising because most knowledgeable teachers, school administrators, and school board members know that their communities are composed of interest groups that have different and often opposing expectations. They also know that these interest groups wield differing amounts of power. When one takes the idea of accountability out of its rhetorical context—where it is often used as a political slogan—and attempts to implement it in a pluralistic community, it becomes obvious that it is not as clear and as workable a concept as its advocates claim.

The principle of accountability, when it is applied in a community composed of diverse interest groups, has the effect of politicizing the educational process. The decisions and performance of the teacher may become a social issue that arouses intense political activity—much of which is directed at the board members and school officials. Even when the issue is not likely to arouse the controversy that results from sex education, or a discussion of whether pacifism is not more consistent with American ideals than militarism, there is still the question of which interest groups are being served by the teacher's actions. By claiming that the teacher must be held accountable to the public the teacher is being placed in the impossible situation where his method of discipline, assigning homework, recommending outside reading, etc. may be approved by some individuals and groups in the community but disapproved by others.

If we were to follow the principle of accountability to its logical conclusion, the person who believes in prayer in the classroom would have as much right to expect the teacher to conform to his wishes as the person who believes that the teacher should maintain the separation of church and state by omitting religious instruction. Similarly, the trade unionists in the community could legitimately ask that American economic and social history be presented in a light that serves their cause, just as the business group could demand that this same history be interpreted in a way favorable to business interests. The teacher would also be as accountable to minority groups—both economic and racial—as he is to values of the white, Protestant majority. I suspect, however, that the advocates of accountability would not want to have the principle interpreted so literally that every interest group in the community would feel they had a right to control the schools for their own ends.

In addition to serving as an invitation to all individuals and social groups to assess the adequacy of the school's program in terms of their own needs, the current discussion of the virtues of accountability implies that everybody has the right to pass judgment on the teacher's performance regardless of their own competence. For example, the parent who is a school drop-out and an anti-intellectual would have the right to pass judgment on the teacher who holds a master's degree in his teaching subject. The idea of accountability is part of the populist ethos to which politicians and educators appeal when they want to win over more supporters. T. S. Eliot identified the limitation of this position when he wrote in *Notes Toward the Definition of Culture,* "A democracy in which everybody has an equal responsibility in everything would be oppressive for the conscientious and licentious for the rest." In view of this problem, it would be useful if the advocates of accountability would clarify whether they really think everybody, regardless of their qualifications and responsibility for the outcome, should be allowed to pass judgment on the teacher's competence.

The academic freedom of the teacher is a related issue that has been totally ignored by the advocates of accountability. Few of us would regard the teacher as competent if he used the classroom for the purpose of indoctrinating students with his own ideas or with the ideas of a powerful special interest group in the community. It can be argued that one of the characteristics of a competent teacher is that he attempts to foster independent and responsible thinking among students by encouraging them to consider conflicting evidence, ideas, and values. This process is essential to developing the student's self-confidence in the power of his own intellect, and to developing his ability to assess the evidence and to formulate his own conclusions. For example, in a social studies class where the settlement of the West is being discussed, unless the viewpoint of the Indian is presented along with the white person's explanation of events, the student would get a distorted interpretation of this period in American history. A presentation of the Indian's side of the story would undoubtedly include the long list of broken treaties, the Trail of Tears, and the battle of Wounded Knee where Indians were senselessly massacred. According to the principle of accountability, a parent could intervene in the classroom if he felt that the teacher in presenting the Indian's interpretation of these events was being unpatriotic in teaching about the settlement of the West. Such intervention would jeopardize the teacher's academic freedom, just as it would be threatened by the parent who thinks that the teacher should be accountable to his point of view by not teaching the theory of evolution. In both examples the freedom that must exist in the classroom if we are to avoid having the truth determined on the basis of which social group can exert the greatest pressure on the school board is being sacrificed for a political slogan.

No matter how the issue is argued, the idea of holding teachers directly accountable to individuals in the community is incompatible with academic freedom. It is ironic that those individuals who are advocating greater teaching accountability, presumably out of a genuine concern for improving public education, have not realized that they are threatening the very thing that is necessary for the teacher to function properly and to keep the classroom free of partisan politics.

There are some other pertinent questions about how the idea of accountability will be interpreted and applied to education. Will the teacher be held accountable for teaching students, in addition to the basic tools of communication, to raise their own questions, to make their own synthesis of ideas, to trust their own insights, and to understand their culture so they will no longer be influenced by its unexamined premises? These intellectual qualities are the ones usually associated with the mature and responsible citizen. Yet, I suspect that teachers will not be held accountable for fostering these traits. This approach to education would involve an intellectual treatment of the subject matter, as well as academic freedom for the teacher. That the advocates of accountability have been silent on this aspect of education suggests that either they have overlooked its importance—which indicates that they do not really understand the mental traits of a mature and responsible person—or they have been unable to reconcile the intellectual process which academic freedom is designed to protect with their populist interpretation of accountability.

I suspect that another reason the advocates of accountability have not talked about education as an intellectual experience is that they have committed themselves to a quantitative system of measurement. There is some usefulness in knowing the rate at which a person can perform a skill. But I am not sure that we can measure objectively and quantitatively what a student learns in the social sciences and human-ities unless they are rendered lifeless by being reduced to names, dates, and places. The true-false and the fill-in examinations—which provide the quantitative score—necessitate transforming the complexities of the phenomena being studied into an overly simplified view of reality where it can more easily be labeled as true or false. Educational measurement encourages teachers to offer a simplistic view of life, conditions students to look for the right or wrong answer without doing the hard work of thinking and wrestling with ambiguities, and allows the educator to maintain the illusion that he is conducting his enterprise on a scientific basis. Perhaps this is the only approach to education that our present system of accountability in education will tolerate. Here I am referring to control of education by local boards that must be responsive to diverse and often conflicting interest groups.

In reading the literature on accountability, especially such docu-ments as the recent report of the Society of Educational Engineers, a group in Oregon composed mainly of superintendents, one has the feeling that history indeed repeats itself. The values of efficiency, scientific measurement, and accountability, which seem so new and full of promise to some of these educational reformers, have been tried before, and, it must be added, without the great success that was hoped for. In the early nineteen hundreds attempts were being made to measure and increase the efficiency within the schools. In his book, *Education and the Cult of Efficiency,* Raymond Callahan reports that by 1915 there were special "efficiency bureaus" set up in major cities where "educational efficiency experts" worked full time developing rating procedures to measure the teachers' performance, and to apply the principles of scientific management to public education. Then, as now, the ideas came from the areas of business and industrial engi-neering. Perhaps if we were better aware of the history of American education we would be able to place the following statement by Leon Lessinger, which he made to the Society of Educational Engineers, in its proper context. Lessinger told his audience that

Clearly, a new educational movement is under way. We seem to be entering the age of accountability in education. This is a most radical departure from present-day practice. It attempts to put us in a position to tell the public and ourselves what we accomplished by the expenditure of a given amount of the funds. It permits us to judge our system of instruction by the results we produce. There is hope that it will lead to cost-benefit data and insight.[3]

The principles and techniques that are being heralded as new are the same ones that dominated public education between 1900 and the Depression, although the labels have been updated. Callahan summed up the consequences of applying business-industrial procedures and values to that period of education by noting:

> that educational questions were subordinated to business considerations, that administrators were produced who were not, in any true sense, educators; that a scientific label was put on some very unscientific and dubious methods and practices; and that an anti-intellectual climate already prevalent, was strengthened.[4]

There is a certain tragic irony in the fact that while many educators are attempting to transform education into a technology that will make the control of students more efficient, the students themselves are turning against the technological view of reality because of its dehumanizing effects. Theodore Roszak, the author of *The Making of a Counter Culture: Reflections on the Technocratic Society and Its Youthful Opposition,* found that many of the youth are seriously addressing themselves to the question of "how shall we live?"[5] They are asking questions about what constitutes personally and socially meaningful work, whether excessive reliance on technology and the world view it promotes are partly the source of our alienation, whether our social priorities are morally sound, and what constitutes an adequate sense of personal and social responsibility. If the student looks to the educator for help in clarifying the assumptions and values that underlie these pressing issues, he will find that the "efficiency" oriented educator can only respond by talking about systems analysis, management by objectives, accountability, performance contracting, and the technology of modifying behavior. It should not be a great surprise to anybody when the students reject the educators for attempting to turn them into technologists, rather than assisting them in clarifying the assumptions they wish to live by. I am afraid, however, that as the students increasingly rebel against the spiritual emptiness of their technologically oriented educators, the efficiency hungry educators will respond by calling for more and better techniques for controlling behavior rather than examining their own assumptions and goals.

I should like to suggest that we begin to think of accountability in terms of what the student needs in order to realize his fullest potential as a person, rather than what it is the public wants—which is often defined in self-serving economic and social terms. The problem can be stated in a way that makes clearer the danger of looking to the public for the answers to the purpose of education. Determining the purpose of education is the same as determining the potential and purpose of man. It is an important philosophic question, and thus it cannot be answered by finding out what the consensus is in the community or state nor can the answer come from individuals and interest groups who attempt to settle educational questions by using economic, social, or religious criteria without considering their implications for education.

One way to answer the question is to determine those characteristics that are associated with maturity, and I think we know enough to identify some of these characteristics. We would all agree, I believe, that the mature person is one who is aware of his own freedom and has a well developed sense of values that enables him to use it in a personally and socially responsible manner. Moreover, he has a positive self-concept that is derived from a feeling of self-mastery of his own rational and physical abilities, rather than from the crowd that gives approval in exchange for blind conformity. He would certainly be proficient in using the symbolic and communication skills of his culture, and he would be knowledgeable about his culture and its underlying assumptions. While he would not represent the final answer to the question of man's potential, his life-style and creativeness might cause those interested in the question to see new potentials that were not seen before.

The educator has to make a decision about whether he is going to use his talents and energies to help each student develop in the direction of his own maturity or whether he sees himself as being accountable to interest groups who may want the classroom to be used for such varied ends as maintaining the community's status system, providing a compliant work force, or indoctrinating students with the beliefs and values held by the dominant interest groups in the community. Those educators who think they can serve both the needs of the students— and I am not talking only about needs the students themselves can identify—and the interests of local groups are engaged in a game of self-deception. For in order to limit the student's understanding and abilities to what can be tolerated by interest groups it is often necessary to manipulate the student's self-identity so that he feels confident about himself only when his behavior conforms to the norms of the interest groups. The teacher would also have to condition him into believing that the range of his freedom is circumscribed by the expectations of others. This is really what socialization is all about, but when it is carried on in the unexamined manner demanded by many interest groups, it becomes debilitating for the person undergoing the process.

If, on the other hand, the teacher feels himself accountable to the long-range needs of the students, he will attempt to create an atmosphere of trust in the classroom where genuine inquiry can take place. In this atmosphere the student does not have to earn a positive self-image by meeting somebody else's terms. He can begin to develop a positive self regard as he learns to trust his own intellectual and emotional responses as he encounters different aspects of his culture. The teacher must also have the ability to teach him the information gathering skills without turning off his interest in learning by using fear and guilt as a means of controlling his behavior. Equally important to the student's future development is the teacher's knowledge of the culture and his awareness that he cannot know what, among all the ideas, assumptions, and values he teaches, will prove dysfunctional at some future point in time. When the teacher is sensitive to the risks the student faces in learning from others, he will discourage the students from uncritically accepting as real what are actually the notions, imaginings, and longings of a particular people at a particular point in history. For when the student unquestionably accepts the truths of other people he may be trapped into reliving the problems connected with their form of cultural blindness.

We are reminded almost daily that some of our most basic cultural assumptions about the environment, meaningful work, the nature of scientific technology, our view of progress, and our Protestant attitude toward the nature of time, need to be re-thought as we face a deepening crisis with our environment, and in our relations with each other in urban centers. These inescapable facts should make educators more conscious of being accountable to students for insuring that their education does not become simply a matter of training for a job that may shortly be eliminated by advances in technology. The students need to learn about their culture, particularly about those assumptions and values that are at the root of current social and ecological problems. They also need to learn how to deal with social issues at an intellectual rather than an emotional and fearful level—as many adults now do. If the current advocates of accountability were genuinely concerned with this form of education, they would be talking about the importance of academic freedom, the problems of recruiting more intellectually mature and socially representative people into the field of teaching, the kind of education that teachers need in order to be culturally literate, and the kind of education that administrators need in order to understand the educational process and their role in protecting it from fearful and anti-intellectual elements in the community. Instead, we hear them talking about input-output indicators, auditing the teacher's performance, applying systems analysis and design to education, and the need for establishing an Educational Engineering Institute in Oregon so that all schools may be controlled more efficiently.

The language of the educational engineer has a great power for mesmerizing people, but it does not tell us anything about the vital issues in education. Before we can talk about accountability we must first clarify the issues that relate to the purpose of education. Otherwise, the technological aspects of education will become ends in themselves.

FOOTNOTES

1. Dale Bratten, Corline Gillin and Robert E. Rousch, "Performance Contracting: How It Works in Texarkana," *School Management,* August, 1970, p. 10.
2. Leon Lessinger, "Evaluation and Accountability in Educational Management," *Academy of Educational Engineers* (published by the Society of Educational Engineers, 1970) , pp. 7–8.
3. *Ibid.*
4. Raymond Callahan, *Education and the Cult of Efficiency* (Chicago: The University of Chicago Press, 1962) , p. 246.
5. Theodore Roszak, *The Making of a Counter Culture* (New York: Anchor Books, 1969, p. 233) .

The "Relevance" of Accountability[1]

DON DAVIES

Don Davies describes the Career Opportunities Program (COP) as a model for a new educational experience. His concept of accountability implies a change in people by changing the educational institutions that serve them. Educators must be responsible for what their pupils achieve. Greater emphasis needs to be placed on the child, especially the disadvantaged child. This can best be accomplished through a shift in teacher education programs. The Education Professions Development Act will play an important role in this movement towards "relevance" in American education.

I have it on good authority that accountability will soon replace relevance as the "in" word among educators. I hope this is a reliable tip, for two reasons: First, along with most people, I am stuffed to the

Don Davies, "The 'Relevance' of Accountability," *Journal Teacher Education,* 21: 127–133, Spring 1970. Reprinted by permission.

eyeballs with relevance, irrelevance, semirelevance and pseudo-relevance of people, programs, projects, and promises. Second, and more important, accountability, I hope, will be more than an "in" word, a current fashion in semantics. I see it as an "in" *concept* that comes to grips with a notion too many schoolmen have too long rejected, the notion that schools and colleges should shoulder the responsibility for the learning successes or failures of their pupils.

This concept of accountability calls for a revamping of much of our thinking about the roles of educational personnel and educational institutions at all levels. It links student performance with teacher performance; it implies precise educational goals; it forecasts the measurement of achievement. It means, in effect, that schools and colleges will be judged by how they perform, not by what they promise. It means that we are moving in a direction we have been contemplating for a long time—shifting primary learning responsibility from the student to the school. It also means that a lot of people are going to be shaken up.

Now the word accountability can be interpreted in several ways. For instance, there *is* such a thing as accountability to taxpayers. Contrary to our American oversimplification, our free public schools are not free; they are paid for with taxes, and the taxpayers have a right to know what they are getting for their money. And there *is* such a thing as accountability to the Congress and to state and local legislative bodies. They are responsible for appropriating funds for educational programs, and they have a right to know how productive these programs have been.

I have no objection to making the schools accountable to taxpayers or legislators. But I am talking about another type of accountability, the kind that holds teachers and aides and principals and superintendents and school board members accountable for the educational achievements of all of their clients—those who come to school well prepared to share in its benefits as well as those who have nothing in their backgrounds that would equip them for a successful learning experience.

I said a few moments ago that the concept of accountability implies precise educational goals. Let us look at the primary goal: to create a society that is free and open and compassionate, nonracist, multicultural, and productive. To achieve that kind of society, we somehow have to learn to create an educational system that is free and open and compassionate, nonracist, and productive.

That kind of educational system requires one basic thing—changing people; that means changing ourselves and all of the people who have anything to do with running and serving the schools—teachers, aides, parents, counselors, superintendents, and school board members.

It means changing the institutions that control education—the colleges and universities, state departments of education, local education agencies, the federal agencies responsible for developing education programs—by changing the concepts and attitudes of the people who control them. We need people and institutions capable of continuous change, continuous renewal, and continuous responsiveness to the needs of a variety of children from a variety of backgrounds and with a variety of hangups, as well as a variety of talents.

The federal government has for several years now put a great deal of money and effort into compensatory programs designed to equalize educational opportunity for children from low-income families. I am referring especially to programs under the Elementary and Secondary Education Act. And we have tried to increase the expertise of teachers under provisions of both the National Defense Education Act and the Higher Education Act. Add to these the efforts to tackle adult illiteracy, to upgrade vocational education, to finance the purchase of equipment, and to provide for the construction of libraries and laboratories and other facilities. The sad fact is that none of these programs has made much of an impact; none has been effective in equalizing, individualizing, or humanizing instruction.

The Education Professions Development Act is an acknowledgement that we put the cart before the horse. The Act says, in effect, that none of the new education measures, no matter how meticulously designed, how noble in intent, or how expensively financed, can be effective without people prepared to make them effective. It says that the only way we can bring about change in education is by bringing about change in the people who control and operate the schools and colleges.

Such a drastic change in concept is bound to arouse anxiety and fear in the people and institutions embarking upon such change. That is what I meant when I said that a lot of people are going to be shaken up. I would like to go into that further in a moment, but in the meantime, a look at some of the problems we face.

As we move in new directions, it is clear that teaching is becoming a more demanding and more sophisticated profession than it has been in the past. In our search for ways to meet the goals we have set for ourselves, we are faced with more questions than answers. Teachers and all school personnel are involved in the search for answers to critical questions such as these:

How do we move from a mass approach to teaching and learning to a highly individualized approach?

How do we go about the "simple" task of treating each child as an individual human being?

How do we succeed with those youngsters who have never experienced
   success?

How do we substitute a vigorous, enjoyable classroom atmosphere for
   one that has too often been marked by competition, pain, fear,
   and failure?

And last, how do we build into ourselves the capacity for continuing
   self-renewal, for meeting increasing demands, for adapting to new
   roles?

We do not know the answers to all of these questions; but we do
know that if we are to find the answers, new techniques, new skills,
new attitudes—in fact, a whole new concept of teaching and learning—is called for. No individual teacher in a self-contained classroom
can put into practice all of the changes inherent in the goals to which
we aspire.

We also know that we will not find the answers by looking at
curriculum changes, relying on technology, or by simply allocating
more money to the schools. We will find them by taking a hard look at
a variety of people who can be trained to augment the work of the
teacher, leaving him free to teach. We will find them by looking at
arrangements that make for more effective staff utilization. We will
find them through cooperative efforts that link the schools that employ
educational personnel with the institutions that train them.

We are not without models for this new educational experience: by
now, we have witnessed the results of team teaching; of interns working in the Teacher Corps or similar programs; of teacher aides and
other auxiliary personnel, who have helped numerous school systems
individualize instruction; of differentiated staffing where it has been
tried. In fact, I plan to spend most of tomorrow looking in on some of
these projects here at the University of Minnesota.

One of the most promising models, and one I want to take an
especially close look at while I am here, is the Career Opportunities
Program (COP). Planning for the program has been going on for
some time, and it will be launched early next spring. The Minneapolis
program is one of approximately one hundred and thirty throughout
the country designed to produce a system for orderly change in two
directions: first, in the very organization and structure of the local
school system; and second, in the alignment of priorities in teacher-
training institutions.

COP has to do with attracting bright, ambitious, and deeply concerned people from low-income communities into the schools as
teacher aides or technicians. Now this is not a new idea, but COP
encourages all of the institutions that control opportunity in education to take a fresh look at these people and place a new value on

them. It requires that they be viewed as individuals who may, with a combination of in-service work experience in the school and academic courses in the college, develop from aides to assistant teachers; to interns; and eventually, to fully certified members of the education professions.

COP is designed not only to open education's gates to persons from low-income areas but to enhance the careers of overburdened experienced teachers by providing them with much-needed assistance and support. One major goal of COP is to put the teacher in a position to reorder his time, reduce the number of children who require his personal attention, and concentrate on his real job—diagnosing and prescribing for the learning processes. It is our belief at the Office of Education that the teacher can be placed in that position if the talents of community people are tapped, if we court people able to serve a variety of functions, starting with simple supportive tasks and eventually sharing in more sophisticated responsibilities.

The most important goal of COP, of course, is to improve the education of children in urban and rural low-income areas. It draws upon experiences in Mexican-American communities, for example, where bilingual auxiliary personnel are helping to bridge cultural and language gaps between students and teachers.

We also know that in many cases teachers have found the aide's manner of relating to the children so good that it could be duplicated; in some instances, teachers started changing their style of communication with children and made new efforts to understand their problems. For many children, seeing adults from their own communities involved in the schools helped them build expectations for themselves and a confidence in the educational process.

The reason I have great hopes for the success of COP, and the reason I dwell upon it here, is that the whole concept is one of partnership—something that until now has been alien to all of the parties involved. New alliances and new working arrangements were required before sites could be funded for COP projects. Local education agencies, for example, had to involve their staffs in developing the work experience aspect of the project; training institutions had to provide appropriate academic training; state departments of education had to participate so that necessary modifications in certification requirements could be made; the community had to provide committed and talented persons who were stimulated by the prospect of interaction with children, by the opportunity for college experience, and by the anticipation of an open-end career.

Most important of all to you people here, I think, is the radical departure from traditional training programs that COP imposes. It gives major responsibility to local school districts and their staffs instead of to colleges and universities. It provides power for the school system to buy packages and programs deemed significant and essential from teacher-training institutions and to reject others. This approach reflects a change that affects not only those being trained but the trainers as well.

Many local education agencies take the position that they have a role to play in staff development, that they can accommodate themselves to the needs of poverty area classrooms, that the school itself has many of the necessary components for sharing in teacher-training responsibility. For one thing, there is a practical setting—a pupil population, administrators, a community environment, contact with parents. All of these factors take training out of the abstract and give recruits an opportunity to see it "like it is."

School districts also say they could improve teacher preparation efforts if they had options that allowed them to work with the colleges and universities in determining training needs that pre-service applicants must have in order to be effective. The Office of Education is answering: Fine. We think you have a point. The colleges and universities are not doing the best job of training personnel to be effective in low-income neighborhoods; we think a better job can be done if both institutions work together.

Early in this speech, I said that the new design for educational reform would shake up some people. I am certain the movement toward sharing training responsibility with the schools is doing just that. Let me hasten to add that the Office of Education is not preaching the demise of teacher-training institutions. We are, instead, suggesting that they strengthen their positions and their programs by venturing out from under the protective ivy to explore new domains, new relationships, and new alliances. We are further suggesting that school districts draw upon the expertise of their own experienced teachers and put it to work in training new people. It is not too farfetched to think that this kind of arrangement can yield a rich body of information that would be of tremendous value if plowed back into the college curriculum. I would hope to see this kind of activity develop; and I would hope it would precipitate a thorough examination by teacher-training institutions of their courses, their methods, and their relationships with the consumers of their products. Such an examination is long overdue.

I would also go a step further and suggest that teacher-training institutions take a close look at what they mean by "training." A recent study conducted by the American Association of Colleges of Teacher Education and Ball State University, with an Office of Education grant, delves into this subject expertly and in great depth. Out of that study came a paperback that some of you may have seen, *Teachers for the Real World.*[2] The burden of this book, especially as it relates to colleges and universities, is that there must be two major shifts in the field of teacher education: (1) A far more orderly and systematic procedure must be created for the preparation of the teacher in relation to the tasks of teaching. (2) This can best be accomplished by adopting procedures that are clinically and case-study oriented. In short, the study calls for a movement toward clinical training and an end to courses dominated by lectures and discussion. It also challenges colleges and universities to develop a systematic body of information, including audiovisual material, that will help prospective teachers analyze their behavior, clarify concepts, and interpret situations.

This whole idea, of course, is also guaranteed to shake up a number of people. Just the word "training" is enough to do it, for educators have long considered that word inapplicable to them, and it offends their sensitivities. However, all that we know about training in other occupations would indicate that there is room for some second thoughts on this subject. Surgeons are trained, and so are airplane pilots; and because they are trained, they can perform their duties with relaxed control and respond to new situations constructively. What the study says is that there is no difference between training a surgeon and pilot and training a teacher; both require practice under controlled conditions.

These are the types of changes that are in the wind and about which we are doing a lot of thinking and planning. The U.S. Office of Education will be taking a national leadership role in stimulating the kinds of changes I have been discussing. This is in accordance with Commissioner Allen's recent statement pledging that the Office of Education will advocate needed reform and improvement in meeting education's problems and needs.

What this means for teacher training—and indeed training of all kinds of educational personnel—is that federal programs for meeting educational manpower needs under the Education Professions Development Act will be funded only if they can be evaluated on the basis of performance. The essential element in evaluation will no longer be the means by which educational personnel are trained but the effectiveness of the learning that takes place as a result of that training. In line with this policy, we have established priorities that represent a transition from former training activities that were popular under the National Defense Education Act and other legislation to activities consistent with the goals of the Education Professions Development Act.

Previous EPDA programs—those inherited from earlier legislation —had little concern for the target population of children to be served by the personnel being trained. Our new priorities put the child first.

The programs have a very heavy, but not exclusive, emphasis on the preparation of personnel to work more effectively with disadvantaged and handicapped children; and all EPDA programs are oriented toward the elimination of race, family income, and physical and mental handicaps as deterrents to equal opportunity.

Why the emphasis on personnel to work with the disadvantaged? Admittedly, for the majority of the population, our school system has been productive; but for a substantial portion, it has failed and continues to fail. Leaving aside the moral issue completely, experience proves that every citizen pays a price in money, in uncertainty, in fear, in social problems for the school failures, the dropouts, and the undereducated.

It has been estimated, for example, that every dropout costs the nation about $1000 a year while he is unemployed. Add to that the cost of crime and penal institutions, the price to the country of high military rejection rates, the cost of welfare and the many other services required to support persons who either reject or are rejected by society, and you will see why we are forced, as Commissioner Allen has said, "to move or to face disaster."

We are also making a transition from programs that were remedial in their efforts to upgrade the subject matter competencies of teachers to programs that emphasize change—changing the system by which educational personnel are prepared. Ultimately, this should eliminate the need for remedial training programs.

A third transition is from primarily short-term, exclusively college-based training to an emphasis on long-term projects that involve a partnership of colleges and universities, state and local school systems, and the community to be served by the personnel to be trained. And finally, there is the transition from programs that are limited in focus, that concentrate on specific subjects, to programs that focus on priority fields.

What has emerged from the convergence of these transitional forces are three priorities that cut across the lines distinguishing one part of the Act from another:

1. Programs for training personnel in fields of critical shortages, such as early childhood education, vocational-technical education, special education, bilingual education, educational media, school administration, and education in correctional institutions.
2. Programs to train personnel to meet critical problems in the schools. These include a program designed to aid black teachers in the South, particularly those threatened with displacement through desegregation. A new rural-urban program will assist experienced teachers in urban and rural poverty area schools in raising the level of pupil achievement.

3. Programs to bring new kinds of people into the schools and to demonstrate, through training, new and more effective means of utilizing educational personnel and delivering educational services. These include five programs—the Career Opportunities Program, which I described earlier; the Teacher Corps; programs for trainers of teacher trainers; programs on school personnel utilization to explore a variety of differentiated staffing patterns; and the state grants program for meeting immediate critical shortages of teachers and aides.

These are the directions in which we are moving and the philosophy behind that movement. As you can see, when I suggested earlier that accountability may become the new "in" word in education, I had some specific indication that this may prove to be so. Under the Education Professions Development Act, accountability will be the hallmark of progress. Teacher-training institutions and local school systems will be accountable to the community for the quality of educational services delivered, and teachers will be accountable for what children learn. And this, I submit, has some relevance to what American education is all about.

FOOTNOTES

1. Address before Dean's Conference on Teacher Education, sponsored by College of Education, University of Minnesota, Radisson Hotel, Minneapolis; December 4, 1969.
2. Smith, B. Othanel; Cohen, Saul; and Pearl, Arthur. *Teachers for the Real World*. Washington, D.C.: American Association of Colleges for Teacher Education, 1969.

The New Look of Federal Aid to Education

TERREL H. BELL

The problems of education have been building for generations. Now the federal government is actively engaged in the search for solutions to these problems. The new look of federal aid to education can be characterized by the word "results." Federal resources need to augment state and local resources to obtain effective schools. Program reform, research, performance contracts, and information dissemination are some areas to which federal dollars are going. Will the increase in federal influence lead to quality education?

Terrel H. Bell, "The New Look of Federal Aid to Education." Speech to the Michigan Association of School Boards, Grand Rapids, September 24, 1970. Reprinted by permission.

Since these are serious times, I have asked that no bonfires be lit, fireworks scheduled, or commemorative medals struck. In fact, since the press unaccountably failed to cover the event, you are the first to know that yesterday I celebrated my centennial. I have been Acting U.S. Commissioner of Education for exactly 100 days. I don't want to give you the impression that I have been marking them off on the walls of my office. It's just that I didn't expect such a long run in the part.

If you are asking yourselves if 100 days comprise a sufficient length of time in which to become profound on the subject of the federal government's role in education, I want to hasten to reassure you on *that* score: I've actually been at the Office of Education a total of 163 days.

In all seriousness, I admit that my exposure to one of the most massive and complex domestic programs ever undertaken has been brief. Yet it has been time enough to persuade me that compared with some of its recent history federal aid to education has taken a new and very hopeful turning. It has a new look, particularly with regard to your interests in the states and localities. I am convinced that new initiatives have been adopted and new policies shaped that will enable us to build and operate a far more cooperative and effective partnership, a partnership based on a solid understanding of our mutual interests and shared objectives.

I must admit that when I arrived in Washington last April I was not quite so optimistic. The 1960s had witnessed intensive federal involvement with all levels of education for the first time in our history. The Office of Education had grown prodigiously; in budget, from less than $500 million to $4 billion; in programs, from 15 or so to approximately 100. Many of these were crash efforts to pour literally billions of dollars into the schools. The schools in so many instances were almost comically unprepared for the sudden largesse.

Federal aid seemed to me to present the classic image of the man leaping on his horse and galloping madly off in all directions. The problems of education had been building for generations. The federal solutions to those problems were conceived and executed in a matter of months. Much was accomplished, of course; Americans, particularly those Americans isolated in their good fortune from the problems of their less happy countrymen, became fully aware for the first time of the vital need for educational reform throughout the nation. Yet the federal actions to achieve reform were often blunted because they were undertaken in a rather profound ignorance of local conditions, local attitudes, and local preferences.

The results of this flurry of activity, it becomes clearer every day, have been sadly disproportionate to the amount of the investment. A

lesson that had begun to emerge long before I arrived on the scene is reaffirmed and strengthened by each new study: money alone is not enough; money, even when accompanied by high-decibel rhetoric, will be wasted if it is not also accompanied by understanding and planning; money, simply stated, can't buy a good education system in the United States.

There is probably no solution to the school problem that will not cost large sums of money. But a checkbook is not an adequate substitute for the proper methods. There is little to be gained by spending unless we spend in a way that will produce tangible results.

And, if there is one word that characterizes the new look of federal aid to education, it is that word—*results*. Washington is no longer pursuing expensive will-o-the-wisps with no regard for what happens as a consequence. We are no longer equating success with increased expenditures. We want to be sure that every dollar invested in an educational program will produce a payoff for the people of this country, particularly the children, that can be measured and that can be proved.

We now seek, as President Nixon said in his Message on Education Reform, a thoughtful redirection of the federal effort to help achieve a genuine reform of the entire educational enterprise in America. The President spoke in that message of the need to strengthen state and local initiatives. He said—and I quote—"I am determined to see to it that the flow of power in education goes toward, and not away from, the local community. The diversity and freedom of education in this nation, founded on local administration and state responsibility, must prevail."

In other words, Washington has abandoned, forever I hope, the parochial notion that wisdom flowers only on the banks of the Potomac. I can assure you that Washington bureaucrats now realize that there is wisdom in Grand Rapids and throughout the State of Michigan. That there is wisdom in *every* state and community in America and our children deserve the benefit of all of it. Our children deserve—and the people are demanding more vocally every day— schools that produce results. They deserve schools that are, as your convention theme states, accountable for their performance.

PROGRAM REFORM

The Office of Education is exploring several ways in which we can help you get performance for your educational system. We are giving a great deal of attention to ways in which our programs can be redesigned for greater utility and effectiveness. For, in terms of accountability, the federal aid effort has apparently operated as much in the

dark as the schools themselves. Many of our programs simply haven't worked as well as had been anticipated. Or if these programs have succeeded in accomplishing what their authors intended, we do not have the information we need to measure their effects.

We know, for example, that 10 percent of Title I funds have been spent in life support (hot lunches and so on), 70 percent in improving reading, and another 8 percent in attempts to improve leadership. That means that 88 cents out of every Title I dollar have gone into programs that can be objectively evaluated and assessed. Yet our evaluative techniques need much improvement if we are to gauge the true cost effectiveness of this program, the largest in the Office of Education.

We believe our studies will enable us to achieve immediate and substantial improvement in the program at the federal, state, and local levels. This is of a high order of importance if we are to take advantage of Title I's early gains. Because there is no question in my mind that Title I—whatever its faults—has given the nation's educational system an awareness and a know-how that can make a significant and continuing difference to our eight million disadvantaged children.

RESEARCH

Accountability is, as you have been discussing for the last three days, a very promising concept. No longer can we be satisfied with traditional standards of measurement—the number of teachers, or books, or trombones. We must search for the proper combination of all factors so that we can guarantee that our children will leave high school well equipped for higher education, jobs, and the general business of living itself.

We can no longer hold the student wholly responsible for success or failure, sharing the credit for his success while completely escaping all blame for his failure. Rather our schools must assume as Governor Russell Peterson of Delaware has rightly said, a commitment as simple as it is just: *that every child shall learn.*

The Office of Education is supporting a broad variety of research and development activities designed to help make accountability an operating principle of American schools.

We are supporting the National Assessment of Education being conducted by the Education Commission of the States under the chairmanship of Governor Peterson. We hope Assessment will provide an understandable reliable national measuring device in the major subject areas against which all schools can measure their performance.

A good share of our research effort is being devoted to the development of concepts such as *education engineering.* This is the name

given the whole system of interrelated techniques which may be used to make an educational system accountable for student learning as well as the use of money, manpower, and equipment.

PERFORMANCE CONTRACTS

We are also exploring the use of performance contracts in the schools to help achieve accountability. This is a new concept to the Office of Education though it is familiar to business-oriented agencies such as the Department of Defense. The school buys student achievement rather than books or teaching techniques. It is up to the contractor to do the job, using the methods and technology that seem best suited to the particular situation. Since the contractors are accountable for results, they recover no costs if they fail to meet minimum standards of student performance.

Although a number of firms are active in this field and more are asking to come in all the time, we are convinced in the Office of Education that if performance contracts prove workable and useful in public education, the school systems themselves should function as the contracting agents. The profit motive will have a particular attraction for our underpaid teachers. Given the proper incentives, I know that our teachers will be more than willing to put in extra time in an effort to accomplish extraordinary results. The Office of Education has been supporting, in preliminary experiments, the use of performance contracts in a number of school districts. Initial results are encouraging though we should be aware that performance contracting is a complex business, difficult to integrate into a traditional system and difficult to measure for results. But it does bring a healthy degree of market competition and cost effectiveness into education. And it does focus instruction on the student because, in the final analysis, it is the student's achievement that determines who gets paid and how much. Performance contracting also places the schools in the advantageous position of searching the market for what will be the most effective instructional system in each individual case, rather than being forced to stay with programs that have been demonstrated to be inadequate.

INFORMATION DISSEMINATION

The Office of Education is, in short, working to help the school systems find out what works. We are examining a whole series of concepts that are new to education including producer-consumer schools, renewal capital, comprehensive planning, educational accomplishment auditing, and many more.

But in addition to development of new ideas, we are also very

concerned with the *transportation* of new ideas, their dissemination throughout the entire educational system. The goal of all federally supported education experiments is the same: improving the quality of American education. Obviously not all are successful, but many are. But we do not intend to strengthen scattered target areas only. Pilot efforts demonstrated to be successful new classroom practice can and must be applied in other localities and regions if federal aid to education is to reach its full potential for effecting permanent improvement.

Multiplying the good effect of the best programs demands dissemination. Educators constantly speak of the need for information on exemplary programs—where they are, how they operate, the results they have achieved. We are attempting to meet that need through our newly established National Center for Educational Communication. This organization is intended to link together information of all types, from pure research through concrete program results, to be able by various techniques to retrieve this information rapidly and make it available widely.

INSTRUCTIONAL TECHNOLOGY

Productivity is a core issue for American education today. The cost of schooling is increasing at a rate far exceeding the growth of our ability to pay for it. Over the past 20 years, enrollment in the public schools has gone up slightly more than 80 percent; school revenues during the same period increased some 350 percent in *price-adjusted* dollars.

Instructional technology offers the best hope for meeting this crisis in cost. Television, in particular, multiplies an educational program's impact many times—upon a school, or a community, or, indeed, an entire nation. Witness the amazing *Sesame Street*. This television production is one of the best investments of research money ever made by the Office of Education and the other organizations funding it. *Sesame Street* reaches an estimated six million youngsters between the ages of three and five. Preliminary studies show that the impact of *Sesame Street* on disadvantaged children, the prime target audience, is impressive. The first formal evaluation, made in January of this year, showed that children watching the show gained in their ability to recognize letters and simple geometric forms at a rate *two and one half times* that of nonviewers.

We're all addicted to the use of initials these days but I would like to call your attention to three letters—CAI—which we feel have great potential for education. They stand for *Computer Assisted Instruction,* a technique being developed with funds by our National Center for Educational Research and by Title III of the Elementary and Secondary Education Act. CAI is vital to the use of three more

letters—IPI—*Individually Prescribed Instruction*. Both systems tailor instruction to a child's individual needs, rather than forcing him into one common mold. Like television, CAI has long-range impact. A computer at Stanford University, for example, provides drills in reading and math to children seated in Kentucky and Mississippi, half a continent away.

My point is this: we in education are at long last becoming aware of the marvelous potential of technology for educational purposes, both in the school and outside the school. These new tools and techniques can literally revolutionize our ability to instruct millions of American youngsters in an effective and interesting way. The methods exist; the problem we face now is putting them to immediate and widespread use.

In closing, let me say that I believe American education is busy in this decade of the 1970s building a new tradition. It is a tradition made up of efficiency, adaptation, and participation. Perhaps you could call it a businesslike tradition. We want to find out what works in education; we want to find the solutions to our problems; we want to give our children the educational preparation they must have to build their own lives and to contribute effectively to the progress of this great country.

The people in Washington are through arguing, I believe, about territorial rights, contending about the federal share of educational responsibility, or the state share, or the local share. Since all of us benefit from the quality and effectiveness of our schools, all of us share the responsibility of helping each other, of using the resources each of us possesses to augment the resources of the others, and being accountable for results.

That's the way it looks to me from Washington. And I think it's an excellent perspective.

Performance Proposals for Educational Funding: A New Approach to Federal Resource Allocation

LEON M. LESSINGER AND DWIGHT H. ALLEN

Many federal aid programs have been poorly conceived and improperly managed. A program that offers promises of greater economy is performance contracting. It has been used successfully for years by private industry and the armed forces. Now performance criteria are proposed for measuring the effectiveness of instructional programs funded by the federal government.

The dam which, historically, has kept back all but a trickle of federal funds to education has been opened to produce what is now a small flood of federal money to all levels of education. There is some question whether such funds are flowing into the most appropriate channels, however, and there is occasional evidence that a good part of it is drained off in poorly conceived and improperly managed programs not conducive to sought-for results. Much of this loss might be avoided if proposals requesting federal funds were based upon specified performance objectives and if it were clearly stated how and when evaluators might know these objectives had been met. Such proposals would be optional; they would in no way jeopardize the freedom of the agency applying for the funds. But they would do a great deal to cut down on misapplication of funds. If educators were required to describe and measure the behavior expected of each student upon completion of the programs they propose for funding, they, the taxpayers, and—most important—the students would profit immeasurably.

The fact is that educators have failed to develop performance criteria for measuring the effectiveness of instructional programs, and many programs have been funded and are now under way which at no point describe what students are expected to gain from their educational experiences. What such programs should (but do not) include are agreed-upon standards which would demonstrate that, as a result of the instruction, a change in student behavior has occurred, a change in the direction desired which meets criteria formulated before instruction began. These criteria would clearly specify what it is the

Leon M. Lessinger and Dwight H. Allen, "Performance Proposals for Educational Funding: A New Approach to Federal Resource Allocation," *Phi Delta Kappan*, 51: 136–137, November 1969. Reprinted by permission.

student is expected to do, the circumstances under which he should be able to do it, and the degree of accuracy expected.

Instead of brave, vague promises to provide students with "an opportunity to learn to communicate effectively," instructional program objectives should be stated in terms as specific as those in the following example:

> Given three days and the resources of the library, the student completing this program will then be able to write a 300- to 500-word set of specifications for constructing a model airplane that any wood-shop student could follow and build to specifications.

A clearer formulation of goals could not help but clarify the instructional means to be followed in achieving them. When a student is able to demonstrate in concrete terms what he has or has not learned, the educator will be in a better position to judge where and why his program succeeds or fails.

In effect, contracts for federal funds, wherever possible, should be performance contracts. Thus a proposal for funds to back a reading program might stipulate that 90 percent of the students participating in a proposed reading program would be able to satisfy criteria demonstrating that they had achieved a particular grade level increase in the time proposed. In requesting funds for a teacher preparation program the agency making the request should be able to prescribe the teaching skills to be imparted and the criteria for measuring the "proficiency level" at which these skills will be exercised by participants in the program. The funded agency should be prepared, indeed compelled, to explain any failure to achieve the performance levels on which such a contract is based, and, preferably, in terms of suggested changes in the program that might be expected to guarantee the results initially stipulated. Lest the idea of performance criteria strike anyone as novel or bordering upon the impossible, it should be pointed out that they have been formulated and applied with great success by both industry and the armed services for years.

True, there are and should be larger objectives in education that are difficult to define and impossible to measure as the consequence of any given program—objectives measured by maturity and all that it implies, by faith in a future upon which we can only speculate, and by aspirations that lead achievement by exceeding it. But the fact that the many results of education are subjective and not subject to audit should not deter us from dealing precisely with those aspects of education that lend themselves to precise definition and assessment. Rather, it demands that we do make maximum use of these individual parts that tell us what the change in the whole has been. If it is truly our goal to help our children transcend their education in completing it, we must begin by giving this education a strong basis in fact.

There are, of course, creative endeavors in basic research that do not lend themselves to a performance criteria approach. If Edison, who failed in thousands of experiments to develop the light bulb, had had at once to propose and promise that outcome within two semesters for his early experiments, we might all be living in a darker world. Admittedly, the objectives of proposals for basic educational research may be limited to defining processes and procedures of investigation— methods specification vs. results specification. But this should in no way absolve the school or agency requesting funds for an instructional program, however experimental, from the obligation to state its objectives in terms of results. Certainly the federal government has the right to ask whether an operational program deserves priority if its objectives are stated as hopeful generalities instead of measurable outcomes.

This discussion does not relate to proposals for federal money to which performance criteria obviously cannot be appended and are not. The obvious advantages of a proposal demonstrating that the writer has carefully evaluated his program in terms of anticipated student performance should not only patently favor its selection, but such proposals should be encouraged further by a government policy that offers special incentives to this model. Virtue should be its own reward but often is not, and the government could further educational progress and safeguard the taxpayer by rewarding precision and compelling honesty.

The following items represent some examples of performance criteria for which incentive payments might be productive:

1. An amount of $_____ per student to the school for achievement on a General Education Development Equivalency Test (GED) demonstrating that the agreed-upon students have completed all five subtests (such tests to be administered by a certified administrator) and have received a standard score of not less than 40 on any one subtest or achieved an average of 45 on all five subtests.

2. An amount of $_____ per school for each student for demonstrating at least N percent per month increase in appropriate behaviors, as recorded by the use of a Behavior Checklist, such appropriate behaviors to be ascertained jointly prior to the signing of any contract.

3. An amount of $_____ per school for each student who demonstrates progress through the academic vocational and social skills program units to the extent that he completes a defined course, completion of such course being defined as curricula and clusters of curricula in existence at the institution on the date the herein referred-to contract is signed.

4. An amount of $_____ per school for each student who demonstrates progress through any and/or all units of new and program content which may be added subsequent to the negotiation of this contract and upon which agreement is achieved by all parties to the contract to the fact that such additional units do constitute relevant and appropriate program content.

5. An amount of $_____ per school for each student who successfully passes such situational performance tests as shall be developed and/or agreed upon jointly by all parties to the contract prior to and after signing.

6. An amount of $_____ per school for each student who demonstrates no antisocial activities, such activities being defined as those that would/should result in a written report on them within the administrative and management criteria presently in existence. No corporal, physical, or mechanical constraints shall be used in efforts to eliminate the antisocial behaviors.

7. An amount of $_____ per school for each student who achieves a high school diploma, to be defined as a verification that 16 credits have been attained in the following areas with proportional allocations: English, 3 credits; social studies, 2 credits; mathematics, 1 credit; science, 1 credit; electives, 9 credits. A credit is defined as 72 hours of successful classroom study.

8. An amount of $_____ per school for each student who enters and participates in VISTA and/or the Peace Corps, such entry in those programs to take place within N months of his departure from the school.

9. An amount of $_____ per school for each student who is a registered student and in attendance, within six months of his departure from the institution, at a certified, accredited college, university, or junior college.

10. An amount of $_____ per school for each student who is employed within N days of his departure from the institution, such employment to be gainful, meaning that the employer must be a state, federal, or governmental political subdivision or that such employer must be a bona fide representative of the private sector of the economy, including privately financed nonprofit organizations.

11. An amount of $_____ per school for each student (first year only) per calendar month who is gainfully employed after departure from the institution, such employment to have been continuous with the employer of record, at the completion of 12 calendar months, for at least N months.

12. An amount of $_____ per school for each student who, while gainfully employed, receives payment for his services 20 percent in excess of the minimum wage rate required by any and/or all applicable state, local, and federal regulations and statutes.

A performance-criteria approach to writing educational proposals promises greater economy in the allocation of education resources. Educational objectives pinned to predictable, measurable student performance would offer a much-needed basis for measuring program cost against program effectiveness. Such cost accounting, in turn, would promote more effective allocation of existing resources among competing educational programs. When monetary and other educational resources are focused on arriving at observable measurable outcomes, the resources required to bring a given student to a level of performance that does justice to his capacities can be identified and applied. When this happens, we will be on the verge of a renaissance in education for which we have all been waiting. Certainly it is asking little enough to expect that proposals for federal funds to education be directed toward this goal.

The Business of Education

EDITH GREEN

U.S. Representative Edith Green states that society, the community, and the teaching profession must share accountability with the classroom teacher. The teacher rather than private enterprise holds the greater promise for education. The Congresswoman's staff is currently examining federal educational contracts with private firms. In this interview, Mrs. Green advocates increased federal aid in the form of revenue sharing with the states or block grants with very little federal control.

What do you oppose as far as the education-industrial complex is concerned? Your name has been linked up with it many times. Eisenhower warned of the growth of the military-industry complex when he left office. Now that the over-all military budget is being cut—from around $80 billion for military procurement two years ago to about $65 billion this year—the amount of money we're spending on education and poverty programs has been increasing. So a new kind of complex may follow the money.

The facts speak for themselves. Some of the biggest defense contractors have spun off corporations to get contracts from the Office of Education and the Office of Economic Opportunity. AVCO has. Volt

Edith Green, "The Business of Education," *Nation's Schools*, 86:40–45, December 1970. Reprinted by permission.

Corporation, which has had both Defense and NASA projects, had about $25 million worth of OEO contracts about two years ago, when we were taking a special look at it. This is true of other corporations, too. This is where the money and future is apparently going to be—and they're hedging their bets.

What is the danger you see in all this? I happen to agree with Admiral Rickover, who is as well informed on defense contracts as anybody in the country. I was talking to him one day about the use of profit-making companies in education, and he said, "Well, Edith, profit-making companies and corporations are interested in one thing first of all—above everything else—and that's profit." And I think that if we're talking about quality of education, the first consideration ought to be education. My basic concern is that we are diverting millions of dollars—that should have gone into classrooms or to the poor—to profit-making corporations and consulting firms.

Some criticism of the nomination of Sidney Marland as U.S. Commissioner of Education is based on his alleged connection with the education-industrial complex through his post as president of the Institute for Educational Development. What is your reaction to this? I have not been trying to block his appointment because I don't know his past record of leadership.

I am concerned, however, about whether his nomination indicates a desire on the part of the administration of the Department of Health, Education and Welfare—the HEW secretary—to use private companies more and more for education. If it does, then I would be concerned.

I might add that IED, which Marland heads, is not a profit-making corporation, but I think that the profit or nonprofit label is a distinction without a difference, when they pump the profits back into the corporation, pay high salaries, and furnish cars and everything else. IED brings up another problem—the way educational research is being carried out. We have taken a look at the research contracts IED has, and the results, for the amount of money that was given, are so far disappointing, to say the least.

Do you think that private corporations are doing an adequate job of research for the government? We have in all the laws that no university or college is eligible for federal funds unless it is accredited, unless an evaluation is made of the work it's doing. There's no "accreditation system" as far as the new consulting firms and corporations are concerned. Oftentimes, contracts are put out to bid, and a new corporation or consulting firm bids the lowest and gets the contract. It is my judgment that we are spending hundreds of millions of dollars on education research that is absolutely worthless. Nobody looks at it. Nobody studies it. We're looking at contracts now where this is the case.

Two members of my staff have been spending considerable time looking at the contracts that have been let. Right now we are concentrating on the Office of Education where there are just under 1,400 live contracts. We've been looking at contracts for $130,000, $500,000, $900,000, and we've found that it's really complete chaos at OE. They don't know to whom the contracts have been given, or for how much, or for what purpose, or what's been done with them after the final reports have come in. Of course, lots of the contracts are on a sole-source basis—there's no competitive bidding.

In OEO, we've found conflicts of interest. For instance, a man who administered a program in the OEO then formed his own corporation and contracted to evaluate the program he had formerly administered.

Is this look a preview of Congressional hearings that might be held later on? It depends on what our conclusions are, after looking at the contracts. There is certainly a possibility of hearings, yes.

It's well known that not enough money is spent on educational research and development. Since you are skeptical of contracts with private, profit-making firms, just how would you go about doing this research? Would you have the federal government set up a separate research agency like the proposed National Institute for Education? Well, you state a conclusion that you have drawn: that it's well known that not enough money is spent on research and development. I don't know that I would agree with that in the first place, and I'd be more willing to discuss that part of it after we've spent this year studying the contracts.

The problem of research was brought up in hearings on educational needs in the 70s—that education spends a lower percentage on R&D than do other sectors of the economy. Well, I don't know if that proves anything. I'm not sure that the billions we've spent on research and development for the space program, the ABM, or the SST prove that we have to spend the same amount on education. I don't know that we're getting the best results for what we're spending now. I don't think I would agree with you that it's well known that we need to spend the same percentage as is spent on getting to the moon or developing the SST, both debatable enterprises.

I think the amount of money that we've spent in the 21 regional education labs around the country—now they've been reduced to 15—

has paid for questionable results. I'm in favor of some research if we know what we're doing, but I'm not in favor of spending billions without sufficient planning.

I think we know a lot of things that we should be doing in education, but we don't have the money to do them. I'd like to see us do that first. I think that we would be better off in terms of the quality of education if more of the money spent on research had actually gone into the classroom.

What do you think of the money that's gone into classrooms via performance contracts that OE and OEO have let recently? You know, as individuals we go on binges with particular fads—miniskirts or maxiskirts, long or short hair, etc. I think that as a society we go off on binges. A few years ago, it was sensitivity training. Right now, I think we've gone off on a binge on performance contracts. We've decided that we can hire a private, profit-making corporation that has been successful—that is, they're in the black instead of the red—and they will go in and measure the performance in the classroom and, for a certain sum, bring up the student's grade levels in reading or math or whatever. This is really quite the fad in education now. How many millions the federal government is spending in performance contracts, we don't know yet—or how much state and local governments are spending.

So you think that the answer to problems of the public schools is not to take the money and give it to industry but to give it to the schools directly. Is that right? I don't think you could walk into any classroom in any urban area today—certainly not in the ghettos or in most city schools with low or low-middle-income students—where the teachers would not be able to say, "If Susie had glasses, she would be able to perform at a much higher level" or "If Johnnie had a decent breakfast in the morning or nutritious meals at other times of the day, he would be able to perform better. And little Sam has a drunken father who beats him every night. If we could change his residence or his living conditions, he'd be able to perform better."

My own theory is that if we would take half of the amount we're spending on performance contracts with private, profit-making firms and, in a control group, say to teachers, "Here's $500. Spend it as you see fit in your classroom to bring up the performance of your youngsters. And if you think Susie needs glasses, go out and buy her some. And if someone else needs professional help, see that he gets it."

I would bet that if we took the two groups—the private firm that is so hot on performance contracting and the teachers, who were given, for the first time in their lives, a limited sum to bring up performance—we would get better results from the latter.

What do you think of the growing push to make teachers accountable for students' performance? I am aware that there's dead wood in the teaching profession, the same as there is in the civil service, government, Congress, medicine or any other profession. I am also convinced—and perhaps I'm biased because I came from the education profession and I did teach—that the vast majority of teachers are really dedicated and committed and really are trying to help the youngsters with whom they work. They may not have the best tools or the best answers or the best knowhow, but they're really trying very hard.

To say to the teacher alone, "We're going to hold you accountable for the education of this child," I think is absolute nonsense. And I think the teacher has a perfect right to say to society, to the community, and to the teaching profession, "We're going to share this accountability with you. And if you're going to place students from emotionally disturbed homes in our classrooms, then to ask us, in five hours a day, to be accountable for the complete transformation of these individuals, is unreasonable and ridiculous." What is the home, the church, society doing with these young people during the other 19 hours, seven days a week?

But I do think that society and the teaching profession ought to join hands in a program that would bring some kind of accountability for the next generation, to be able to say to those children, "We're going to see that you have a better start in life."

Do you see reading as the primary goal for the elementary schools—as former U.S. Commissioner of Education James Allen has stated? Reading has always been a primary goal for any teacher. I don't think Allen's pronouncement about having reading as the national goal accomplishes anything. I thought it was an awful lot of rhetoric, unaccompanied by funds or specific plans.

Of course reading is essential, but it isn't something you can teach in a vacuum. To single out reading and say this is going to be our goal is idle talk. You're going to have to look at the total child, and if he has dyslexia problems, you must recognize that before you can teach him to read. Or if a child has a very severe emotional problem, you have to do something about that before you can teach him to read.

What about computer-assisted instruction for reading, especially for the disadvantaged? I have serious questions about the path we're taking in computerized education. There are so many more things that are necessary than just sitting at a console and being able to identify words. Especially for the disadvantaged child who comes from a ghetto, I know of nothing that would be more important than the human relationship. Not the presence of a computer that's cold, methodical and unconcerned, but the warmth of a teacher who cares.

Suppose that the computer can produce grade level increases when a teacher cannot. How can you argue against the computer? You're saying *if* a computer can provide a higher level than a teacher. You know that's a big *if*, if the teacher has optimum conditions.

I think computerized education probably has one of its greatest values in adult education. An adult who has not completed the third grade is sensitive about that very fact. For him to be put in a classroom with 30 others and have his ignorance exposed to all 30 is something that many adults probably will not go through. The adult will stay home. But if there is individualized instruction at the computer console, where he is all by himself, nobody knows his ignorance but the computer. This can serve a great purpose. And the adult can also go at his own speed.

I also think, from the results of some limited studies, that computerized education has a great chance with the mentally retarded and in other special education.

But it seems to me for a small child, a warm relationship is much more important than for a 35-year-old, who reads at the second-grade level. I think we have to do a major job with disadvantaged kids when they're two, three and four years old.

Are you talking about day care centers? I'm very much in favor of a massive program of good day care centers.

What about the inadequate mother who lives in a crowded tenement, with five to ten youngsters running around? That mother and her children share their ignorance day after day. It seems to me that we must provide good day care programs and included in this would be the possibility of training ghetto mothers as paraprofessional aides —they could learn how to take better care of their children.

Placing the two, three and four-year-old children from the ghettos in good day care programs—where there are new opportunities and new horizons for them and where there's medical care, where there's the possibility of educational programs started at that age, where nutritious meals are served, where if psychiatric help is needed at that early age, it's given—this is really the only hope we have. I'm quite cynical about how much we can do for the 18- 19- and 20-year-olds who have already experienced failure.

What do you see as the real need for high schools today? My highest priority for the high schools would be a greater emphasis on vocational and technical training. The training of paraprofessionals and the training of service people such as dental technicians, laboratory technicians, engineer aides. Some of us in the Congress—and I take my share of the blame—and the academicians, who are degree oriented, have placed entirely too much emphasis upon the acquisition of a college degree.

We've made a mistake in the last several years in allowing the draft deferment only for the universities and colleges. It ought to have been extended to the technical schools.

John Gardner once said something that sums up my views in regard to this emphasis on the acquisition of a degree and the looking down on anybody who works with his hands, even an expert craftsman, as somebody who has not achieved success. Gardner said society must demand excellence in every phase of its activity and any society which looks down upon plumbing, because plumbing is a humble activity, and tolerates shoddiness in philosophy, because philosophy is an exalted activity, will have neither good plumbing nor good philosophy and neither its pipes nor its theories will hold water.

How do you stand on vouchers—the idea of providing parents with the money to pay for their child's education at the public or private school of their choice? I am interested in the experimentation going on in this area. I think it would be disastrous to this nation if the doors of the private schools were closed. And we know that at every level—elementary, secondary and higher education—many private schools face bankruptcy.

What many opponents of the voucher plan forget, is that we have had in essence a voucher system since World War II. And it has never been ruled unconstitutional. The GI bill is a voucher plan: The federal government has given the GI a certain sum of money and has said, "Spend it at the school of your choice."

Do you feel that vouchers are the answer for elementary and secondary plus higher education? I'm not willing yet to say so. I said I'm interested in the research and in studying it more. If we have the voucher system, in elementary, secondary or higher education—and especially in higher education, where the costs are much greater—we would have to have the institutional matching grants, the same as we did after World War II, with the GI bill. Not only was the GI given a certain sum of money, but the institution which he decided to attend was given a corresponding grant. And if the voucher system were to work and save some of our private colleges and universities from going out of existence, I think we'd have to have it.

What other possible solutions could you see for alleviating the financial squeeze on private elementary and secondary schools? My first choice has been shared time—facilities that would be shared by students from both private and public schools. In terms of higher education, in addition to the vouchers, institutional grants may receive great attention. If the government in its wisdom—or sometimes lack of it—is willing to contract with all of the profit-making corporations for various kinds of goods and services, I don't see why we can't have a program where we would contract with colleges and universities to educate a certain number of people. The institutional grant might be based on the number of bachelor's degrees that are awarded or some other formula for four-year colleges and also for community colleges.

Could you go back and elaborate on how you might attack some of the financial problems of public elementary and secondary schools? With school bonds being voted down more than ever before, what do you think they should actually do? There has to be a real policy program carried on to restore the confidence of the public in education. I think things that have happened in the last few years have really contributed to this lack of confidence. We're almost moving into an anti-intellectual period and the support of education is going to suffer a great deal.

As we see certain values ignored in the public school, I think there are going to be more and more parents who will want to send their children to private schools. It's inevitable that, as parents decide the public schools no longer contribute the kind of education that they want their children to have and as they pay the cost of private schools, they're going to lose their enthusiasm for supporting the public schools. I think this would be disastrous.

One of the first things we can do is look at the thousand-and-one programs we have on the periphery of the school system and do away with the multitudinous categorical federal grants.

I'm absolutely committed to the idea that we have to have decentralization of programs. We cannot, as an education committee here in the House, sit as a school board for every city or town in the U.S. and decide that we, in our arrogant way, have all of the wisdom and knowledge to make the decision for Nome, Alaska, Portland, Maine, Fresno, California, the ghettos of Chicago, and the rural areas of South Dakota. All the studies show that these programs aren't working. So instead of 118 programs run by the Office of Education, I favor revenue-sharing with the states or block grants with a very limited number of strings attached.

What would be some of the strings? One would be a fairer formula written in so that the big cities, in those states that are dominated by rural areas, would be sure to get their fair share of funds within the states. The second thing, since you've spoken of defeated tax levies and bond issues, is that with our mobile population and with the tremendous migration we've seen in the last decade especially from the rural towns to the big cities, a much larger share of education costs must be paid by the federal government.

These two positions that I have stated are not in conflict. I want less control from Washington, D.C., fewer categorical grants and more block grants. But I do think there has to be a larger share of the bill paid by Washington, if we're going to avoid the same tax situation we have at the present time with the school districts too often totally dependent upon the local property tax which is becoming confiscatory.

Do you foresee another big fight over the next education budget coming up? If the Congress and the education community are not willing to sit down—and I hold the education community accountable for this—and decide what are the highest priorities in education, then I think there's going to be a fight.

You know, Nixon is absolutely right on federal impact aid. That's the most unfair formula for the allocation of funds that was ever devised. And no educator who knows anything about it argues this point. There's no justification for Montgomery County, Md.—one of the wealthiest, if not the wealthiest county in the U.S.—getting the biggest chunk of money out of that and the poorest counties getting the least.

My ultraliberal friends bleed and die for the poor children of Sunflower County, Miss., and love to blast [Senator] Eastland every day on the hour. It's interesting that when we did a study on Title I of ESEA, three or four years ago, we found that Westchester County, N.Y., which is not known for widespread poverty, was getting three times the amount per poor child as Sunflower County. It's great to engage in rhetoric about the poor little child that is so abused in Sunflower County, but, when it came to cutting up the pie for allocation of education dollars, it required a knockdown battle to get even a partial change in the formula.

I also think that this business of 100 categorical programs is nonsense and so, yes, I think there is going to be a continuous fight over how the money is spent.

Advance funding is another problem. There's no superintendent, no college president who can make a wise decision and plan programs that will really be of help to kids, when he gets the money in March for the school year that began last September. But the thing they had to do, in order to spend all that money before June 30 and the new fiscal year, was go out and buy more audiovisual equipment and more books. The lobbyists back here—the booksellers and those who sell audiovisual equipment—have no reason to want advance funding. I believe advance funding is required.

The education community has a responsibility to decide priorities and not act like a bunch of lions all in there roaring for the lion's share.

Are you saying that the education lobbies aren't strong enough? I'm saying that some of the education lobbies are far too strong and aren't sufficiently interested in the quality of education. I'm talking about part of the influential so-called lobby—the Emergency Committee for Full Funding—the people that finance it and the people who decided what they were going to support. Educators have a first responsibility to look at their lobby groups who decide priorities.

The Emerging Role of State Education Agencies

EDGAR L. MORPHET and DAVID L. JESSER

Technological revolution, knowledge explosion, and population expansion are necessitating a new role definition for state educational agencies. This new role should be tailored through an alliance among the state agency and citizens and institutions with interests in education, an alliance which should ensure that the agency provides creative leadership, as well as assists in developing a planning mechanism to ensure that final decisions of the agency are both defensible by and reflective of the needs and wishes of the people. The state agency, in conjunction with citizens, must seek to improve learning environments, opportunities, and procedures; strengthen the research, development, demonstration, and dissemination; and encourage adequate evaluation of education for a changing society.

In a time of rapid and ever-accelerating social change, the state education agency—that agency which has the fundamental responsibility at least for public elementary and secondary education in a state—cannot reasonably be expected to contribute to the direction of the changes that are occurring, or to the improvement of education and at least

Edgar L. Morphet and David L. Jesser (eds.), "The Emerging Role of State Education Agencies," p. 18–22, *Emerging State Responsibilities for Education, Improving State Leadership in Education,* Denver, Colorado, October 1970, 177p. ERIC Document, ED-047-409. Reprinted by permission.

indirectly of society, if it simply continues to do only what it has done in the past. It must anticipate and prepare for its appropriate roles in the emerging future.

Planning for Needed Educational Improvements

Preservation of the status quo is not a defensible attribute of leadership in an ever-changing society. Efforts to maintain the status quo, however well meaning or sentimental they may be, are, in effect, efforts to prepare for a world that will no longer exist.[1]

One major role of every state education agency, therefore, must be that of providing leadership and services in planning for—and helping others to plan for—meeting educational needs during coming years. Only in this manner will it be possible for the agency to help education to be more responsive to societal needs, and at the same time will enable it to exert some influence on societal change. In assuming this role, the state education agency will have to consider at least the following:

- In an era calling for much greater and more pervasive equality of educational opportunity and for more relevant and adequate provisions, the state education agency has few, if any, options available in responding to the emerging requirement that it actively promote equality and adequacy of opportunities for all children, youth and adults. It does, however, have certain available options in terms of *how* it might or should proceed.
- At a time when society is quite justifiably calling upon education to demonstrate a greater degree of educational accountability for the total educational enterprise, the state education agency cannot very well maintain that professional autonomy somehow makes it immune to public criticism.
- In an increasingly interdependent society, the state agency cannot crawl into a shell of professional aloofness.
- When the increasing demand for a more rational allocation of scarce resources is being legitimately made upon all parts of our governmental and social organization, the state education agency cannot afford to ignore the potentialities of the systems approach as applied to educational planning.
- When traditional authorities are being challenged throughout our society, the state education agency will find it extremely difficult and unrealistic to attempt to preserve an authoritarian paternalism toward its many clients.
- The urgent cry for more relevant—applicable and meaningful—

education is being heard in every quarter, and the state education agency cannot ignore the plea.

Leadership in Preparing for Change

While it is impossible—in a literal sense—to be certain of many things in a society that is characterized by pluralism, contingency and relativism, it is at the same time necessary to assume that the state education agency does and will have a crucial role of leadership in the overall system of education.

If, however, the state education agency is to assume a bona fide leadership role in education, it must move away from the historic organizational and operational concerns—checking on compliance and doling out both money and advice—to new leadership and service activities that are less bureaucratic, less regulatory, less bound by traditions and structures, and more concerned with planning, development, and change.

The term, "leadership," whether used as a descriptive word or as a broad concept, is often either misunderstood or misused. Unfortunately, this term seems to connote different things to different people. However, the fundamental purpose, or function, of leadership consists of providing assistance in—or facilitating—the identification and attainment of goals that have been established by and for the organization. It is in this context that leadership, as both a role and function, is crucial to the state education agency. It is in this vein that the agency can and must provide leadership of the type suggested by Morphet, Johns and Reller[2] who observed that constructive leadership is found when assistance is provided in:

- Defining tasks, goals and purposes of the organization;
- Achieving or attaining the tasks, goals and purposes of the organization; and
- Maintaining the organization by accommodating emerging as well as present organizational and individual needs.

A rather fundamental dilemma relating to the concepts of power and authority often confronts people—and especially educators—who are concerned with leadership. Can a person be a leader without having power and authority? Conversely, does the existence of power and authority necessarily result in bona fide leadership?

As state education agencies prepare to assume leadership roles in education, questions such as these must be raised, and even more importantly, must be answered in a satisfactory manner. Power and authority may be valid components of leadership, but there is a difference between "power over" and "power with." As Wiles observed:

> Under the group approach to leadership, a leader is not concerned with getting and maintaining personal authority. His chief purpose is to develop group power that will enable the group to accomplish its goal. He does not conceive of his power as something apart from the power of the group. He is concerned with developing the type of relationships that will give him "power with" the group.[3]

As state education agencies move from the more traditional supervisory or regulatory roles to greater reliance on the leadership role, they not only must be aware of and utilize the positive aspects of leadership; they must also be aware of and avoid the potential misuse of leadership. The overall role and function of leadership must be clearly understood and accepted by all concerned. As Morphet *et al* have indicated:

> No school group is completely autonomous in authority. All school groups, both formal and informal, are subgroups of the total organization. The ultimate "group" that has the final authority to determine school goals is the people. . . . Participation in decision making by all groups and individuals concerned is now being widely advocated. As groups participate in decision making, it is vital that the limits of authority of each group be clearly defined. The administrator-leader must also make clear to groups and individuals participating in decision making the decisions that he reserves for executive decision making and the decisions in which they can share.[4]

Whyte has offered some challenging observations relating to "democratic leadership" that serve to re-focus attention on some fundamental problems or dilemmas of leadership:

> The leader of a group or organization is expected to be "democratic." He is expected to get results through encouraging "participation" on the part of group members in the decision-making process. . . . We are . . . inclined to be more than a little suspicious toward anyone in a position of authority. At the same time, we recognize that a complex society cannot run without the exercise of some authority and without some limitations upon individual freedom. Perhaps then we can find our way out of the dilemma if we try to make our organization more democratic and substitute "democratic" leadership for "autocratic" leadership.[5]

The specifics of how the leadership role and function may be assumed by state education agencies have been the concern of many recent studies, including those mentioned above. They are also of primary concern in this volume, and further suggestions relating to the specifics will be presented in the chapters that follow. But before many alternatives for action can appropriately be considered, it is necessary to look at some of the persistent problems and new dilemmas that face state education agencies in this changing society.

FOOTNOTES

1. For a meaningful discussion relating to the various "pitfalls" of planning, see Robert B. Howsam, "Problems, Procedures and Priorities in Designing Education for the Future," in *Cooperative Planning for Education in 1980*, Edgar L. Morphet and David L. Jesser, eds. (Denver, Colorado: Designing Education for the Future, 1968), pp. 81 ff. Republished by Citation Press, Scholastic Magazines, Inc., New York, N.Y.

2. Edgar L. Morphet, Roe L. Johns and Theodore Reller, *Educational Organization and Administration: Concepts, Practices and Issues* (Englewood Cliffs, New Jersey: Prentice-Hall, Inc., 1967), p. 127.

3. Kimball Wiles, *Supervision for Better Schools* (Englewood Cliffs, New Jersey: Prentice-Hall, Inc., 1955), p. 164.

4. Edgar L. Morphet, Roe L. Johns and Theodore Reller, *op. cit.*, p. 141.

5. William Foote Whyte, *Leadership and Group Participation* (Ithaca, New York: Cornell University, New York State School of Industrial and Labor Relations, 1953), p 1.

Making the School System Accountable

WILLIAM G. MILLIKEN

Governor Milliken of Michigan states that the primary task of education is to create confidence where little or no confidence exists in public American education. This can only be accomplished by cooperation among all levels of government. The states can no longer take a silent role, but must expand their positions to meet their responsibilities. He proposes educational reform in Michigan by the creation of regional education centers, appointment of a state superintendent of public instruction by the governor, changes in school finance, and a program of state assessment.

What do we mean by accountability? Accountability can mean a strict accounting by educators for the ways in which they spend money or an accurate means of testing how effectively educators are teaching children or any one of several other possible meanings.

William G. Milliken, "Making the School System Accountable," *Compact*, 4:17–18, October 1970. Published by the Education Commission of the States. Reprinted by permission.

Whatever accountability means to each of us individually, I think we hold in common a collective sense of its implications. And the chief implication is that people are increasingly demanding to know how their children are learning, what they are learning, and why they are being taught whatever they are being taught.

To create confidence where little or no confidence exists is the principal task of American education today. We cannot create this confidence by reciting a litany of accomplishments . . . all the money we are spending, all of the schools we are building, all of the new programs we have initiated. We can only create, or recreate, this confidence by eliminating our failures.

The best opportunity we have to create new confidence in public education is to expand the role of the states in the field of education. I believe that this can be done without diminishing local control of the schools. As a matter of fact, I believe if the states meet their responsibilities in education, local school officials will be able to do a better job.

As many of you know, I submitted a far-reaching program of educational reform to the Michigan Legislature last Fall.

The major elements of the plan have not yet become law. But I will continue fighting for this plan as long as I am Governor. For I believe that without bold and sweeping reform in finance and administration, there can be no significant increase in the quality of American education.

Proposals for Reform

The program proposes replacing intermediate districts with regional education centers. These intermediate districts (there are sixty of them in Michigan) now float in semi-autonomous limbo between the state and local school districts. We are convinced that replacing them with regional centers would vastly improve the delivery of such services as special education, vocational education and a variety of administrative responsibilities.

Second, in order to develop a more rational administrative structure, I have proposed a new system in which the Governor would appoint the state superintendent of public instruction, with the advice and consent of the Senate. The qualifications for the director would be spelled out in law, so that there would be no chance of a purely political appointment. In any event, the performance of the department and the superintendent would be the direct responsibility of the Governor. The Governor would be held accountable for the performance of the department, and the people would have a chance to make a judgment at the ballot box.

Third, school financing. I do not have to remind this audience how difficult it is to apply the concept of accountability to educational financing. I think all of us would like to finance schools and colleges on the basis of proven pupil achievement. But we cannot agree on a definition of learning, nor am I sure that we should. Financing reform is at the heart of proposals that I have submitted to the people of Michigan.

The most significant statement on state responsibility in the area of school financing was made at this meeting two years ago by Dr. James B. Conant. Largely on the basis of Dr. Conant's arguments, I became convinced that most of the responsibility for financing elementary and secondary education should be transferred to the states.

Dr. Conant has proposed that all authority to levy taxes for schools at the local level be eliminated and that the local share of school financing be taken over by the states. My proposals do not go as far as those of Dr. Conant and others. But they do move significantly in the same direction.

Specifically, the program which I have submitted calls for a uniform and limited property tax for school operations. This tax, which would require a constitutional amendment, would equalize the property tax burden. The total property tax levied throughout the state would be decreased substantially, and the state income tax would be increased to offset the cut in tax on property.

I believe that the distribution of funds to local districts should be related directly to need. My proposals recognize the varying need among districts—special needs for vocational and special education and the needs of under-achieving students. In addition, the budgeting process provided in my program would recognize differences in educational costs throughout the state.

Assessment in Michigan

Finally, accountability in the sense of accomplishment, what the students learn, and how to measure it. In this regard, Michigan, like the Education Commission of the States, has embarked on a program of educational assessment, which I have supported strongly. Much more work needs to be done in the area of educational assessment, for until the measurement of educational progress can be clearly defined, we will be unable to develop a system for correcting educational deficiences which have been revealed.

The fact that less than one percent of our total national education investment goes into research and development is indefensible. The federal government has made some important new commitments in educational research and development. President Nixon's National Institute of Education is one of the most exciting programs in national education policy in recent years. Recognizing this need at the state level, I am presently considering the establishment of an educational research and development organization in Michigan, combining the expertise of state government, the universities and the private sector.

We live in a time of multiple crises, and no approach to the solution of these crises is as promising as education. The quality of American education must be raised if we are to survive the Twentieth Century. Somehow, in the process, we must give our young people something more than the technical skills to earn a living. We must give them respect for the past, confidence in the present and a faith in the future.

We must introduce into the American education system a spiritual dimension which it does not now possess. We must show young people all along the line that we regard them as individuals—not to be folded, mutilated or spindled by an educational establishment which treats them as products instead of human beings.

Our goals cannot be reached by the federal government alone, or by the state governments alone, or by local school districts alone. They will only be reached by all units of government working together in creative partnership. And the time has come for state government to be something more than a silent partner.

Accountability as a State Function

RUSSELL W. PETERSON

Traditionally, the American commitment to education has been stated in terms of dollar inputs with little attention to output. An important ingredient in an accountability system is the feedback available to professional educators and lay personnel in the decision-making process. The ultimate in accountability requires a commitment that each child accomplish one specified increment of learning for each period of attendance in the school district. Would these increments of learning necessitate a state or even a national curriculum to provide for population mobility? In this paper, the Governor of Delaware addresses such questions.

Russell W. Peterson, "Accountability as a State Function," *Compact*, 4:19–20, October, 1970. Published by the Education Commission of the States. Reprinted by permission.

There is no doubt that accountability is the most important of the state's functions in terms of need, opportunity and cost. State governments and their agencies such as local school districts provide services to people. Many of the state's services can be fairly easily measured. For instance, the number of miles of highway built or rebuilt can be counted along with the number of people using the roads. We have automated monitors to record pollutant concentrations which tell us how effective pollution control is. In crime, even though it is more difficult, we do have statistical measures of performance.

I have set out specific output goals for Delaware state agencies over the next one to ten years. Some examples are: Reducing the amount of violent crime 25 percent by 1976, 50 percent by 1980. Getting 1,000 welfare recipients off the rolls and into jobs by a specified date. Having Delaware, within five years, lead the nation with the lowest number of deaths and injuries per automobile passenger mile. As Governor, I am accountable for achievement of these specific goals.

I winced a little in reviewing my objectives for education. All the goals are inputs, such as: completing the institution of state-supported kindergartens, making all schools in Delaware community schools, completing the upgrading of occupational-vocational education in all high schools and establishing prekindergarten programs for all four-year-olds by 1976.

Why couldn't I have listed as goals for education such things as: reducing high school dropouts by 50 percent; insuring that every child who left the schools could read and comprehend political and economic news, so that he could function effectively as a literate voter; reducing to less than three percent the number of kids graduating from high school who are racially prejudiced by 1976 when we will celebrate the 200th Anniversary of our Declaration of Independence?

Educators traditionally think in terms of inputs—new programs, more dollars for materials, higher teacher salaries and the like. We have files, and wastebaskets, full of statistics about education—how many schools, how many teachers, how many strikes and campus rebellions.

In principle, the American educational commitment has been that every child should have an adequate education. This commitment has been stated in terms of resources such as teachers, books, space and equipment. In fact, most of the outside accreditation techniques for elementary and secondary education still use measures of input as prime criteria for performance.

When a child fails to learn, school personnel have all too often labeled him "slow," "unmotivated" or "retarded." Our schools must assume the commitment that every child shall learn. Such a commitment must include the willingness to change a system that does not work, or to find one that does; to seek causes of failure in the system and its personnel, instead of entirely in students.

Let us adopt Lessinger's definition of accountability. That is, "Holding the school accountable for results in terms of student learning rather than solely in the use of input resources."

Underlying Concepts

From the acknowledged prejudices of my scientific and industrial background, let me share with you some concepts in accountability.

First, most pupil achievement in elementary and secondary education can be measured. Second is the importance of detailed, measureable educational objectives. Third is the necessity for evaluation by the independent accomplishment audit procedure. Fourth, the absolute necessity for complete, unvarnished performance feedback to the decision-makers. Finally, a real commitment "that every child shall learn."

Let's talk about measurement. The common cry from educators, particularly those working with disadvantaged children, is that education is too intangible to be measured. There are many methods of assessment, and teachers should specify the method of measuring what the student has learned. It does not have to involve standardized testing.

Very important is the establishment of detailed, measurable educational objectives. Even those educators who cry "It can't be measured" must admit that we teach with the notion that there is something to be learned. It is absolutely essential that a detailed list of concepts, skills and attitudes for each learning unit be set out in advance. The objective must be stated in measurable terms and should specify the method of evaluating whether the concept has been learned.

I would like to stress the necessity of independently evaluating results by using independent accomplishment audits. We want to evaluate results, not inputs. Results are the products, services or other effects created by the school. Results stand in contrast to resources consumed by the school.

Next, but very important, we must talk about the evaluation or audit process which can be an important stimulus to accountability. To be effective, the audit must be based on the objectives of the course or program as developed by the staff, students or even the community. The objectives must be specific and the auditor must agree with the program people on the method of measuring whether the locally developed objectives have been met.

The next point covers a fundamental of all systems—feedback. The continuing reluctance of professional educators to allow the newspapers to publish comparative standardized achievement test scores for examination by the citizens is a real problem. The newspapers contend that it is public information. The educators say that publishing comparative test scores will give misinformation because results do not indicate the inherent capability of the students. This argument must be resolved; indeed, it has been resolved in some large cities by publishing of test scores along with other socio-economic indicators of inherent pupil ability.

I am less concerned with whether newspapers publish test scores than whether or not the lay citizens who set the educational priorities and allocate funds are getting proper feedback. It is imperative that these decision-makers get all the facts—good and bad, pleasant or disquieting.

Commitment

Someone has stated that in America education has become our God. This is a general mystical belief—a blind faith that somehow education will solve all our problems.

I am for the commitment to education. But not the blind faith of some professional educators who say just give us more dollars, let us alone and we'll get the job done. We have been doing pretty much that and the evidence is pretty conclusive: We are making headway but the job is not getting done for many of the children in our society.

How do we get started in making teachers and administrators accountable for results? First, local school boards, with their professional educational leaders, must make a commitment that each child will accomplish one specified increment of learning for each period of attendance in the school district. The economists would call this accountability for the value added during each year of education. This is the ultimate in accountability.

What are we going to do about the children who don't achieve? It will take much more individual testing, special programs of remediation, summer schools, programs for children with learning disabilities and many more. Sure it will. But some states, like Delaware, have stated legislative policy that "the State Board of Education and local school districts shall provide special classes and facilities to meet the needs of all handicapped, gifted and talented children." In any case, it will be far easier to sell programs to assist children who are lagging if the district has agreed to be accountable for results.

It is well known that individuals, teams, business organizations and governmental agencies achieve considerably more when they are being held accountable for specific, measurable goals. This is particularly true when the goals have been set by individuals in the organization through participative management.

Now is the time when professional educators and key lay decision-makers must make a commitment to deliver on one of the most radical ideas in history—allowing every child in America to develop to the limit of his ability.

Problems Connected with Equalization of Educational Opportunity

JOHN W. POLLEY, and OTHERS

This paper traces the changing concepts in school finance that have implemented equality of education in New York State. Some financing methods are reviewed, such as the foundation program approach based upon state and locally financed minimum dollar levels, state financing of schools, and a voucher system. The paper also considers the definition of equality.

A definition of equalization of educational opportunity is extremely difficult in this time of rapidly shifting social relationships. Any final definition is likely to be highly controversial. However, practically such a definition is made in each session by the legislatures in each of the 50 states. Therefore it is useful to examine the concept as it has evolved over a period of years.

The concept was certainly present in 1812 when a system of common schools under a State Superintendent of Common Schools covering the entire area of New York State was instituted. These schools were to be supported by state funds matched equally by local taxation. Unfortunately the funds did not cover costs and rate bills in the form of tuition charges persisted for another 50 years. It was not until 1867 that the rate bill was abolished and free common schools achieved. The concept of equalization was extended with the development of a system of free high schools over the late portion of the 19th century.

John W. Polley, and others, "Problems Connected with Equalization of Educational Opportunity," New York State Education Department, Albany, Bureau of Educational Finance Research, July, 1970, 13 p. ERIC Document, ED-046-098. Reprinted by permission.
Mr. Polley is Assistant Commissioner, New York State Education Department.

As some states began to provide significant funding for education beyond that available from property taxation in the local district, the need for a theory on which to base action became more pressing. Cubberley, in his major analysis of state financing, 1905, advocated a weak fiscal equalization. Under his plan poor districts would receive minor additional funds because they were low in property valuation per pupil, and all districts would receive subventions to encourage numerically more adequate staffing.

As Burke states it "the early equalization schemes were developed for very primitive or simple operations—they presumed one teacher schools and a rudimentary elementary school program."

What perceptive individuals in the early 1900s thought of as a task involving a few hundreds of thousands of dollars of state funds, in each state changed into an undertaking involving many millions by the 1920's when the present basic system emerged.

This system has been called the foundation program approach and with many variations has guided the development of school finance from that time to this. It consists of a set number of dollars defined in legislation and assured to each district by a combination of state aid and a given level of local taxation which is constant among all districts. There is, of course, authority to supplement this foundation program through local effort. This produces inequalities in per pupil revenues, arising from differences in local taxable resources and from differences in the willingness of local citizens to support education.

Mort, writing in the late 1950s, defined equality of opportunity as follows:

> Equality of educational opportunity is a principle that is fundamental in American education—a principle based upon the assumption that our democracy is best served by extending to all children an equal minimum opportunity to attend schools adequate for the achievement of self-realization, economic efficiency, civil efficiency and efficiency in human relationships.
>
> Equality of educational opportunity means not an identical education for all children, but the provision by state and local means of at least certain minimum essentials of financial support. The acceptance of education as a function of the state and the insistence that, in the main, certain minimum educational standards are the concern of all people in the state rather than that of certain minorities make it incumbent upon the state to provide the machinery through which the principle may be effectively realized. The classical statement of the implications of the principle of equality of educational opportunity, as given by the Education Finance Inquiry Commission in 1923, recognized the obligation of the state to require at least minimum schooling for all the children, to place the support of this minimum schooling

squarely on the resources of the state, and to make supervision an important element in the state's program.[1]

The achievement of equalization of educational opportunity by the provision of somewhat adequate state and locally financed minimum level of dollars was not quick. Efforts at this had been going on for many years. These came to a climax in the pressing need for funds which occurred in the 1920s. Following a decade of special aids for such things as physical education, farm schools, and industrial education and the rapid increase in the costs of education, the National Educational Finance Inquiry was mounted. One of the states studied was New York. About the same time the Committee of Twenty-one developed the Rural School Survey, an eight-volume study, in which Updegraff proposed aid in relationship to tax effort. The Legislature had in 1919 established the Special Joint Commission on Taxation and Retrenchment. As a result of the continued studies of this Commission over the period of the 1920s, Mort in 1925 proposed refined measures of educational need and defined and set a minimum program. Mort extended this work through the Friedsam Commission in 1929 and 1930. The essential elements of the equalization program under which schools presently operate were defined in that period.

Yet this concept didn't offer a guarantee that anything other than a relatively low minimum number of dollars would be equalized—and this only as well as the property system functioned. Typically, expenditures have varied tremendously from district to district, usually closely in accordance with the level of taxable resources in the local district.

This led to a rule of thumb used extensively by some school finance people over a period of years from the 1930s on. When educational expenditures vary by more than 25 percent from the top to the bottom it is time to readjust the level of the foundation program upward. The inequalities created by fiscally able districts expanding their provision for education has in the past two decades provided a powerful stimulus for redefining and increasing the state's minimum program.

The concept of equalization has had a wide variety of side effects. It is premised on local control of education. Mort, troubled by the need to provide funds for all districts and not just the poor evolved the theory of adaptability which includes the concept that the more able districts tend to pioneer innovation. It has also led to widespread consolidation of school districts to even out local resources and to bring about more effective utilization of these resources.

In recent years, the fact that equality of educational opportunity can be defined as a set minimum number of dollars has been called into serious question.

The confusion over the question of what constitutes equality has been compounded by the fact that basic measures which determine the distribution under any system, whether it be a state-local sharing or an entirely state financed system, are not and, probably, can never be defined to everyone's satisfaction.

For many years the "need" measure has been defined in terms of one student equals one unit of need. While this was never completely true, in a less complex time such a measure was acceptable. While it is unlikely that the need for education by a given individual will ever be measured precisely, present knowledge should enable differentiation among broad groups of students.

A number of specific suggestions have been made for changing the unit of need. One is to substitute a per capita for a per pupil grant. The basic difficulty with this is that the educational system is not presently concerned with the total population of the community but only with children of elementary and secondary school age. Higher education is financed separately. Children of elementary and secondary school age are much more highly concentrated in certain communities than in others. Normally the suburbs in New York State contain a higher proportion of public elementary and secondary school students than do other types of districts.

It has been suggested that the use of enrollment rather than attendance would improve the measure. This argument is based on the fact that those communities which have the most difficult children to educate, normally the cities, have both the highest rates of absenteeism and the highest dropout rates.

Still another suggestion is that the need measure can be improved by giving a weighting for certain groups of children; e.g., the disadvantaged, or those in occupational education, or those who are handicapped. In essence this is already done at least to a degree through ESEA, Title I and the State Urban education program. The use of a weighting would tend to change the categorical nature of the present programs to general aid programs although this would not of necessity be so. Furthermore, whatever the system of weightings, it would be important to insure that duplication is avoided. For example, an economically disadvantaged student may also enroll in an occupational course.

The ability measure has also been called into question. Ability is presently based on property valuation in New York State. Property values become less and less an adequate measure of wealth. Generally, property remains, however, the only part of the tax base available for use by school districts. The only other measure would be income and this presents almost as many problems of measurement as does property, including that of incidence and a most difficult administrative problem; namely, that income figures are not available by school district.

Redefinition of the unit of need might remove much of the objection to the use of property valuation as the measure of wealth. Shifting to another local measure of wealth such as income doesn't seem especially desirable as long as school districts may tax property only.

As an alternative to revising and repairing the present system the proposal for complete state financing of schools has been revived. Most Southern states operate on some variation of that theme at present. Delaware, an industrialized state like New York, depends on approximately 80 percent state financing and has done so since the early 1920s. Hawaii, a state much different than New York, is a 100 percent state financed system.

Complete state financing of education must be judged on tax and administrative considerations as well as in the context of centralized versus decentralized governmental structure. It does not automatically provide for equality of educational opportunity even though it may provide for an apportionment of approximately equal dollars per child in every community.

Providing for complete statewide financing will tend to eliminate some of the worst of the inequalities due to variations among districts in property valuations. It will not assure that each child has equal access to educational resources, however. From the point of view of state equalization this must depend on the definition of need adopted. A child from a ghetto area may need more education than does a child from a wealthy suburban community to bring him to a given level of competence.

In recent years for a variety of reasons and there are many, there have been a number of radically new proposals for financing education. The ferment in school finance is perhaps greater than ever before including the battles over the rate bill and the equalization efforts of the 1920s. The concept of equalization of educational opportunity has taken on a new meaning. As currently stated it means that every child shall have access to a minimum amount of funds necessary to educate him for responsible citizenship.

How to achieve this is a more difficult matter than developing a definition. Shall some new measure of educational need be devised and written into the law as was done in the 1920s in New York State? Shall the district system which first evolved in New York State in 1812 be abolished? If the district system is retained, shall there be a recognition of the relationship between the need for educational aid and the need for other municipal services in the local school district? Shall the parent be made responsible for determining the level of his child's educational need and be enabled to meet that need?

Among the first of the new proposals to emerge is a call for a voucher system. Originally it was advocated as a means of overcoming the monopoly characteristics of the public schools and of increasing competition. More recently a variable voucher has been advocated as providing a means of equalizing the opportunity for the education of the poor, especially those caught in the ghetto areas of the cities or those in smaller districts where local resources make any program but the barest minimum impossible. Many variations of this theme have been presented.

District power equalizing is a different kind of plan and resembles in some part the present New York State system plus high tax aid. Variations on this theme exist presently in Wisconsin and Rhode Island. A poor district with an interest in education as measured by its tax effort would be enabled to support the same level of program fiscally as a rich district with the same tax effort. The choice of what tax effort beyond a required minimum would be made would be left to the community.

Greatly oversimplified, the family power equalizing plan originated by Clune, Sugarman, and Coons is described below. The plan has its genesis in the attempt to assure the same level of educational opportunity for the poor as for the well-to-do.

Local, political units (the districts) would be eliminated. However, both public and private schools would be permitted. The entire system would be state operated. The level of spending for education would be set by the state. Several different levels would be designated. The parent could then choose the level of spending by his choice of the school his child would attend. Parents willing to make the greatest financial sacrifices would send their children to the highest cost schools. Parents would pay an educational tax which would be progressive and would vary according to the cost of the school selected. There would, however, be a ceiling on the taxation at approximately twice the most expensive class of school permitted.

The family's yearly educational tax liability would range from nearly zero to $3,400. This would not, of course, fund the entire system. The funding would be based on the state income tax, thereby eliminating the property tax for school purposes.

It would appear that the equalization of educational opportunity has meant a variety of things over the past 200 years. From a beginning when a free common school education was the goal, it has been gradually extended to include high school education and to broaden the base of the adequacy of provision right on up to the present. The goal has always been expanded to include more education for more children. The present challenging concepts should continue to move the provision of education in this same direction.

FOOTNOTE

1. Mort, P. R., Reusser, W. C., and Polley, J. W. *Public School Finance,* New York: McGraw-Hill, 1960.

Our Accountability Problems

LUVERN L. CUNNINGHAM

Accountability is a broad concept which includes providing constituencies with an information base upon which outputs of educational systems can be judged. Because of the huge size of our educational system, only segments of it are visible to anyone at any one time. This necessitates sharing accountability. Local boards of education serve as initial appeals in accountability matters, but state agencies are ultimately responsible for education. The federal government and the education profession are also involved in the accountability process of responding to feedback from the citizenry.

Today's much used new concept is accountability. It is bantered about in many institutional environments but especially in education. Its most general meaning is that public officials must be responsible to their constituents in specific ways. In oversimplified terms, it implies that policemen must police, educators must educate, court justices must adjudicate, public administrators must administer.

Accountability and evaluation, as I use the terms, are not synonymous. Accountability is dependent upon evaluation, obviously, but it is a broader concept. The accountability responsibility extends beyond appraisal; it includes informing constituencies about the performance of the enterprise. Similarly, it implies responding to feedback.

For most educators, especially educational administrators, the term accountability is new but the need to be accountable is not. Administrators have for decades been concerned about public support. Many citizens (sometimes after some cajoling and coaxing) have turned out year after year to support bond issues and other referenda in the interest of improved education. These friends of the schools have asked for very little in return. The nearly blind American faith in the "good" of education has carried the burden. Most Americans still languish in the sunshine of deep belief in the virtues of education, especially public education. They want their children to reap the benefits of social and occupational mobility which public education has provided over the years. They want terribly to believe and most probably do believe that our schools are doing a good job.[1]

We live in an age, however, when citizens are seemingly hungry for information about institutional effectiveness. It was the rare occasion

Luvern L. Cunningham, "Our Accountability Problems," *Theory Into Practice*, 8 (October 1969), 285–292, College of Education, The Ohio State University. Reprinted by permission.

in the past when people asked for definitive, hard data. This is no longer the case. People are asking for visible evidence of success, and their inquiries are now appearing in accountability language. The press for accountability is real, takes many forms, and appears at many decision points within the educational system.

Citizens must have an information base upon which to make accountability judgments about their institutions. The principal response of school officials when accountability issues arise is either to become defensive or to begin an immediate search for information. Usually, as school people, we do quite well in providing evidence relative to inputs into the educational process. We can go to school documents and prepare attractive reports on such input indices as levels of expenditure per pupil, relationships between size of administrative staff and teaching staff, teacher-pupil ratios, numbers of dollars spent for library books, and the variation in expenditure for special education in contrast to regular educational efforts. Where we have difficulty is producing data relative to school outputs or product or performance. This is our chief accountability bind.

For a long time educators were able to sell the public on the relationship between level of expenditure and quality. The decades of work at Columbia University, especially under the leadership of Paul Mort, led school people and laymen alike to believe that there was correlation between level of expenditure and educational quality. Indeed this is true. Few people will quarrel with the overall generalization.[2] The argument grows thin however as one tries to correlate levels of quality among programs to particular levels of expenditure. Moreover, it is hard to break out quality differences (cost-benefit) *vis-a-vis* alternative allocations of resources within a school district or school building.

In times of scarce resources (which appears to be almost all of the time), we find it difficult to assemble data that would allow us to make judgments on the value of one internal allocation contrasted with another. Indeed, we are impoverished by the absence of criteria to aid us in making such judgments. If we were to decide whether to add courses in foreign language, black history, or enrichment work in social problems, we could find it almost impossible to produce easily and readily cost data that would help us make such a decision.

We are, in education, now adopting research methods which will allow us to make better input-output assessments. Thomas pioneered such analyses several years ago.[3] He has borrowed research models from the field of economics and has made applications of economic concepts to the field of education. At present, methods and techniques are primitive, but they promise to evolve into a more substantial set of tools. His students are currently at work on costing out internal allocation choices. If successful, these approaches will be useful in meeting public accountability demands.

A galaxy of companion developments is leading in the direction of rationalizing our decision-making in society. The NASA achievements will be fantastically persuasive in a political sense in effecting public acceptance of cybernetic sciences and more importantly their applications to a larger set of problems. Further examples include the adoption of program planning and budgetary systems, the acceptance of the Program Evaluation and Review Technique (elaborated by Desmond Cook at The Ohio State University), the continued press toward some form of National Educational Assessment, and the development of Computer Assisted Instruction. Each of these has in common the specification of objectives, gathering of data about achievement, organizing and analyzing information, and feeding it back. There is accountability potential in such devices.

The total institutional system of public education is so gargantuan that it is never visible to any person or group at one time. We see only pieces of it either as citizens or professionals. The disaffected can only nip away at its heels. Because of its size, accountability is necessarily shared. Herein lies a terribly difficult dilemma, particularly for the layman. We witness his frustration in so many places.

In a recent study, reported by Nystrand and myself, we described the problems of the would-be participant in school affairs.[4] First of all, the participant is staggered by the time problem. It takes fantastic amounts of time to be active. Second, it requires astonishing perseverance and tenacity to pursue participation objectives in the face of large scale impediments. It also takes patience and understanding—a third set of ingredients for effectiveness. Finally, effective participation requires leadership—in fact, unusual leadership.

The total education bureaucracy (all its parts and layers) is like a gigantic marshmallow. External pressures against it result in a little depression here, a little displacement there. But when the pressure is relaxed it quickly restores itself to its original form. It is exceedingly resilient and self-protective.

The Board of Education. In the thirteen-city study mentioned above, we found that one of the most important purposes of new efforts by citizens to participate in school affairs was an accountability drive. I would like to quote from that report:

> Citizen concern for accountability is being expressed in many ways.
> One of the first actions of the Citizens Committee on Public Education
> in Philadelphia was to work for procedures to select board of education
> members which would make the board more accountable to the public.
> The Pupil Placement Committee in Rockford wanted to know if stu-

dents in different but presumably equal schools achieved at different levels. Student unrest in a Detroit high school led to formation of a city-wide commission and a number of neighborhood citizen committees to study the total program in all city high schools. The Ad Hoc Pickett Committee in Philadelphia asked for and received permission to partici-pate in the formulation and application of criteria to evaluate the school principal. Oceanhill-Brownsville Governing Board members have assumed the right to dismiss teachers whom they deem ineffective.

Accountability as sought in these instances appears to have two dimensions. The first is access to information about performance. The second is ability to change those factors thought to be responsible for unsatisfactory performance. Like mechanisms established to articulate citizen expectations, those which attempt to maintain accountability have little if any authority to alter conditions. Many of them have con-siderable power in this regard however. The facts seem to be that some citizen participation mechanisms have resources which they can em-ploy in such a way that formal school authorities yield to their requests to change factors which the citizens consider responsible for unsatis-factory performance. Instances were identified, for example, where school officials removed or transferred a teacher or principal because of citizen dissatisfaction.[5]

We are witnessing similar phenomena today, all across the country. People really do have anxieties about the performance levels of schools. Packed galleries at school board meetings are common oc-currences.

In a recent study of the Columbus Schools, citizens questioned assessment and accountability. Quoting from the report:

> Throughout the period of our work . . . we have heard one ques-tion repeatedly: "How well are the Columbus Public Schools doing?"
> . . . The question is asked honestly and humbly and in many cases by parents who are not particularly uneasy about the schooling received by their own children. People would like to know within reason how their educational dollars are being spent. Even more important, they would like to know the quality of the return on their educational invest-ment. This is a modest request. . . .[6]

The board of education stands as a most visible target when citizens want to know how well the public school enterprise is performing locally. Citizens can bring their questions to the administrative team within the school district and satisfaction often is achieved through that inquiry. But in today's climate of sometimes exaggerated and increasingly emotional concerns about education, more and more accountability questions are being brought to the attention of boards of education.[7]

It is quite appropriate, too, that this occur. Within legal structures for the governance of education, the local board of education is the responsible public body for initial appeals on accountability matters. However, many laymen forget or are not aware that the board of education is not the court of last resort. The state and its state-level agencies are ultimately responsible for education—both its provision and its quality.

The State. State legislatures wrestle at least biennially with educational legislation that includes appropriations for the support of schools. Their work often turns on issues which in some measure are decided on the basis of feedback about the effectiveness of the educational enterprise. A legislator hears from his so-called constituencies in several ways. They provide him with their interpretations of facts, especially local ones as they see them. They offer responses (most of which are intuitive) to questions that a legislator might raise with them about institutional performance. These data frequently are contradictory. He questions their validity. Often he falls back upon his own visceral feeling about things.[8] Much of his contact with constituencies is negative, since things perceived to be wrong get communicated while things that are right seldom do. His confrontations are with problems not successes.

The "accountables" at the state level are a mixed lot. They include the governor, legislators, the like. In fact, the most responsible people state department personnel, budget officers, and legally in America for education are state legislators. The Constitution of the United States is clear on that point. The "buck stops here" should indeed be their slogan—more so for education than other public services. School board members are agents of the state responsible to state authorities, not to the local constituencies which may select them. It is an anomaly that we expect things of our local boards which often legally are beyond their capacities.

State legislators, as a population, and especially the committee structures (education and appropriations) have been ignored by the students of educational politics by and large. Yet, they comprise the most powerful decision group in education. They are the accountables. We should know a lot more about them.

The Nation. The mid-1960's was a period of rapid expansion of federal interest in public education. The celebrated Elementary and Secondary Education Act of 1965 provided for a host of new federally sponsored and financed educational programs and activities. There was a marked upswing in federal expenditures although appropriations lagged behind the spirit of enthusiasm surrounding the creation of those efforts. These programs, unlike most of their predecessors, gave more than lip service to evaluation. Small amounts of money (clearly not enough) were earmarked for this purpose as an attractive new beginning to a hoped for era of interest in appraising our product.

In this Congress, with a new administration, the accountability consciousness appears to be at an all-time high. Congressmen in general, but especially the education committee, are asking hard, penetrating questions. They want to know what has happened to strengthen public education as a consequence of stepped-up federal investment. They have a right to ask, they need to ask, and they should expect to get solid, definitive answers.

They apparently are not getting those answers. As a consequence, their restlessness about education has increased. The United States Commissioner of Education, James Allen, and his top staff, testify before congressional committees regularly. This is not a new exercise, but the harshness of the questioning, according to old-timers on the Washington scene, appears to be more severe than it was in the past.

The Commissioner is expected to have clear-cut, concise, and accurate data to support his answers to accountability questions. Congressmen appear to be serving notice that in the future hard data will be anticipated. It remains to be seen, however, whether the solons will provide the appropriations to do the accountability data gathering job.

The federal establishment not only is subject to inquiries from the administration and Congress, but it also is subject increasingly to intensive review on the part of its client systems. Large cities and states are not given to sitting back quietly and accepting federal mandates and directives. They now fight back and with a vengeance. They reach out for political support from all sources which partially accounts for the new vigilance on the part of senators and representatives as they in turn seek data from the United States Office of Education.

The Washington nervousness is understandable. The data which do come to federal bureaucrats and politicians are disturbing. The Coleman Report, the Study of Racial Isolation in the Public Schools, and analyses of the impact or effectiveness of Office of Economic Opportunity programs such as Headstart are not reassuring.

The justifications of further spending on old programs or the invention of new efforts directed at old targets does not come easily. Roche, writing in *The New York Times,* comments about the "changing of the guard" in Washington and the programs of the Johnson era:

> Nixon's actions and his inactions since his inauguration indicate his full awareness that he was elected Chief Executive to preside over the liquidation of the Democratic empire—that is, the vast expanse of pro-

grams designed to implement the rhetoric of freedom at home and abroad. He is far too shrewd to tackle these policies head-on. On the contrary, he affirms their abstract, theoretical merit—and allows them to be garreted in the soundproof dungeons of the Bureau of the Budget. He will sponsor no dramatic executions, which could be a unifying catalyst for the shattered liberal Democrats, but one by one the major Democratic programs will be administered to death.[9]

Roche is not without his biases. As a professor of politics at Brandeis, he was also a special consultant to President Johnson a couple of years in the latter days of the Johnson administration. I offer his observations partially in support of the point that accountability has its national face and partially as evidence of the problems inherent in the politics of accountability, a notion developed more fully later.

The Profession. We are a mixed profession; we have many fragments. Historically, we have held together rather well, but in the past decade we have given some evidence of coming apart at the seams. In Ohio, as in other states, sharp divisiveness exists between the chief administrators' organization and the teachers' organizations. Nationally, we have witnessed disaffection among the several departments of the National Education Association. At that level, too, we have what has been described as a death struggle between the National Education Association and American Federation of Teachers.

Testimony to the professional establishments' historical solidarity comes from many sources. Martin, a political scientist of reputation, describes it this way:

> Education's peaceable kingdom was not achieved by sudden flight, but resulted rather from arduous and purposeful effort exerted over a long period of time. Not to put too fine a point on it, the leaders of education have erected for their enterprise a fortress which seems all but impregnable.[10]

His appraisal was made about seven years ago. More recently, Mayer made these observations:

> On a higher level of generalization, our problems in education are merely a special case of the root problem of politics in a modern society: the control of professional performance. It is nonsense to believe that amateurs (gentlemen scholars or black militants) can successfully operate the immensely complicated machinery of modern government. . . . Because they are the masters of their own mysteries, the professionals must be given a large measure of self-direction, but they are after all part of a larger society which supports them, and when they ignore the needs and purposes of that society to serve their own shibboleths (as educators especially tend to do), they become parasites. The failure

of public education to respond to societal demand is especially discouraging, because here there is a public institution—the school board—
which presumably exercises some continuing authority.[11]

In both of these observations, there are explicit as well as implicit
references to the power of the kingdom and its unwillingness to respond to accountability inquiries. Part of the professionals' nonrespon-
siveness is because the expectation of accountability is not highly
visible within the norms of the profession.

I recently examined a study entitled "The Normative World of the
Elementary School Principal."[12] The research instrument, purported
to explore the professional norms of this group, did not contain any
questions having to do with a sense of responsibility on the part of the
principal for evaluating the performance of the enterprise he heads. If
we are to trust this research, we must conclude that elementary principals value an accountability obligation modestly at best.

The Exploratory Committee on Assessing Progress of Education
(more affectionately called National Assessment) sponsored by the
Carnegie Corporation in cooperation with the U.S. Office of Education
represents a recent attempt to gather data about the national educational product.[13] The work of ECAPE is to result in periodic reports
to the nation on the state of its educational health. Many professional
educators have attacked this development frontally and obliquely.
Their salvos have slowed down the Committee's progress; possibly its
opponents will administer the death knell. The posture of educational
leaders toward assessment suggests the subdued nature of the accountability ethic within the fraternity.

To transfer this conclusion to the entire profession obviously would
be unfair. However, we cannot dismiss lightly the feeling that the
profession has an ill-formed posture on its own accountability.

In the past, we professionals have refused to believe that we pos-
sessed adequately refined evaluation technology to make judgments
about ourselves and/or our colleagues. We have rationalized our way
out of intensive performance evaluation on the basis of inadequately
perfected technology, when the reason really has been that we have
been unwilling to face prospects of negative appraisal.[14]

Educational institutions, although they are brutally inhuman in
many of their behaviors, are starkly frightened at the prospect of
presenting to their members evidence of inadequate performance.

We tend to pass educators' fear of evaluation off as a "naturalistic"
phenomenon and in so doing underestimate its power and significance. For example, on the topic of passing judgment, Gardner says:

> It is in the modern mode for us to shrink from making judgments,
> even to believe that it is somehow presumptuous or arrogant to make

judgments. We feel that it is more seemly to devise a system and let the system make the judgments, or invent a machine and let the machine do the judging, or gather statistics and let the statistics make the judgments.[15]

We withdraw intuitively from circumstances where we distrust the evaluator. We strike out against the linking of power with judgment. Thus, we retreat to the institutionalization of judgment and to the depersonalization of appraisal. Our language reflects these postures. Seldom do principals say "Miss Abernathy, you are a lousy teacher." The principal will say, "Miss Abernathy, the custodian reports paper on the floor in your room." Or, "The test scores indicate that the children are not reading up to grade level." Or, "Seven parents complained today at the open house about their children's spelling." The language of evaluation is couched in indicators, some neutral, some not.

Waller described parents and teachers as ". . . natural enemies, predestined each for the discomfiture of the other. The chasm is frequently covered over, for neither parents nor teachers wish to admit to themselves the uncomfortable implications of their animosity, but on occasion it can make itself clear enough."[16]

Teachers and parents can at times discuss a child (even one with severe problems) in an aura of fantasy, as if the child were of peripheral interest. Parents verbalize frequently in masked form their private anxieties about their failures in the parent role; teachers counter in kind evidencing concern about their own performance. In addition, parents and teachers want to do different things with the child. They want the child to prosper in different ways. They wish him well according to different standards of well being.[17] It is a situation where the child becomes the excuse for playing out other accountabilities.

We have become very skillful at subduing interest in appraisal, both as a society and as institutions. We mask our deficiencies at all levels within the society and within institutions in the society. Again, I find it hard to improve on Gardner's language:

> We fear the judging mind. Even more, we fear the judging and purposeful mind. And let's face the fact that we have reason to fear it. All of recorded history tells us what tyranny and dogmatism can flow from that mind. A good deal of social organization is designed to protect us from that tyranny. . . . Our own society is rich in social and organizational arrangements that protect the individual from being at the mercy of some other man's dogma and tyranny.
>
> It would be catastrophic if we were to forget this distilled wisdom of the race. Yet the paradoxical truth is that the same judging, pur-

poseful mind that can cause us such trouble is an important instrument
of creativity and change and the source of all form and style.[18]

There is substantial reluctance within the society to unleash its
powers to appraise itself.

The politics of accountability is an exceedingly tricky domain. It is
difficult to sort out those phenomena that are essentially political from
those that are organizational. Perhaps I can illustrate what I mean
under the phrase "the triumph of bureaucracy over democracy."

Lowi has observed that bureaucracy is a relatively new basis of
collective action in the United States and as yet we don't quite know
what to do about it.[19] Reform governments with destruction of the
Big City political machines as their objectives have led to the disintegration of those machines, but they have not led to the exciting
revitalization of the cities that the supporters of reform may have
hoped. The new breed of mayor such as Lindsay, Cavanaugh, Stokes,
and Naftalin ran headlong into the entrenched power of city bureauc-
racies. Those "establishments" in fact run the cities, but do not
govern them. The highly bureaucratized departments (sanitation,
transportation, health, etc.) are powerful "principalities" each ruled
independently and presided over by increasingly professionalized bureaucrats.

If, in broad terms, we conceive of the school system as a public
institution responsive to the public interest then we would expect that
demands for change or reforms with salient political support within
the broader community would be reflected in change. This is not
always the case. The struggle in New York City (generating out of the
proposal to decentralize the school system) is in large measure a story
of the irresistible force encountering the immovable object. There was
a coalition of external or public interests (Ford Foundation, Mayor
Lindsay, Civil Rightists) attacking what proved to be an impregnable
"bureaucratic principality." The attacker, finding the New York City
arena itself untouchable, chose to move the conflict to the state level.
There the coalition proposed decentralization alternatives that would
crack the solidarity of the New York Federation of Teachers and
challenge severely the power of the Association of Administrators and
Supervisors. The decentralization concept threatened the establishment severely but its responses were adequate to the test.

The New York City School System represents possibly the tightest
bureaucratic "goliath" in the country. As Lowi has remarked about
New York City's earlier (1963–65) turbulence: "The superintendent
of education, an outsider, (Calvin Gross) was forced out. He was
replaced by a career administrator. One education journalist at that
time said: 'Often . . . a policy proclaimed by the Board (of Educa-

tion), without the advice and consent of the professionals, is quickly turned into mere paper policy. . . . The veto power through passive resistance by professional administrators is virtually unbeatable. . . .' ''[20]

Rogers in his controversial study of the New York City schools describes the extent of professionalism and the accountability of the school system to the public it serves as contributing more to the disintegration of the system than desegregation.[21]

Let me quote from Rogers' first chapter:

> Of great significance is the Board of Education's active role in shaping and promoting a 'politics of futility' that exists in New York City around the public schools. The institution has *organizational defenses* that allow it to function in inefficient, unprofessional, undemocratic, and politically costly ways without evoking more of a revolution or push for radical change than has yet emerged. It has an almost unlimited capacity for absorbing protest and externalizing the blame, for confusing and dividing the opposition, 'seeming' to appear responsive to legitimate protest by issuing sophisticated and progressive policy statements that are poorly implemented, if at all, and then pointing to all its paper accomplishments over the years as evidence both of good faith and effective performance.[22]

The implicit tension (professionalism vs. community interest) is growing across the nation. It promises to become more and more explicit in the months ahead and warrants our attention as persons interested in schools.

Provus, writing in the 1969 NSSE Yearbook on evaluation, fingers school administrators as the villains in school system evaluation but reserves some of his complaints for the university-based evaluators. He chides the practitioners:

> It is entirely possible that most public school evaluations are meaningless because they reflect the confusion of administrators regarding educational programs which are equally meaningless. It is also possible that most evaluators do not know their business. No doubt, the weakness of educational programs, evaluation methodology, and the training provided in institutions that prepare both administrators and evaluators are related.[23]

Later he comments on another issue: "There is surprisingly little theory on which to base good evaluation practice."[24] It is precisely on this point that I find the work of Stufflebeam and Hammond at The Ohio State University and Guba at the Indiana University promising.[25] They are trying to understand institutional change and the function of evaluation in achieving such transformations. Evaluation can be seen as a form of applied research and in this context the evaluator is concerned with finding immediately relevant answers for decision-making.

Skillful evaluation makes accountability feasible. We need to keep in mind that the parameters of accountability at any given level in the school organization are broader than those implied in the term evaluation. Similarly, those who are the "accountables" have responsibilities that differ in important ways from the evaluators.

Our classic approaches to evaluation have been rather narrowly defined and designed without particular reference to needs of the organization for decision or accountability purposes. As a consequence, one datum on performance, for example achievement test scores, becomes information sought after by the public and protected by administrators. School officials are not yet comfortable with openly sharing such data with their communities. The total hardware of accountability and evaluation should include theoretical frameworks comprehensive enough to incorporate data sharing and the management of feedback.

The Columbus School Profile[26] produced recently under the direction of Howard O. Merriman of the Columbus Public Schools is a strong beginning along the path of meeting a community's accountability expectations. The decisions of the school administration and the board of education first to produce such a document and second to share it extensively with the community were courageous actions. Few school systems have been so forthright. Most systems protect data that are in some measure unfavorable or are difficult to interpret by laymen.

Columbus school officials felt the sting of public response to their boldness in releasing test data to the community. Some critics offered their "I told you so's." Those who suspected that inner city children were performing below grade level found evidence that this was so. Professionals understand that there are reasons why such young people are performing inadequately. Sharing and clarifying such reasons with the schools' constituencies becomes a second and more difficult step. In this effort, achieving community understanding of the data will depend upon skillful interpretations. The teachers and administrators who will carry the burden will require some special preparation.

This is what accountability means. This is what friends, as well as critics, of the schools are requesting.[27] A Task Force of The Urban Education Coalition of Columbus, directed by Arliss Roaden of the College of Education at The Ohio State University, has developed a splendid set of guidelines to assist the Columbus Public Schools (and others for that matter) with several accountability objectives.[28] The work of the Task Force represents a rational attempt to link schools and communities in a mutual assault on accountability problems. It is a sound beginning to a large assignment.

The professionals and laymen interested in schools are confronted with problems as well as opportunities. We will hear much more about accountability. It will become a household word much as the IQ or the "whole child." Thus, we must search for ways to understand what it means to be accountable, what accountability expectations are among the many constituencies of the institution as well as among professionals within the institution. We must find ways to evaluate our product that permit us to meet our varied accountability expectations.

As we become more adept at appraisal and as we incorporate the accountability norm into our profession, the fear of appraisal will diminish. Strengthened understanding of organizational constraints that mitigate against evaluation will permit more rapid progress too. The same is true for unraveling the political mysteries that confuse and add to the complexity.

Evaluation technology is gradually being improved and updated but progress is slow, inhibited by organizational constraints and slowed because of low priority on the lists of educational needs. As imperative as the invention of new technology and the refinement of existing tools is the creation of new interpretive capabilities.

I make no apology for our primitive levels of accountability progress. At the same time, I am confident that the clients who support us will not tolerate our impotence much longer.

FOOTNOTES

1. Nystrand, Raphael O. "Home-School Communications in Big City School Systems," paper presented originally to the National Conference of Professors of Educational Administration, August 19, 1968.

2. For a discussion of Mort's role *see* Stephen K. Bailey, *et al.*, *Schoolmen and Politics: A Study of State Aid to Education in the Northeast.* Syracuse: Syracuse University Press, 1962, pp. 24–25.

3. Thomas J. Alan. "Educational Decision-Making and the School Budget," *Administrator's Notebook,* December 1963, *12*, 4 pp.

4. Cunningham, Luvern L., and Nystrand, Raphael O. *Citizen Participation in School Affairs: A Report to the Urban Coalition.* Washington, D.C.: The National Urban Coalition, June 1969, pp. 39–41.

5. *Ibid.*, pp. 19–20.

6. The Ohio State University Advisory Commission on Problems Facing the Columbus Public Schools. *A Report to the Columbus Board of Education.* Columbus: College of Education, The Ohio State University, 1968.

7. For a description of the problems of today's school board members *see* Morris, Jack H., "A Thankless Task," *The Wall Street Journal,* April 16, 1969, *173*, 1, 25.

8. Bailey, *op. cit.*, pp. 50–52.

9. Roche, John P. "A Vacation from Responsibility," *The New York Times Magazine,* July 20, 1969, p. 26.

10. Martin, Roscoe C. "School Government," in *Governing Education,* Alan Rosenthal, editor. Garden City, New York: Doubleday and Co., Inc., 1969, pp. 282–83.

11. Mayer, Martin. *The Teacher Strike: New York, 1968.* New York: Harper and Row, Publishers, 1969, pp. 118–19.

12. Foskett, John M. *The Normative World of the Elementary Principal.* Eugene, Oregon: The Center for the Advanced Study of Educational Administration, University of Oregon, 1967.

13. For a review of the origin and development of national assessment *see* Jack C. Mervin and Frank B. Womer, "Evaluation in Assessing the Progress of Education to Provide Bases of Public Understanding and Public Policy," in *Educational Evaluation: New Roles, New Means,* Ralph W. Tyler, editor. Chicago: The University of Chicago Press, the Sixty-eighth Yearbook of the National Society for the Study of Education, 1969, Chapter 13.

14. Carter comments on this problem. "It is surprising how frequently we resist the idea of assessment. We will deplore some existing condition or state that a serious problem exists without being willing to undertake the necessary effort or even to recognize the necessity for a quantitative assessment of the existing situation." He continues: "Similarly, we should not be satisfied with introducing ameliorative efforts in the social and educational areas unless we are willing to undergo the stringent test of objective assessment so that an evaluation of the effectiveness of new methods can be made and cost/effectiveness estimates derived." Carter, Launor F. "Knowledge Production and Utilization in Contemporary Organizations," *Knowledge Production and Utilization in Educational Administration,* Terry L. Eidell and Joanne M. Kitchel, editors. Eugene, Oregon: Center for the Advanced Study of Educational Administration, 1968, pp. 16–17.

15. Gardner, John W. *No Easy Victories.* New York: Harper and Row, Publishers, 1968, p. 119.

16. Waller, Willard. *The Sociology of Teaching.* New York: John Wiley and Sons, Inc., Science Editions, 1965, p. 68.

17. *Ibid.*

18. Gardner, *op. cit.,* p. 122.

19. Lowi, Theodore. Introduction to *Machine Politics,* Howard F. Gosnell. Chicago: University of Chicago Press, 1968, p. xv.

20. *Ibid.,* p. xiii.

21. Rogers, David. *110 Livingston Street: Politics and Bureaucracy in the New York City Schools.* New York: Random House, 1968, p. 3.

22. *Ibid.,* p. 13.

23. Provus, Malcolm. "Evaluation of Ongoing Programs in the Public School System," in Tyler, *op. cit.,* (footnote 13) , p. 242.

24. *Ibid.,* p. 243.

25. Professors Daniel Stufflebeam and Robert Hammond of The Ohio State University and Egon Guba of Indiana University are collaborating on the refinement of promising new evaluation theories.

26. *The Columbus School Profile, A Report of the Columbus Public Schools to the Community* by Howard O. Merriman, director, Department of Education and Research. Columbus, Ohio: Columbus Public Schools.

27. For a discussion of the imperatives of accountability *see Education and Urban Renaissance,* Roald F. Campbell, Lucy Ann Marx, and Raphael O. Nystrand, editors. New York: John Wiley and Sons, Inc., 1969.

28. Roaden, Arliss. *Citizen Participation and the Need for Public Accountability.* Columbus, Ohio: Assessment Task Force, Urban Education Coalition, 1969.

Client Criticism of Urban Schools: How Valid?

AMOS WILDER

Amos Wilder's theme is that school boards and professional educators are unresponsive to citizen groups. The educator-client relationship is a failure; parents feel that such things as professional accountability should become part of collective bargaining. The schools need to be accountable to the community and should function under community control.

The client in a school system is the community, the parent, and the student being served by education professionals. The commonly accepted literal interpretation of the word "client" is a *person, company, or organization receiving a professional service*. The dictionary also refers to a client as 1) a poor or humble person in ancient Rome depending on a noble or wealthy man for assistance, 2) a person who is under the patronage or protection of another, or 3) one dependent on another.

If these definitions adequately describe the educator-client relationship today, then this relationship is a dismal failure in the city of Detroit. Relevant education for the majority of black and poor students is nonexistent. Pilot projects and compensatory programs are a local as well as a national failure. No matter how well-intentioned, educational equality through integration is a geographical and mathematical impossibility, and a political improbability. Unrest among disenchanted and frustrated black students is increasing. The public schools are now symbols of social dynamite, reflecting generations of society's neglect and indifference.

The practice of citizen groups presenting their concerns to board of education officials is now regarded as an exercise in bureaucratic gymnastics and futility. Parents will no longer experience the humiliation of presenting their vital concerns to school officials only to have them courteously received, then rationalized and compromised into inaction.

Teachers, administrators, teachers' unions, and other professional groups look the other way when the question of professional accountability arises. Many in the school system still believe that the primary

Amos Wilder, "Client Criticism of Urban Schools: How Valid?" *Phi Delta Kappan,* 51:129–130, November 1969. Reprinted by permission.

causes of their professional failure are cultural deprivation and lack of resources rather than their own policies and attitudes and the indifference of society in general.

To further complicate the educational dilemma, black parents now overwhelmingly reject the view that our children *can never be rescued, can never be educated,* unless subjected to the benign influence of white, middle-class children.

Traditionally, parents exercised a "blind faith" in believing that education was the exclusive domain of the professional. Decisions affecting the operation of schools were not to be challenged. Parents were once urged not to teach their children at home so that the child would not be confused when later he encountered the methods and techniques being employed by the professional. Even the teaching of the alphabet was once considered taboo. In contrast, schools today claim that parents are not doing enough for their children at home. This contradiction is underscored by the thousands of children who can neither read nor write.

School officials, teachers' unions, and the profession in general have thus far successfully isolated themselves from serious public criticism. But today parents are asking: What kind of a school system is it that systematically relegates poor and black children to a status of academic inferiority and intellectual mediocrity? They wonder whether they can permit the schools to be run by a bureaucratic fossil, dedicated to the status quo and uniformity, which protects the vested interests of its members through a legalistic device called "tenure." Parents question a system which seldom if ever discharges a member for incompetence while incompetence is widespread and commonly accepted as the standard for most schools.

Admittedly, teachers and administrators, like all other groups of workers, should have the opportunity to bargain collectively for economic and other benefits in order to guarantee their competitive status as a profession. Parents wonder, however, just how much of this improved status must be gained at the expense of students and communities.

The president of the Detroit Federation of Teachers, at the time of ratification of the 1967 teachers' contract, said: "The collective bargaining procedures through which this contract was negotiated have given these educational experts [teachers] a real voice in school decisions." If in fact these "educational experts" have a "real voice" in school decision making, then they must also shoulder their share of the responsibility for the massive academic deterioration found in our schools.

The community is now asking some serious questions about this bargaining process: Where is the voice of the community during such one-sided negotiations? Who protects the vital interest and concerns of parents and students? Not the school system's bargaining officials; certainly not the teachers' unions.

Why, for example, cannot teacher and administrator salaries be geared to measurable levels of professional performance and/or student progress? Why is not professional accountability the subject of collective bargaining? How can parents and citizens continue to tolerate the growth and assertion of teacher power with no corresponding educational benefit for their children or their communities?

Until and unless citizens organize and develop effective community power which will neutralize and diminish the power now held by teachers' unions and top-level school officials, all that we can hope for is higher salaries and more layers of ineffective administration. Student achievement will continue to deteriorate while the teachers and professional educators will be relegated to the role of petty civil servants.

As the momentum for community control of schools moves forward, there is increased opposition from those who feel threatened by elimination of the "old established ways." In any discussion of the concept of community control, the voices of opposition—whether speaking for the board of education, the teachers' union or the administrators' organizations—sound the same.

In view of the near complete failure of public schools to educate black and poor children, it is an affront to their parents, whose vested interests are paramount to all others, that their right to control their own destinies and decide what is in their communities' best interest is being challenged. And it is particularly disturbing that these rights are being challenged by those who have no personal stake in the community and who have demonstrated beyond doubt that they cannot or will not educate the children of these communities.

The new mood of the black community is placing different demands on the educational professionals who would work in this community. Professionals who cannot demonstrate competence should not serve this community. Teachers and administrators who are incompetent ought to be identified and if necessary removed. Clear-cut, well-defined standards of conduct and performance ought to be demanded by this community from its administrators, its teachers, and *its students.* Principals and teachers ought to be freed from rules and policies which prevent them from being held accountable. They ought to see themselves as part of the community rather than merely working in it. Since everything else has failed during the last 15 years to educate black children, the community must develop the psychological freedom to declare that its schools are its own, and that they must function under the community's rules and be accountable to the community.

Accountability and Governance in Public Education

EDWARD J. MEADE JR.

The ingredients of accountability are measurements, evaluations, and assessments, according to Edward Meade. Traditionally, lack of money and resources have been used as excuses to defer the question of accountability in public education. With the increase in aid from all levels of government, this is no longer a valid excuse. The recent innovations in education have added to the difficulties of assessment and caused a shift from the classroom to the school as the accountable agent.

Had I addressed this group some eight or so years ago, it is highly likely that the substance of my remarks would have dealt with the internal aspects of the school itself. The chances are I would have discussed the emerging innovations and technologies that make schools more vital and effective instruments of education. Team teaching, nongraded schools, flexible scheduling, large- and small-class grouping, educational television, teaching machines, and better staff utilization are a few of the concerns that preoccupied us as educators at that time.

I'm not suggesting that improving the ways in which schools help youngsters to acquire and apply knowledge, and help them learn to think for themselves, are not matters of continuing importance, particularly to you as principals. But, to a large degree, they are professional concerns. Although society has an interest in these matters, primary responsibility for them belongs to you and the teachers. Rather, other broader and more public issues are today emerging—issues in which the community at large is becoming more and more interested, and less and less patient about their resolution. I shall speak about two of them: accountability and governance.

My definition of accountability in public education is the conventional one: It is the holding responsible of someone or group for the success or failure of individual schools and pupils. Until now, the hard questions of accountability have been avoided or deferred, and generally for good reasons. Legitimate excuses have been offered why

Edward J. Meade Jr., "Accountability and Governance in Public Education," Ford Foundation Reprint, 1969. Address delivered before the Committee on the Smaller Secondary School at the annual convention of the National Association of Secondary School Principals, Atlantic City, New Jersey, February 12, 1968. Reprinted by permission.

measurements, evaluations, and assessments—the ingredients of accountability—should not be applied to determine the effectiveness of public education.

One reason was poverty. For years it was claimed that the federal, state, and local governments needed to provide more money for education before schools could be improved and do the job expected of them. This lack of funds prevented the difficult questions of educational assessment from being raised. Everyone was too busy trying to feed the system rather than question it. Today, however, there are more federal, state, and local funds available—not enough, but more than many educators realistically expected.

Internal Improvements in the School

Educators also have argued that schools were undernourished in other respects, particularly in regard to teachers. Today our schools have better teachers—still not as good as they could be, perhaps, but better nonetheless—and there are more of them. Teacher-training programs are more sophisticated, and class sizes are getting smaller. In addition, schools have more professional specialists and an array of technological resources at their disposal—everything from a television set to a computer. School organization has been studied and improved by experts in management and organization. There is hardly a school today that has not had a consultant within its walls over the past academic year or two. College professors have found working in schools a useful and productive enterprise—for them and for the schools.

What all this means is that many of the traditional excuses used to defer the question of accountability are no longer valid. Perhaps the only excuse remaining is the lack of technical know-how to develop and implement more precise methods of measurement. Still, even that excuse has a hollow ring since a number of good measuring tools are available.

So, whether we like it or not, the issue of accountability is before us. Already, educators and social scientists are devising guidelines for a national assessment of education. The great outpouring of funds through such legislation as the Elementary and Secondary Education Act, the Vocational Education Act, and the National Defense Education Act has brought demands for an evaluation of the results of these programs.

Still, the issue has been drawn in only very general terms. Congress is receiving only a general outline of a national evaluation of the major programs it has funded. State legislators have not done much more than ask about the effect of increased state aid on school programs. Questions raised by the community about the effectiveness of the local schools are not expected to be answered in precise terms. As yet, it is still not possible to measure exactly the effect of individual school programs on the student.

At the outset, I suggested that eight or so years ago a discussion of the pressing issues in education would have focused on internal improvements in school organization, staff, and program. A decade of innovations in education has now passed and what has happened? Whatever the innovation, almost all have had the effect of breaking down the isolation of the individual class and the individual teacher. Team teaching, flexible schedules, non-graded programs, technological aids, and improved staff utilization have all made it increasingly difficult to identify the individual class and the classroom teacher in a system of accountability.

The Shift in Accountability

After a decade of improvement in the content, pedagogy, and organization of education, accountability has been shifted from individual classes and teachers to individual schools and school staffs. The shift has been accomplished by improving the process and the content which go to make up the particular school. A school can now be identified, as it may not always have been, as an organization with a specific set of goals for the pupils it serves. Pupils, teachers, schedules, facilities, and technology are combined and mixed in order to make the school, and not merely the individual class or course, a better vehicle for learning.

Little real change has occurred on a system-wide basis. If there has been any change at the level of the school district or school system, it is cumulative change made up of many different changes in individual schools.

What does this shift in accountability from class to school mean to the principal? Similar to the plant manager in a large industrial corporation, the principal is the key person responsible for the productivity of the organization. The school, like an industrial plant, represents a process. Raw material goes in and a product comes out. The change that occurs between input, that is the entering pupil, and output, the departing pupil, will be determined by the ways in which you apply and coordinate the available resources of your school. It is the change in the individual pupil from what he was upon entering the school to what he is when he leaves that measures the school.

How can accountability be accomplished? We know it is possible to make a quite sophisticated assessment of the academic, social, physical, emotional, vocational, intellectual, and attitudinal attributes of each child. Given this assessment and given a malleable system of education in which pupils, teachers, and technology are deployed in an infinite variety of ways, substantial change should have taken place in the child when he leaves school—provided the schools know in advance what the direction and goals of this change should be. If so, then it is simple to conceive of an equally refined set of evaluations to measure the product—that is, the degree of change that has taken place in the pupil during the years he has spent in the schools.

Thus, after a number of years of working on improvements in the process of education, we are now coming closer to two ends: (1) a more efficient, effective and sensitive individual school with more and better resources for helping children to learn, and (2) more sophisticated ways to measure human potential and productivity. Approaches to these two goals are making it possible for education to be more effective and for its effectiveness to be measured in relation to the students, the community, and its contribution to the social system at large.

THE GOVERNANCE ISSUE

If we are able to measure what goes in and what comes out with some precision, it should have a strong bearing on governance, which is a second pressing public issue confronting schoolmen today. Governance is a term long-favored by the political scientist. Today it is being used by the men and women who pay your salaries—the parents and taxpayers in your communities. In some communities, governance is an issue being raised by your teachers. In still fewer communities, the issue is even on the minds of high school pupils.

Originally, the public schools were extensions of education in the home. Almost all the citizens in a community had a direct hand in determining school programs, hiring teachers, and establishing means of support for schools. Later schools began to be governed primarily by boards of education or school committees—bodies made up of a few citizens who accepted the responsibility for determining the general policies and programs of public education. Often, these citizens took on this task because no one else wanted it. A historian in the 1940s once remarked that education was something that most Americans wanted but did not care about, and so it was in many communities. It was not too long ago that what the school board said about curriculum, school programs, textbooks, teachers' salaries, athletic programs, administrative style, and so forth determined both the form and substance of American public school education.

As the public schools grew to become an even more important and vital part of our way of life, many school boards and school committees realized that they could not deal with what were becoming increasingly complex matters. To a large degree, these citizen boards passed the issue of governance on to a new group—the professional administrators. The dominance of the professional administrator is perhaps the most dramatic in some of the larger city and county school systems where administrative policy and procedure have a far greater effect on the way in which schools operate than do the general policies established by the school board. In some communities, the school principal, particularly the secondary school principal, has become literally lord of the domain.

THE ROLE OF THE COMMUNITY

Today, however, other forces are emerging—each wanting to play a significant role in the governance of schools. Many teachers now believe they have a right to participate in the determination of school policies and programs. The community is also striving for power and control. This is not the traditional community that schoolmen are accustomed to—the PTA, the Home and the School Association, or the Citizens Advisory Committee. The community I am referring to is not that well organized and in some cases is not even identified. Still, from the town meetings in rural New England to the ghettos in the cities, these community forces are building and raising important questions about our schools. They ask, "How public is public education?" and "To what extent can we, the public, design the kind of education which we, the public, support?"

How the issue of governance will be resolved is not clear. Doubtlessly most of us yearn for the best of all worlds, the best of all schools, and hope that the governance of our schools is a shared responsibility among the community, the school board, the administrator, and the teacher. Some suggest adding the student, and while at the moment "student power" is not an issue in secondary education, it may soon emerge, just as it has on college and university campuses.

It may be that the issue of governance may well turn on who is to be held accountable for what comes out of our schools. After all, governance is based on responsibility, and responsibility implies accountability. If administrators are not able to account in reasonable ways for what is mandated to be done in schools, it would seem to me that they may lose their acquired rights to govern schools. After all, the schools are public. It is, therefore, easy to make a case for governance by community. If administrators default on the question of accountability, they—and particularly principals—will lose their right to govern and will become more technicians than governors.

This holds for teachers as well. Teachers do the primary work in schools and represent the majority in the professional staff. They have a right to share in governance but just so long as they are willing to be held accountable. In fact, I am eager to see what happens when teachers' organizations realize that accountability is equated with governance. Will the demands of teachers then focus more on welfare than on program or instructional issues? Will they be anxious to be held more accountable? I do not know, but I am not encouraged by the unwillingness of some teachers to be held accountable for the progress of their pupils, any more than I am by the unwillingness of some parents to accept their share of responsibility.

Holding accountability to the level of the school may help to re-solve the governance issue. After all, it is the school—whether it is Intermediate School 201 in New York City, Meadowbrook Junior High School in Newton, Massachusetts, or Oakland Technical High School in California—where the controversy over governance is taking place. Rarely do teachers and communities rise up against a class or an individual teacher on the issue of accountability. Similarly, protests at the level of school systems seldom are based on accountability. Usu-ally, those protests have to do with more general and diffuse matters—overall costs, excessive administrative overhead, promotion rules, and so forth.

It is at the level of the school, with you as principal, where the question of governance and accountability will be most visible. It is in your school where these issues stand the best chance of being faced squarely and resolved fairly.

CHAPTER 2.
ROLES OF SCHOOL PERSONNEL
AND EDUCATIONAL INSTITUTIONS

Teacher Education: Why, What, and How?

E. KUNO BELLER

In this article, the author discusses teacher evaluation within the context of three major questions: What is the function of teacher evaluation in education? What should be evaluated? What methods of evaluation should be used? Within this framework, Beller identifies a limited number of issues, including evaluation of the teacher's role, style, and techniques.

A comprehensive understanding of teacher evaluation necessitates careful scrutiny of several questions: What is the purpose of such evaluation, what should be evaluated, and how should the evaluation be carried out? Teacher evaluation will be discussed in the context of these three questions, each of which will be examined in turn.

The Question Why: Or What Is the Function of Teacher Evaluation in Education?

1. In the broadest sense, one might say that evaluation of the educational system is necessary because we want to determine whether the objectives of education are being achieved. However, any evaluation of teaching must come to grips with the definition of its objectives since the outcome of the evaluation can never be clearer than the objectives of the education which are being evaluated.
2. A second major objective of evaluation is to identify effective and ineffective teachers, to help administrators in the assignment, promotion, or other changes in the status of teachers.
3. A third objective of evaluation may be its contribution to the im-

E. Kuno Beller, "Teacher Education: Why, What, and How?" *Peabody Journal of Education*, 48:125–139, January 1971. Reprinted by permission.

provement of education by providing a basis for in-service training and for supervisory activities. It may accomplish this by helping in the development of instructional practices and in the improved selection of curriculum material.

4. Evaluation may provide a source for motivation and self-improvement, especially if the teaching staff is included in the planning of evaluation. Criteria for evaluation can serve as standards for excellence in teaching and if they are clearly and explicitly stated, and well publicized, they will help every teacher to know what is expected of him. Moreover, carefully defined and publicly stated criteria for evaluation may assure objectivity in the evaluation of individual teachers.[1]

5. Another important function of evaluation might be to give evidence of the quality of services rendered and thereby justify to the community the investment of public funds in educational institutions.

6. Finally, a major objective of evaluation could be to determine to what extent educational programs produce changes which are compatible with the goals of the culture.[2]

What Should Be Evaluated or the Content of Evaluation

One can distinguish three aspects of teacher functioning: role, style, and technique.[3] Teacher role has been defined as behavior which concerns the duties, responsibilities, and functions of the teacher.[4] For example, in a maternal role, the teacher addresses herself to the gratification of the child's needs and to the protection of the child from injury and harm. In the role of socializer, the teacher addresses herself to developing socially accepted conduct and attitudes in the child. The instructional role refers to the development of cognitive skills, strategies, and interests in the child.

Teacher *style* refers to personality traits and teacher attitudes which are not a planned component of the teacher role. Any reaction or attitude which becomes a planned component of the teaching function is a technique and not a style element. Characteristics, such as controlling or noncontrolling, friendly or unfriendly, warm or cold, sensitive or insensitive, relaxed or tense, intimate or detached are style variables. However, when such characteristics are the result of training to bring about certain effects, they become a technique of teaching.

Technique of teaching refers to specific strategies employed by the teacher to carry out her role or to accomplish her objectives. For example, a teacher may use varying amounts of reward or punishment, praise or criticism to socialize a child. A teacher may provide factual information or create opportunities for the child to discover such information on his own; he may use questioning, suggestions, or active direction as his preferred technique for developing knowledge in the child.

Discussion of the literature about evaluation of teacher functioning will be organized along dimensions of role, style, and technique as has been outlined.

EVALUATION OF TEACHER ROLE

Investigators have attempted to evaluate teacher role as perceived by the teacher himself and by others. Bush reports that teachers perceived their main role to be that of purveying knowledge to students, directing their learning, and keeping the youngsters under direct control at all times.[5] Administrators agree with this definition, but also want the teacher to keep their pupils happy. In another study, which investigated perception of teacher role by teachers, administrators, pupils, and parents, found that teachers perceived themselves less in a disciplinarian role than did parents.[6] Parents not only want the teacher to maintain order and control deviancy, but they also want the teacher to participate in community affairs. Teachers do not share the latter expectation. It is interesting that when the teacher agrees with this role of guardian of the adult culture assigned to him by many parents, he is found to manifest arbitrary attitudes towards authority and to lack warmth in his reaction to children.[7] Teachers who see themselves in this role of guardian also have high expectations for the mastery of academic skills. By contrast, teachers who have child-centered role concepts emphasize pleasure and creativity in their activities with pupils rather than obedience and imitation of adult behavior. To judge from one study in which over 2,000 sixth-grade students were asked to evaluate teacher role, it would appear that students prefer a pupil-centered rather than adult-centered teacher.[8] In that study, the effective teacher was perceived as a friendly, warm, supportive person who communicated lucidly and who motivated students to greater effort.

Sorensen, et al. who investigated divergent concepts of teacher role, found five dimensions of teacher role functioning: information giver, motivator, counselor, disciplinarian, and referrer.[9] When teachers and non-teachers evaluated teacher role with regard to discrepancy between real and ideal teachers, it was found that young teachers perceived a greater discrepancy between teachers as they are and teachers as they ideally should be than was the case for older teachers.[10] Younger people altogether, regardless of whether they are teachers or non-teachers, tend to assign a more pupil-centered role to teachers, while older people tend to assign a more adult-centered role to teachers.

A further source of discrepancy between the perceptions of teacher roles is contributed by other professions on the educational team, such as counselors or therapists. The latter are concerned with the treatment of learning disturbances or other difficulties a pupil might have in school. A therapist is more concerned with the child's experience history and with understanding and bringing to the fore the central conflicts which underlie the child's problems, while the teacher is more interested in guiding the child's normal development of skills, interests, and values in his daily functioning.[11] Attempts to modify a teacher's role must be undertaken with caution. Kemp, who carried out a comparative study of the need of structures of teachers, administrators, and counselors, came to the conclusion that these three professionals cannot interchange roles without changing the purpose, functioning, and outcomes of their new roles and without failing to meet their own needs.[12] However, one should not conclude from studies such as the one cited that teachers' roles cannot be modified without detrimental results. For example, Tuckman, et al. investigated the possibility of modifying the discrepancy between the teacher's self-perception of her role from the observer's perception of the teacher role.[13] These investigators found that teachers change both the perception of their behavior as well as their behavior as a result of feedback. Moreover, it is known that some teachers can carry out multiple roles without feeling conflicted.

It would seem reasonable to conclude from the available evidence as viewed above that future evaluation of teacher roles should never rely on one source alone but should include the perception and judgment of all groups involved in the teaching of the child, e.g. the teacher himself, the administrator, other professionals in the school system (such as counselors, psychologists, and special teachers), parents, and pupils. Moreover, the literature throughout the last decade shows that education is considered to be a concern of both the professional and non-professional members of a community and, therefore, a wide range of interested parties need to be included in the definition, evaluation, and redefinition of the teacher role.

TEACHER STYLE

Although teacher style results largely from experiences other than professional training, it has been found to have an effect on the techniques which the teacher uses and, in some instances, on the effectiveness of his teaching. Since teaching style is not a function of outside formal training, it needs to be evaluated for the purpose of selecting and assigning teachers to certain duties.

Evaluative studies of teacher style can be grouped into those which attempt to relate personality traits outside the educational situation to teaching style in the classroom and others which attempt to relate teacher style to effectiveness of teaching.

Two studies represent the first group. Harvey, et al. examined teacher belief systems with regard to such factors as ethnocentrism, use of platitudes and normative statements, belief in Divine fate control or Religious Fundamentalism.[14] The investigators divided the teachers into abstract and concrete groups in which concreteness was associated with high scores on the items indicated above. The teachers were then rated on the basis of observations of their behavior in the classroom. It was found that the more concrete teachers were more controlling, less warm, less perceptive of children's needs, less flexible in meeting these needs, and less relaxed in their relationship with children than abstract teachers. Thus, these investigators demonstrated a very clear relationship between a teacher's belief system and his teaching style. Paraskevopoulos found that Jungian character traits, such as Extroversion versus Introversion, Sensing versus Intuition, Thinking versus Feeling, and Judging versus Perceiving, related consistently to teaching style.[15] For example, Sensing teachers were perceived as more friendly and warm than Intuitive teachers. Intuitive teachers were rated higher on understanding and flexibility. Sensing teachers responded more quickly to the needs of children but with less depth of understanding than Intuitive teachers. The same investigator also found that high divergent teachers were judged to be friendlier, warmer, and more understanding by their pupils than high convergent teachers.

Several studies have investigated relationships between teaching style and effectiveness of teaching. One group of investigators examined this relationship on the basis of judgments of both teaching style and teacher effectiveness by the same judges. One of these investigators, Kerlinger used a wide range of judges, i.e. professors of education, elementary and secondary teachers, and teachers from parochial and military schools. He found two major clusters for effective teachers.[16] One of these clusters, named traditional, associated effective teaching with being self-controlled, trustworthy, refined, industrious, reliable, healthy, moral, religious, and conscientious. The second cluster, which was named progressive, associated effective teaching with imagination, insight, warmth, openmindedness, flexibility, sympathy, sensitivity, patience, and sincerity. Hamachek concluded after a representative review of the research literature concerning aspects of good and bad teachers that good teachers are basically warm, responsive, flexible individuals who seem as sensitive to relationship variables as they are to cognitive variables.[17]

Bullock reports that superintendents considered principals effective who manifested personality traits such as ambition, ability to relate well to people, confidence and a tendency to be energetic.[18] Watkins investigated the hypothesis that effective leadership in task-oriented groups is characterized by an impersonal style of the leader in his relationship with group members.[19] The study did not confirm this hypothesis. Watkins found that an impersonal principal was less aware of his teachers' feelings and values, and inhibited teacher self-actualization. A limitation of these studies which needs to be pointed out is that teacher effectiveness and personality or style characteristics of teachers were not investigated as separate variables nor was teacher effectiveness defined or measured explicitly in these studies.

There are a few studies in the literature which took greater care in separating the measurement of teacher effectiveness and teacher style. For example, Heil and Washburne grouped teachers on the basis of their responses to an interest schedule into three groups: (a) turbulent, impulsive, variable; (b) self-controlling, orderly, work-oriented; (c) fearful.[20] On the basis of observations in the classroom and academic progress, they found that b teachers were most effective, and c teachers least effective, academically and socially. B teachers were especially effective with opposing and wavering children. A teachers were quite ineffective with opposing and wavering children, but were found to be successful in teaching mathematics and science.

Scott observed children of teachers who fell at both extremes of an effectiveness continuum as judged by supervisors. Effective teachers were found to exhibit more positive and less negative emotional feeling tone in their contacts with the children, were more involved and showed more spontaneity than ineffective teachers.

Beller found that preschool Head Start teachers judged as the best and most effective teachers by a supervisor, when subsequently observed in the classroom, were found to allow their children a wider range of free choices and to be more responsive to the needs of children than other teachers.[21]

The evaluative studies reviewed in this section have yielded evidence that both the teacher's personality outside educational situations and his perceived effectiveness as a teacher relate to his teaching style in the classroom. However, the studies cited here are too few and a portion of them too weak methodologically to use existing evidence for the selection of teachers, in-service training, and direction for research on the modifiability of teaching styles. Future evaluative studies of teacher style need to pay more attention to explicit definition and measurement of teacher effectiveness and greater methodological sophistication in obtaining independent measures of teacher effectiveness and of teacher style in order to establish with greater validity the relationships between these two sets of variables.

TECHNIQUE

The greatest advance with regard to the evaluation of teacher functioning has been made in the area of teaching techniques and outcome or product of teaching. These advances have occurred in the refinement in measuring and evaluating an individual's techniques, the concentration on patterns of techniques, the study of teacher-pupil interaction rather than of teacher functioning as a one-way traffic and, finally, the greatly improved methods of measuring and evaluating effects of teaching on pupil achievement and functioning. Evaluative studies of techniques will be discussed in the order just outlined.

In the extensive review of teacher performance criteria, Rosenshine and Furst conclude that among a series of teaching techniques, clarity, enthusiasm, and task orientation were found to be consistently and significantly related to improved performance of students.[22] Positive but weaker support was found for the effectiveness of such single techniques as use of criticism, use of student ideas, probing or encouraging a student to elaborate on his answer, and perceived difficulty of the course.

Praise and criticism are good examples of single techniques which gain in importance as a result of refinement in studying and evaluating them. Neither verbal nor non-verbal praise by itself was found to be related to pupil achievement.[23] When the study of praise was further broken down into brief verbal expressions such *ah-ha* and *right,* it was found to be positively related to improved academic performance of pupils.[24] It is possible that this improved relationship was due to the fact that brief verbal praise has a more distinct cue value than non-verbal expressions of praise and is more specific and less distracting than elaborate verbal statements of praise. However, certain types of elaboration, such as restating and analyzing the response of the pupil or explaining what was good about the response, were found to make praise more effective.[25] It would seem that this particular breakdown or refinement of praise involved a separation of motivational components and cognitive clarification of the response being praised, which may have resulted in an additive effect on learning. Criticism offers another example of the benefit derived from more refined measurement. When criticism was broken down into strong and mild criticism, it was found that only strong criticism showed consistently a negative effect on pupil achievement.[26] No negative effect has been found for mild criticism, which has sometimes shown positive effects on cognitive performance.[27]

With regard to patterns of technique, Soar found a higher ratio of inquiry to drill activity most effective in producing better pupil achievement.[28] Thompson and Bowers found that an equal mixture of convergent and divergent questions were most successful in producing results in students.[29] A third finding along the same line has been that combinations of praise and criticism have yielded positive relationships with academic achievement as the proportion of praise increased and exceeded criticism. There are other types of patterns of teaching techniques which have been studied and evaluated. One example is use of student ideas which represents a breakdown of elaborating student responses in particular ways, i.e. acknowledging, modifying, applying, comparing, and summarizing what was said by an individual student.[30] Another use of patterning of techniques can be seen in studies of *variability* which refers to the use of various cognitive levels of discourse and the use of a variety of instructional materials and classroom techniques by the same teacher. Beller found in a recent study that the use of a variety of teaching techniques was positively correlated with the child's ability to learn a cognitive problem solving task.[31] Rosenshine and Furst cite eight studies in which variability as defined here, resulted in significant improvement of pupil performance.[32]

The third area of advance in evaluating teacher techniques has been the inclusion of both teacher and child in the evaluation. This approach has made it possible to investigate individualization of teaching. For example, Gray and Klaus attempted to improve children's language in the context of encouraging achievement and by keeping the teacher-child ratio low enough to permit individual attention and responses from teachers to the particular needs of the child.[33] Language was stimulated by making it necessary for children to ask for attractive toys. The result of this approach was that both language and IQ performance was significantly better in the group receiving this type of training than in a matched group which did not have this program. In another study an attempt was made to individualize language training for pre-school children enrolled in Head Start classes.[34] Methods of language training were constructed to match the individual cognitive styles of children. It was found that children whose language training was adapted to their preferred cognitive style improved significantly more on a wide range of language functioning than children with non-individualized language training or with no language training. Other examples of individualized techniques and their evaluation may be seen in the work of Withall,[35] Flanders,[36] and Amidon and Hough.[37]

It is important to discuss one other consideration in the application of findings from evaluative studies. One needs to pay close attention to the conditions under which the evaluative study is carried out. Three major conditions may affect teacher functioning and its effectiveness: the environment and setting in which teacher functioning is being observed, certain background variables of the teacher, and character- istics of the pupil, such as age, social class, and ability. Outcomes of evaluative studies which are qualified in terms of these conditions will gain in their usefulness for application.

An extensive study of teacher functioning in day-care centers by Prescott, et al. yielded a series of findings which lend themselves to illustrate the points made above.[38] With regard to environment, Prescott found that teacher functioning varied as a result of center size. Teachers in large centers were found to make more frequent use of control and restraint and to emphasize rules of social living; teachers of medium-sized centers were found to use more often encour- agement as a technique and to emphasize pleasure, creativity, and interaction with other children rather than obedience and rules of social living; teachers in small centers related more closely and inti- mately with the children than teachers in large centers. Another environmental condition which was found to affect teacher function- ing was the particular program unit or activity setting in which the teacher was observed. Programs dealing with basic routine activities evoked greater amounts of direction and restriction than free-choice and free-play settings, which, in turn, evoked the highest incidence of encouragement.

With regard to teacher background factors, Prescott found that the amount of training was an important condition for teacher function- ing. As a teacher's amount of training increased, her attitudes towards authority became less arbitrary and her attitudes of warmth increased. Role concept was also found to be related to her functioning as a teacher. Teachers who perceived themselves as adult-centered, that is as a representative of the adult culture who has to teach children ways of behavior which are valued by adults, used arbitrary authority more frequently and manifested less warmth than other teachers. In con- trast, teachers who perceived themselves as pupil-centered used en- couragement more frequently and emphasized pleasure as well as creativity in their activities with children.

With regard to characteristics of children affecting teacher function- ing Prescott found that the child's social class had an appreciable effect on teacher behavior. For example, teachers of children in low-income centers were less likely than teachers in other centers to show affection for individual children. Teachers serving high-income families were particularly prone to giving individualized affection to children.

Although it is quite evident that teacher functioning must vary as a function of the child's age, little, if any, evidence has emerged from research on that point, that is studies observing the same teachers functioning with children on different age levels. However, there is a good deal of evidence concerning the effect of a child's brightness or

Another aspect of the intervention that needs to be carefully controlled is the program itself. The investigator needs to get a large enough sample of program periods to make his findings applicable to other situations. Examples of such program periods are one-to-one contacts between teacher and pupil versus teacher contact with small or large groups of pupils, written assignment or oral reports or, in the case of preschool, indoor versus outdoor, organized work versus free-choice activity, etc. If the technique under investigation is such that it can be applied to a variety of content or behavior, such as reward, criticism, use of student opinion, or probing, it might be advisable to record not only the frequency of influences of a given technique, but also the specific content material or behavior to which it was applied. Similarly, the timing of the technique may be important. For example, if the technique is type of question asked or probing, it may be important to relate the application of technique to the beginning, middle, or end of a lesson.[48] Even though such added steps make the evaluative study more cumbersome and more expensive, the gain may be considerable because the availability of such specific data may make the findings more meaningful than a mere frequency count of the technique and increase the replicability of the study. It makes more sense to consider a repeated study or replication when the technique is applied to the same material and at the same time as in the original study.

A final point with regard to intervention and teacher functioning is the value of sharing with teachers the purpose as well as procedures of the evaluative study. Teachers are more likely to accept and actively support the decisions when they are an active part of the whole process rather than simply the pawns in a game.[49] This consideration is important in relation to both systematic evaluative studies as well as individual evaluation of teachers by principals. When principals base their evaluations on such indirect evidence as casual teacher contacts outside the classroom, what parents say about teachers, appearance of the classroom, and teacher participation in extracurricular activities, teachers often feel that such evaluations have been incomplete and unfair.

Finally, with regard to the evaluative study of intervener, that is the teacher, it should be pointed out that observers are often affected by their beliefs and values. Brown points out that "observers see what they already believe and tend to lean towards their fears rather than their hopes." In some cases it has been found that differences among observers were larger than differences among teachers. In order to guard against such sources of errors, it is important that observer reliability be established. Brown also reports that ratings are higher if the observer-judge and the teacher are of the same sex, and that older teachers and elementary teachers receive higher evaluations than younger teachers and secondary school teachers.

Several factors need to be mentioned with regard to pre/post testing of pupils in evaluative studies. It is best for the investigator to make up his own test procedures so that they will be maximally relevant to the effects he attempts to produce with his teaching technique. Standardized tests are easily available but are often too narrow or not sufficiently relevant to measure the various aspects of pupil behavior and growth which particular techniques or educational programs attempt to effect. Another consideration is that factors such as general intellectual abilities of students, the motivation of particular students, and other pupil characteristics discussed earlier in this paper, if controlled may greatly improve the accuracy of the effect of the technique evaluated in the study. Specifically, when such factors are controlled, they will protect the investigator and others from over- or underestimating the effects of teaching techniques under study since these pupil characteristics may account for a large portion of the change from pre to post testing, or work against the effects of the experimental intervention.

The present paper has focused on a limited number of issues concerning teacher evaluation. An attempt was made to examine these issues in the light of several major studies in the recent literature and to propose directions for future study of teacher evaluation.

FOOTNOTES

1. National Education Association, *Programs for Evaluating Classroom Teachers,* Research Bulletin No. 42 (Washington, D.C., 1964).
2. Gner D. Phillips and Adolph Manoil, *Appraisal in Education,* Vol. 246. No. 1 (Boston, 1963).
3. E. K. Beller, "Adult-child Interaction and Personalized Day Care," E. Grotberd, ed., *Day Care: State of the Art* (Washington, D.C., in press, 1970).
4. Lilian Katz, *Teaching in Preschools: Roles and Goals.* ERIC No. 70706-E-AO-U-26, 1969.
5. Robert Bush, "Redefining the Role of the Teacher," *Theory into Practice,* VI (December 1967), 246–251.
6. J. Pascal Twyman and Bruce J. Biddle, "Role Conflict of Public School Teachers." *Journal of Psychology,* LVI (January 1963), 183–198.
7. Elizabeth Prescott and Elizabeth Jones, *Group Day Care as a Child-Rearing Environment: An Observational Study of Day Care Program* (Pasadena, 1967).
8. William Beck. "Pupils' Perception of Teacher Merit: A Factor Analysis of Five Postulated Dimensions, *Journal of Educational Research,* LXI (November 1967).
9. A. Garth Sorenson, T. R. Husek, and Constance Yu, "Divergent Concepts of Teacher Role: An Approach to the Measurement of Teacher Effectiveness." *Journal of Educational Psychology,* LIV (December 1963), 287–294.
10. Thomas E. Smith, "The Image of High School Teachers: Self and Other, Real and Ideal," *Journal of Educational Research,* LIX (November 1965), 99–104.
11. E. K. Beller, *Clinical Processes* (New York, 1962).
12. C. Grattan Kemp, "A Comparative Study of the Need Structures of Adminis-

trators, Teachers, and Counselors," *Journal of Educational Research*, LVII (April 1964), 425–427.

13. Bruce W. Tuckman, McCall M. Kendrick, and Ronald T. Hyman, "Modification of Teacher Behavior: Effects of Dissonance and Coded Feedback," *American Educational Research Journal*, VI (November 1969), 607–620.

14. O. J. Harvey, J. B. White, M. Prather, R. D. Alter, and J. K. Hoffmeister, "Teacher's Belief Systems and Preschool Atmospheres," *Journal of Educational Psychology*, LVII (December 1966), 373–381.

15. Ioannis Paraskevopoulos, "How Students Rate Their Teachers" *Journal of Educational Research*, LXII (September 1968), 25–29.

16. Fred N. Kerlinger, "Attitudes Toward Education and Perception of Teacher Characteristics: A Q Study," *American Educational Research Association Journal*, III (May 1966), 159–168.

17. Don E. Hamachek, "What Research Tells Us About the Characteristics of 'Good' and 'Bad' Teachers," Don E. Hamachek, ed., *Human Dynamics in Psychology and Education* (Boston, 1968), pp. 187–203.

18. William Bullock, Jr., "The Relationship of Educational Training and Years of Administrative Experience to Role Perception of High School Principals," *Journal of Educational Research*, LXII (September 1969), 3–5.

19. J. Foster Watkins, "An Inquiry into the Principal-Staff Relationship," *Journal of Educational Research*, LXIII (September 1969), 11–15.

20. Louis Heil and Carelton Washburne, "Brooklyn College Research into Teacher Effectiveness," *Journal of Educational Research*, LV (May 1962), 347–351.

21. E. K. Beller. "The Evaluation of Effects of Early Education Intervention on Intellect and Social Development of Lower Class, Disadvantaged Children," E. Grotberg, ed., *Critical Issues in Research Related to Disadvantaged Children* (Princeton, 1969).

22. Barak Rosenshine and Norma Furst, "Current and Future Research on Teacher Performance Criteria," paper presented to AERA-Prentice Hall Symposium on Teacher Education (Minneapolis, 1970).

23. R. L. Spaulding, *Achievement, Creativity, and Self-Concept Correlated to Teacher-Pupil Transactions in Elementary Schools* (Hempstead, 1965); R. S. Soar, *An Integrative Approach to Classroom Learning* (Philadelphia, 1966); A. J. Harris, C. Morrison, L. Gold, and B. L. Serwer, *A Continuation of the Craft Project: Comparing Reading Approaches with Disadvantaged Urban Negro Children in Primary Grades* (New York, 1968).

24. N. E. Wallen, *Relationships Between Teacher Characteristics and Student Behavior—Part III* (Salt Lake City, 1966).

25. H. V. Perkins, "Classroom Behavior and Underachievement," *American Educational Research Journal*, II (1965), 1–12; J. D. Fortune, *A Study of the Generality of Presenting Behaviors in Teaching Preschool Children* (Memphis, 1967); B. M. Morrison, "The Reactions of Internal and External Children to Patterns of Teaching Behavior," unpublished dissertation, University of Michigan (Ann Arbor, 1966).

26. Perkins, 1965; Soar, 1966; Spaulding, 1965.

27. Perkins, 1965; Spaulding, 1965.

28. Soar, 1966.

29. G. R. Thompson and N. C. Bowers, "Fourth Grade Achievement as Related to Creativity, Intelligence, and Teaching Style," paper presented at the meeting of the American Educational Research Association (Chicago, 1968).

30. N. A. Flanders, *Analyzing Classroom Behavior* (Boston, 1970).

31. E. K. Beller, "The Evaluation of Effects of Early Education Intervention on Intellect and Social Development of Lower Class, Disadvantaged Children."

32. Rosenshine and Furst, 1970.

33. Sue Gray and R. A. Klaus, "An Experimental Preschool Program for Culturally Deprived Children," *Child Development* XXXVI (December 1965), 887–898.

34. E. K. Beller, "Cognitive Styles and Methods of Language Training," paper

presented at the Annual Meeting of the American Educational Research Association (New York, 1967).

35. J. Withall, "The Development of a Technique for the Measurement of Social-emotional Climate in Classrooms," *Journal of Experimental Education,* XVII (March 1949), 347–361.

36. Flanders, 1970.

37. E. J. Amidon and J. B. Hough, *Interaction Analysis: Research Theory and Application* (Boston, 1967).

38. Prescott and Jones, 1967.

39. A. H. Hoehn, "A Study of Social Class Differentiation in the Classroom Behavior of Nineteen Third-grade Teachers," *Journal of Social Psychology,* XXXIX (May 1954), 269–292.

40. H. Wilensky, "Observational Techniques in Preschool Classrooms," in *ERIC Bibliography,* No. 3 (Urbana, 1968), pp. 15–23.

41. E. K. Beller, "The Evaluation of Effects of Early Education Intervention on Intellect and Social Development of Lower Class, Disadvantaged Children," 1969.

42. W. L. Herman, J. E. Potterfield, C. Mitchell Dayton, and K. G. Amershek, "The Relationship of Teacher-centered Activities and Pupil-centered Activities to Pupil Achievement and Interest in 18 Fifth Grade Social Studies Classes," *American Educational Research Journal,* VI (March 1969), 227–240.

43. Samuel Messick, "Educational Evaluation as Research for Program Improvement," *Childhood Education,* XXXXVI (May 1970), 413–414.

44. Arthur Combs, "Can We Measure Good Teaching Objectively?" *National Education Association Journal,* LIII (January 1964), 34–36.

45. Gertrude M. Lewis, *The Evaluation of Teaching* (Washington, D.C., n.d.).

46. M. Hughes, "What Is Teaching? One Viewpoint," *Educational Leadership,* XIX (June 1962), 25109.

47. For a good discussion of the use of research design in evaluation studies see Edward A. Suchman, *Evaluative Research* (New York, 1967).

48. Rosenshine and Furst, 1970.

49. Robert B. Howsam, "Who's a Good Teacher? Problems and Progress in Teacher Evaluation," Joint Committee of Personnel Procedures, 1960.

Who's Accountable to Whom?

ARTHUR L. COSTA

In many demands, the teacher is being identified as the accountable agent. Can a teacher really be held accountable without a high degree of teacher self-governance? Arthur L. Costa identifies several levels of autonomy and the teachers' relationships within these levels.

We are becoming increasingly aware of the thrust toward more personal power—power of the individual to direct his own education, shape his own environment, and derive his own value system. On the other hand, educators are being called on the carpet to make an accounting for the time, money, and energy being poured into the

Arthur L. Costa, "Who's Accountable to Whom?" *Educational Leadership,* 28:15–19, October 1970. Reprinted by permission of the Association for Supervision and Curriculum Development and Arthur L. Costa. Copyright © 1970 by the Association for Supervision and Curriculum Development.

educational complex intended to develop "responsible citizens." Some educational leaders are in a quandary as they anticipate the implications of the quest for more autonomy by students and teachers while at the same time trying to satisfy the demands for increased accountability, assessment, and justification.

Autonomy or Immunity?

There seems to be some confusion as to the meaning of autonomy in the educational lexicon. While autonomy connotes self-governance, auto-regulation, and self-modification, it may be that some students and teachers are demonstrating their interpretation of autonomy to mean immunity, exemption, or lack of restriction. Autonomy and freedom are not synonymous. Using these definitions, the autonomous person would consciously search for the implications of his behavior on others in order to modify himself; while an immune person would feel no obligation to determine the consequences of his actions.

A graffito, recently viewed emblazoned on a college wall, manifested this search for immunity: "If it feels good, do it!" In a discussion with some students about their interpretation of this declaration, they agreed that another phrase should have been added: ". . . as long as it doesn't hurt anyone." The addition of this dependent clause is enough to shift the intent from immunity to autonomy. The autonomous person would be responsible for and sensitive to the effects of his actions on others. He would assess the situation to determine appropriate behavior; he would evaluate the power of his decisions in relation to the effect they produced; he would behave in similar situations based on his evaluation of previous performance.

Is there ever a state of complete immunity? To identify any living person who is totally immune would be difficult indeed. Perhaps a hermit who has chosen to sever all social interaction is neither influenced by nor influencing of others. Yet as soon as two or more humans choose to interact in each other's social setting, there are restrictions placed upon their immunity. They are then obliged to act autonomously since their interaction will have mutual effect. Therefore, there will be no person, functioning in a social situation, who is totally immune.

Is there ever a state of complete autonomy? Many individuals have never been educated to make decisions based upon the assessment of their effect on others, and it is often difficult to obtain feedback as to the effect of one's presence and action. Furthermore, the particular situation may allow or demand more or less autonomous behavior. Intuitive, sensual, and aesthetic acts of love and play may allow for interaction at the immediate, feeling level rather than the mediated, conscious level. Therefore, there may never be a totally autonomous person. There are only those who act more or less autonomously as the situation permits. Autonomy and immunity, then, may be thought of, not as states, but as degrees along a continuum.

It has been suggested that the artist may be in a position to achieve greatest freedom. He may be free to create any expression of art which pleases him. However, as soon as he releases his products for others to interpret, to compare, and to judge, he is no longer immune. If his works continually find no significance in the eye, mind, and heart of others, he may decide to alter his performance. Although artists need courage to take the consequences of their individual expression, they are probably the most sensitive people in the world and therefore are the most highly influenced by others and by the emotional climate of the times. They may be greatly autonomous in that they are sensitive to and restricted by those influences.

Likewise, the scientist is free to create any theory he wishes. However, the availability of data to substantiate his theories places restrictions on the power and usefulness of those theories. If he is to be honored by his colleagues, he must demonstrate how his theories predict, control, or explain events in the environment. He is therefore not only accountable to his profession, but also to nature. Scientists may be relatively autonomous in that they subject their theories to the scrutiny of others and to the test of experimentation and prediction.

Autonomy, for our purposes then, might mean that a person is self-governing: Deciding for himself how to behave based upon evidence of the effect of his behavior and ideas on other people, objects, events, and conditions in the environment in which he exists; and altering himself accordingly.

THE AUTONOMOUS TEACHER

We are all basically teachers. Teaching is an artistic act, based in science, and having social consequences. Yet too many educators "do their own thing" because it "feels good." Studies have shown that many teachers derive greatest satisfaction from their classroom experience because of the emotional rewards rather than from the achievement of objectives.[1] While it may be valid to evaluate some educational endeavors at the intuitive, "feel good" level, there are increasing data which indicate a teacher's interactive behaviors *do* have a direct effect on classroom learning. These behaviors can create the conditions which maximize or detract from the achievement of educational objectives.[2]

An autonomous teacher, therefore, is one who would be conscious of the educational goals and objectives which he, his students, and his community have selected or developed, and he would be conscious of his own behaviors which facilitate the acquisition of those objectives. He would create or employ instructional strategies intended to provide conditions in which students demonstrate desired learnings; he would observe, analyze, and interpret students' behavior; and he would experiment with his own behaviors to determine their usefulness as tools which affect learning.

INSTANT AUTONOMY

We may believe that the main purpose of education is to help students get along without the teacher. However, we find many practices in our schools which increase dependence rather than autonomy. Teachers (or other persons) set goals. Textbooks decide what ideas are important and select the data to support those ideas. Myriad school rules dictate which behaviors are appropriate. Lock-step curricula determine levels of conceptual entry for the student. Inflexible schedules impose time limitations on student interests and rates of learning. Grades impose hidden criteria. Then, upon graduation, students are suddenly expected to demonstrate autonomous behavior.

Autonomy, like any other learned behavior, is acquired through practice. Developmental curricula with corresponding instructional strategies are being developed which increasingly trust the student with more decision making, goal setting, self-analysis, and sensitization to others. Inquiry is an instructional strategy intended to help the student direct his own thinking processes.[3] Self-enhancing education is an interactive strategy intended to help the student take charge of his own emotions.[4] Role playing is intended to sensitize students to the effects of their own behaviors and those of others in social situations.[5]

Some students will come to school with the ability to behave more autonomously than others. There are also situations in the school day which elicit more autonomy on the part of students than do other situations. Yet with any set of instructional objectives, be it reading with comprehension, forming letters accurately, or responding to beauty in the environment, the student must ultimately come to perform this behavior by and for himself—autonomously, without the initiation and direction of the teacher. If the student graduates with more dependence on the teacher for the initiation of desirable behavior than when he entered school, then what has been gained? Behavioral objectives for any curricular goal must be sequenced along a continuum or taxonomy of increasing autonomy. In other words, descriptions should be made of how students behave differently as they are progressing toward more self-direction, self-evaluation, and self-modification.

As students develop increasing autonomy, the teacher needs to diagnose this growth and alter his own behavior accordingly. As the student becomes more and more self-directive, the teacher would correspondingly become less and less of the decision maker for him. He would gradually resign himself to become only a part of the student's rich and responsive environment.[6]

Supervision for Autonomous Teachers

A militant cry for increasing teacher autonomy is being heard today. Perhaps some educational leaders are hesitant to accept this appeal. If these outbursts seek immunity, then the leaders' reluctance may be justified. However, if teachers are truly interested in becoming autonomous, then educational leaders should enhance that endeavor.

Few teacher education institutions today prepare teachers with the skills and techniques of self-analysis and self-modification. Yet this should be a goal of all teacher preparation programs. The many forms of interaction analysis, micro-teaching, and self-other awareness training are but a few strategies being employed to develop more autonomous educators. But since some teachers enter the profession with a greater degree of autonomy than others, the leaders of teachers must be able to diagnose this ability and plan in-service strategies which will develop greater autonomy. And, parallel to the classroom, taxonomous descriptions should be made of what teachers do as they are progressing toward more autonomy. Likewise, the leader's role changes as the teacher acquires the skills of and inclination for self-supervision. Perhaps Chart I expresses the idea more concisely.

ACCOUNTABLE TO WHOM?

Somehow we have developed the notion that the classroom level is the locus of responsibility for the achievement of educational objectives. Some state legislatures hold school districts accountable for performances on achievement tests. The taxpayers hold the school boards accountable for running the schools. Boards of education, in turn, hold school administrators answerable for the expenditure of time and resources, and building administrators hold teachers accountable for the achievement of educational objectives. Teachers, in turn, hold students accountable for demonstrating the acquisition of desired behaviors.

An examination of some of the strategies and practices employed at each of these levels reveals neither the accountability for nor the development of autonomy in others. To illustrate this point, one state adopted reading texts for statewide use and also selected standardized reading achievement tests to evaluate and publicly compare each dis-

Levels of	Autonomy ⟶			
Accountability	Identifying Performance Objectives	Facilitating Growth in Autonomy	Diagnosing Growth in Autonomy	Altering Self-Behavior in Response to Growing Autonomy
Students	What student behaviors are desired?			
Teachers	What teacher behaviors are needed to facilitate development of those student objectives?	What strategies will teachers employ to help students become more autonomous?	By what behaviors can teachers recognize that students are becoming more autonomous?	How should teachers behave differently as students become more autonomous?
Leaders	What leadership behaviors are needed to facilitate development of those teacher competencies?	What strategies will leaders employ to help teachers become more autonomous?	By what behaviors can leaders recognize that teachers are becoming more autonomous?	How should leaders behave differently as teachers become more autonomous?

Chart 1. Levels of autonomy

trict's performance. One fallacy, however, was that the tests did not measure the same performance objectives as those of the textbook program. Who is accountable?

A common practice is for district administrators to consider the building principals as the "instructional leaders" of the schools. Yet at the same time the principals are given burdensome tasks, meaningless audits superfluous inventories, and other "administrivia."

At a recent music in-service meeting, a district music consultant told a group of teachers they were expected to be on page 25 by Thanksgiving, 67 by Christmas, 118 by Easter, and to finish the text (intended to develop joy and understanding of music) by the end of the year.

This recalls to mind the professor of education who droned on about the importance of establishing interest and motivation; and all the while his students slept. By our own actions, are we developing autonomy or immunity in others?

ACCOUNTABILITY FOR PRODUCT AND PROCESS

Accountability for our educational products is with us. We are busy developing behavioral descriptions of learning for students. The next step is to develop descriptions of desirable teacher competencies to achieve these objectives. Then someone will describe the desirable performances of leaders of teachers. Then . . . etc.[7]

Yet we can never develop autonomous products until we examine those processes and strategies we use in developing autonomy in others. Every quarter of the educational institution needs to examine the effect of its actions and decisions on others. If teachers examine their own behavior to determine how it develops autonomous learners; if administrators and consultants devise and evaluate strategies to develop autonomous teachers; if school trustees and superintendents examine the constraints and limitations which they place on the autonomy of the building principals; then we might more realistically answer the question: "Who's accountable to whom?" That's autonomy, baby: Accountable for ourselves!

FOOTNOTES

1. Philip Jackson and Elizabeth Belford. "Educational Objectives and the Joy of Teaching." *School Review* 73: 267–91; 1965.

2. N. A. Flanders. *Teacher Influence, Pupil Attitudes, and Achievement.* U.S. Department of Health, Education, and Welfare, U.S. Office of Education Cooperative Research Project No. 397. Minneapolis: University of Minnesota, 1960.

3. Arthur L. Costa, Charles Lavaroni, Fred Newton, and Ben Strasser. "Inquiry: A Strategy for Developing Autonomous Learners." *Modern Trends in Education.* Unit III. Chicago: Science Research Associates, 1967.

4. Norma Randolph and William Howe. *Self-Enhancing Education.* Palo Alto, California: Stanford Press, 1966.

5. Fannie R. Shaftel. *Role Playing for Social Values: Decision Making in Social Studies.* Englewood Cliffs, New Jersey: Prentice-Hall, Inc., 1967.

6. Arthur L. Costa. "Strategies for Developing Autonomous Learners." *Audiovisual Instruction* 13 (8) : 832–34; October 1968.

7. Albert J. Harris. "The Effective Teacher of Reading." *The Reading Teacher* 23 (3) : 195–204; December 1969.

The Profession's Quest for Responsibility and Accountability

D. D. DARLAND

In the movement towards accountability, the American teacher could become the most likely candidate for scapegoat of the 1970s. D. D. Darland identifies some of the steps the teaching profession must take before guaranteeing competent performance and ethical behavior of its

D. D. Darland, "The Profession's Quest for Responsibility and Accountability," *Phi Delta Kappan,* 52: 41–44, September 1970. Reprinted by permission.

members. Can the teaching profession acquire the status and posture whereby it can be accountable?

George Bernard Shaw once noted that there are five major ways in which civilizations go wrong: by falling out of date in their economics, politics, science, education, and religion. What happens in each of these five areas depends a great deal upon teaching.

Never has so much been expected of teachers in this country. New conditions and demands have multiplied to produce a national crisis in education. Accordingly, the American teacher has become a most likely candidate for scapegoat of the 1970's. Evidence can be seen in the current drive to hold teachers responsible for assuring quality education in our schools. Indeed, this movement called accountability has all the characteristics of a panacea, and one which it appears difficult to fault. Quite generally, demands for teacher accountability are accompanied by blunt threats that if teachers don't achieve this, others will. This is the time-honored strategy to force conformity by threating reprisals by legislatures, the public, or the federal government. It is, at best or worst, poor psychology.

After all, why shouldn't a teacher be accountable? What could possibly be more reasonable? One USOE official predicts the following;

> Teacher training institutions and local school systems will be accountable to the community for the quality of educational services delivered, and teachers will be accountable for what children learn.[1]

The use of the word "will" in the quote should be noted. There is widespread acceptance among teachers, and fortunately so, that neither they nor their profession is in a position to assume very much responsibility either for assuring quality education or, in many cases, even quality teaching. They do not, however, deny the urgency of the problem. The president of the National Education Association has noted:

> It is pure myth that a classroom teacher can even be held accountable, with justice, under existing conditions. The classroom teacher has either too little control or no control over the factors which might render accountability either feasible or fair.[2]

For a society to provide and assure quality education requires a whole series of interrelated guarantees, including adequate finance; wise administration and organization; optimum social policy, facilities, and equipment; parental involvement; and the maintenance of adequate educational manpower. Assuring quality education then requires a whole series of groups, agencies, and institutions being held accountable, not the least being the individual citizen.

Obviously, it is impossible in a short space to deal with all aspects of accountability for quality education. Therefore, this discussion is limited to one imperative—namely, what needs to be done before the teaching profession can become accountable for guaranteeing competent performance and ethical behavior for its members. Even when the profession arrives at such a point, it should be obvious that the guarantee, while a giant step forward, is only one of the necessary aspects of quality education for children and youth. It would enable the profession to pinpoint and fix others responsibilities related to delivering quality education. And more important, it would establish clearly some perimeters of responsibility. Teachers cannot be all things to all people.

What Is the Profession?

If the teaching profession is to move toward assuming accountability for competent and ethical teachers, it is essential to delineate what is meant by the teaching profession. The teaching profession is not a simple organization but rather a complex composed of persons functioning in a variety of capacities—in selected agencies, institutions, and organizations designed for specific purposes. These include:

1. Those who teach or carry out other professional activities in preschool programs and in elementary and secondary schools.
2. Those who teach or carry out other professional activities in colleges and universities.
3. Professional personnel in state departments of education and other governmental agencies, such as the U.S. Office of Education.
4. Professional personnel in organizations directly related to teaching at any level.
5. Professional personnel in voluntary accrediting agencies involved with accreditation of educational institutions.[3]

Very little thought has been given to creating a physiology of the teaching profession. The collective organic processes required for teaching to be an accountable profession are not in existence. Instead, certain segments of the profession are very likely to see themselves as the one imperative rather than perceiving that to function as a professional entity requires the development of a variety of interrelated functions, each working toward similar goals but also acting as a check and balance on the others.

Accountability and Responsibility

If a profession is to be accountable for its own, obviously it must have some form of self-governance. Such is not the case as yet for teaching, although the process of establishing such self-governance has been under way for many years. The legal right for local organizations of teachers to bargain collectively with school boards is one aspect of such governance. Although seen by teachers as an imperative function, bargaining has not become universally accepted. In many cases it is underdeveloped. The process will continue to mature, and numerous sophisticated models exist. Ultimately, professional governance will require other internal procedures and machinery, including better established legal rights and responsibilities.

The NEA holds, as a beginning, that the profession must have authority for the following:

1. Issuing, suspending, revoking, or reinstating the legal license for educational personnel.
2. Establishing and administering standards of professional practice and ethics for all educational personnel.
3. Accrediting teacher preparation institutions.
4. Governing the in-service and continuing education programs for teachers.

To accord the teaching profession such authority has legislative implications for every state. Some 16 states have enacted legislation related mostly to practices and ethics (professional practice acts). These acts create independent practice commissions. In some states these acts are beginning to function in responsible ways. However, some of these laws are very weak in that they do not provide for means of financing or powers of subpoena. They are simply paper tigers. In at least one case, the commission is becoming more of a political arm of the governor than a professional body designed to protect the public welfare and the profession.

There is great reluctance toward giving the teaching profession the legal control over entrance to the profession, but a start has been made. Some 16 states have certification review boards. These boards represent an effort to involve the profession in making exceptions where deviations from precise prescriptions are deemed wise.[4] Also all stats now have some form of advisory body (usually called a council) on teacher education and certification. Some even have two such bodies. In 30 states these bodies are voluntary and extralegal; in 14 states they are created by law. In the remaining states, varied practices are followed with reference to advisory bodies.[5]

Oregon is somewhat unusual in this regard, in that it has a legally stratified teacher standards and practices commission which can deal with both certification and practices, but it is still only advisory. Maryland's new certification regulations include an Advisory Professional Standards Board; Washington has a new plan whereby the state education legal authority describes only in general terms the essentials of preparation programs and then, through involvement of colleges, associations, and school districts, precise programs are developed for individuals. This approach probably has gone the furthest toward the concept of performance criteria rather than the traditional use of courses and credits for initial licensure of teachers. However, the chief state education agencies (but for a very few exceptions where certification power is shared by the state and a city or district) still wield the power over entrance to the teaching profession. This may be as it should be, but evidently not in the thinking of educators. A recent survey of NEA members[6] reported that 90% responded "yes" to the question, "Should a state board composed of educators establish standards for teacher preparation?"

It does appear illogical to ask a profession, especially classroom teachers within it, to be accountable when such persons are little involved with developing controls over entry into the profession. Currently the conglomerate state-by-state approaches to professional governance result in much confusion and frustration. Progress toward national approaches to the problem is very slow. Examples: What about national reciprocity for certification? Should the teaching profession move toward national certification? What about reciprocity for retirement?

An Evolving National Effort

The NEA is mounting a national effort to bring about the necessary legislation in each state whereby the profession approves programs, issues licenses, enforces standards of ethics and practice, and promotes studies and research designed to improve teacher education, including initial entry programs and continuing education.

The NEA is saying that if a profession is to be accountable, why not delegate the responsibilities which are concomitant with being accountable? For a legislature to delegate such a right to a profession is not to give up the right, but rather to place responsibility with those directly involved. Moreover, there is always the right of legislative review.

Invariably the question is asked, "How would a professional board dealing with licensure, accreditation, etc., be any better than the present procedure?" One answer is that the existence of such a board would remove any valid argument for the profession not to be held accountable for the performance of its members. But far more important, practitioners in the field would be in a position to participate in the establishment of policies related directly to their continuing needs and problems. In this regard, teachers and all school personnel are too often placed in the position of having something done for them or to them rather than having decision-making powers in professional matters. This is a very critical issue and one that is complicated by our failure to distinguish between the control of education and the governing of a profession. Equally disconcerting is the internal power struggle among the various segments of the teaching profession itself. Many would seemingly rather continue to depend upon the benevolence of the educational establishment—upon state and local boards' decision-making powers over entrance and all that this implies.

Often those persons in the profession who hold this point of view in reality do control such entrance through their relationship to lay boards. However, this arrangement is a shortsighted solution which neglects the total problem. The teacher who has to obtain initial license and advanced credentialing will be kept in the perennial posture of being advisory to those with the legal power. However, as was mentioned earlier, there is growing recognition that classroom teachers, especially, must be more directly involved in the entire complex of professional governance activities.

A number of state departments of education are diligently searching for ways of involving the practitioner, but there is still very little inclination for either state departments or preparing institutions to accept the idea of professional legal boards having such authority as would be logically consistent with establishing practitioner accountability. One result is that many teachers are not merely upset with what often passes for in-service education, they are indignant. In some cases they are about ready to declare a moratorium on being subjected to any more of what they consider irrelevant requirements and regulations over which they have no control. This in no way denies their needing help from colleges and others. It is how this help is applied that is the problem.

Indeed, teachers are the victims of paternalism at the very time education is in need of reform. However, reform is likely to be seen as threatening rather than liberating if policies are superimposed. This probably accounts for the expanding dimensions of many negotiated teacher-board contracts to include items dealing with in-service education. In curriculum development and professional governance, it is now becoming clear that the teaching profession must necessarily design its own establishment if it is ever to become mature and in a position of parity with external forces.

Educational-Professional Establishment

But for rare exceptions, state departments of education and preparing institutions still see themselves as being required to deal exclusively with the educational establishment and not at all with the rapidly developing professional establishment. This attitude is bound to cause further polarization unless ameliorative activities are instituted. That teachers feel put upon must be recognized and dealt with lest opportunities for reform to be lost.[7]

Earlier, the term "professional establishment" was used in juxtaposition with "educational establishment." This was done to emphasize the fact that teachers have largely given up expecting their interests to be entirely served through the educational establishment. In fact, basic role conflict between the two establishments is clearly more evident.

The educational establishment deals with the creation, maintenance, and survival of institutions, and these involve determining public policy, erecting an administrative structure, and generating public support of the system. The ultimate goal is survival. The professional establishment, however, is more concerned with sustaining the tenets of the teaching and learning process. Such a concern is sometimes the antithesis of conserving institutions. The conflict is often difficult to deal with, but such is the nature of a free and open society. To educate is to undermine the status quo.

> In short, then, those who are responsible for managing institutions— that is, the educational establishment—and those responsible for teaching—that is, the professional establishment—in a sense have built-in conflict roles which can produce progress, provided each establishment deals with the other productively and intelligently as they carry out their respective functions. This is one of the perpetual paradoxical dilemmas of a free society. Surely, to understand the paradox is prerequisite to serving the public interest. This dilemma will not go away if we remain a free society. Conversely, it will grow stronger the freer we become. Role conflict need not deteriorate into an adversary context, especially if there is major goal agreement on maintaining a free society.[8]

What continues to baffle public school teachers is the obvious distrust implicit in excluding them from parity in matters of professional governance; and this has complications far beyond legal rights and responsibilities. Teachers also perceive that many practitioners in higher education, state departments of education, and accrediting agencies don't seem to understand their plight. Teachers claim to be hearing the same clichés and paternalistic pap emanating from some of these sources as they heard from many boards of education prior to the advent of collective bargaining. For example, teachers are admonished that professional behavior does not have to depend on legal sanctions or rights. But who doesn't know this? The issue goes much deeper. If legal rights are so irrelevant, why not give them to teachers?

Accountability Demanded

Surely the time is ripe for a thorough study of the sociology of the teaching profession. It is paradoxical that many of those who are quickest to condemn the teaching profession for becoming a craft are the very ones who would deprive the profession of the right of self-governance and thus the opportunity to be justly accountable for competent and ethical teaching.

The present demand for accountability may turn out to be a blessing. Modern parents are wise in the ways of child development and learning; they are beginning to demand more and more sophistication of teachers. Such demands will surely pressure the teaching profession toward more vigorous involvement and search for ways of being more responsible.

Moreover, the younger people preparing to teach are a new breed. If anyone doubts the rebirth of altruism, just listen to the young people. All across the nation a new mood is evolving. Professionals are being forced to turn toward social change. They are being pressed to assume new and more sophisticated roles in society. The consumer is demanding change. People are placing greater importance on performance, less on courses, credits, and degrees as ends in themselves. There is a growing disdain for all credentials, primarily because they have so often been misused, or, especially in recent times, have had little relevance to professional needs. There is a greater feeling of vested interest, and not merely one which is narrowly conceived. Such vested interests are critically oriented and sometimes driven by great compassion.

It would be naive to believe that the teaching profession will have an easy time acquiring the status and posture whereby it can be accountable. A whole fabric must be dealt with. First, as stated earlier, those segments of the profession possessing power have little inclination to share it within the profession. They feel it is theirs. Others view teachers as being overly militant and therefore not ready for greater involvement in professional governance. But even with all the obstacles, real and imagined, the teaching profession is systematically moving toward creating the self-governance machinery and processes necessary for their being accountable. This will happen because there are those in all segments of the profession who know that teaching must become a professional entity, one responsive to both the public welfare and the individual practitioner.

FOOTNOTES

1. Don Davies, "The Relevance of Accountability," *Journal of Teacher Education*, Spring, 1970, p. 133.
2. Helen Bain, "Self-Governance Must Come First, Then Accountability," *Phi Delta Kappan*, April, 1970, p. 413.
3. Margaret Lindsay (ed.) , *New Horizons for the Teaching Profession*. Washington, D.C.: National Commission on Teacher Education and Professional Standards, National Education Association, 1961, p. 24.
4. T. M. Stinnett, *A Manual on Certification Requirements for School Personnel in the United States*. Washington, D.C.: National Commission on Teacher Education and Professional Standards, National Education Association, 1970, pp. 43–44.
5. *Ibid.*, pp. 40–41.
6. NEA Research Division, *Teacher Opinion Polls*. Washington, D.C.: National Education Association, 1969.
7. For documentation, see "Some Inhibitors to Professionalization as Reported by Teachers" in *Negotiating for Professionalization*. Washington, D.C.: National Commission on Teacher Education and Professional Standards, National Education Association, 1970, pp. 66–70.
8. "The Context and Purpose of Professional Self-Determination," a working paper. Washington, D.C.: National Commission on Teacher Education and Professional Standards, National Education Association, 1970, p.7.

SUGGESTED READINGS

Broudy, Harry S. "Teaching—Craft or Profession?," *The Educational Forum*, January, 1956.
Dummont, Matthew P. "The Changing Face of Professionalism," *Social Policy*, May-June, 1970, pp. 26–31.
Smith, B. Othanel, *et al. Teachers for the Real World*. Washington, D.C.: American Association of Colleges for Teacher Education, 1969, 181 pp.
Sparks, Richard K. "Are We Ready for National Certification of Professional Educators?," *Journal of Teacher Education*, September, 1970.
Stinnett, T. M. *A Manual on Certification Requirements for School Personnel in the United States* (1970 Edition) . Washington, D.C.: National Commission on Teacher Education and Professional Standards, National Education Association, 1970, 221 pp.

Professional Accountability in the Schools

ROBERT LOVETT

Education is multifaceted and cannot be examined in isolation from the rest of society. In the quest for accountability, the question must be asked: can schools be held accountable for all the ills of society? If not, then who is accountable? To whom is he accountable? And for what is he accountable? Teachers must be prepared to accept their share of credit or blame for the state of education, but other social elements must also agree to an accounting.

Robert Lovett, "Professional Accountability in the Schools," *Kappa Delta Pi Record*, 7: 4–6, October 1970. Reprinted by permission of Kappa Delta Pi, an Honorary Society in Education, owners of the copyright.

I was very interested in the remarks of Mr. Whitney Young, Jr. in the April, 1970, *RECORD*. Statements by a person with the impressive credentials of a civil libertarian like Mr. Young's deserve to be taken seriously.

It was distressing, therefore, to find in the article an attitude that seems to be shared by many today who seek explanations for educational failure and methods for attaining success. Mr. Young seems to insist that full accountability for educational success or failure lies with the classroom teacher and assumes that we know what a given child should know at a given grade level. He seems sure that if the pupil does not meet this standard, it is the teacher who is to be adjudged incompetent and—without euphemisms—fired.

I have been very concerned with the matter of accountability and as result of conversations I had with officials of the United Federation of Teachers in New York City, I was invited to present my views on teacher accountability at their annual Spring Conference in March, 1970. The enclosed article summarizes some of the concepts developed at the Conference.

Perhaps you would like to offer these ideas to your readers.

Yours truly, Robert Lovett, Gamma Iota Chapter.

At the March, 1970 United Federation of Teachers Annual Spring Conference, Mrs. Blanche Lewis, president of the United Parents Association, defined "accountability" as the right to insure a good education for the children of a community and to sever from the school system those who do not contribute to that end. Mr. Whitney M. Young, Jr., in the April, 1970, *RECORD* agreed with this view.

Theoretically, there has always been this kind of accountability in the New York City schools—indeed, in all school systems. Teachers and supervisors can be charged and, after proper hearing procedures, fired. In practice, this has seldom been done. There are two principal reasons. One is that the procedure involved in dismissing a teacher has been so laborious that supervisors are loath to initiate it. Depending on one's view, this can be considered a screen to protect incompetents or a shield to defend professionals from the caprices and heartlessness of bureaucracy. The second reason is need. Until very recently there have not been enough teachers to fill classrooms. Principals have tolerated mediocrity because they could not be sure of replacing the malfactor with anyone better—or anyone at all. Now, however, several factors are acting to change the attitudes about accountability. One is the rising demand for educational achievement from local communities—white and black alike. Another factor, at least in New York City, can be attributed to the United Federation of Teachers.

Although the UFT has often been accused of protecting incompetents, it has increased the pressure for professional responsibility by creating one of the best teacher pay scales in the country. The writer has often heard people express the rather anomalous opinion that the public had no right to expect educational excellence when teachers were sorely underpaid, but now that salaries are improving teachers should be expected to produce. At the same time, the better salaries are attracting more candidates for teaching positions, thus portending the day when schools can be more selective about whom they want to have teaching. Recognizing these conditions, in their 1969 contract the UFT and the New York City Board of Education promised to ". . . join in an effort, in cooperation with universities, community school boards and parent organizations to seek solutions to this major problem and to develop objective criteria of professional accountability."

The inclusion of this clause in the contract indicates the belief that the present concept of accountability requires some change in direction or emphasis. A review of the question would seem to involve three basic considerations: (1) Who is accountable? (2) To whom is he accountable? (3) For what is he accountable? These are the points that will be examined here.

Who Is Accountable?

If we accept as part of the definition of "accountability" the evaluation of how well a professional is doing his job, teachers believe that they are accountable. In a survey by the NEA, 75% of the teachers surveyed believed that both probationary and tenured teachers should be evaluated regularly.[1]

However, when a teacher's classroom work is observed and evaluated by a supervisor, the major emphasis is on *how* the lesson was taught. If a test of teacher performance is to be methodology, it must be remembered that a teacher comes to his job equipped only with the tools he was given at college—the methods he learned in his education courses. If these methods do not work (and the current cry is that they do not) will the teacher training institutions be accountable for the failure of *their* methods?

The role of the school supervisor is often defined as that of a teacher of teachers. His basic responsibility is to help improve the quality of education. If a teacher does not meet the standards of performance that may be mandated, will his supervisor be held accountable for the aid and expert on-the-job training the teacher has or has not received?

If the teacher's performance is hindered by children in his class who have psychological, emotional, or social difficulties, will guidance and pupil personnel services be held accountable for the support they have offered the pupil and his teacher?

If a child does not learn because he is unfed or abused or because his family is emotionally upset, who is responsible? Is the parent then accountable? And if the child is poorly cared for because the community does not give all its citizens the means and opportunity to see that their children are well fed and clothed, is the community to be accountable? If a community's children have been psychologically traumatized either by the deprivations of ghetto life or the pressures of affluence without affection, will that community accept the economic responsibility for reducing class sizes or providing auxiliary personnel in schools or will it insist on giving a teacher 35 psychologically and socially damaged children and then insist on arbitrary levels of achievement?

It may well be that the question of who is accountable for good learning cannot be discussed only in terms of the teacher and the classroom. It may be necessary to create a chain of accountability if practical, long-lasting results are to be found.

To Whom Is He Accountable?

We have not yet really decided who "he" is who is to be accountable, but if we assume that it may well be the classroom teacher, we must again consider the accountability chain. In a very true sense, the teacher is first accountable to his pupils. He is then most directly accountable to his supervisors. However, a paradoxical situation exists. A new teacher has presumably learned the newest, most effective teaching methods in his training courses. Experienced teachers must continue in-service learning in order to advance to maximum salary levels. Supervisors, on the other hand, may not have been in classrooms or even taken a single course for 15 or 20 years. Yet it is assumed that their standards will be those of experts in the field and will reflect current educational philosophy and research and are to be given strong weight in determining teachers' fitness.

Then, teachers have always been accountable to parents. Parents have been free to question and complain. Their complaints could go to principals and to district superintendents. Now, under decentralization in the larger cities, complaints can go to the parents' representatives on the community school boards. Increasingly the demand is heard that teachers must be accountable to these parents. It therefore becomes imperative that community boards be truly representative of their district. Mrs. Lewis, in her remarks cited above, warned that, "Special interest groups are trying to take over the boards, disenfranchising the parents!"[2]

Perhaps teachers should be accountable to themselves, as many other professionals are. In the 1969–1970 New York State legislative session, the Committee on Rules of the New York State Senate introduced a bill (S5105) to give teaching legal recognition as a profession. It would have designated teachers as licensed practitioners and proposed a board to govern admission to the profession and regulate its practice. Fifteen of the twenty board members were to be teachers, the other five were to be educators from the university level. Professor Myron Lieberman of the City University of New York has expressed a similar view, saying that professional questions such as a person's right to be a teacher (as opposed to what Prof. Lieberman calls "employment" problems like lateness or whether to hire someone) should see professional organizations taking a more active role.[3]

It may come to the point where mutual trust and respect on the part of community, supervisors, and teachers will allow for an effective sharing of responsibility and each will acknowledge that it is inevitably accountable to the others and can neither monopolize nor evade its part.

For What Is He Responsible?

If we can ultimately decide who bears (or shares) the burden of accountability and to whom he is responsible, we still must try to define the area of this responsibility.

Several questions arise. Can we set a standard for every educable child? Are we to assume that every child can learn the same thing at the same time as all his peers? Who devises and administers tests objective, valid, and reliable enough to evaluate learnings in all areas precisely? Will the teacher be responsible for improving only academic skills? What about fostering creativity, patriotism, critical thinking, social responsibility, good health habits, psychological maturity, and social development?

In addition to the bill mentioned above, another one (A807) was filed in the session of the New York State legislature. It would have mandated 5 credit hours in dangerous drug addiction identification as a requirement for state certification. To one assemblyman, identifying drug users should be part of a teacher's responsibility. This may be a commendable aim, but at some point it must be decided whether it is intended that a teacher will be held accountable if he fails to recognize an addicted pupil.

If a teacher—or an educational system—is to be accountable for *anything,* society must first establish what its goals are. Does it want purely cognitive learning? Will it stress affective learning? Just as the social community has manifested its intention of being involved in educational matters, it seems reasonable that the educational community will also become involved at this point. It must declare for what it is *willing* to be held accountable.

A teacher may accept responsibility for teaching subject matter, but to what extent will he be accountable for detecting drug use? If drug detection is so essential to society's welfare, should only the teacher be responsible? It may not be too extreme to hold that those who accept the responsibility of parenthood should take mandatory "in-service" courses and assume their share of accountability.

As the concept of accountability becomes more real and specific, teachers may well demand a larger say in determining the things for which they will be accountable and for defining the limits of those responsibilities they are prepared to accept as appropriate to their professional obligations.

What If It Doesn't Work?

If it is possible to decide for what teachers are accountable and to whom, the possibility of failure must still be considered. Failure is not necessarily synonymous with incompetence or irresponsible performance. It is generally agreed that some things are beyond a professional's control. Psychologists, engineers, doctors, lawyers, legislators all fail sometimes, but they are not automatically branded as irresponsible or incapable. Will more be demanded of teachers? The answer is "yes" if society does indeed decide that *only* the teacher controls success and failure. Whether this is a reasonable hypothesis is what we are questioning here.

Conclusion

At this point there are clearly more questions than answers about professional accountability. To many teachers this concept may represent the threat of laymen interfering in professional matters beyond their competence. To lay persons it can mean a chance to defend their children and communities from the dangers of indifference and incompetence. The Professional Organizations foresee an effort to amass a large body of statistical data so that meaningful comparisons can be drawn between similar educational situations. Then it might be possible to isolate those factors in a given situation which might affect teacher adequacy and use them as a yardstick to measure performance. At the moment, there is no reason to think this yardstick must apply only to teachers. Teachers must be prepared to accept their share of the credit or blame for the state of education. But education is a multi-faceted construct and all the social elements that articulate with it must also agree to examination and accounting.

To do less would be the biggest cop-out of all.

FOOTNOTES

1. Evaluation of Teacher Competence, *NEA Research Bulletin,* October, 1969, p. 70.
2. *The United Teacher;* United Federation of Teachers, April 5, 1970, p. 8.
3. *Teacher Education News and Notes;* Division of Teacher Education, City University of New York, Vol. 21, No. 1, October, 1969, p. 19.

Administrators and Accountability

CONRAD BRINER

Traditionally, educational institutions have reflected the moral principles and values of the adult society. Parents employed educators to operate the schools but retained the power to determine the nature of the schools. Administrators must be accountable for explaining to the public the discharge of their responsibilities. Accountability requires combined efforts of community and educators in determining the educational purpose, defining functions, judging results, and taking corrective actions.

What makes education accountable? Who determines what is being done in the schools? Who answers for its instructional and management problems?

Historically, educational policy and administration have been fundamentally the people's business. Schools are domesticated organizations: we, the public, allow little self-determination, competition, and radicalism in them; we dote on them, often being attentive, protective, and sometimes generous in our care for them. We are used to being watchful of schooling—of the behavior of personnel, of the costs and quality of activities and facilities. We watch the students, too, for the effects of schooling, especially in terms of what each of us expects the effects to be.

Conrad Briner, "Administrators and Accountability," *Theory Into Practice,* 8 (October 1969), 203–206, College of Education, The Ohio State University. Reprinted by permission.
Editor's Note. This article is based upon a position paper the author prepared at the request of Leon M. Lessinger, Associate U.S. Commissioner for Elementary and Secondary Education, August 1969.

We, the public, are emotional about the need for good schools because schools are the means of personal success; they are the road to the future of our society.

But the public is not alone in its concern for education and its problems. School board members, legislators, congressmen, and other spokesmen for our social consciences are increasingly fostering inquiry into "who is responsible" and "what's being done."

Because of the extent to which education sorts human destinies, it must represent public sentiments. But should the public go it alone in defining the required nature of teaching and learning, governmental responsibility and educator expertise are denied. Should the educators go it alone, technology is worshipped as king. The answer to the question "who is responsible" lies somewhere in between.

Local public concern in education is illustrated by the old practice of groups of people establishing their own schools to represent their beliefs about what education should be. Schools, both public and private, represent the deeply embedded moral principles and values of their sponsors. Parents and others presume and even arrogate to themselves the power to determine the nature of schools. Educators are employed to operate schools, not to define them. This fiercely held public right to local control is mediated only by occasional deference to needs that are of general benefit in our society.

One result of the public's interest in education has been a continuation of the traditions of both common and elitist schools. Generally speaking, elementary education has meant providing common schools and secondary education has meant elitist schools. In elementary schools, each student is expected to attend and to achieve minimal achievement standards before being eligible for "release." Secondary schools have been obstacle courses designed and operated so only the fittest survive. Today these distinctions are less sharp, but they are far from being eliminated. As a result, educational accountability is faced with the special purpose of achieving equity of educational opportunity at all levels. Equity is increasingly a popular demand to improve education.

Equity is an exciting challenge for a number of reasons. Schooling today to a large degree still involves the classification of young people, sorting out those who succeed from those who fail and the various levels in between, rather than functioning to help each succeed to the best of his abilities. Students still get "turned off" in school and fail to finish in many ways what they had intended initially. But worse, some finish their schooling functionally illiterate and unemployable. This condition is inconsistent with our democratic tenets; it does not operate for the common good.

Spiraling costs represent another hindrance to better education.

Revenues for education, like all governmental services, probably always will be scarce. Probably too, the demands for educational services will continue to grow and exceed any existing financing arrangements. Such are the consequences of a dynamic society. Consequently, administration must involve expressing educational needs, proposing priorities, planning comprehensively, and inventing, all within the limits of policy, expertness, and cost. An up-dating of management practices is long overdue.

In human terms, the need to overcome neglect of individual integrity and welfare is most at stake in achieving equity on education. There obviously exists a lack of commitment to the moral responsibility of furthering, as a democratic pledge, the emancipation of individuals from the bondages of poverty, discrimination, fear, and lack of optimism about the future. This lack of commitment is evident whenever one looks closely not at what we say needs to be done in education, but at what we actually do and what happens as a result. The typical instructional and management practices in education are in many ways inhumane; schools are intolerable to students, teachers, parents, and others.

As a consequence, popular activity in education is increasing. Attention is being focused on how to update policy processes, educational purposes, and technologies. The public demands greater involvement in the schools, in policy-making, and administrative activities to achieve basic literacy skills, fewer dropouts, and vocational education that is relevant to present and future manpower demands. Vocational education is also being questioned in terms of whether or not each student learns to believe in himself and whether or not schools have overcome the stigma, so subtly taught and learned, that preparation for work after school is less respectable than preparation for college. Some of the demands are controversial because they reflect emerging values more than traditional ones; for example, sex education in the schools, increased student determination of curricula, and planned racial and socioeconomic integration of student bodies and faculties.

The public drive for accountability and equity represents a demand for constructive action to eliminate education's failures.

As a concept, accountability can only be understood as a derivative of a number of social and technological contexts. After all, learning is not only the result of formal educational experiences; it is also a matter of human conditions that reflect a broad array of societal components. The concept means more than measuring and evaluating the outcomes of teaching; it is a mixture of social problems, political processes, and educator expertise.

Education is a basic social institution and its organizational forms are human contrivances based not just upon an empirical plan for schooling but also moral judgments about what is good and bad about our society. The real nature of administration, instruction, and learning is many faceted; intertwined inextricably are social, political, and economic forces influencing the technical means of doing the educational job. Accountability is, thus, a matter of knowing and using cooperatively both public and governmental, as well as professional resources. I wish to argue in this context that the responsibilities for policy, organization, and management do not reside alone with the public at large, with any governmental agency, nor with the educator. We, the public at large; we, the governmental representatives; and we, the educators, know too little about how to guarantee maximum educational achievement for all. The nature of human capability to learn is still something of a mystery, as are the political, administrative, and teaching arrangements required to realize individual potential.

A dramatic implication of this political-educational complexity is that instructional and management practices must go public. This means more than people voting, courts rendering judgments, and governments taking action. Educational accountability, geared to the continual improvement of teaching and learning, must involve participative communication and decision opportunities both for the public and the educator. Operationally, this can mean localizing educational administration more so than exists now, differentiating various functions to open up the educational system, and bringing new resources into the task of improving learning. It also means making systematically developed information about educational success, failure, and the limits of expertise available for all to see.

In localizing administration, the practices of each school will become the object of lay and porfessional diagnosis, experimentation, and innovation. Teachers and community representatives must be indirectly accountable for advising and counseling administrators about educational purposes and means that are to be realized. Administrators must be accountable for stating and explaining directly to immediate publics the discharge of their responsibilities. This will require that administrators know the dispositions of their public, including teachers and students, the quality of their educational programs, and the ways of learning how to do better the educational job.

Teachers, parents, and others apparently don't want to be fully accountable for improving education. They tend to be consumed by their typical social and professional roles. On the other hand, administrators must be directly accountable. It is their essential reason for being. They are the ones upon whom the hands of approval and disapproval will be laid. Accordingly, their roles require orientation and commitment to educational success and the elimination of failure. In their performance, they can be expected to explain both success and failure; they must be capable of proposing educational improvements to the satisfaction of students, teachers, parents, and others.

Administrators are not to be feudal lords, however. Schools should be managed with the assistance of public expression of need, teacher and student advice and counsel, and knowledge of human development. They should be managed by administrators who can accept the challenge and career risks attendant with admitting that instructional, learning, and management problems do exist, and they are difficult because we are not sure how to solve them.

There will be conflicts over policy and professional decision. Such is the nature of freedom and political process. Schools embody and thrive on these ideals, as do other social systems. The educational process is, thereby, of necessity a dynamic rather than a static arrangement for social development.

School administrators must literally take to the sidewalks. They must know their publics, programs, and operational limitations. They must be articulate and aggressive in revealing successes and failures to the public and arranging participative efforts to eliminate the failures. The administrator must be an educational planner and a statesman. He, by his actions, generates open assessment of educational need and function and, hopefully, a popular respect for schools—a respect based upon educational success.

Accountability as only a professional exercise is unrealistic. Accountability as a combined community and educator political exercise is workable.

In support of this thesis, I propose certain assumptions and strategies. First, that in one manner or another students can be taught and they can learn; second, that human and financial resources will continue to be scarce; and third, that the educational management process can include participation of various publics in determining priorities of educational needs, source and manner of allocating resources, and types and uses of evaluation. These assumptions all defer to a new management technology that involves stating instructional objectives, defining performance criteria, monitoring, auditing, and correcting instructional activities within the context of local, state, and national political processes.

The basic strategy of accountability in these terms is to employ participative decision-making to shaping educational policy and evaluation and a highly detailed plan of educational management. What should be incorporated in educational management is careful reasoning about teaching and learning that is similar to engineering work. The desired result of instruction is made explicit; known alternative ways of accomplishing this are simulated to ascertain feasibility in terms of needed public and professional approval, available personnel, space and time, and of course, cost. The activities selected are then evaluated. Should the known ways of doing an educational job not be successful enough, invention is required and, accordingly, research and development work including experimentation and innovation will be the handmaiden of the engineering-like management practices.

Tying together these two basic strategies of participation and engineering is continuing assessment of both governance and technology. This is a matter of always knowing how well any educational job is being done according to the beliefs and perceptions of the people involved. Students, teachers, parents, and others will be asked repeatedly how well the participative decision-making arrangements are working. Instructional and management technologies will be judged similarly. Where possible, formal evaluation of instructional results such as standardized testing will add significance to the effects of assessment.

These strategies are based in the traditional nature of instruction and administration. It is not possible to hold teachers accountable for the quality of learning. They are too little involved in educational management, including the allocation of resources; and surprisingly, the pronouncements of teacher organizations to the contrary, they do not want to be involved greatly. Teachers do wish to believe, however, that they have the opportunity of access to policy-making and administration processes.

For administrators, it is a different story. Their primary responsibility is educational accountability. Administrators must be the ones to acknowledge eloquently what is being done in education, what should be done and why, to strive to free hopeless educational conditions. Such boldness will require considerable personal courage. The various publics must judge administrators in terms of the clarity and sophistication of their reasoning and the morality of their explanations and proposals. Administrators cannot be sufficient masters of all forces buffeting schools, but they will be helped to overcome the liabilities because the management will be a public affair and therefore represent all the power of the democratic political system.

Accountability in education must be the result of rational understanding and communication between the public and educators about the discharge of responsibility for determining educational purpose, defining function, judging results, and taking corrective actions to improve learning. Even the new expertise involved in modern management technology such as cost-benefit analysis and program budget planning can only function in terms of the tradition of educational government—bringing social problems and educational responses together locally. Localized popular participation—give-and-take between the public and the educators—is still the most productive way to determine educational policy and administration. Schools are the people's business.

School Administration by Contract

CHARLES H. WILSON

School administration is becoming so complex that it requires specialists in many areas. School superintendents and their staffs are being asked to assume roles they are not professionally prepared to handle. To meet this problem, Charles H. Wilson proposes that school trustees contract with a respectable management firm to provide all administration for a given period of time. Would the efficiency of administration by contract lead to increased pupil learning?

A new type of school administration could be in store for us, if it is not already just around the corner. It will utilize the best features of industrial and business management without eliminating the cherished virtues of local control. It will bring an element of competitiveness into a profession heretofore marked by degrees, years of service and even favoritism. The outline of its future may be seen emerging in the large consulting or managerial firms being organized—and reorganized—throughout the country.

Today it is a rare school district that does not rely to some extent upon the recommendations of outside management or educational consulting firms. Sometimes these recommendations are sought simply to reassure local citizens on proposed bond issues. Increasingly, however, the local district, large or small, requires the expertise of managerial specialists who are prepared to make recommendations ranging from site selection to curriculum development.

All of which leads to a quite simple question: If expert management is desirable in school operation, why is it not purchased outright by a district rather than superimposed on an already costly administration? Why cannot a local board of trustees contract with a respectable management firm to provide all administration for a given period of time, as it presently contracts with an individual superintendent?

If this be heresy, then so be it. But before I am nailed to the wall as a traitor to my profession, let's examine the reasons why this proposal makes sense from the standpoint of the school district *and* the school administrator.

In the first place, there has always been an element of the macabre in educational administration. Presumably, superintendents have been head teachers chosen to lead the teaching staff because of their outstanding classroom ability. But they are nothing of the kind. Teachers have no voice in the selection of their so-called leadership. Superintendents are employed by boards of trustees and are responsible solely to boards for their salaries and continued employment.

But superintendents, when employed, are expected to administer the schools through an established, on-going hierarchy of subordinate administrators that comprise an almost unmovable bureaucracy. I do not exaggerate greatly when I say that the superintendent is dependent solely upon the goodwill of his subordinates to tolerate him in office. Any efforts on the part of the superintendent to "get things done" will go for nought without the support of his associates, assistants, directors, principals, supervisors and what-have-you. Indeed, if a superintendent were so inclined, and some are, he could simply float along for years on the shoulders of his administrative bureaucracy without making serious decisions or solving critical problems.

Even this, however, fails to touch the hard-core reality of American school administration—the fact that it is the largest and most costly of any in the world. The State of New York, for example, is reputed to have more administrators than all of France. I know from personal experience that a school in Great Britain managed by one head master and a secretary would require a superintendent, three or four principals, a buildings and grounds director, a business manager, a curriculum supervisor and a half dozen counselors if it was relocated in a typical American suburb.

Why all this proliferation of administrators? There are several reasons. The nature of local control, for one thing, places the major burden for raising tax money on the administration. Every principal, if he is worth his salt, is a good public relations agent, a sort of educational ward healer. More than this, however, administration provides status and financial rewards for teachers otherwise tied to poor salary schedules. Then, too, the complicated nature of modern education and financial support demands specialists of many different kinds.

This last factor, in my opinion, may hasten the coming of the managerial firm. For instance, a superintendent simply must have on his administrative staff today, in addition to the customary financial and building specialists, a person to prepare federal reports and another to negotiate with teachers. Now unless the district is exceedingly large, it is unlikely that either position is a full-time assignment. It is still more unlikely that one person can serve in both capacities. Therefore, we employ two people and fill up their time with whatever busy work we can find. Eventually this work becomes so burdensome that there is not enough time for the original assignment, thereby requiring, with Parkinson's Law predictability, the employment of an administrative assistant and an additional secretary.

I know of no district where there are not far more administrators than are really needed if personnel could be used efficiently. Actually, the situation is so bad that in some districts over half of the certificated (professional) employees are in non-teaching assignments. And all, or nearly all, are frozen into position by a combination of tenure and tradition.

Nor am I, as a superintendent, able to make any significant reduction in the non-teaching staff. Every year or so, when someone retires or leaves the district, I can possibly consolidate two positions into one or spread the retiree's duties among several people. But I get only suspicious glares from those remaining, who step up the pace of their busy work to protect their own jobs and avoid additional assignments.

What Advantages?

How many of these problems could be eliminated with professional management employed by trustees for a period of three to five years as the superintendent is presently employed? And what would be the benefits?

First, there would be the benefit that would result from competitive bidding. The trustees would specify in broad terms the character of administration they desired, whereupon the competing firms would appear for interview and bid upon a contract.

What exactly would the trutees buy, and how would this differ from existing practice? Today, as I pointed out, the trustees employ only a superintendent, who is obliged to accept an administrative staff which he knows little or nothing about and cannot dismiss or transfer except at great peril to himself and the system by which he is employed.

Under a managerial contract system, however, the trustees would employ a managerial team. The director (superintendent) might or might not be specified in the contract. In either event, he would be appointed by, and responsible to, the managerial firm, as a school building architect is responsible to and paid by the architectural firm that assigns him to a specific job. Indeed, the parallel is pronounced. When school trustees build a building, they employ an architectural firm, which assigns a member of the firm to be in charge, who in turn uses his firm's engineers, draftsmen, architects and other specialists to the best possible effect. No one has ever questioned the loss of "local control" in the process.

We should think it madness if a board of trustees employed a single architect, however competent, to direct the board's own engineers and draftsmen in designing a new building. Similarly, no one should find it in the least surprising that a firm employed to manage a school district appoint its own director, who in turn would choose his own managerial team.

Later, I shall say something about why the lives and welfare of existing administrators need not be unduly threatened in the transitional process. Before I do, let us see what advantages an independent managerial system would have over our existing practices.

One thing that immediately comes to mind, of course, is that every managerial firm, large or small, would be obliged to recruit the best administrators it could find, and to pay these people whatever is necessary to retain their services. It is conceivable that particularly able superintendents or business managers would be offered bonuses and stock options on top of high salaries. Certainly, we should see an end to salaries and promotions based upon the length of service in a school district or the attainment of an advanced degree.

Next, and equally important, we should witness a higher order of efficiency introduced into school administration. No longer would an individual be employed to fill a particular slot and be expected to perform dozens of functions he is incompetent to perform. A firm would not employ a business manager, or a maintenance supervisor, or a personnel director, or a data processing director, or a teacher negotiator for every school district it serves. Rather, it would have specialists who would serve many districts. Unburdened by rigid tenure laws and seniority rights, the management firm, pressed to maintain profits, would employ only the minimum number of executives to get the job done.

As employees and representatives of a particular firm, desirous of obtaining a renewal contract for that firm, the administrative team would be universally solicitous to work with teachers and citizens of the community. No longer would we see the authoritarianism for which many administrators, protected by tenure, seniority and tradition, are known throughout the land. That school principal, long suffered for his fuddy-duddy paternalism, would become as polite and cooperative as a rising young bank executive.

Furthermore, when that principal or other administrator unexpectedly encountered a situation he could not handle, a management firm would not have to wait until the end of the year, or until the poor man reached retirement age, to offer a replacement. That could be done in a fortnight with a temporary or longterm substitute.

Let's face one fact squarely: whatever the strengths and shortcomings of those who enter school administration, there's not one in a thousand with the skill and fortune to avoid all disaster. Any one of us deserves at least a second, if not a third, fourth or fifth chance before permanent discard! And who is best qualified to assess an administrator's talents—an elected board of trustees or a group of professionals with their reputation on the line?

Out in the Cold

This brings me back to the matter I referred to a moment ago: why the lives and welfare of existing administrators need not be jeopardized by such a change. How would this be possible? How can you avoid disastrous treatment of a run-of-the-mill administrator, who, through no fault of his own, finds himself out in the cold when a board of trustees decides to employ a management firm?

Some people would say, of course, that if a man is run-of-the-mill or incompetent, he deserves to be put out to pasture. Isn't this the way business and industry operate? Well, yes and no. Many enlightened and socially responsible commercial firms take adequate care of individuals who have given long-time service to the enterprise, even when time has passed them by. Besides, when an executive is dismissed from a company, there is an endless number of companies for the executive to apply to. Where would the released school administrator turn?

First, one must keep in mind that most of us would find employment with the managerial firm, as many have already done.

Second, an administrator generally has a degree of tenure protection that a business executive does not have; while he may be dismissed from his $15,000 a year principalship, he does have tenure as a $10,000 or $12,000 a year teacher.

Third, we must remember that the new managerial concept, if it does materialize, will not come about all at once. It will be a gradual process that may require a decade or two to complete. And herein is still another element of competition that will be introduced. Where a management firm may be employed in school district A, school district B next door may continue to rely on the traditional administrative bureaucracy. Both the public and the trustees will have a good opportunity to compare the two systems.

Will the managerial firm face opposition from universities and legislatures? Obviously, any change meets with resistance. However, I would predict less resistance than might be expected. The firm-employed administrator would still require certification, just as the firm-employed architect or lawyer requires certification. Universities would continue to provide this training; but it would become a more precise and professional sort of training rather than the broad, ambiguous and somewhat directionless training that attempts to make all things out of all administrative candidates.

Personally, I can foresee little resistance from economy-minded and business-oriented legislatures. Whatever technical changes in the law might be required should be forthcoming with little opposition. After all, who could object to more efficient administrative practices at less cost?

How will a start be made? A start has already been made by a number of large consulting firms, who are admirably staffed by ex-administrators, college professors, architects, data processors and a host of other specialists. I have a suspicion that most of these firms are competent right now to take over the management of any school district, whether large or small.

Where It Will Start

I would guess, however, that the first significant inroads in firm-management will be made in small school districts where an inadequate jack-of-all-trades administrative staff might be unprepared to cope with the contemporary world of computers, negotiations and the growing complexity of federal and state financing.

Let me be among the first to admit that without a fairly large staff of administrative specialists, I could not begin to administer a school district today.

But while I cannot survive without a business manager, a building and grounds director, a personnel director, a public relations coordinator, a curriculum assistant, a data processing director and at least two people in charge of state and federal reporting, I will admit that this is something like double or triple the administration I need. My problem is that a highly skilled public relations coordinator cannot direct the data processing division. As a consequence, I run something of a managerial firm myself, seeking other districts who can use the services of these two specialists.

Do I hear someone suggest that administrators might soon come from professions other than teaching? Yes, possibly a few, such as accountants and data processors. But what better training ground is there for educational administration than teaching? The great majority of administrators would continue to come from the classroom.

However, they would not necessarily be talented teachers or aging football coaches to be rewarded with administrative assignments. Aside from the fact that competent teaching and coaching are needed the same as good administration, our schools have tended to drain the best teachers from the classrooms for administrative assignment.

Under the system that I envision, a teacher interested in administration would train specifically for employment with a managerial firm. Here he would serve in a variety of administrative capacities and rise within the firm as a junior executive rises to corporation president. No longer would he be thrown directly from the classroom or the gridiron into a full scale administrative assignment for which he may have had little training, experience or talent.

Do I hear the objection that competent administrators may not be willing to accept assignments where they must travel and move around a lot? But why not? Many of them do now. Our own building consultant lives 500 miles to the north. Our architects live in another state over a thousand miles distant. A large consulting firm from New York is handling a major assignment for some California schools.

By and large, of course, administrators would live in the general area where they work, as architects and engineers presently do. It is probable that most of them would serve a single district for many years.

But no longer would an administrator, whatever his rank or age, be subject to the whims of a changing board of trustees or superintendent. As an employee of a firm, he might be able to transfer from one assignment to another, even in another state, without loss of rank, salary or retirement benefits. In view of the hopelessly chaotic differences that presently exist among the states, retirement benefits alone should be enough to attract most would-be and practicing administrators to a managerial firm.

How would teachers receive this new breed of administrator? I am tempted to say—what difference? Haven't teachers, in their current militancy, asked for it? But, in matter of fact, I have a suspicion that teachers would welcome a more efficient and professional management. In the long run, it is to the advantage of teachers everywhere to have effective and economical administration.

Would local boards of trustees lose any degree of control? No faster than they are losing it now to the state and federal governments with the fantastic inefficiencies they are obliged to tolerate. "Local control" in the United States has always been something of a myth perpetuated by trustees who relished, and thought they had, power. Local boards have no power whatsoever except that granted to them by the state. As many people are coming to see, there is only one board of education in every state—the legislature.

Therefore, if the myth of local control is to be preserved (and there are good reasons why it should be preserved) it is essential that trustees seek to obtain the highest form of managerial direction at the least cost. And where can this best be obtained—from a haphazard system of teacher trained administrators, or from a professionally trained and skilled administration?

Educational Arthritis

Perhaps the point I should stress is this: we are a young nation turning arthritic before our time. Painfully and grudgingly, we are making progress in the area of human rights; but we are remaining hopelessly arthritic in education.

I would not pretend that a professional, business-like administration is the cure-all for our educational arthritis. In theory, at least, I believe that teachers must ultimately be responsible for the management of schools, as doctors are largely in charge of the administration of hospitals. But if, and when, that day arrives, there will still be a need for skilled and specialized administrators.

For that matter, I would not pretend that it is ever possible to maintain a satisfactory system of education. No generation can conceive that its successor is equally well educated, let alone superior. Yet it must be obvious that we cannot correct a fundamental weakness in a system by doubling, tripling or quadrupling the weakness.

If it has been an error, as it surely has been, to separate and relieve teachers from administrative responsibility, we cannot correct the situation with more and more administrators. For the time being at least, the best we can do is to provide an efficient administration. Once that is established, perhaps next we can talk in terms of a teaching profession—a group which selects, polices, dismisses and governs its own ranks.

And when this day arrives, what professional group would not desire the best management? Again, every dollar less for administration is a dollar more for teachers. And every dollar for good administration is overwhelmingly likely to produce more dollars for teaching.

Considerations for Administrators When Big Business Moves into Education

RICHARD GILKEY

Big business is taking over some of the basic instructional skills in a few selected school systems. Instructional systems being promoted by business depend heavily on educational media and technology. Richard Gilkey identifies some advantages and disadvantages within these systems. The question arises as to whether the objectives of these instructional systems are consistent with the overall objectives of the school system.

Much of the current literature on education in both the popular and professional press has dealt with turning over certain aspects of the instruction in basic skills to business firms. This takes the form of either turning over the entire school to a business (as is now being tried in one Gary, Indiana elementary school) or a part of the school program with selected students (as in Texarkansas). In both cases defined levels of performance are guaranteed and a part of the basis by which the firm is compensated.

Performance contracting systems have a basic philosophical soundness once the instructional-behavioral objectives have been defined and means for evaluation set forth. The danger lies in the scope of the objectives and whether or not they are consistent with the overall educational objectives of the school or system.

Today there are a number of firms beginning to promote a variety of instructional systems which they claim will solve total educational problems or a major component of these problems. Educational media and technology are usually central components of these systems. The systems are well articulated, smoothly presented, and address themselves to areas of primary instructional concern such as reading and computational skills. These educational merits are somewhat offset by certain problems inherent in any total "system" adoption.

When various companies present their concept for a systems development, they stress that their plan offers a complete program and as such accomplishes what no other program can. As an added incentive they offer in-service programs with various degrees of completeness

Richard Gilkey, "Considerations for Administrators When Big Business Moves into Education," *The Clearing House*, 45: 191–192, November 1970. Reprinted by permission.

which are designed to assist teachers in carrying out the program which they usually state must be followed as outlined or failure will result from deviation rather than inherent errors in original design.

There are many obvious advantages to any of these systems:

(1) They provide for an articulated, integrated vocabulary and concept development in which all components build on each other.
(2) In-service activities and consultation are provided to insure effective program execution. This is an essential ingredient of any innovative activity and by itself is one of the real strengths of these systems.
(3) Generally the objectives are clearly stated and are very specific. Meeting the objectives, therefore, becomes a task of following outlined strategies.
(4) There are marked savings in research and development funds which can be utilized for other activities when a proven system is employed as compared to having to develop a system within the district. In addition, the time lag is overcome since it is not necessary to spend a year or more in organizing a variety of resources into a proven and tested system.
(5) The inherent philosophical and psychological tenets are usually those which have been subjected to rigorous study over a period of time and are educationally sound.

While the above are significant advantages, there are a number of disadvantages which must be considered:

(1) Almost all of these programs focus on a limited range of skills—usually various aspects of reading or computation. They often develop these skills for the skills themselves rather than as a part of the total instructional program.
(2) The resources in personnel and funds required to implement these systems may restrict curriculum activity in other areas or operate such a fashion that the skills are not readily transferred to other areas.
(3) The programs are seldom concerned about developments within the affective domain. The work of Glasser, Holt, and others have clearly indicated the essential characteristics of the affective domain. A child which comes from a home in which learning receives little recognition may be motivated to develop reading and computation skills, but may never use these skills productively to do the necessary reading and analysis to understand social issues, to broaden his background in the humanities, or to develop the type of attitude towards vocation essentials in today's society.

Mere skill development is not enough. Change in attitudinal behaviour is also essential.

(4) Motivation in these systems is often extrinsic rather than intrinsic, with prizes or rewards being substituted for grades.

What should be the course of action for school administrators in considering these various systems?

(1) The total school program should be studied and modified rather than simply attacking the matter piecemeal and putting "band-aides" on these aspects which cry out for primary attention.

(2) The assignment of funds should be made with consideration of long-range developmental priorities. Failure to meet anticipated goals should be reported along with the successes. Analysis must be made then of why some aspects succeeded and others failed.

(3) There should be a focusing on the total needs of both the students and the society rather than merely modifying pieces of the school program to solve particular problems.

(4) There should be a demand for a demonstration and experimental program before any major commitments are made in order that the system can be tested with the pupil population with which it is to be used.

No one would suggest that we should take lightly the fact that many junior and senior high school students have never developed even minimum levels of reading and computational efficiency, but the solution of this problem must also be in terms of insuring that we are doing something more than merely conditioning students to perform certain skills. The school program must change the attitude of these students towards learning and their responsibility to keep on learning throughout their lives. The print and nonprint media resources available today offer ideal opportunities to be combined into systems that can assist in achieving these objectives. What is needed is the commitment of educators to solve these problems rather than merely to turn their solution over to commercial sources.

Educational Accountability Starts at the Top

TERREL H. BELL

As pressures for accountability in education continue to grow, the concept of local control will come under increased attack. The school board, as the ultimate responsible agent at the local level, will need to become accountable to the public. The school board member needs to be more than a trustee; he must be a guardian of the pupils' welfare. Accountability does not require complex and expensive hardware to audit learning output. If educational accountability really starts at the top, what are some performance measures of a good school board member?

I am sure that by this time a good share of the present audience knows my sentiments on returning to my home town. I suspect it's quite apparent that I take an absolute delight in coming back here—even if only for a day or two.

I miss Salt Lake City very much, of course, though to be fair, I must tell you that life in Washington has its compensations. For example, as a newcomer to government, I have been very deeply impressed by the willingness of the American public to be helpful. You'd be surprised at the large number of people who take the trouble to write in and tell the Commissioner how to improve the Office of Education.

Since turnabout is fair play, I thought I would use this occasion to give you a little free advice on how to improve things in your territory.

I know that you, too, get lots of help from your constituents and, indeed, have gotten some free advice from Ted Bell in years past. You might wonder whether any more is really necessary! But since I have spent seven months in Washington and have thereby qualified as another of those universal experts on everything, I'll go ahead anyway. Your Executive Secretary, Mr. Darld Long, asked that I speak on a subject that has gotten a great deal of exposure in the educational press recently—accountability. At the outset I want to make it clear that I come with no illustrated, step-by-step, how-to-do-it government accountability manual. The best I can do is to offer my views on the ways in which this interesting new concept applies to your concerns as school board members and to list a few questions that seem to need answering.

Terrel H. Bell, "Educational Accountability Starts at the Top." Speech before the annual convention of the Utah School Boards Association, Salt Lake City, November 19, 1970. Used by permission.

Actually, accountability in education as practiced by school boards could be a very down-to-earth thing. It calls for no complex and expensive hardware, but merely the introduction of measurement and control practices that have been in operation for years in virtually every sound business establishment.

We have fairly good measurement and control practices on the financial management side of education. However, we have a void where measurement and control are needed most, on the learning accomplishment side. This is the point I want to make tonight: that school boards will not be accountable until they audit learning output the way they audit dollar output.

Contemporary pressures demand that school boards become more than administrative groups primarily concerned with budgets and construction. As trustees to the community, school boards are now being forced to look more searchingly and intently at the educational welfare of the pupils within their jurisdiction. This, of course, is part of a growing movement toward grassroots government taking place all over the country. School boards are the most "grass green" of all such movements.

And that is where "accountability" enters the picture. "Accountability" may be an overworked word as applied to teachers and school administrators, but it is virgin soil where school boards are concerned. We know that in any organization the most logical place to begin the application of performance criterion is right at the top—the school board.

Before I develop this concept further, it is only fair that I explain why I feel this new point of view is worth your consideration. As you all know, in an era of social unrest such as we are living in today, education tends to become the key to the solution of many diverse problems. People of all types turn to educational institutions for guidance and help. This begins in the kindergarten and carries through to higher education.

Today, for example, parents send into our schools children who seem to need more help than they did in the past. On the surface they may appear more independent. That is, many of them no longer accept things on faith, as we did. Whether it's television or parental permissiveness that has made them more skeptical, today's children have to be hit with gut issues that emotionally involve them or they'll tune the teacher out. This of course has its advantages from a purely educational point of view. There's certainly nothing wrong with relevancy in teaching. But it also forces today's teachers to carry additional burdens. Teachers must compete not only against the excitement and lure of television entertainment, but must also compensate for an increasing lack of home training.

This runs all through primary education. Teachers become arbiters for all the problems not solved at home. In a growing number of cases, they also find themselves having to rebuild the personalities of children with wounded egos, again the result of parental neglect. Today's teachers, in addition to teaching, must play the roles of doctors, psychologists, actors, or what have you. Guiltily or ignorantly, many parents today give their children a morning shove in the direction of the school and hope for the best. I recognize that this does not typify the actions of most parents but it is representative of a significant number.

On a higher level the dependence on educational institutions is equally patent. We all now the great hue and cry that went up throughout the country when the Russians sent Sputnik into the sky. "Make our schools teach more mathematics and science subjects," the citizens demanded as our effort to catch up with the Soviets in space. Today we find similar examples in the social sciences, where people feel that education is the answer to all their environmental problems.

This dependence of the public on educational institutions has of course burned the spotlight directly into the hides of the educators. No longer do they operate a cloistered establishment. Parents now demand specific performance results. This may be an unconscious expression of self-inadequacy on the part of parents. But regardless of the cause exciting their sudden interest in education, the interest is there, and it is growing more intense with each passing year.

As members of school boards, you are well aware of one way—a rather painful way—this parental interest in education is expressing itself. Increasing numbers of parents are now demanding of the schools that they demonstrate their effectiveness before asking for more funds.

Recent polls taken by Gallup bear this out. Parents are insisting that they be informed of their children's status in comparison with the rest of the country. Three-quarters of the adults recently polled by Gallup said they want students in local schools to be given national tests for their educational achievement so that the results can be compared with students in other communities. When asked if they would favor or oppose a system that holds teachers and administrators more accountable for the progress of students, some 67 percent said they favor the idea.

All of this indicates the growing importance of accountability in education. It directly involves the teacher, the superintendent, and, in my opinion, now reaches the school board. As educational trustees of the community on questions concerning the ultimate welfare of your schools, you find that the buck stops with you.

What would constitute an adequate list of performance measures for a school board? Well, I personally feel that the most fundamental characteristic of a good school board member is reflected in his attitude. His concern for education and learning should never be overshadowed by his interest in administrative matters such as budgets, buildings, transportation, and the numerous other items that plague him.

I know that some of you will claim a foul right here by saying you are not qualified to intrude into professional educational matters. Before I consider this aspect, let us take up the more conventional performance measures for a good school board.

Your first task, of course, is to create conditions that make for the success of the superintendent and his staff. This means putting up a fight for an adequate budget. It also means overseeing the budget to the extent that there is a balance of funds to provide for all the wider aspects of education—innovation, experiments, adoption of new methods, and the opening of new directions that will keep the school system up-to-date in a fast-moving world.

It also means giving psychological support to the administrative staff when you feel its members are in the right. This calls for getting the facts on controversial issues and not buckling under to pressure groups. It means not committing yourself to a decision until all the facts are in and studied. In other words, hearing the superintendent and staff out before reaching your conclusions.

The response of school boards to pressure groups is becoming an increasingly important factor in modern education. Our highly organized society is composed of all kinds of special interest bodies and many of these groups, sad to say, are attacking the schools. Constructive response and sophisticated management of frustrating pressure from many sources will make school board accountability in this area a vital element to success in the future.

Except for added pressures, there's nothing really new in these requirements. Most of you face them throughout the year. I mention them only to keep the picture in balance. For though we see your shadows, as members of school boards, constantly lengthening in terms of potential accomplishment, we nevertheless recognize that there is a certain routine necessary for making the machine go.

Switching from here into a more subtle area of accountability, the school board must ask itself whether it is supporting conditions for the school's governance to operate as an "open" system. For some time now, American public schools have been moving to become more responsive to major changes in our society and economy. We have been more consciously and practically involved with the goal of providing equitable education for all children regardless of race, creed, or economic-social background. This has placed a greater burden on our educational system. It has had to attain increasing flexibility so that it could respond not only to the demands of the middle class, but to those of the newly emerging minority and disadvantaged and handicapped people as well.

To be able to cope with these new challenges, a school board must now ask itself just how "open" is its system. Are channels being established within the school for parents to express their concerns under sympathetic conditions? The struggle that occurred to make the Brooklyn, New York, Public School system more responsive to the community should be studied closely by all of us. In that case, the inability of parents to reach the top of the educational hierarchy, either through normal channels or "direct action," eventually produced an explosive situation that threatened to rip asunder the entire public school fabric. A school board should ask itself if its school is facing this community challenge.

Teacher input should also be welcomed as part of the "open" system. In every school there is a yearly influx of young new teachers carrying young new ideas. The board should be aware to what extent its schools are giving serious consideration to these contributions. In the trade, schools are known as backward or progressive. Some are considered good, others bad. Certainly an alert school board should be sophisticated enough to discern where its schools stand—locally, countywise, statewise, and even in the national pattern.

Students' rights should also not be overlooked or slighted by the school board. We have learned that small things, considered ridiculous by the administration of the school system but terribly important to the student, can often grow into major tests of authority. In devising a plan of accountability, members of school boards certainly should ask themselves whether their schools are really "open" to the consideration of such claims. Teachers' rights are equally important, and of course there should always be protection for the right to appeal.

If you will look into some of these factors, I think you will find that no great professional educational know-how is needed to assess the extent to which your schools are "open," and thus in a more strategic position to cope with the problems of the new age. As a matter of fact, most of these accountability requirements fall into the area of good common sense.

Something that touches more of the professional, however, also should occupy a key position in your accountability appraisal. Here I am referring to teaching and learning performance accountability.

A school board today must insist that it be provided, by the professional educators it employs, a student progress surveillance system and evaluative processes broad and comprehensive enough so that the board knows at all times the relative strengths and weaknesses of its schools.

This is a rather tall order, but something which no one can afford to close his eyes to, least of all a member of a school board. In Utah, overall, we are not in such bad shape, but let us consider what has turned up in the national situation under the glare of professional surveys and evaluation.

In reading, the results are disturbing.

About seven million public school pupils in the United States (16 percent of the enrollment in grades 1–12) require special instruction in reading.

In those of the nation's public schools in which at least half of the pupils come from poor homes, more than one out of five of the elementary, and more than two out of five of the secondary pupils, require special instruction in reading.

Board members should also keep a close eye on their dropout statistics. Nationally this is another rapidly deteriorating situation.

In the 1969–70 school year, there were around 800,000 dropouts from high school, an increase of 100,000 from the previous year. This 800,000 figure is based on the number of fifth graders in school in 1962.

Youth unemployment is directly related to dropout rates and presents still another dismal aspect. Twice as many dropouts are unemployed as high school graduates. Jobs calling for high school graduates have increased 30 percent while jobs for non-graduates decreased 25 percent. The unskilled are the last to be hired and the first to be fired.

Among the disadvantaged the educational statistics are equally disturbing. Here disparity widens as age increases. When at the twelfth-grade age level, the ghetto child may be as low as the sixth grade in actual achievement.

At least once a year each school board should sit down with its staff and perform an educational accomplishment audit. This exercise should include a review of dropouts, youth unemployment, reading failures, and other easily measured outputs. Such an appraisal on a school-by-school and also on an age-level basis is part of a school board's accountability to the community that elected it. Appraisal, of course, should be followed by *action,* plans by which the system can grow to a higher level of educational excellence. A system of renewal and recognition for accomplishments of schools and of individuals in the system would be another quite obvious outcome of a performance-oriented school system.

As I look at it, the greatest mistake a school board could make is not to comprehend the gaps existing between what "is" and what "ought to be" in the school system. Industry has long ago faced up to this challenge by devising a plan of procedure known as management by objectives, or MBO, to use the abbreviated term.

The process is relatively simple in concept. Objectives or goals are established after a free flow of information pertinent to the subject has determined what areas need to be improved. This of course calls for a careful and unbiased perusal of weaknesses and strengths. Then once the objectives are clarified and put into mold, a management procedure is established to monitor for results. Through this monitoring there is early detection of any shortcomings, and it is then possible to make timely correction to set the work back on its true course.

Though I have given you the briefest abstract of Management by Objectives, its theories and procedures can be applied to education as well as to business. The results of education's failures and breakdowns in such vital afeas as reading and dropouts—figures which I have just listed on a national scale—indicate that many school systems are painfully in need of a comprehensive plan to identify and correct their shortcomings. School boards are really the only people who can effectively demand that their institutions develop and implement plans adequate to coping with such situations.

It is platitudinous to assert that the problems facing the American educational system today are enormous. It is more important to find out what we can do about them. One of the first things is to obtain reliable, practical information on student progress and goals. A Management by Objectives type operation could put this responsibility for performance into the system with a minimum of expenditure and effort. Members of the Board, as educational trustees to the community, are logically the ones to make certain that such adequate monitoring and evaluation exist in their schools.

As long as education continues to be a cornerstone of our free civilization, education will remain a subject of vital importance to most Americans. The first requisite of school board performance has always been to see that quality education is developed. I urge you to evaluate yourself as Board members so that accountability in education can start at the top, where it must begin if it is to be a success. Once the spirit of accountability begins to permeate the school boards of our nation, it will move strongly from there through the entire educational system.

When the school board appraises itself and then holds itself to high standards of performance, the staff and students will respond in kind. Nothing is so infectious as a good example. What you apply to yourselves others are more ready to accept.

How enthusiastically board members accept accountability as an idea applying to themselves as well as to school employees might well determine how long we will keep our present system of local control of education. My recent experiences in Washington convince me that our system of local control of education will face some strong attacks if we do not become more responsive to the educational urgencies of our era. But dramatic improvements must be made, and they will have to come primarily from you. Accountability starting at the top is one answer—perhaps one of the most sensible and practical answers we can make to the educational problems of the day.

The School Board and a Model for Educational Improvement

BURTON KREITLOW and TERESA MACNEIL

This model for educational improvement developed by a research team at the University of Wisconsin suggests two key roles for the school board member. He can stimulate improvement, and he can be an important force in organizing for improvement. The model represents a three-dimensional conceptual scheme of the school district as a social system which can offer a board of education the chance to appraise what happens in its district. The article underscores the importance of interaction among all the major entities within the system.

I. Introduction

In a culture of change there must be concern for improvement. The fact of school change during the past decade is accepted as is the potential for continued change during the next. This being true, boards of education will deal with the change process either by design or by default. It is by design that the focus can be switched from mere change to positive action culminating in improvement.

School boards will miss the potentials of improvement if they think they alone are responsible for introducing change. Teachers, administrators, and the community need to be in on the act. These three, along with the board, make up the groups who have an opportunity to direct the process of change if they want to and if they understand it. Their "minds' eye" needs to focus on a picture of what the improvement process is like.

A research team at the University of Wisconsin has pictured this "minds' eye" image of the improvement process in a school district.

Burton Kreitlow and Teresa MacNeil, "The School Board and a Model for Educational Improvement," Practical Paper No. 10, Research and Development Center for Cognitive Learning, University of Wisconsin, Madison, April 1970. Reprinted by permission.

The image is called the Model for Educational Improvement. This Model may be used as a guide to those school districts wishing to organize for improvement or it may serve as a backdrop against which to compare what a district is already doing. It took shape after carefully study of the work completed by other social scientists who have pictured the change process in both agriculture and education and after observations in five Wisconsin school districts. In these five districts, change-agent teams were formed and the school improvement action of these teams was either orbserved or tape recorded for later analysis.

II. Improvement—Its Structure and Process

There are a few things that all 26,000 U.S. school districts have in common. Figure 1 illustrates some of these. It is a representation of a

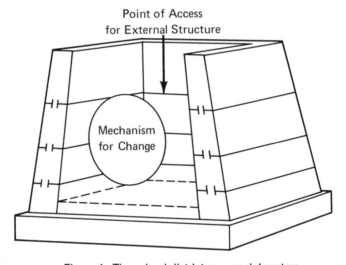

Figure 1. The school district as a social system

three-dimensional conceptual schema of the school district as a social system. The outside boundaries of the Figure represent both the actual boundaries of the district as a physical unit and its boundaries as a social unit. Thus included are land and people as well as school buildings and other community institutions along with those who manage them.

Is it wrong to assume that all school districts have access to resources outside of the district or that outside influences have a way of getting to the district? We believe not. The opening at the top of Figure 1 represents the assumption that it is an open system. It is the point of access to the school district and the avenue for influences within the system to move out.

Another characteristic that all districts share is an internal structure. When Figure 1 is viewed as a three-dimensional model, its internal structure may be more readily visualized. It is within this internal structure that the program of the school takes place. Because programs are not the same in all school districts there are consequently variations in internal structure.

In addition to the regular school program and its operation is the social machinery that is responsible for change, innovation, and improvement. There are changes, innovations, and improvements that can be made by individual teachers in the classroom; by supervisors in their relationships with teachers; by boards in the way their meetings are run. These individual or unit changes are not our major concern. In total school improvement the concern is with those gross adjustments that involve and relate to the entire system. The social machinery necessary for this kind of adjustment is located within the Mechanism for Change in Figure 1. It is the cauldron of change that every community institution concerned with service must have if it is to "keep up" or "move ahead" in a dynamic society.

Figure 2 is an expansion of the cauldron, or social change mecha-

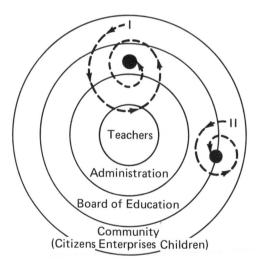

Figure 2. The improvement module: a mechanism for change

nism. We call it the Improvement Module and it is the key to unlocking the planning and decision resources of those who are in a position to improve an educational system. In a school district those with the greatest potential to lead or to impede improvement are board mem-

bers, administrators, teachers, and citizens (including the students).
With formal or informal interaction among representatives of these
key groups comes the chance for commitment decisions on improvement. Without this interaction change may come without unifying
purpose. The interaction among the four key groups is noted in Figure
2 by the arrows at Point I.

It is possible for some improvement to occur without total group
interaction. Point II in Figure shows such an example. In this instance
there is interaction only between the community and the board of
education. In our observations we have noted a number of schools
where there is far less than a complete and interacting Improvement
Module such as that illustrated at Point I. What we often see is a
number of Mini-Modules similar to that noted at Point II. It can be
predicted that Mini-Modules will lead to mini-improvement. Strong
commitment to change requires a decision in which the total group
has participated.

Developing a model as has been done in this research required
visualizing the process and drawing it. The process flows from a
concern with purposes, problems, and needs to solutions and action.
The arrows in Figure 3 illustrate the path of this flow from problem to

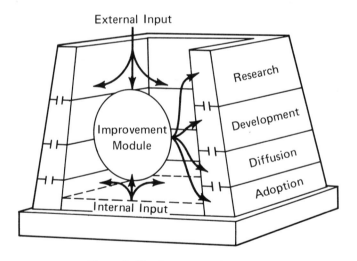

Figure 3. The improvement process

solution. There are a number of alternate routes which the path may
follow. First, the Internal Input or the External Input may not be
acted upon. The open area around the Improvement Module is
symbolic of the inefficiency of all educational agencies. There are
places where improvement ideas can get lost. Thus, an input may
disappear before it reaches the Improvement Module. In a school

district where there is not a specific organization for improvement, the chance for inefficiency is greater than that shown in Figure 3. That is, the space surrounding the Improvement Module is large and ideas are easily lost. Second, if the input is acted upon (gets into the Improvement Module) and a commitment decision is made with subsequent administrative follow-through, the action can next go to any level: research, development, diffusion, or total adoption. There is no necessity for the flow of action to start with research and move through each level until it reaches adoption. The processes occurring within the Improvement Module make many shortcuts possible. The internal structure of the model shows that it is possible for a proposed improvement to move easily from one level to another. The proposed improvement may move toward adoption or away from it depending on the level of assurance that the decision makers have about its appropriateness for the school district.

III. The Model in Operation

Observations in schools and a review of tape-recorded meetings of change-agent teams in cooperating schools provided evidence that there is a structure and process similar to that pictured in Figures 1, 2, and 3. The Model helps explain what goes on as a school moves to an improved practice.

Figure 4 places in a single drawing the total structure and process described above. A few words are added to complete the picture. The

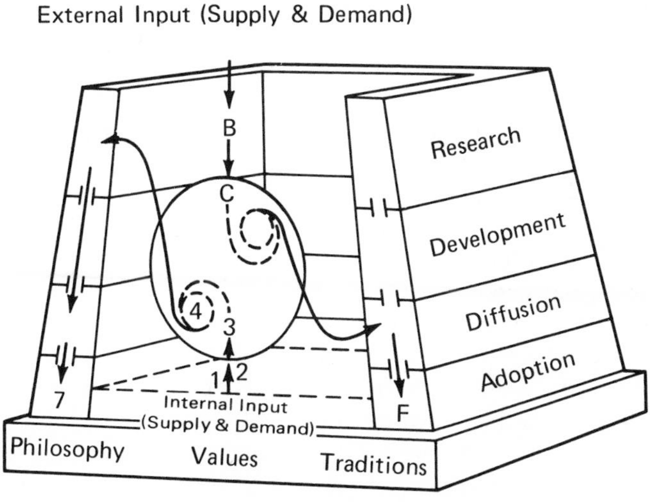

Figure 4. A model for educational improvement

base of the pyramid includes the philosophy, values, and traditions of the district. These are the long-term stabilizers. The external and internal input is identified as being "supply-" or "demand-" oriented. The use of supply and demand in this context is to indicate whether the solution to a problem is sought (demand) or whether it is available (supply). The results of research by a university or any other agency can provide an external input to a school district by either the "supply" or "demand" route. If the school asks for help, the input is "demand-" oriented. If a university professor disseminates the results of his research in an article such as this one and it reaches the school district, it is a "supply-" oriented input.

The process flow of an external input ("supply-" oriented) is demonstrated by letters "A" through "D" in Figure 4. In this instance, and on the basis of experience, a professional section within the State Department of Public Instruction believes that rural community schools should work out cooperative arrangements with neighboring districts for the employment of school social workers. A spokesman for the department decides (Point "A") to disseminate (supply) this belief in his monthly newsletter to schools. It is at this point—"B"—that the idea is noticed by the guidance counselor and gets into the school system. This could be the end of the idea. In this instance it is brought to the attention of several staff members and the administrator. After some informal discussion the administrator decides to turn the suggestion over to the school's committee on improvement (Point "C"). Here it is discussed in detail by all concerned groups (Point "D"). Recommendations and decisions are made to diffuse (Point "E") the idea into the system in order to have the teaching staff become acquainted with its potential. At Point "F" the determination is made to adopt the idea in full and commit the institution to the joint employment of a school social worker in cooperation with a neighboring district.

An example of an internal input (demand-oriented) in the same district is shown by numbers 1 through 7 in Figure 4. Beginning near the bottom of the model at Point 1 is an illustration of an input brought to the system by a teacher. The teacher has a major reading problem in her Fifth Grade. She brings the problem to the attention of her principal (Point 2). On the basis of his contact with the reading problems experienced by other teachers, the principal is convinced that the problem is one that affects the entire school. This being the case, he suggests that it be reviewed by the committee for improvement (Point 3 in the Improvement Module). A search for solutions is made (Point 4) by an interacting and concerned group. Help is sought and obtained from many sources both within and outside the system. In the process, information on a non-graded reading program is studied and special committees are established to determine whether a nongraded program would appropriately solve the problem for the district. At one point in discussions a suggestion is made to have the system establish its own research program to test out a non-graded program. Later information received from a research and development center (external input on the basis of demand) convinces the committee that a non-graded program would work if carefully developed to meet the special characteristics of the children in the district. On this basis the committee on improvement proposes and receives administrative sanction to research a few aspects and to develop the overall nongraded idea (Points 5 and 6) in the lower grades in 1968–69. If it works well, they will diffuse it throughout the system (Point 7) as soon as possible. If success continues, they would bring the practice to full adoption (Point 8).

IV. The Role of the School Board in Educational Improvement

A careful examination of the Model clarifies the fact that improvement is not the sole responsibility of the school board. Yet the board has a vital part to play if improvement is to occur. The board is one major entity in the improvement module.

The Model suggests two key roles for the board of education if it is to be an effective participant in school improvement. First, the board should and can be the stimulator of improvement. A board's potential for being the bottleneck blocking improvement is so great that every effort should be made to lead toward improvement rather than to stand in its way. Second, the board is in a position to deliberately organize for improvement in its district. Every school board can compare the structure and the process for improvement that exists in its district with the Model for Improvement described in this report. This Model gives the board of education a chance to appraise what happens in its district and compare it with what would happen if it were to organize an "Improvement Module" to do the job.

Performance Contracting: Is It the New Tool for the New Boardmanship?

HAROLD V. WEBB

The business of performance contracting is dependent upon the amount and purpose of expenditures which are controlled by boards of education. In order for performance contracting to be successful, it must have the support of school board members. A recent survey indicated that a full two-thirds of the nation's school board members looked with some favor on the concept of performance contracting. This results in part from a sensitivity to public demand for humane education, plus a belief by some board members that some teachers have modified their primary commitments from children to occupational interests.

It is a tidy idea and easy to express: the board decides what should be done and the administration carries out the order. That, essentially, is how the action is—in theory. And that is pretty much how it is *not* in reality. The line of management division in school district operation—as boardmen across the nation know all too well—is hardly holding, if in fact it ever did.

An increasingly vocal public keeps getting in the way. It is a public less inclined by the day to respect or care about fine differentiations in administrative theory. It is a public that wants solutions to the enormous problems of the schools. Citizens, especially in the cities, are bypassing even the superintendent's office; they are taking their grievances directly into the boardroom, and they are dramatizing the jarring truth that underlines the role of school boards in the 1970s:

An aroused and incredibly diverse public is making complex vocal demands on its schools and is insisting on a measurable accounting from the people it selected to be immediately answerable for what the schools accomplish or fail to accomplish.

The result already is visible: the emergence of a totally committed, totally involved school board member, determined—sometimes forced —to assert a vigorous presence not witnessed for a long while in American education.

I am not suggesting that this is likely to mean open conflict between school board members and the school staff, but I am stating that staff is going to have to get used to the idea that board members increas-

Harold V. Webb, "Performance Contracting: Is It the New Tool for the New Boardmanship?" Reprinted, with permission, from *The American School Board Journal,* November 1970. Copyright 1970, The National School Boards Association. All rights reserved.

ingly are awakening as functional managers of the educational process, with a sense of responsibility for the *productiveness* of what we call the teaching-learning process. That is really a principal reason that various methods of educational accountability to the public are being adopted by school boards and very likely will grow in application and number during this decade.

"Performance contracting" (see example on facing page) could very well turn out to be one such workable method. It is being tried out, under federal auspices, by a number of school boards in several parts of the country this year.

In addition to its obvious, albeit not fully tested, implication as a means for boards to demonstrate pupil achievement to their communities, performance contracting may suggest a new kind of relationship between school boards and industry and, as portentous, between boards and teachers.

So far as either is concerned, no factor in public education is more crucial to the success or failure of performance contracting—indeed to its very idea—than is the school board. Industry is already cognizant of this, realizing that, if the school board—the functional manager of education which determines the amount and purpose of education expenditures—is not committed to performance contracting, the idea can never amount to anything more than another of the passing fancies that have plagued public education on and off for decades. For this truth is more evident than ever: education's policy makers—its elected and appointed school board members—are chiefly among the people who can and will decide whether the concept of performance contracting is to become widespread educational policy.

Whether they will, and to what degree, is still unclear, but the nationwide scientific sampling of school board members on the subject, conducted by the *Journal* and summarized on page 35, provides important clues. A full two-thirds of the nation's school board members, the survey found, look with at least some favor on the concept of performance contracting.

Why? As the article on page 35 points out, board members offer numerous explanations, but generally these can be refined to two major points:

• *A sensitivity to the public's demand for a humane education with opportunities for each child regardless of his personal, racial or economic circumstances.* This is compelling evidence of the emergence of school board members determined to take more seriously than ever before their responsibilities for all aspects of the school system for which they are responsible—to demand of their staff demonstrable *results* of the teaching-learning process, and to account to the public for those results.

• *An apparently widespread belief on the part of boardmen that teachers have turned, at least to some degree, from commitment to children as their primary responsibility to a commitment to their own occupational interests.* Board members participating in the national survey cited the overwhelming increases in the number of teacher strikes in recent years—along with intensified collective bargaining activities on the part of militant teacher groups—as indications of a new teacher preoccupation, not so much with whether children learn, but, as it was put by a board member from a school district on the East Coast, "with winning the highest possible pay for the least possible effort." Whether that conviction is entirely accurate or even completely fair is not the immediate question. What is significant is that this belief appears widespread among school board members and may indicate that school boards are willing to give aggressive consideration to new arrangements to achieve demonstrable results in getting children to learn—new arrangements with their own teacher employees, or indeed, beyond the teachers, perhaps to private contracting agencies.

Both points expressed in the survey by school board members deserve examination.

About the first—it is easy to state, as I did at the beginning of this article and as did so many school board members who participated in the *Journal* study, that the demands of an increasingly vocal public to share in the educational decision-making process mean that school boards will have to become more sensitive to their constituents and more thoughtfully demanding of their staffs. But it is a little more complicated than that.

Board members are not likely to ignore the demands from their new electorate for a voice in making decisions that affect the lives of the community's children. At the same time, neither can they abandon their legal responsibilities for making final policy. Even though there is room for a new democracy in education—indeed, room must be *made* for it—we cannot embrace the extreme of regarding educational policy making as a populist free-for-all. While the new educational electorate is entirely within its rights in complaining about school deficiencies, it remains the task of the school board and its appointed superintendent to translate complaints about educational deficiencies into *programs.* So the school board cannot abdicate—to private contractors, to teachers or to anyone else—its legal obligation to make the final decisions about prudent public policy and effective plans for education.

That seems to be the real challenge facing school boards in their relationships with the new educational electorate. How are they to convince an apathetic, sometimes hostile, financially threatened middle class *majority* that only truly major changes can bring the schools into line with the needs of the Seventies?

General agreement has it, probably rightly, that this will be achieved by offering some measurable, believable proof of performance—performance *contracting* being one of several possible methods for achieving that, and, to be sure, the method currently receiving the greatest degree of national attention and experimentation in school districts.

The need for offering proof of performance is clearly recognized by many of the board members who expressed favor to the concept of performance contracting (page 35). But, as these participating boardmen also pointed out, there is reason to conclude that teachers, as a group, do not yet seem to share the belief that some measurable proof of performance is needed in education. Or, if they do, that they are unwilling or feel unable to accept responsibility for it—indeed, if recent statements by spokesmen for national teacher groups are to be taken seriously, teachers are hostile to the specific idea of performance contracting.

Yet the facts tell an almost incredible story.

Our public schools enroll more than 44 million students, employ nearly two million teachers, and account for the expenditure of at least $35 billion in tax dollars each year. We have all kinds of measurements of where this money goes: We can pin down per-capita expenditures nearly to the penny, state how much any school district in the country spent for construction and debt service, and enumerate pupil-teacher ratios.

But we have virtually no measurement of the *results* that such an enterprise yields. We do not know, for example, what it costs on the average to increase a youngster's reading ability by one year; all we know is what it costs to keep him seated for that year.

Fortunately, the evidence, born of long and close association with school boards in all parts of the nation, is encouraging. It indicates strongly that in the Seventies we will see school boards moving beyond showing the public where its education dollars went (teacher salaries, textbooks, new buildings) to showing the public what it *received* for those expenditures—how youngsters moved from one level of learning achievement to a higher one.

It is reasonable to conclude, in view of the *Journal's* survey findings, that performance contracting seems to have a better than even chance of becoming one important means that school boards will employ to accomplish that.

It also seems reasonable to predict that school boards will enter into performance contracts not only with private corporations but, just as likely, with their own local teachers. The reason for that likelihood is this: boardmen, as they hold *themselves* accountable to the public for learning results, will in turn hold their administrators and teachers accountable to the board for the same results. The evidence of this change may manifest itself fairly early in this decade—in collective bargaining. If it does, it may indeed involve school boards with performance contracting of a very real sort, although not always with private corporations.

Collective bargaining between boards and teachers thus far has been largely one sided. In general, teachers have taken the offensive, boards the defensive. That teachers intend to retain and enhance their initiative seems clear enough from the plans teachers are announcing nationally with the intent of strengthening still further their bargaining position with boards. In the face of that, nevertheless, school board members are now being heard arguing forcefully that teachers have an inescapable *performance obligation,* an obligation that must be translated into measurable performance levels and written clearly into contracts.

Many board members are recognizing that it is futile and unfair to perpetuate the notion that some "mystique" about education precludes the spelling out and measuring of learning outcomes. The public no longer will accept that. A new conviction, in fact, is that learning outcomes can and must be spelled out and introduced as legitimate and essential items in bargaining between school boards and teacher groups.

The public has a right to expect a defined standard of performance by its teachers and it is holding the board itself accountable for that performance—to a greater degree each year. The buck is stopping with uncomfortable frequency at the boardroom door. It is this hard fact of life that is likely to spawn school board performance contracts both with private corporations *and* with teachers.

The degree to which the public is beginning to hold school boards accountable isn't entirely fair, of course. Perhaps as much as 75 percent of what school boards do is predetermined by (a) state law, (b) federal guidelines, (c) negotiated agreements, and (d) budget limitations. But to quibble about what is fair is useless. Some one agency must accept prime responsibility for education, and since accountability is thrust upon the school board, it is accepting that responsibility—and proceeding to act accordingly—with the knowledge that the options exercised in that 25 percent gap can spell a significant difference in the quality of education children are afforded.

A Program of Accountability
for Elementary Schools

AARON WILDAVSKY

Accountability has been compared to the economic concept of "value added" for services performed. This requires the use of comparison tests coupled with identification of significant norms. The establishment of local achievement norms could become the subject of bargaining among parents, administrators, and teachers. The author proposes a program of accountability for elementary schools based on local norms with the focus of accountability on the principal of the school.

The request for accountability in the sense of holding the school system responsible for the achievement of children in critical areas is a good one. Consumers of governmental services are entitled to know what they are getting. Truth in packaging applies just as much to government as to private industry. Indeed, the field of education may be on the verge of making a contribution to the general evaluation of governmental programs. The ability of ordinary citizens to appraise whether they are getting what they want is of critical importance in a system of democratic government. Yet no one today knows what citizens will do with this kind of information. In view of the inevitable tendency to oversimplify, it is desirable to add to public understanding through an assessment of what accountability means and what it will and will not do. The best way to get these ideas across is to set up procedures for accountability that embody them.

A student's ability to read is critical for later achievement. His ability in mathematics is indispensable for a whole range of occupations. Achievement in these two areas must be evaluated in terms of standardized tests. It is true that such a test does not by any means measure all that a teacher does or attest to all of his impact. No such test can be devised. Nor is it necessary to do so. To say that what a teacher does is so exotic that it cannot be measured is simply to say that he ought to do what he pleases, and that is not tenable. All the impalpable qualities of "growth" mean nothing if students cannot hold jobs as clerks in drugstores because they cannot make change correctly or cannot be messengers because they cannot read street signs. Before a student can do other things he must be able to read, and it is

Aaron Wildavsky, "A Program of Accountability for Elementary Schools," *Phi Delta Kappan,* 52: 212–216, December 1970. Reprinted by permission.

sufficient to say that he must develop in this direction as well as in others. The deprived child needs this skill more than other children.

It may be said that the standardized tests are culturally biased, but I think this is beside the point. Few doubt that if one took an article about the life of the Yoruba tribe in Africa or the city-state of Benin, equally remote from the experience of all students, those students who read well would be able to answer questions about the material and those who read poorly would have difficulty. The same would be true of a book directly concerned with the black man's experience in America. To say that one must wait until tests without cultural bias are developed is simply to say there will be no accountability. I should add that there is a great deal of difference between tests designed to help parents hold schools responsible and tests that work to exclude people from opportunity for higher education and better jobs.

At this point I would like to add a word of caution about the problem of cheating on tests. As the pressure grows to improve student performance on standardized tests, teachers will be tempted to cheat. It is one thing for teachers to prepare students by giving them exercises similar to ones on the test; it is another for teachers to feed their students the exact words and phrases that will be used on the test. That practice should be discouraged. I find here an analogy with the New York State regents' examinations I used to take when I was a high school student in that state. One learned a great deal by going over previous examinations, and that was not considered a form of cheating. Rather than relying merely on negative sanctions I would suggest providing a lengthy series of sample "previous" examinations, so that teachers will feel quite free to use them.

All standardized testing should be turned over to an extra-school organization—a state agency or a private business that will administer the tests and see that they are fairly conducted. Tests should not be brought into the schools until the morning of the testing day, and observers from the testing organization should be present. One drawback of this proposal is its expense, but if there is to be confidence in accountability, there must be assurance that the test scores mean what they say.

Teachers I know have told me that they fear spending most of their time gearing students to pass certain examinations. My reaction is: What is wrong with that, if the examinations are good indicators of what we wish students to learn? Learning a limited vocabulary by rote may be useless. If we wish to increase cognitive ability by enabling students to read material with understanding within a certain time, however, a test that measures that skill is a good idea. The ideal situation is one in which a student's ability to do well on this exam means that he can also pick up any other similar body of material and understand it well.

I am aware that reading ability may be affected by many things. Reading may be a function of the personality. It may be a result of motivation; children may not read because they see no reason to do so. It may be a function of certain high-level cognitive processes that are imperfectly understood. And so on. Let us say, then, that reading is a very complex matter, a product of many circumstances, most of which are badly understood and some of which may not be known at all. So what? Who said that one must know the causes before propounding the cure? The history of medicine has taught us that many diseases may be cured before their etiology is perfectly known. For present purposes it is sufficient that students be enabled to read a certain level of material with a certain degree of comprehension, whether or not the teacher or the researcher fully understands the processes by which this is done. No doubt more basic research should be conducted in reading. Surely, few would suggest waiting 20 years before we begin our efforts to improve performance through accountability.

There may be quick ways of getting at motivation to read by developing measures based on the amount of reading done by students. All the discussion of developing motivation would be beside the point unless the motivated student read more (or perhaps even a greater variety) of literature than his fellows. I would not wait until such a measure was perfected, however, before beginning a simpler use of accountability.

There are important conceptual difficulties with a program of accountability. Presumably we are after something like the economic concept of "value added." We want to know what impact exposure to a particular teacher or school has had on a child's reading or mathematical ability, compared to what it would have been in other circumstances. This requires some base-line knowledge of where a child would be expected to be, given his previous rates of achievement and those of other students similarly situated. Since reading and cognitive ability are not simple matters, the requisite talents may be developed in more than one class. How much of a student's progress (or lack of it) is due to his reading teacher versus other teachers would be exceedingly difficult to determine. How much is due to school versus home environment is a tricky question. Parceling out a single cause from many is never simple. I believe that rough and ready answers can be found to these dilemmas if the problem of causation is approached in a practical spirit.

To hold someone accountable is to assess how well he is performing. A program of accountability requires standardized tests on the one hand and significant norms on the other. Yet it is not easy to decide what these norms should be. The first that suggests itself is a national standard for reading or mathematics by grade. If this standard, however, is much higher than present performance, it will appear unrealistic to teachers and students alike. They may despair at ever achieving it and therefore not make the required effort. Should an accountability group be performing above the national standard, they would have no way to measure their progress. Another way to handle the problem of setting the norm is to make it a subject for bargaining between local school boards, parent groups, teachers, and principals. This approach would have the advantage of allowing participation in setting norms and might have the effect of committing the participants more strongly to their achievement. Unfortunately, however, the negotiations may simply reveal who is more powerful or determined or aggressive. The result may be terribly low norms in some places and unfairly high ones in others. It would become impossible to determine either how the city as a whole was doing or how the various subgroups were faring. The level of conflict would surely rise without much hope of corresponding benefit.

A third alternative would be to divide all elementary pupils in the city into five or six groups based on the mean score by grade on the standardized tests. Students would be tested each September, and the focus would be on the rate of change during the year. Each school would then be rated on the basis of its ability to secure more rapid changes by grade in the mean scores of its students. Immediately we are faced with a major dilemma. One of the purposes of modern reform in education is to escape from the syndrome of helping those most who need it least. If the students who perform better initially are also the students who are capable of showing the greatest rate of change, teachers and principals will find it most efficient to concentrate attention on these students in order to improve total performance. We will be back again to the adage "To him that hath shall be given." One way of surmounting this difficulty is to require not only the mean but the median scores, so that schools are rewarded for securing improvement in the largest number of students as well as for the total rate of improvement. Another way of dealing with the problem is to use tests that have a "top" to them so that those who score the highest have difficulty in improving by a large percentage. Whatever the formula used, the principle is clear: The school gets rewarded more for improvements among those students who start out at the lower levels of performance than it does for the students who start out at the higher levels. The rational man will, therefore, exert his effort to bring forward those who need it most.

My preference is for a fourth alternative in which different norms would be set for different groups of students. It should be possible to compare groups of students with similar backgrounds. Groups can be defined largely in terms of previous opportunity. I would suggest working up a *short* list of the principal extra-school variables that appear, in terms of current knowledge, to be relevant to student performance, such as socio-economic level, rate of movement from one neighborhood and one school to another, and so on. It would then be possible to place each elementary school in one of five or six groups. Each group of schools could be rank-ordered according to student performance on standardized tests, with the results given three weeks after school starts and again sometime around the first week in June, so that progress during the school year could be measured. (The early test are necessary because many students lose a lot of learning over the summer.) The norms against which progress is measured would not be the same for the entire city, but would differ for each of the five or six accountability groups.

The five top schools within each subgroup could be taken together and their current achievement and average growth used as the normative standard. In this way participants in each school's activity would know that the norm set for them had in fact been achieved by students in situations comparable to their own. Norms would be reasonably objective and realistic. Selection of these norms, however, is critically dependent on factual information about the degree of homogeneity within elementary schools. If the differences in achievement between schools are greater than the differences within schools, this proposal is feasible; if the heterogeneity within schools is great, however, it will be difficult to make sense out of the performance of the school as a whole, and it will be necessary to deal with different classes of students throughout the entire system.

Determination of the level of accountability within the school system is also a difficult problem. Should it be a single teacher, a school, a district, or the entire school system? In a sense, all levels must be accountable and the efforts of all must be appraised. Determination of the center of accountability, however, cannot be avoided because if all are in some vague sense accountable it will be difficult to hold anyone responsible. Making a large geographical district or the entire system accountable will prove too imprecise. Nor will holding individual teachers directly accountable work. The problem of causality —how much does that teacher's effort contribute to the total result?— will prove insuperable. Teachers may also prove unable to cope with the pressures that come directly at them.

I recommend focusing accountability on the principal of the school because he is the one with the essential power in the system. My understanding is that the district superintendent, although nominally responsible for what the teacher does, usually gives him wide latitude. Local boards may change the situation, but it is too early to tell. The principal, therefore, is the one who is capable of limiting and usually does limit the teacher's discretion. The principal, moreover, could be assumed to have a longer-term commitment to the school system. If his work can be improved, or if he is replaced by others whose work is better, that is bound to have a profound impact throughout the system. If principals are to be held accountable, however, they must receive training in teaching. I do not believe that the concept of the principal as the master teacher is accurate today in view of the mechanisms of recruitment that obtain. For the moment it would be sufficient for principals to hire qualified people to assist them. Principals should also be given adequate administrative help or at least each one must have the same kind of help. In some school districts the amount of administrative help per pupil varies considerably from school to school. Either administrative help per pupil must be equalized or principals with a relative lack of administrative help must not be required to do as well. If accountability is to get support it must be as fair as we know how to make it.

However good a system of accountability is worked out, it will always have defects. Some teachers will find that their students are especially difficult to teach; others will find that their students make more rapid progress than they had thought. Some teachers may be especially gifted in dealing with children with special reading difficulties, while others do better with different kinds of students. If accountability is placed on the teacher it will be difficult to take account of their differing capabilities. By placing accountability on the principal, however, he will be able to take these special circumstances into account and not require the same level of performance from all his teachers regardless of the difficulty of their assignments. The requirement he must face is that the school as a whole show reasonable progress. While the principal is, in effect, charted with maximizing a kind of educational production, he may set different goals for his teachers in order to make the best showing for the school as a whole. In a different context a number of teachers could perform the same function by forming accountability groups with a school.

In order to envisage the problems encountered by making schools accountable through their principals, let us imagine that such a system were adopted. Everyone would presumably know which schools were performing better and worse than others. There would naturally be a tendency for parents to send their children to the schools shown to be performing better for children like their own. One way of handling this problem would be to prohibit movement from one school to another based on this criterion. Otherwise the normative basis of the school would change rapidly because those parents and students most interested in improving performance would go to the better schools. The result would be a reallocation of students, leaving certain schools worse off than they were before. A long-run solution, after accountability has been in force for a number of years, would be to treat the phenomenon as part of a market system and give the better school additional resources to accommodate new pupils. Here accountability would merge with some of the proposals for giving parents vouchers allowing them to send children where they hope to get better education. In the short run, however, it would be better to restrict movement and to place emphasis on improving the performance of schools that show the least progress in meeting the norms.

Realism compels us to recognize that there is more than one way to improve the performance of children: There are ways we would like, and there are ways we would hate. One of the easiest ways to improve school performance, for example, is to remove those children who are most troublesome and whose scores on achievement tests are likely to be the lowest. It would be sad to see accountability used to justify defining children as behavioral problems or as victims of mental disturbance just so they would be eliminated from the school population. Schools should be allowed only a very small proportion of transfers on these grounds; otherwise they will be in the same position as a football team that finally achieves a winning schedule by choosing only the weakest opponents. A trigger mechanism could be used so that any transfers on these grounds above a certain minimum would result in an investigation.

The problem of sanctions for failure to perform is an integral part of a system of accountability. If those who do badly are allowed to continue, the system will not work. If those who do well are not rewarded, there will be no incentive for them to continue. My preference is to accentuate the positive. Teachers and principals who show the greatest progress should receive recognition, promotion, and freedom. By "freedom" I mean that those who show excellent progress should be given the right to innovate in teaching methods and curriculum. Rather than attempt to control their behavior through prescription of detailed curricula, we should let them devise their own with broad limits. As a contribution to this effort, the superintendent of schools should make available a diverse number of curricula for various grades and of methods for teaching various subjects among which teachers might choose but to which they would not be limited if they performed well. One can choose to direct teachers by inputs—standard curricula and teaching methods—or by outputs—norms of achievement—but not by both. If the output norms are met, the inputs should be left to the teachers.

Before sanctions are applied, principals and teachers should be given supervisory help. Their administrative superiors should work with them to improve performance. Additional personnel and financial resources should be provided. The imposition of negative sanctions should be downgraded but cannot be entirely avoided. For the most part, teachers will simply have less freedom. Should a teacher or principal reveal consistently poor performance, it should be possible to transfer him, or ultimately, remove him from the system. Agreement should be sought with the teachers' union on procedures to be followed in this eventuality so that abuse will be minimized. If the union will not agree, then accountability is not possible.

In order to reduce anxieties and take cognizance of the difficulties of the enterprise, the procedure for accountability should be reviewed every two years. The groups that serve as the normative schools should be revised according to their performance.

No plan for accountability can succeed unless all the major participants in the educational process—parents, teachers, students, principals, superintendents, and board members—see something in it for themselves. It is worthwhile, therefore, to explore the advantages and disadvantages of this plan as the various participants might see it.

The hard part for teachers would be the fact of being judged on a rather narrow level of performance according to strict standards that may not be entirely valid. If they consistently fail to move their students toward the norm, teachers would be subject to sanctions. Under current conditions, however, teachers suffer psychological punishment due to a feeling of failure. Their ability to show progress, indeed even to know the direction toward which they and their students should be moving, may provide tremendous relief. Standards of accountability may also give teachers a mechanism for guarding against arbitrary action by principals. If a teacher can show that his students have made excellent progress toward the norm, or have even achieved it, he has prima facie evidence of competence. He should thus be entitled to a reward in the form of permission to work under less supervision with greater leeway to introduce his own ideas.

The initial reaction of principals to the idea of accountability may well be negative. It will be hard for them to see themselves as responsible for behavior of students and teachers which they find it difficult to control. As the most visible manifestation of the school authorities, principals are easy to blame and to pillory in public. Fear and defensiveness by principals would be understandable. Yet first thoughts are bound to give way to deeper considerations. Principals are already being held responsible according to vague standards and under rules that guarantee dissatisfaction. National norms are held up as appropriate by some and are condemned by others. Principals may come to believe they will be better off if they have a hand in shaping reasonable norms. If they are held to account by their administrative superiors and by parents they will also gain additional leverage in regard to recalcitrant teachers. If performance is poor, a principal can move to change teacher behavior with more than the ordinary amount of justification. He can also show his administrative superiors that he is doing a good job in a more convincing way than before. Accountability has its defects, but the norms it enforces on the principal are superior to "keeping out of trouble" or "pleasing the boss" or others one can think of.

Parents may be expected to give initial endorsement to a program of accountability. They should feel that at last they have a mechanism for appraising the performance of their children and the school in which they are taught. (Accountability not only means that the school is responsible to the parents, however, but that the parents are responsible for the school. They need to help teachers whose children fail to make adequate progress.) It is often difficult for parents to gauge the legitimacy of complaints made by their children or school critics; knowledge of whether their children are making progress with regard to the norms of accountability should help them decide where reality lies. When parents are asked to mobilize themselves concerning school policy, they may decide whether to become involved by consulting public information on school achievement.

Accountability, defined in terms of achievement in reading and math, will not satisfy those parental and neighborhood groups that are looking to schools to inculcate their cultural and/or political values. To them, accountability may be a barrier to control of schools, because it (in their view) falsely suggests to parents that schools are doing well. There is no escaping the fact that accountability is not a neutral device—it encapsulates a view of the educational function in which basic cognitive and mathematical skills are primary. Cultural, artistic, or political values would still receive expression (it could hardly be otherwise), but they would not be dominant.

The job of the superintendent of schools has become increasingly frustrating. He is placed at the very center of every controversy. At times he appears utterly surrounded by swirling clouds of controversy. Yet when all is said and done, he is too far from teaching and learning to know whether his efforts are worthwhile. Often he must feel that all he does is stay alive while the purposes for which he originally became an educator become increasingly remote. For such a man a program of accountability must have great meaning. It is his opportunity to affect education directly. It is his opportunity to participate in an innovation that could make his tenure in office worthwhile. The drawback is that progress, if it can be achieved at all, may be painfully slow. No one can be certain that the statement of educational goals will lead to their achievement. The factors that guide improvement in reading and mathematics for large populations may not be known to anyone. The special problems faced by deprived children may not respond to available techniques. While various schools and teachers may meet with notable success, average rates of growth may not change at all, or may even decline for reasons no one knows. Yet the superintendent may be regarded as a failure because a particular norm of accountability has been specified, when he might have escaped under the nebulous criteria which would otherwise exist. Still, he is unlikely to escape unscathed, and norms of accountability are as good a measure of progress as he is likely to get.

The board of education can find accountability of great use in defining problem areas and questioning the superintendent about them. The board can choose to hold the superintendent responsible for systematic performance or it can investigate problems according to the geographic area, grade, or level at which they occur. The board's greatest role, if it is so willing, will be to monitor the system of accountability and suggest revisions of it to the interested parties. It should take the lead in suggesting changes in the norms by which measurement is accomplished, the incentives and sanctions employed, and the tests used.

Very young children are unlikely to question these arrangements. As they get older, students may well be the people most difficult to satisfy on the question of accountability. They may feel that *no* system of norms gives them sufficient freedom. They may dislike the idea that a single set of norms appears to define them when they know that each individual is much more than that. They may fear that they will be stigmatized if greater publicity is given to test results. They may not even want their parents to know how well or how badly they are doing. Part of the difficulty may be overcome by holding individual and class scores confidential except to parents. Another part will be dealt with by giving students special liberties in taking courses if they perform at an acceptable level. Ultimately, however, they must be persuaded that accountability is a useful mechanism for improving the performance of school children in general and that it is therefore of special benefit to those whose performance is now at a low level. Some students, like some teachers and principals, will have to accept sacrifices for the common good. It will not be easy.

Accountability, Commitment, and the Community School

ROBERT L. WHITT

The concept of the community school is tied very closely to the concept of accountability. A community school cannot function without being directly responsive to the needs of the people it serves. By decentralizing the schools (a process Whitt perceives as more a matter of the mind than of fact) and by providing for community control, the concepts of both accountability and the community school can become practical considerations.

In today's society we hear a great deal about a new sense of commitment and a call for clear accountability. Although the call is clear, our ability to relate the two to education as it is now organized in difficult.

Harold Taylor, in a position paper on educational commitment starts his paper with the following lines:

Tomorrow has broken out to-day:
Riot in Algeria, in Cyprus, in Alabama;
Aged in wrong, the empires are declining
And China gathers, soundlessly, like evidence.
What shall I say to the young on such a morning?[1]

These lines are quite applicable to a sense of commitment and accountability because we must continually answer the young in their morning of growth.

A sense of commitment and accountability is essential if we are to turn this nation around. The public is calling for this in its request for a new sense of teacher and administrator accountability.

In the October "Kappan," the second annual Gallup Poll concerning the public's attitude toward schools indicates that the public is demanding that the schools take a new look at themselves in relation to accountability and commitment. The first question asked:

Would you like to see the students in the local schools be given national tests so that their educational achievement could be compared with students in other communities?[2]

Robert L. Whitt, "Accountability, Commitment, and the Community School," *Community Education Journal*, 1: 21–24, January 1971. Reprinted by permission.

In answering this question, 75% of the adult public approves of this factor of accountability.

A second question raises this question in a more direct manner:

> Would you favor or oppose a system that would hold teachers and administrators more accountable for the progress of students?[3]

Again, a substantial majority of the public feels that this is necessary. Similar majority opinions were held in regard to paying teachers on a basis of quality work rather than on a single salary schedule. Tenure was in question by a majority of the public.

It is fairly evident that the public is trying to say something to those in education.

In the public secondary school the students are asking, perhaps demanding is a better word, for a larger sense of commitment to their personal development in terms of increased responsibility. Literally, "Tomorrow has broken out to-day" for our young. Their education has come largely from outside the school through media, music, festivals, moratoriums, sit-ins, and other complex psycho-social phenomena.

For too long now pupils in our secondary schools (elementary and college also) have been placed in a demeaning role, in many instances requiring "permission to go to the pot." (Pot here does not refer to a type of material used in smoking.)

I recently had the experience of meeting in a high school where the students were holding open hearings in order to convince the general public and school officials of the need for an open campus. Early in the meeting it was evident that though the quality of the presentation by the students was high, the commitment to this idea by the educators and other adult power figures in the local area was not linked to the educational needs of the students. The general consensus by those in power was that the students did not need this for educational development since the school was the place to learn. A great deal of hostility was engendered. Fear was expressed in the concern for student behavior. An open campus was considered tantamount to chaos and anarchy. In essence, the adult view was that the controlled student was a good student, and that students would not nor could not accept responsibility, this based largely on the fact that they had never had any previous experience in this realm. When the students asked when they would ever have the chance to become responsible through a meaningful learning situation, there were no answers.

The pay-off for this type of behavior comes when the student enters a university. Joseph Tussman, writing in "The Center Magazine" illustrates this well when he writes:

The educational imagination of a product of an American high school is not very significant. What he wants is to avoid some obvious difficulty like reading something he doesn't like to read, or having a sadistic exam or having to sit still for three hours a week listening to some bore talk about something the student feels he ought not to be required to listen to in the first place. It's stupid to expect genuine educational insights to come from kids who are the products of our high schools.[4]

Within the profession itself there is a new sense of commitment to new priorities in education with a definite demand for more money. They are saying that we must make some hard decisions about the quality of life. In a society that has nearly a trillion dollar gross national product, it is immoral to place education at the bottom while placing military demands at the top. It is irrational and unreasonable for a people's democracy to continue to spend itself beyond its limits in the art of aggression and killing. Such a sense of priorities cannot go unheeded. This is exploitation of the rankest kind. At the same time that society is asking the profession to become accountable for its teaching and use of economic resources, the members of the educational establishment are asking the individual members within that society to become accountable in terms of its values and sense of priorities. This clash does not augur well for the schools.

Where does the Community School fit into all of this? How does accountability and commitment relate to this concept of education:

We need a general program aimed at the decentralization of schools, workable forms of community control, and diversity of method. This means smaller schools, many kinds of schools, education outside the schools, vast changes in curriculum, work-study programs, independent study, systems of apprenticeship.[5]

What Peter Marin is asking for as a modern answer to a latter day problem is nothing but the Flint Program of Community School Education. Let's analyze what is needed for a new sense of commitment and accountability.

DECENTRALIZATION

The Community School is decentralized. The citizens in the community use this school as their own and are encouraged to do so. Decentralization is more a matter of mind than a matter of fact. If I perceive the local school as serving me, then it is decentralized. If it is a closed system, rarely responsibe to my needs and concerns, then it is a monolithic, centralized system.

COMMUNITY CONTROL

The Community School recognizes the need for and provides for community control, both in terms of community wide and local attendance center participation. The Community School Director and the principal know the local community members. Through them there is a relationship established with the school that recognizes the inherent right of local citizens to have a say in the education of their children and in their own education as well.

EDUCATION OUTSIDE THE SCHOOL

The Community School has long recognized this as a viable alternative to the traditional school program. Afternoon and evening classes for all ages are as important a part of the community school program as the regular day programs. Too, courses are not limited to the traditional academic courses, although these play an important role. Curriculum offerings in a multitude of areas and individual interests are planned, sponsored and encouraged. The educational programs move across the whole spectrum of the community in terms of location and facilities. Education is outside the school in terms of tradition and structure.

COMMITMENT

One need only to work within a Community School for a short time to understand what this word really means. The concern for the individual, the sense of priority that is brought to the educational process, the involvement of people in a meaningful way, the concern for the community as a whole rather than within narrow limits indicates the degree to which Community Education defines commitment. Community Education brings to the people it serves a "sense of community," a feeling that establishes new criteria for the welfare of mankind and a sense of freedom indicative of the concept of what it means to be Man.

ACCOUNTABILITY

Accountability is not a new concept. Those in the Community Schools have recognized this for a long time. The Community School is more than an educational process organized around a well-designed building. It is spirit with a purposeful thrust toward responsibility for designing continuous community involvement. This continuous involvement insures a high level of accountability. It is impossible to develop a full blown Community School program without being held accountable by the people. They demand it. What is often a threat to other educators is an every day reality to the administrators with a district that provides real community education. The broad base from which this type of an educational program operates is one which essentially eliminates indifference and negative criticism. To believe that the public does not have a stake in education belies a basic premise of Community Education, that of acknowledging the fact that the schools are accountable to the total public which they serve.

Accountability, Commitment and the Community School are all inter-related. They are part and parcel of each other. It is the opinion of this writer that public education will not have either accountability or commitment until the Community School Program becomes the practical as well as the philosophical. In working with school districts in three states over the last twenty years, I have found that the Community School concept is generally accepted at a philosophical level. "It is a great idea, but it can't work," is the most frequent comment. The question before us in our society is how can we have accountability and commitment on the part of educators and within the educational system without a vehicle that allows for full participation, full cooperation, intentional flexibility and an underlying philosophy that says there are no barriers to learning. Community education designed around the Community School provides that necessary vehicle.

We face today a need for a realignment of our national priorities. Within each community the same need exists. The citizens within the confines of individual neighborhoods cannot overcome societal problems without a base from which to operate. Out of the local neighborhood Community School can come a new way of life that allows people to deal with the vast changes necessary to bring accountability and commitment back into our national life and rearrange our system of priorities.

Commitment and accountability will enable all of us to say something to "the young on such a morning." The people will have a large voice in determining the quality of their educational program and through this commitment will hold themselves accountable. This is the essence of democracy.

FOOTNOTES

1. Harold Taylor, "The Meaning of Commitment," *Fiscal Planning for Schools in Transition,* Proceedings of the Twelfth National Conference on School Finance, Committee on Educational Finance, N.E.A. (March, 1969), p. 9.

2. George Gallup, "Second Annual Survey of the Public's Attitude Toward the Public Schools," *Phi Delta Kappan,* Vol. LII, Number 2 (October, 1970), pp. 99–112.

3. *Ibid.,* pp. 101–102.

4. Joseph Tussman, "Selling Out to the Students," *The Center Magazine,* Vol. II, No. 1 (January, 1969), p. 35.

5. Peter Marin, "The Schools," *The Center Magazine,* Vol. II, No. 1 (January, 1969), p. 52.

Accountability in the Two-Year College

JOHN E. ROUECHÉ, GEORGE A. BAKER III, AND RICHARD L. BROWNELL

The concept of accountability applies to all levels of education, including the two-year community college. The authors feel that if the community college is to meet the community's needs and fulfill the promise of an open door, accountability must permeate all levels of the institutional spectrum. To accomplish this, the community college must be responsive to external demands of the community and the internal needs of its students.

Accountability is becoming an increasingly popular and controversial concept among educators. Accountability is both fundamental and complex; it can be applied to the activities of an individual, a department, a division, or an institution. To some people accountability suggests finance and business operations; others think of instruction and student learning. In practice accountability can apply to these and many other activities. Judging from the growing number of magazine and newspaper articles, it is indeed an idea whose time has come.

A favorite question is, "Why has accountability suddenly become popular in certain educational circles?" After all, the concept has been around for many years. Perhaps the best explanation for the historic rejection of the concept is what might be called educational determinism and the consequent acceptance of student failure. Simply stated, educational determinism is the belief that people have a predetermined capacity for learning, a capacity best defined by intelligence quotient. This being the case, it is reasonable and acceptable that an increasing number of students will fail as they climb the educational ladder. Or, to put it in the language of Darwinism, in the educational jungle only the fittest survive. Until recently this belief in a limited and predetermined capacity to learn precluded the idea of accountability for learning. How could anyone, with the possible exception of the learner who might be lazy and therefore fail to utilize all of his capacity, be held accountable for something determined by divine will or the chance of heredity? It would certainly be unreasonable to hold educators accountable for something over which they had no control.

John E. Roueché, George A. Baker III, and Richard L. Brownell, "Accountability in the Two-Year College," *Instruction and Curriculum,* a publication of the National Laboratory for Higher Education. Reprinted by permission.

Currently this belief in educational determinism is being discarded by a growing number of people. Studies have revealed self-fulfilling tendencies in the measurement of student achievement when educators are informed in advance of student "intelligence quotients" or "learning abilities." Furthermore in many colleges students have been graded in accordance with normal curve distributions, another way of demonstrating that only a few students can really excel at learning. But now, given the evidence of many studies and the re-examination of basic beliefs about learning, many notable educational researchers and writers are arguing that almost all students can learn if a variety of instructional approaches are available and if sufficient time is allowed each student. Now the question becomes, "Why do so many students fail?"

The re-orientation in beliefs about learning and what can reasonably be expected of students, schools, and education has led to a growing interest in accountability. No longer is widespread student failure and attrition acceptable. As Charles E. Silberman so aptly states in his recent book, *Crisis in the Classroom*, "It is only when men sense the possiblity of improvement, in fact, that they become dissatisfied with their situation and rebel against it."

The Concept of Accountability

The word accountability is laden with a host of meanings. It may seem threatening and unreasonable to educators who are reluctant to accept responsibility for academically inept and poorly motivated students; it might be viewed as a fashionable slogan by those with a penchant for launching naive attacks upon academe's disordered strongholds; it has profound implications for community colleges. In the following paragraphs four essential characteristics of accountability will be discussed.

(1) *Accountability Accents Results:* Accountability aims squarely at what comes out of an education system rather than at what goes into it. If educational institutions exist primarily to cause learning, then educators should scrutinize the results of their efforts. Teaching causes learning. If no learning occurs, no teaching has taken place!

Why speak glowingly of academic buildings and salaries when the failures of the education system contribute to social discord and violence? Educators must remove their heads from the sands of irrelevance or risk becoming irrelevant themselves.

Leon Lessinger, former Associate Commissioner of Education, has stated succinctly the urgent need for accenting results:

. . . the American educational commitment has been that every child should have an adequate education. This commitment has been stated in terms of resources such as teachers, books, space, and equipment. When a child has failed to learn, school personnel have assigned him a label—"slow" or "unmotivated," or "retarded." Our schools must assume a revised commitment—that every child shall learn. Such a commitment includes the willingness to change a system which does not work, and find one which does; to seek causes of failure in the system and its personnel instead of focusing solely on students; in short, to hold the school accountable for results in terms of student learning rather than solely in the use of resources.[1]

(2) *Accountability Requires Measurement:* Accountability suggests that we stop counting the number of volumes in the library, quit measuring square footage per full-time student, and start looking at how well students are being taught. We must use relevant criteria to evaluate teaching. Learning, the only valid evidence of teaching, can be further defined as a change in behavior. If specific behavioral objectives are established, educators can be held accountable for students who are able to demonstrate learning by acting in ways that were impossible before teaching took place.

In January 1970 Lessinger quantified accountability in easily understood terms:

If an air conditioning contractor promises that his installation will reduce interior temperatures 20 degrees below outside temperatures, it takes only an accurate thermometer to determine if the promise has been met. Similarly, if an educational manager promises that all children attending his school will be able to read 200 words per minute with 90 per cent comprehension on their twelfth birthday, as measured by a specific test, simply giving the test to all children on their twelfth birthday will readily reveal if the promise has been fulfilled.[2]

Although learning cannot always be measured as easily and as accurately as in Lessinger's example, modern educational techniques enable us to achieve acceptable evidence of learning. The concept of accountability is based on specifically defined objectives, measurement techniques that deterimne exactly what the teacher intends to accomplish, and instructional methods that guarantee most students will obtain the objectives.

(3) *Accountability Assumes and Shifts Responsibility:* Accountability assumes responsibility for the success or failure of individual schools and pupils.[3] Students have traditionally been held responsible through tests and recitations for whatever they may or may not have learned. Accountability shifts the emphasis of that responsibility away from the student.

Another associate commissioner, Don Davies, has said:

> This concept of accountability . . . links student performance with teacher performance. . . . It means . . . that schools and colleges will be judged by how they perform not by what they promise. It means . . . shifting primary learning responsibility from the student to the school. It also means that a lot of people are going to be shaken up.[4]

(4) *Accountability Permeates the College Community:* Although some people (as Mr. Davies predicts) may be shaken up, teachers should not become scapegoats. Teachers cannot be accountable unless the concept of accountability permeates the entire spectrum of institutional responsibility.

In a broad sense accountability means that boards of trustees, presidents, administrators, and teachers will be held responsible for the performance of their students.[5]

Accountability implies that two-year colleges must be accountable externally to the community and that colleges must be accountable internally to the students who pass through their open doors. This state is achieved when students from the community enter the college, find a program that is compatible with their goals, persist in college until the goal is reached, and then become productive members of the community.

In short, the entire college body including the board, the president, the administration, the students, and the instructors will become accountable to the community.

CONCLUSION

Accountability is far more than a glib term or "in" word. It is an operational concept "that comes to grips with the notion that schools and colleges should shoulder responsibility for . . . their pupils."[6] Accountability is a privilege—not a burden. It calls forth the best within us. It challenges us to examine our purposes, to find better ways to make education responsible to the society that pays the bills. It holds equal promise for all of education's clients, "those who come to school well prepared to share its benefits, and those who have nothing in their backgrounds that would equip them for a successful learning experience."[7]

Accountability is inevitable because it is needed so desperately.

The Need for Accountability

An October 1970 issue of *Time* contained an education feature entitled "Open Admissions: American Dream or Disaster?" The article expressed the notion that an "open access" policy could either "invigorate colleges" or lead to "academic disaster," and pointed out that education officials meeting at the American Council on Education in St. Louis displayed opposing attitudes towards a policy of open admissions. "To some it seemed a triumph of democracy; to others an omen that colleges may soon be overwhelmed with the wrong kind of students."[8]

Are ignorant, culturally deprived, and poverty-stricken youth the "wrong" kind of students? Should they be branded undesirables because they are academically inept and need education desperately? The American academic system is already on the brink of disaster because of the "wrong" kind of educators. Why fear the "wrong" kind of students? Overwhelming educational inefficiency can be traced to archaic attitudes and self-serving institutional callosity. Arthur Cohen in *Dateline '79* pictures traditional faculty members making "desperate attempts to plant sprigs of ivy at the gates so that the barbarians will be dissuaded from entering."[9]

The time for "planting ivy" has passed; the gates are open. Educators must leave their comfortable retreats and become accountable by joining the ranks of other professions in a common effort to solve national problems. A tangible expression of educational accountability in the form of honest "open door" policies supported by a willingness to assume responsibility for student learning may be the only way to prevent "academic disaster."

HISTORICAL FOUNDATIONS OF THE COMMUNITY COLLEGE

The community college in the United States has been described as the only educational institution that can truly be considered an American social invention.[10] Sometimes called "democracy's college," it adopted a philosophy of equal educational opportunity for all and espoused an ideal of open admissions.

The community college is not an offshoot of classical higher education in America. Its ancestry can be traced to 19th century educational innovations developed to fill needs that traditional institutions of higher learning could not meet. The classical colleges, with their limited curriculums, existed to transmit culture and class values to a privileged elite. Those institutions were neither willing nor able to respond to 19th century industrial and social demands for broader curriculums or choice of subject matter including business, technical, and agricultural courses. The nation's educational framework had to be supplemented with additional colleges and different types of institutions. Land grant colleges, created by the Morrill Land Grant Act of 1862, gave substance to the concept that each individual, regardless of his economic or social status, should have the opportunity to progress educationally as far as his interests and abilities might permit.[11]

The belief in extending educational opportunities to all people led to a philosophy of the "open door" that has become the hallmark of the community college movement. Its democratic style, positive philosophy, and social promise appealed to the American people and won great popularity and support. The unprecedented educational benefits accompanying the G.I. Bill of Rights after World War II further enhanced and expanded the community college movement.[12]

PHILOSOPHICAL FOUNDATIONS OF THE COMMUNITY COLLEGE

In addition to the idea that universal higher education is the right of any person who can profit from it, the community college movement was also founded on the conviction that colleges exist to serve the society that supports them.

A democratic society cannot sustain itself without a well educated citizenry capable of influencing its destiny in a responsible manner. The increasing polarization and violence of American society emphasize the need for more education for all citizens. Education's role in enhancing the civic competence of the American people is crucial to the nation's economic, social, and cultural welfare. Education helps to equalize opportunity by stressing the concept of individual worth and serving as a vehicle for personal and social advancement.

The pending crisis in American society represents a particular challenge to the community college because it is more closely identified with social needs than is any other segment of higher education.

NATIONAL NEED FOR COMMUNITY COLLEGES

The community college movement is much more than a democratically inspired attempt to meet educational demands that have been ignored by other institutions of higher learning. In the United States today post-secondary education is a vital national need—not a luxury. Community colleges are in a unique position to answer that need.

The role of unskilled workers becomes less important as technological society grows more complex. There are few jobs available for high school graduates who possess no other training.[13] Conversely, there is an insistent national demand for manpower trained in sophisticated skills. The obsolete concept of scarcity of educational opportunity is not applicable to highly developed nations. At one point in its history, this country needed only a few highly educated persons and thus provided economic support for only a small number of students to complete advanced education. The academic system was designed to select the talented few and to reject the majority. Today the nation cannot afford to waste human resources. Educational institutions must impart essential skills to all students.[14]

In an age of burgeoning enrollments and increasingly selective admissions at senior colleges and universities, the community college's familiar role of meeting the educational needs of society becomes more and more important. While the university continues to cater to relatively homogeneous groups from a dominant stratum of society, the community college embraces a heterogeneous group that represents a cross section of the total population.[15] Two-year college students are more likely to come from the lower two-thirds of the socioeconomic spectrum. The "open door" is a matter of national concern, for the community college performs a vital service in removing barriers to education.

Geographic location of academic institutions is a crucial factor in education. (Most community college student bodies are localized within fifteen miles of the campus.) Colleges constructed within commuting distance of potential students extend educational accessibility to the total population and facilitate attainment of our national goal of universal higher education.[16] And the fact that community college fees are either modest or nonexistent removes financial barriers and provides an economical avenue to higher education. However, even if all gographical and financial barriers could be eliminated, racial minorities, women, and children from low socioeconomic classes would still be sparsely represented.[17] These groups contain human talents that cannot be wasted even though potential students might be poorly motivated. The concept of accountability demands active efforts to seek, recruit, enroll, and retain every possible student in the community; the community college must "make readily available, programs of education . . . that match a wide spectrum of community needs and relate economically to the total pattern of educational opportunity in the area."[18]

THE CHALLENGE OF THE OPEN DOOR

Today more than two million students are enrolled in community colleges. Over 1000 two-year colleges already exist in this country and more are being added at the rate of one per week[19] The community college movement has solid historical and philosophical foundations. It occupies a unique position and seems to promise a solution for many of the nation's pressing social and educational needs. The community college is now faced with the critical challenge of becoming accountable for its unfulfilled potential by translating ideals into reality.

The open-door policy of the community-junior college implies acceptance of the concept of universal higher education. The basic criteria for admission is graduation from high school; however, all individuals 18 years of age and older, who appear capable of profiting from instruction, are usually eligible for admission. Community colleges have become the primary vehicle for social and economic advancement for the lower two-thirds of the population. The typical student body is an extremely heterogeneous and diverse group that is often drawn from backgrounds characterized by low economic and social status, low educational achievement, marginal employment, and limited participation in community organizations. Students from these environments are disadvantaged to the degree that their culture has failed to provide them with experiences typical of the youth that traditional colleges are accustomed to teaching. The community college must recognize, however, that a considerable number of disadvantaged, low-aptitude students in its student body creates diverse problems that necessitate drastic modifications in traditional instructional techniques, as well as requires an expanded curriculum.

Unfortunately, few community colleges faced with these problems have lived up to their bright promise. The "open door" is too often a glib admissions statement rather than a true concept of accountable reality.

UNFULFILLED PROMISES

Although the community college movement should be credited with pursuing the ideal of universal higher education, accountability demands that the success of that venture be judged by results. Student success (both persistence and achievement in college) is the only accurate measure of the open door.

Attrition rates at community colleges generally are alarming. The typical urban community college reports annual student dropout rates of more than 50 percent.[20] As many as 75 percent of low-achieving students withdraw during their first year.[21] In one typical California public junior college, 80 percent of the entering students enrolled in remedial English, but only 20 percent matriculated into regular college English classes.[22] Remedial courses are generally poorly designed, poorly taught, and seldom evaluated carefully.

The problem of unacceptable attrition has led critics to refer cynically to the open door as a "revolving door." The obvious lack of accountability behind these shocking attrition rates seems particularly reprehensible when one realizes that they reflect the shattered hopes of disadvantaged youth who were led to believe that the open door offered them a chance. "There is a marked difference between allowing a student to learn and taking responsibility for the direction and extent of that learning."[23]

The glaring inadequacies of many community college programs should lead educators to seek new approaches geared to individual learning and learning deficiencies. If community college instructors can be taught to become effective teachers, and are willing to be held accountable for student learning, the promise of the open door can be fulfilled. Unfortunately, there is a decided difference between the attitudes of many community college instructors and the attitudes that must be developed if they are ever to become effective teachers of community college students.[24] A national survey of community colleges revealed the discouraging evidence that, although 91 percent of the institutions espoused the concept of the open door, only 55 percent provided programs appropriate for non-traditional students.[25]

INAPPROPRIATE ATTITUDES

Emund J. Gleazer, Jr., writing in the winter 1970 issue of the *Educational Record,* stated:

> I am increasingly impatient with people who ask whether a student is "college material." We are not building a college with the student. The question we ought to ask is whether the college is . . . student material. It is the student we are building, and it is the function of the college to facilitate that process. We have him as he is, rather than as we wish he were . . . we are still calling for much more change in the student than we are in the faculty. . . . Can we come up with . . . the professional attitudes . . . [necessary to] put us into the business of tapping pools of human talent not yet touched?[26]

This clear statement of accountability strikes at the heart of the community college problem. The promise of the "open door" will never be realized until teachers change their attitudes and accept the professional responsibility of becoming accountable for students. When educators point a finger at the "wrong" kind of student, their own three fingers point back at the "wrong" kind of educators!

Accountability must permeate every level of the institution, but the individual instructor is by far the most important element in the success of community college programs.[27] Unfortunately, the typical faculty member is seldom in complete accord with the generally acknowledged purposes or with the principles of admission applying in most community colleges.[28] Although some teachers appear genuinely concerned about the high rate of student attrition, many simply attribute the dropout rate to the notion that the students were not "college material."[29] How can a unique multi-purpose institution catering to a highly non-traditional student body be successful if the faculty—who

are the key element in implementing the purposes of the institution—
do not agree with those purposes?

The typical community college faculty member is a subject matter
specialist. The instructor is usually male, a full-time instructor, and a
former elementary or secondary school teacher.[30] His graduate education has developed his interests and abilities along a narrow spectrum.
This faculty member is "academically inclined," finding his greatest
satisfaction in transmitting the knowledge of his chosen discipline to
able students who can comprehend and appreciate his discipline. This
accounts in large part for the instructor's preference for teaching
advanced and specialized courses: they afford him the opportunity to
teach that which he knows best.

Few community college instructors have had any preparation for
teaching in that unique institution.[31] Most have served internships in
schools other than junior colleges; they do not understand the community college setting and tend to think of it in terms of their own
senior college or university experience. Thus, these instructors cannot
fulfill the responsibilities imposed by the open door if they insist upon
"aping the practices of . . . universities which were designed in other
times to provide services to different populations."[32]

Four-year institutions undoubtedly serve a necessary and valuable
educational function. They are selectivly geared to upper socioeconomic levels and the upper third of the student population. They are
research oriented and pursue the task of advancing basic knowledge
rather than providing training for immediate job application. While
the defined task of the university faculty member includes teaching,
this is essentially subordinate to his other functions.[33] Traditional
four-year institutions are neither willing nor equipped to offer educational opportunity to all—especially when increasing numbers of those
individuals seeking higher education lack the academic prerequisites
for successful performance.

The community college is not a basic research institution nor a
home for a "community" of scholars. The main function of the community college instructor is to teach; he must be committed to this role
and specialize in instructional processes.[34] He must be willing to be
held accountable for student learning.

Like their university counterparts, community college instructors
are concerned about "status" and being properly identified with
higher education. They "view themselves as members of a profession
in which they are independent practitioners who specialize in interaction with students in groups."[35] They may believe that the "person
of the instructor" has some intrinsic "worth in itself"[36] and many
cherish the center stage role of dispensing knowledge to the less
learned. They fail to understand that being identified with higher
education does not automatically confer respect, and that "an in-

structors is worth only as much as he contributes to the purposes of the institution."[37]

If instructors feel that teaching specialized and advanced courses affords them prestige, while the onerous chore of teaching remedial or developmental courses is below their dignity, they certainly do not belong in community colleges.

Accountability demands that the best qualified instructors available be assigned to well organized courses of remedial instruction. Those who believe in the philosophy of the community college should seek personal and professional prestige by carrying out the promise of the open door. Yet it is the inexperienced instructor, without preparation or understanding of the basic objectives of the course, who is most often found in remedial classrooms.[38]

Many community college instructors persist in the practice of norm-referenced testing and curve-based grade-marking practices, even though these archaic mechanisms were designed to screen and sort students in the days when only a talented elite merited higher education. These traditional methods assume from the start that all will not succeed.[39] Such practices have no place in any community college that is willing to open its doors and be accountable for the learning of all students.

Research has shown that specifying learning objectives in precise terms and using well organized, self-paced instructional sequences to reach those objectives can guarantee learning for up to 90 percent of all students.[40] Yet many community college instructors resist the very methods that could help them become accountable for student learning. Some are reluctant to give up their "star" role and fear a loss of status in becoming a "manager of learning" rather than a "dispenser of wisdom."[41] Others seem unwilling to do the considerable work necessary to systematically organize self-paced instruction. They prefer to hide behind "a feeling of elitism manifest in such statements as 'Hold me accountable for their learning? They don't belong in college anyway! In my day we had to work for what we got!' "[42]

Changed attitudes are the key to fulfilling the promise of the open door.

CONCLUSION

If the community college is to meet the nation's desperate educational needs and fulfill the promise of the open door, a genuine acceptance of accountability must permeate all levels of the institutional spectrum. This will require changes in the attitudes of governance and administrative officials and even more drastic changes in the attitudes of instructors. "Administrators can supervise . . . and make assistance available, but instructors must implement the process. If teachers refuse to spell out ends or to accept accountability for their being achieved, the enterprise will not succeed."[43]

Community colleges can no longer exist selfishly as ends in themselves, stifled by obsolete traditions and ignoring their democratic heritage. Their calling is too dynamic and too important to be rejected in favor of posing pathetically as poor cousins of the university.

Faculty members and administrators must change their attitudes and work together to gear curriculum to student achievement, to define objectives, and to accept accountability for their efforts. By "guaranteeing some form of minimum educational achievement" they can turn their institutions into places where learning takes place. By working towards equality of educational results they can transform their communities and fulfill the unique promise of the open-door community college philosophy.

NOTES

1. Lessinger, Leon, "Accountability in Education." (National Committee in Support of the Public Schools, February 1970) , p. 1.

2. ———, "Accountability in Public Education." *Today's Education*, May 1970, p. 52.

3. Meade, Edward J., Jr., "Accountability and Governance in Public Education." (Address to the Annual Convention of the National Association of Secondary School Principals, Atlantic City, New Jersey, February 12, 1968) , p. 3.

4. Davies, Don, "The 'Relevance' of Accountability." *The School Administrator* 1: April 1970: 11.

5. Schwartz, Ron, "Accountability." (Special Editorial Report) *Nation's Schools* 85: June 1970: 31.

6. Davies, p. 11.

7. *Ibid.*

8. *Time* 96: October 19, 1970: 63–66.

9. Cohen, Arthur M., *Dateline '79 Heretical Concepts for the Community College.* (Beverly Hills: Glencoe Press, 1969) , p. xvii.

10. Gleazer, Edmund J., Jr., ed., *American Junior Colleges*, 6th ed. (Washington, D.C.: American Council on Education, 1963) , p. 3.

11. Roueche, John E., *Salvage, Redirection, or Custody?* (Washington, D. C., American Association of Junior Colleges, 1968) .

12. Gleazer, Edmund J., Jr., "The Community College: Issues of the 1970's." *Educational Record*, Winter 1970, p. 47.

13. Cohen, p. 54.

14. Bloom, Benjamin S., "Learning for Mastery." *UCLA Evaluation Comment* 1: May 1968: 2.

15. Lombardi, John. "The Challenge for the Future." (Speech given at Developmental Studies Workshop, Los Angeles City College, June 3, 1967).

16. Roueché, *Salvage, Redirection.*

17. Cross, K. Patricia, "The Junior College's Role in Providing Postsecondary Education for All." (Berkeley: Center for Research and Development in Higher Education, and Educational Testing Service, 1969) , p. 5.

18. Wattenbarger, James L. and Godwin, Winfred L., eds. "The Community Colleges in the South: Progress and Prospects." (A report of the Southern States Work Conference Committee on Education Beyond the High School, sponsored by State Departments of Education and State Education Associations, 1962) .

19. *Time* 96:65.
20. Cohen, p. 5.
21. Schenz, Robert F., "An Investigation of Junior College Courses and Curricula for Students with Low Ability." (Ed.E. dissertation, UCLA, Graduate School of Education, 1963) , p. 141.
22. Bossone, Richard M., *Remedial English Instruction in California Public Junior Colleges; An Analysis and Evaluation of Current Practices.* (Sacramento: California State Department of Education, September 1966) .
23. Cohen, p. 8.
24. Roueché, *Salvage, Redirection.*
25. Schenz, p. 22.
26. Gleazer, "The Community College," p. 51.
27. American Association of Junior Colleges, *Selected Papers* from the 47th Annual Convention, February 27–March 3, 1967, San Francisco. (Washington, D.C.: The Association, 1967) , p. 62–63.
28. Medsker, Leland L., *The Junior College: Progress and Prospect.* (New York: McGraw-Hill Book Co., 1960) , p. 185.
29. National Conference on the Teaching of English in the Junior College. *Research and the Development of English Programs in the Junior College.* (Tempe: Arizona State University, 1965) , p. 32.
30. Medsker, pp. 171–173.
31. Cohen, Arthur M. and Brawler, Florence G., *Focus on Learning: Preparing Teachers for the Two-Year College.* (Occasional Report No. 11, Junior College Leadership Program, UCLA Graduate School of Education, March 1968) .
32. Cohen, p. xvii.
33. Blocker, Clyde E. et al., *The Two-Year College: A Social Synthesis.* (Englewood Cliffs, New Jersey: Prentice Hall, 1965), p. 144.
34. Cohen, p. 21.
35. Ibid., p. 96.
36. Ibid., p. x.
37. Ibid., p. 45.
38. Bossone, pp. 12–13.
39. Cohen, p. 86.
40. Bloom, p. 1.
41. Cohen, p. 100.
42. Ibid., p. 199.
43. Ibid., p. 201.

Higher Education's Contribution

JOHN D. MILLETT

Recently there has been a great deal of criticism of our institutions of higher education and very little mention of the contributions they have made to society. If the university is to continue to serve society, it must gain public support to obtain the resources necessary for its operations. In broad terms, higher education is accountable to the general welfare.

John D. Millett, "Higher Education's Contribution," *Compact*, 4:25–26, October 1970. Published by the Education Commission of the States. Reprinted by permission.

In recent years we have heard a great deal about academic freedom, about inadequacies and irrelevancies in the process of higher education, about failures of higher education to change society. We have heard very little about academic obligations, about achievements in expanding enrollment two and one-half times in the last ten years, and about the contributions we have made to society.

Some of the criticisms voiced during the past decade about the shortcomings of higher education have had certain validity. Some have completely misconstrued both the mission and the social role of the university. The dialogue about higher education is not ended but may be expected to continue for some time to come.

The accusation is often made by some student spokesmen that university leaders do not listen to them. Communication in terms of shared understanding of shared concerns is at best a delicate process. But frequently it appears to me that students seem to believe that agreement with an action to implement their point of view is the only proof that university officials have listened to them. The possibility that university officials might reasonably disagree with some student positions on many issues seems to be absent from much of the campus rhetoric we hear today.

No gulf more widely separates certain student and university attitudes than does this gap in understanding about the social accountability of higher education. Many students seem to hold the belief that the university is or should be accountable only to students. These students seem to conceive of the university as an institution for youth to perpetuate a youth culture in our society.

If the university in our society is to obtain increased resources for its operation and for its capital plant, then society must be convinced that the university serves a useful purpose. Individuals of wealth and governments which spend the tax income of their citizens will not distribute funds to an institution serving no useful social objective.

The endeavor to define university accountability has a long history in Western culture. Societies extending a large measure of personal freedom to their citizens have found it equally desirable to extend considerable academic freedom to their universities. But this freedom has had its obligations. Academic freedom will be preserved only so long as it has social utility, and our universities will survive only so long as they advance and do not threaten society.

In the past one hundred years, American society has expected its universities to transmit the knowledge and values of our culture to the young. It has also expected universities to carry on research which will advance the general welfare and to perform certain public services incidental to the diffusion of knowledge. Furthermore, a very sizable public investment has been made in higher education, reaching a larger proportion of our youth than in any other nation.

The accountability of higher education is simple: In broad terms, it is to contribute to the general welfare. Large segments of the whole population, not just the young, must be convinced of that contribution.

Furthermore, it must be widely believed that these contributions do in fact enhance the general welfare of all society. If these contributions come to be doubted, and if the general welfare is negated rather than advanced by our universities, then public accountability by higher education will have been lost.

Higher education sees its contribution to the general welfare as improved performance on behalf of a society committed to environmental quality, social justice and world peace through international goodwill rather than through conflict. No greater accountability can be asked or should be expected from American higher education.

Accountability and Autonomy

T. R. McCONNELL

There is an increasing demand for colleges and universities to justify what they are doing. Even though public institutions are directly accountable to their governing boards, they are also ultimately accountable to the public interest. T. R. McConnell first discusses institutional accountability to external agencies; later he discusses accountability as it relates to the faculty member. He envisions conflict between accountability and faculty autonomy.

Turmoil and disruption on the campuses; political action by students and faculty members; severe shrinkages in governmental, corporate, and individual incomes, coupled with rising taxes; and mounting distrust of higher education by the public are behind the increasing demand for colleges and universities to justify what they are doing and to disclose the effectiveness and efficiency of their operations. Perhaps as never before, institutions, administrators, faculty members, and even students find themselves accountable to a wide range of both internal and external agencies. Institutions and faculties, much to their concern and distress, have discovered that their autonomy is by no means absolute, and that in fact it is often highly vulnerable.

T. R. McConnell, "Accountability and Autonomy." Reprinted from the *Journal of Higher Education*, XLII (June 1971), pp. 446–463. Copyright © 1971 by the Ohio State University Press and reprinted with its permission. The author acknowledges the assistance of the Carnegie Corporation in the preparation of this paper.

An individual loses autonomy to the extent to which he is answerable to an external agent. Likewise, a university faculty cannot be completely autonomous if it is accountable to administrators or trustees. The corporate university is not completely independent if it is answerable to donors, the legislature, or the electorate. We may then ask, to whom are the institution and its constituents responsible, and for what are they accountable?[1] Public institutions, obviously, are accountable for their expenditure of appropriated funds. Even constitutionally autonomous universities are subject to governmental post audit, but this is not the only check on their expenditures. Since they must return to the legislature annually or biennially for their support, they become in fact accountable for the use of their appropriations. If support requested for a particular purpose is diverted to other purposes—and if these uses happen to be matters of particular interest to the legislature—the institutions will have to be prepared to justify their reallocation of resources. I suspect that a study would show that it has become increasingly common, too, for legislatures to attach riders to appropriation bills, even for constitutionally autonomous institutions, mandating expenditures for particular purposes.

Fiscal regulation is not the only means by which legislatures strike at institutional autonomy. A survey of recent threats to institutional independence and to faculty autonomy by Robert M. O'Neil[2] turned up such other kinds of interference as these:

Shortly after the Kent State killings, the lower house of the Ohio General Assembly passed legislation under which the arrest of a faculty member initiates a complex course of hearings. If a criminal conviction ensues, dismissal is automatic without any further university proceedings. In another instance, the Pennsylvania legislature enacted a statute which required colleges and universities throughout the country to report certain criminal convictions or disciplinary actions against Pennsylvania students resulting from campus offenses. The refusal of an institution to agree in advance to report such information would render it and its students ineligible to receive Pennsylvania state loans and scholarships.

In still another case, the Michigan legislature attached a resolution to the 1970–71 appropriation bill which stipulated that faculty members at the University of Michigan, Michigan State, and Wayne State should teach ten classroom hours each, those in four-year colleges twelve, and those in community colleges fifteen. The resolution provided that those who teach less than the required load should have their salaries reduced proportionately. In 1969, the California legislature passed a concurrent resolution urging on public institutions certain regulations concerning probation and tenure. In his State of the State message in January, 1971, Governor Ronald Reagan went further. He advocated the abolition of faculty tenure, saying:

> The original and legitimate reasons for tenure no longer exist. Tenure has become a haven for the incompetent teacher. It should be altered to include a system of merit pay which provides real incentives for quality teaching. This should not be precipitous; a judicious, sensible phase-out would be a real service to all concerned—the student, the public and the teaching profession.

A summary by the National Association of State Universities and Land-Grant Colleges of restrictive legislation passed in 1970 covered acts providing penalties for disturbances and interference with university functions, including revoking financial aid to students and curtailing salaries of faculty and staff convicted of charges of disruption; establishing special procedures for suspension and dismissal of students, faculty, and staff for certain offenses; and requiring institutions to establish regulations governing campus conduct and sanctions for violation of these rules. Commenting on such legislative erosions of academic autonomy during 1970, O'Neil concluded that "these intrusions have clear and dangerous implications for faculty autonomy as well as institutional independence."[3]

Executive branches of government also often exercise onerous controls over academic institutions. Reporting in 1959, the Committee on Government and Higher Education concluded that "in some states, college and university expenditures are subjected to close supervision by various state officials . . . leading in many instances to administrative limitations which amount to a usurpation of the responsibility of university governing boards. . . . Beyond question, centralized budget-making is the most powerful of the devices created as instruments of central control. With the development of the executive budget, the judgments of the state budget agency may have a decisive effect upon the decisions of the Governor and the legislature on appropriations for higher education."[4] I believe that a new investigation would show that state budget departments have steadily increased their control over the operations of public institutions during the last decade, and that constitutionally autonomous institutions have by no means been immune from such fiscal supervision. There is reason to believe that unless this trend is checked—and this is unlikely—state finance departments will greatly expand their control over the fiscal administration of public institutions. Among the factors which may strengthen the hand of these departments are a steady increase in many states in the governor's power to supervise and control all state programs; a tendency to tighten controls over spending and program duplication because of the increasing costs and complexity of higher education; and the development of complex management information systems, cost analyses, and program budgeting, all of which provide instruments of review and control for state finance officers.[5]

The examples given above are only a sample of the methods by which government agencies have expanded their control over higher education, and thus diminished the autonomy of public institutions. Some of the recent instances of governmental intervention were responses to what legislators and government officials considered irresponsible and disruptive student and faculty behavior. In other cases, financial stringency and mounting educational costs have provoked greater control. In still other instances, tighter fiscal controls are indicative of long-range trends in government and public administration. In any event, educational institutions have found themselves accountable in manifold ways to the agencies of state government. As private colleges and universities secure state support, they too will find themselves publicly accountable. And as federal support of higher education grows, both public and private institutions will find themselves increasingly accountable to the federal departments which administer the funds as well as the state agencies through which they are channeled.

Although the immediate accountability of public institutions is to the lawmakers and public officials who exercise various kinds of control over them, and more directly to their governing boards, they also are ultimately broadly accountable to the public interest. Stung by the failure of the voters of California to approve a state bond issue providing large sums for the construction of medical school facilities—which ordinarily would evoke strong public support—and by other evidences of widespread public disaffection, President Charles J. Hitch of the University of California emphasized the ultimate public accountability of that university when he said to the Assembly of the Academic Senate:

> Make no mistake, the University is a public institution, supported by the people through the actions of their elected representatives and executives. They will not allow it to be operated in ways which are excessively at variance with the general public's will. By various pressures and devices the University will be forced to yield and to conform if it gets too far away from what the public expects and wants.

Pressures exerted by special interest groups will shape the functions and services which institutions of higher education perform. Some of these groups have been much more articulate and influential than others. The University of California, like the land-grant universities of other states, has long responded with alacrity to the needs of agricultural producers. Only recently, however, has the university shown any interest in the farm workers displaced by machines designed by its agricultural engineers. In the past, the public university has responded primarily to the articulate, the influential, and the powerful in the citizenry, but that it has been socially responsive no one can deny. Now, however, the handwriting is very clear. The public university will have to become responsive to a wider range of economic interests, and to a more diverse pattern of ethnic and cultural backgrounds and aspirations. Whether institutions, including their faculties, like it or not, they will find themselves ultimately accountable to all these publics.

Intervention by state legislatures and government officials is not the only form of encroachment by civil authorities. Colleges and universities are increasingly subject to regulation by the courts. Over some period of time, the courts have required institutions to observe fairness and due process in dismissing students, while at the same time holding that colleges and universities have the right to establish regulations necessary for the orderly conduct of academic affairs. Campus disruption, especially after the Cambodian crisis, provoked a wave of judicial intervention. O'Neil has summarized recent court decisions and their bearing on problems of governance, and especially on institutional autonomy. What follows is taken primarily from his reviews.[6]

Acting in accordance with a resolution of its academic senate authorizing each school or college to set its own requirements for course completion after disturbances following the Cambodian incursion, the law school of New York University permitted its students to take final examinations or not as they chose, and, if they wished, to receive credit for work done to the point at which formal classes were suspended for the balance of the semester. However, on its own initiative the New York Court of Appeals ruled that students who wished to take the state bar examination must complete all their courses by regular written tests.

The father of an NYU student successfully petitioned the New York Small Claims Court for a refund in the amount of $277.40, the pro rata share of the student's tuition and fees for the period during which classes had been suspended, though a higher court subsequently reversed this decision. A group of Queens College students petititoned a court to direct that they be given instruction in several classes that did not meet as scheduled after the Kent and Cambodian episodes. The court ordered the college administration to provide special instruction to the individual plaintiffs in the courses which had not regularly met.

On the afternoon of the Kent State shooting, the campus at Kent

State was closed indefinitely by order of the Portage County Court of Common Pleas, which delegated to the Ohio National Guard complete control over access to the campus. The University of Miami, which had voluntarily closed for a short time after the Kent shooting, was ordered by a Florida state court to reopen. O'Neil comments on these two cases as follows:

> In neither case was the administration even consulted, much less the faculty. The problem is not so much that these decrees were wrong on the merits; one would have to know much more about the facts and circumstances to make that sort of judgment. The fault is that they constituted complete and summary displacement of campus decision-making by external agencies.[7]

A far-reaching decision concerning termination of nontenure faculty appointments occurred in Wisconsin. A nontenured faculty member at one of the state institutions brought suit in the federal district court alleging that he had been denied tenure in violation of his constitutional rights solely because he had made public statements critical of the university administration. The judge held that "minimal procedural due process includes a statement of reasons why the University intends not to retain the professor, notice of a hearing at which he may respond to the stated reasons, and a hearing if the professor appears at the right time and place." This decision contravenes the assumption long held by university administrators that a probationary teacher could be denied reappointment without stating the reasons.

Judicial decisions and the presence on campus of the community police, the highway patrol, and the National Guard symbolize the fact that colleges and universities have increasingly lost the privilege of self-regulation to the external authority of the police and courts. One must concede that recourse to the police and the courts may on occasion be unavoidable, but I believe that the general policy of abdicating internal regulation in favor of external control—and this is the tendency in many places—is unfortunate. Whatever one's views on the matter, it is apparent that colleges and universities have become increasingly accountable to the judicial systems of the community, the state, and the national government.

So far, I have emphasized institutional accountability to external agencies, although legislative actions and court decisions have significantly affected the authority of governing boards, faculties, administrators, and students and the internal distribution of power and influence among these constituencies. I now turn especially to the accountability of one of these groups, the faculty.

First of all, of course, a faculty member is accountable to his own conscience, and especially to his own standards of scholarship and intellectual integrity. The faculty member holds himself accountable to his own ideals.

Faculty members are also accountable in a variety of ways to their students. Presumably, they are answerable for the effectiveness of their teaching, for fair and unprejudiced evaluation of students' academic accomplishment, and for maintaining freedom of expression in the classroom. But faculty are not only answerable for keeping the classroom intellectually open; there are other elements of responsibility which the teacher must respect at the same time, such as accountability to the canons of scholarship, intellectual integrity, and fundamental educational values. Students are justified in insisting that what they study should be germane to their interests and to the problems of their own time. There is nothing new about this, but to me it does not justify a cult of immediacy. Neither does it justify encouraging students to think that the problems of their society are capable of simple solution. Faculty members' accountability to students is not merely to their immediate concerns; it is likewise accountability to the necessity for intellectualizing problems without dehumanizing them or blunting their urgency.

Gerald M. Platt and Talcott Parsons found that in institutions strongly oriented to research and intellectual values the primary mechanism of control is influence rather than power.[8]   They also found that under high stress, a collegial, influence-oriented social system tends to regress to relationships of power and to bureaucratic organization and administration. Under disruption and turbulence of the kinds which have plagued higher institutions recently, we may expect administrators and governing boards to assert greater authority over the faculty, and that the faculties consequently will become more accountable than before to administrators and to boards of trustees. Let me turn first to administrative authority.

At the University of California, the issue of relationships between faculty and administration, which became acute in the series of student disruptions beginning in 1964, was precipitated most recently by alleged faculty irresponsibility in "reconstituting" the university immediately after the Cambodian invasion. There were widespread reports in the press of politicization, improper conduct of courses, abandonment of academic standards, cancellation of class sessions, improper grading, and widespread student and faculty absenteeism. There were demands in the legislature and in the press to hold the university, its administrators, and its faculties responsible for dereliction of duty and perversion of the educational process.

President Hitch responded to these criticisms in a memorandum to the regents which was in reply to an earlier resolution directing him to submit plans for maintaining the future academic integrity of the university. The president took the position that the central problem of administrative governance of the university was the relationship between the administration and the faculty. He then observed that over a period of many years, the Academic Senate had moved toward more and more separation between its working committees and the administration, a phenomenon which Mr. Mortimer recently documented in his study of faculty government at Berkeley.[9] President Hitch's memorandum called for the restoration of a close working relationship between the faculty senate and the administration. To that end, he took the position that "it is the administration's responsibility to allocate the resources, and it is a joint responsibility of the administration and the faculty to work out the best means of accomplishing desired educational objectives with the available resources."

As a means of protecting academic integrity, President Hitch proposed that the roles of department chairman and dean should be strengthened in assigning academic personnel, reporting failure of staff members to carry out responsibilities, and recommending appropriate disciplinary action. The import of this proposal is that there should be more direct lines to administrative responsibility and authority from central administrators to deans to department chairmen. This is exactly what Platt and Parsons predicted would happen under severe organizational stress.

The reassertion of administrative educational responsibility and authority will not be confined to the University of California. For many reasons we may expect faculties, even in the major institutions in which they have won a high degree of autonomy, to become increasingly accountable to administrators. The faculties of distinguished institutions are not likely to accept without opposition such strengthening of bureaucratic authority and hierarchy. What Platt and Parsons called "organizational overemphasis" and the assertion of administrative authority are likely to shatter the delicate balance on which decision making by reciprocal influence depends, and undermine the mutual trust necessary for effective collaboration between faculty members and administrators.

There are signs that governing boards will also demand greater faculty accountability. Platt and Parsons point out that questions of financial and general educational policy ordinarily are formally in the hands of trustees and administrators, although in prestigious institutions the senior faculty are highly influential in these decisions. In matters of faculty appointment and promotion, however, the faculty voice in academically distinguished institutions is decisive even if the final formal approval rests with the president and the governing board. The prerogative of determining its own membership is one of the faculty's principal claims to professionalism, and it may be expected to resist external control over its membership. This issue has been in contention between the Board of Regents and the Academic Senate of the University of California for many years. In the famous loyalty oath controversy of two decades ago, the regents finally became less concerned about requiring faculty members to take a non-Communist oath and more determined to assert the board's authority over the appointment, promotion, and dismissal of members of the faculty.[10] Ultimately, although the Committee on Privilege and Tenure of the Academic Senate found favorably in the cases of nearly all the regular members of the senate who refused to sign the oath, and in spite of the fact that President Robert Gordon Sproul recommended that those reported favorably by the committee should be retained, the regents dismissed thirty-one nonsigning faculty members. Although the state supreme court subsequently struck down the regents' special anti-Communist oath, the court failed to pass judgment on tenure rights, faculty self-government, and political tests for faculty appointment, and especially on the faculty's control of its own membership.

Much later, President Clark Kerr persuaded the Board of Regents to authorize the chancellors of the several campuses of the university to approve appointments and promotions to tenure positions. But within three years, after controversy over the reappointment of Professor Herbert Marcuse on the San Diego campus, the regents withdrew this authority. The issue of the faculty's control over its own membership thus surfaced again. It is doubtful that the delegation of authority over appointments and promotions will be restored for a long time to come. Again, the regents have asserted the accountability of the faculty to the governing board.

There is reason to believe that other boards of trustees may reclaim elements of legal authority previously delegated to faculties and administrative officers or entrusted to them by custom and informal understanding. This trend is suggested by the recent statement on Basic Rights and Responsibilities for College and University Presidents issued by the Association of State Colleges and Universities. This statement first asserts the ultimate authority of the governing board. It affirms that the many constituencies of an institution—faculty, staff, students, alumni, parents—all should be provided with an opportunity to be informed and heard. The statement goes on to say, however, that "legally defined, a college or university does not consist of any one or combination of these constituencies. In the eyes of the law, a college or university is its governing board. . . . Although the president listens to the voices of all constituent groups, it must be recognized that he functions primarily as the administrative arm of the board, and that all legal governing authority resides with the board."

As professionals, faculty members are also accountable to their peers. Sometimes they are answerable only informally, as when other scholars appraise their research. Sometimes they are formally accountable, as is the case when a faculty committee evaluates the individual's performance as a basis for appointment, promotion, tenure, or discontinuance.

Scholars are accountable to their colleagues for the maintenance of the intellectual freedom of the classroom. On campuses torn by violent student disruption, some faculty members have wavered in their commitment to freedom of teaching, freedom of learning, and freedom of expression on all sides of a disputed issue. They have tolerated disruption of classes, intimidation of professors, and suppression of dissenting voices. Since the acts of a few may endanger the freedom of all, faculty members who fail to support the full freedom of the academy fail their own colleagues. Faculty members are accountable to one another for keeping the university intellectually free.

Public criticism and pressure from governing boards, and in certain cases self-initiated concern, have persuaded some faculties to define the responsibilities which are correlative with academic freedom and to formulate methods of self-regulation. It is high time. I think it is fair to say that the academic profession has given insufficient attention to means of assuring the professional conduct of its members. It was therefore highly appropriate for the American Association of University Professors to issue its statement on Freedom and Responsibility.[11]

After expressing only general principles, this statement advises that rules governing faculty self-regulation and possible imposition of sanctions should be adopted on each campus in response to local circumstances. It is the association's position that faculties should establish their own norms of professional conduct and recognize their stake in promoting adherence to them. Faculties recently engaged in this process include those at the University of California, the Oregon state institutions of higher education, the California State Colleges, Stanford University, and the University of Illinois, among others. The code proposed by the Academic Senate of the California State Colleges includes, as most of the others also do, sections outlining the responsibilities of a faculty member to his discipline, to his students, to his institution, to his profession, and to the community at large, all of which have been discussed above. The statement is prescriptive, not proscriptive. Its emphasis is positive and constructive, not negative and punitive, but it recognizes that as a last resort disciplinary action may have to be imposed for flagrant violation of professional standards.

In October, 1970, the Oregon State Board of Higher Education issued a statement relating to faculty conduct.[12] This included sections on faculty roles, the regulation of faculty conduct, and faculty discipline. The criticisms of this statement by the Inter-institutional Faculty Senate of the Oregon system of higher education,[13] some of whose recommendations had not been followed by the board, are indicative of the attitude which faculties are likely to take on questions of faculty responsibility and discipline. The senate report objected to the inclusion of a list of specific prohibitions on the ground that these were proscriptive regulations which smacked of a "criminal code." More significantly, however, the Oregon senate took exception to the failure of the board's statement to relate unacceptable faculty conduct to the faculty's professional responsibilities. The senate had proposed a draft which recognized that the appointment of an academic staff member might be terminated, or other sanctions might be imposed, for cause. The passage referring to cause was as follows:

> "Cause" shall mean failure to perform the responsibilities of an academic staff member, arising out of his particular assignment, toward his students, toward his academic discipline, toward his colleagues, or toward the institution in its primary educational and scholarly functions and its secondary administrative functions.

Thus, sanctions proposed by the senate were to be imposed for serious failure to perform stated professional responsibilities.

We may expect faculties to press for control over their own membership, to insist on establishing the norms of professional performance, to judge the performance of their members, and to propose sanctions for violation of professional standards. To this end, we may anticipate that many more professional codes will be formulated and adopted. We may also conclude that faculties will do everything possible to hold administrators and governing boards accountable for recognizing the professional status of college and university teachers. The code proposed jointly by the Committees on Academic Freedom and Senate Policy of the Berkeley Division of the Academic Senate of the University of California especially emphasized the "mutual and interdependent obligations of the faculty member and his institution."

So far, in discussing institutional and faculty accountability, I have said very little about the effectiveness and efficiency of their operations. In other words, I have said nothing about the extent to which colleges and universities change their students in demonstrable ways; the relative effectiveness of the means employed to produce these changes, including the differential effects of different institutions; and the cost of whatever educational values may have been added between the time the student entered and the time he left an institution or an educational program. These, however, are the questions with which most current discussions of educational accountability in the lower schools are preoccupied. Finding out how and to what extent students change while they are in college, however, turns out to be inordinately difficult. I shall not take the time to discuss all the complexities here, but mention only some of the more obvious problems in studying college impact.

The characteristics of students at a given point in their educational careers are functions of their attributes at an earlier time. The question to be asked, then, is, how has the student changed in relation to his characteristics at the starting point? We now have a great deal of evidence on how students in any one institution vary at entrance, not only in previous academic achievement, but in general and special academic aptitude; intellectual dispositions such as a theoretical or pragmatic orientation; and interests, attitudes, values, and motivations, to mention only some of the dimensions of personality which are relevant to the educational process. Students in some institutions are relatively homogeneous in such characteristics, while in others they vary greatly. Furthermore, the evidence clearly indicates that colleges and universities are differentially selective with respect to the same characteristics. These attributes not only establish the base lines for determining the amount of change over stated periods, but some of them are indicative of students' openness to change, in other words, their educability.

No single measure of educational outcomes or of student characteristics will suffice to measure effects. In addition to measures of academic achievement such as the Graduate Record Examination, the range of outputs assessed should be as varied as that of the inputs listed above. I should note in passing that although a good deal of progress has been made in measuring intellectual dispositions as well as attitudes and values, the methods by which we attempt to assess these outcomes are for the most part still relatively crude. Nevertheless, there is widespread recognition among persons interested in college impact, accountability, and management information systems that the major problems with which they are concerned demand defensible measures of many aspects of students' performance. Once satisfactory measurements are devised, however, many problems in determining the amount of change still remain; not the least of these are statistical methods for estimating the differences between measures at successive intervals, problems which cannot be discussed here.

Studies of impact also require means of measuring, or at least describing, college characteristics, "the prevailing atmosphere, the social and intellectual climate, the style of life of a campus,"[14] as well as "educational treatments." These methods range from the analysis of students' and others' perceptions of general campus atmosphere and campus subcultures to organizational analysis involving faculty values, the distribution of authority, public images, student traditions, student subcultures, curricular patterns, teaching procedures, and learning activities.[15] One of the confounding problems which research workers confront in describing college environments is that student characteristics and institutional qualities are by no means independent. Student attributes are potent determinants of institutional character. Another difficult problem in the analysis of sources of potential influence is that most institutions are not all of a piece. Consequently, the "global environment" may have less effect on particular students than the subcultures of which they are members.

But it is in determining the impact of the environment that the greatest difficulties arise. I can mention only some of them. First, environmental variables probably do not act singly, but in combination. Second, changes which occur in students may not be attributable to the effect of the college environment itself. Developmental processes established early in the individual's experience may continue through the college years; some of these processes take place normally within a wide range of environmental conditions, and in order to alter the course and extent of development, it would be necessary to introduce fairly great changes in environmental stimulation. Third, changes which occur during the college years may be less the effect of college experience as such than of the general social environment in which the college exists and the students live.[16] In an article with the arresting title, "The Best Colleges Have the Least Effect," the author concludes that the carefully selected students in these institutions develop in accordance with general cultural and genetic forces of the society; the colleges neither hasten nor retard their development, but provide the "womb" in which it can occur. The article also points out that one can often infer college effects by studying the misfits, and even the drop-outs, rather than the students who are well suited to the college environment.[17] For these and many other reasons, it is extremely difficult to relate changes in behavior to specific characteristics of the college or to particular patterns of educational activity.

The president of the American College Testing Program recently criticized the accreditation of colleges and universities as being highly subjective, based ordinarily on characteristics of the institution which may have little or no measurable effect on student attainment, and bereft of any objective data on changes in students. He predicted that performance contracting of the sort now being tried in such fields as elementary school reading will spread to higher education as a means of assessing its accountability to the taxpaying public.[18] The most enthusiastic proponents of the accountability movement believe that it is possible to assess objectively the effectiveness and also the efficiency of whole school systems, particular schools, individual administrators, and, finally, specific teachers. I am not very sanguine about parceling out the contributions to measured pupil performance, and particularly to the subtle outcomes of education, made by teachers, administrators, and school systems. But I am certain that there is no immediate prospect of doing this in colleges and universities, and I suspect that we will not be able to do so for a long time to come.

Be that as it may, the public will press us even more insistently to justify what we do, to show results, and to use resources efficiently. As professionals, we should proceed with all deliberate speed to define standards of performance and to measure our effectiveness against them, for the general public and various constituencies will be pressing their values on us and attempting to hold us accountable in appropriate and inappropriate ways. The forms of accountability which we will undertake and to which we will be subjected will be multiple and sometimes conflicting. There will be inevitable tension between the demands and requirements of accountability and the desire for autonomy. We will be fortunate indeed if we manage to reconcile all these forces to the benefit of students, to the requirements of critical scholarship, to the purposes of the university, and to the legitimate public interest.

FOOTNOTES

1. I wish to acknowledge the assistance of the Carnegie Corporation of New York in the preparation of this paper.

2. Robert M. O'Neil, "The Eclipse of Faculty Autonomy" (Paper prepared for a conference on Faculty Members and Campus Governance at Houston, Texas, February 17–18, 1971) , mimeographed.

3. *Ibid.*

4. *The Efficiency of Freedom: Report of the Committee on Government and Higher Education* (Baltimore: Johns Hopkins Press, 1959) , pp. 9, 11.

5. Lyman A. Glenny, "State Government and Control of Higher Education" (Paper presented to the Symposium on Systems Applications in Higher Education at the annual meeting of the American Educational Research Association, February 7, 1971) , mimeographed (Berkeley, California: University of California, Center for Research and Development in Higher Education, 1971) .

6. Robert M. O'Neil, "Judicial Overkill," *Change,* II (September–October, 1970) , pp. 39–41; "The Litigators' Response" (Address at a conference on Student Protest and the Law at the University of Kansas, November 13, 1970) , mimeographed; and "The Eclipse of Faculty Autonomy," cited above.

7. O'Neil, "The Eclipse of Faculty Autonomy."

8. Gerald M. Platt and Talcott Parsons, "Decison-Making in the Academic System: Influence and Power Exchange," in *The State of the University: Authority and Change,* edited by Carlos E. Kruytbosch and Sheldon L. Messinger (Beverly Hills, California: Sage Publications, 1970) , pp. 133–80.

9. Kenneth P. Mortimer, *Academic Government at Berkeley: The Academic Senate* (Berkeley, California: University of California, Center for Research and Development in Higher Education, 1970) .

10. David P. Gardner, *The California Oath Controversy* (Berkeley, California: University of California Press, 1967) , p. 143.

11. "A Statement of the Association's Council: Freedom and Responsibility," *AAUP Bulletin,* LVI (December, 1970) , pp. 375–76.

12. *Statement by the Oregon State Board of Higher Education Relating to Faculty Conduct and Amendments to the Board's Administrative Code* (Eugene, Oregon: Oregon State System of Higher Education, Office of Academic Affairs, 1970) .

13. "Report on the 1970 Amendments to the Administrative Code Concerning Faculty Conduct, October 23, 1970," mimeographed (Eugene, Oregon: Oregon State System of Higher Education, Inter-institutional Faculty Senate, 1970) .

14. C. Robert Pace, "When Students Judge Their College," *College Board Review,* LVIII (Spring, 1960) , pp. 26–28.

15. Burton R. Clark, *The Distinctive College: Antioch, Reed, and Swarthmore* (Chicago: Aldine Publishing Company, 1970) .

16. Burton R. Clark, Paul A. Heist, T. R. McConnell, and Martin A. Trow, "Student Change in Selected Institutions" (Berkeley, California: University of California, Center for Research and Development in Higher Education, in process of publication) .

17. Arthur W. Chickering, "The Best Colleges Have the Least Effect," *Saturday Review,* January 16, 1971, pp. 48–50, 54.

18. *ACTivity* (American College Testing Program) , IX (January, 1971).

Commitment to Competency: The New Fetishism in Teacher Education

ROBERT J. NASH

One recent innovation in higher education is performance-based teacher education programs. Robert J. Nash identifies some of the basic assumptions of such models. He poses four questions about the curriculum which will assess the degree we have fetishized the skills dimension of teacher training. With a projected excess of classroom teachers, is now the time for a competency-based teacher education program?

More and more colleges of education are moving toward a competency model in teacher education. This commitment to competency is usually buttressed by the following assumptions:

1. Teaching can be reduced to a series of performance functions and can be analyzed according to types of teaching activities.
2. Because teaching consists exclusively of these various kinds of activities (e.g., explaining, guiding, demonstrating, testing and evaluating, skills imparting) , the best teacher education program is one which develops training protocols that foster these skills.

Robert J. Nash, "Commitment to Competency: The New Fetishism in Teacher Education," *Phi Delta Kappan,* 52:240–243, December 1970. Reprinted by permission.

3. The performance or competency curriculum is rooted in a set of very clear objectives. This competency curriculum provides knowledge and develops skills to reach those objectives. Also, it systematically measures its effectiveness by checking on how well its trainees are fulfilling the objectives.

4. Such a curriculum is not concerned with liberal education, specialized knowledge in an academic area, the values and attitudes of the trainee, or the dilemmas of the larger society within which the school is located. Its primary and exclusive function is to train learning strategists and communicators of skills. Its ultimate goal is to produce the teacher who has mastery of specific professional competencies.

One recent spokesman for competency-based teacher education models has argued that teacher education ought to follow the pilot-training procedure. Like the pilot, the teacher trainee ought to pass through three phases: familiarization flights, supervised flights, and solo flights. And like the pilot program, progress through each of the phases ought to be governed solely by the trainee's performance and the concomitant demonstration that he can perform all of the skills which make up the goals of the program.[1]

According to the American Heritage Dictionary (1969), a fetishism is a belief characterized by an excessive attention or attachment to something. Often this belief impels the fetishist to bestow a kind of mystical or magical power on the thing he reveres. It is my conviction that, as teacher educators, we are racing slavishly to adopt a model for teacher education which is so out of touch with the contemporary zeitgeist that it has become but another unquestioned fetish in the arsenal of pedagogical ammunition. In an overzealousness born out of frustration and defensiveness we are adopting a model which promises to bestow a magical kind of scientific-technological warrant on our professional endeavors. What is happening, however, is that we are fetishizing techniques and trivializing the entire teacher preparation program. One of the consequences of a teacher education model which proposes the *reductio ad absurdum* of the student teacher's being trained as an airline pilot is the loss of many of our brightest, most idealistic students to the neoromaticists. Our students envy the romantic's willingness to question the mechanistic-positivistic assumptions which the competency model presupposes.

In recent years, the commitment to competency in teacher education has often been motivated for unassailably benevolent reasons. We have been deeply concerned about the deterioration of the educational process in low-income neighborhoods. We have realized, after much soul searching, that teachers must be more than self-sacrificing, dedicated sentimentalists. We have understood the necessity for producing the competent educational professional in the inner city who is capable of determining specific skill weaknesses in his students, and who, on the basis of his expert diagnosis, can then proceed to the implementation of a program of behavior modification—in order to increase student skill proficiency. Kenneth B. Clark, a psychologist-educator, has even proposed that teachers in the inner city be paid on the basis of their competencies in raising the reading, arithmetical, and writing skills of their students.[2]

Correspondingly, public school officials are becoming more convinced of the validity of the competency model and the requisite teacher accountability which such a model presupposes. Experiments in Ossining, New York, where a public school principal has "guaranteed" parents of an incoming kindergarten class that by the year's end 90% of their children will be reading at or above the national average, and in Gary, Indiana; Texarkana, Arkansas; and Camden, New Jersey; where public schools have contracted with private business and industry to teach the basic communicative and arithmetical skills to children, exemplify the move to competency in public education. Such programs also illustrate the basically humane motives of educators to deliver in the cities the kind of education which they have for years been promising.[3]

In spite of the above, it is my conviction that the failure of competency-based teacher education programs lies *not* in the humanity or integrity of those educators who have devised them, nor in the zeal with which they have been applied in the cities. Neither is the failure located in the predispositions of those teacher educators who desire more precise, operational training programs. Rather, the failure has occurred because we have made a fetish out of the competency model. We are in danger of reducing the entire teacher training program to such trivializing exercises as the preparation of general and specific instructional objectives. We are becoming excessively preoccupied with performance criteria, behavior modification, and a whole congeries of related competency concepts. We are in the process of gleefully devising an incomprehensible methodological nomenclature based on the precepts of operant conditioning. We are rapidly approaching the point where we are speaking a quasi-mystical language which bears little resemblance to the real world. Thus we hear of modules, entry and re-entry, tandem and chained schedules, differentiated staffing, mands, and tacts. Such mystagogy—the inevitable offspring of fetishistic thinking—would be laughable, if it were not for the legitimacy it is getting in many teacher education curricula.[4] Also, we are hawking the notion that what constitutes learning in any acceptable educational situation is only that which is observable, demonstrable, and objectively defined. Finally, we are conveying the belief that the most "professional" teacher is the one who concentrates solely on imparting a variety of skills to his pupils, while systematically detaching himself from the personhood of his students and from the bewildering social events which rage just beyond the walls of the school.

In retrospect, the ascendancy of such thinking has been predictable. For at least a century our culture has been guided by the values of post-Comtean positivism,[5] pragmatic immediatism, and opportunistic technologism. As positivists, we have insisted that demonstrably visible behavior which can be measured is the most acceptable basis of human learning. As pragmatists, we have maintained that the practical and the expedient in human learning take precedence over the claims of those who say that people can learn in ways that are *not* immediately reducible to utilitarian usefulness. And as technologists, we have devised educational technicways which allow us scientifically to utilize and to exploit our natural environment toward the satisfaction of our multiplying material needs. Small wonder that teacher educators, in the face of all the urgent social demands made on them, would rush with naive expectancy to a scientific model in order to validate and renew the teacher-training endeavor. As products of the larger culture's basic value system, we have embraced a model which promises immediate, demonstrable results. But what we have been asked to surrender is an epistemology which allows for the significance of non-cerebral, or non-intellective, learning. Also, we have been asked to ignore or underplay that dimension of human behavior which is activated by one's value perceptions. And, finally, we have been cautioned to suspend any substantive judgments about the morality of the system we are preparing students to face and to accommodate.

A result of such thinking is that our competency model has failed to inspire many education students. This generation of college students is questioning, at times with clarity and eloquence, the cultural life-style which is rooted in the values of positivism, pragmatism, and technologism. They recognize that solutions to the most pressing crises of our times will emerge only when we begin to challenge the melioristic-mechanistic axioms of progress and the good life which guide our thinking. Research studies by several social scientists have illustrated the extent to which contemporary college students are eschewing values rooted in practicality, achievement, scientific detachment, competitiveness, orderliness, and precision.[6] Instead, students are pursuing values related to self-expression, communitarianism, and a dedication to personalistic and humanitarian objectives. Also, as Theodore Roszak has so convincingly shown, a growing minority of our youth is forming a counter-culture in opposition to those technocrats who, in the name of science or expertise or competency, would reduce our human projects to the illusory busywork of the functionary-professional.[7]

When these students enter a teacher education program, they seek an alternative to the technocratic world view which has terminated in outcomes young people deplore: the narrowness of specialization, the depersonalizing meaninglessness of routinized tasks, and the suspicious interpersonal skepticism bred by a sterile competitiveness. They look to us for help in realizing their most ennobling aspirations. Pathetically, we give them more of what they have renounced. We insist that they temper their "idealism" with the stuff of realistic professionalism. Snidely, we demean their naiveté, while undermining their goodwill. We suffocate them with the paraphernalia of systems theory, behavioral objectives, technological gimmickry, tests and measurements, performance criteria, behavior modification, and other related competency activities. Students implore us to assist them in their pursuit of personhood. We strive to turn them exclusively into competent functionaries by giving them a rigid, skills-centered curriculum which borders on the inconsequential and the nugatory. They ask for a program which balances the need for performative skills with the insights gained from concerted self-understanding and self-definition. We offer them our fetishes and insist on their allegiance.

Occasionally, the bizarre outcome of this is the image of the teacher trainee leaving his micro-classroom, or his simulation session, or his behavioral objective exercise, or his learning laboratory, with a copy of A. S. Neill's *Summerhill* under his arms. Rather than convincing this student of the validity of mastering specialized professional competencies in a laboratory setting, we have merely increased his demand for the neoromantics with their commandments of self-actualization, individualization, and autonomous choice. Men like Neill and Goodman, Kohl and Holt, speak to the subjective concerns of the idealistic and the alienated young teacher-to-be. Such authors share with E. E. Cummings the belief that the dimension of behavior which is most susceptible to quantification is of least importance. They stress that what is of central significance in preparing students to be helping professionals is not the technique or the function which they must perform, but rather how they live their lives and how they manage to subordinate the inordinate demands of a hungry technological social order to the realization of each of their students' finest human potentialities.

It is essential to note here that this is *not* an injunction to return to a pretechnological or prescientific age. Rather, it is my hope that we can begin to retrieve the young, gifted, and idealistic education student only when we understand his disillusionments with the social order. One of the purposes of teacher education ought to be to give young students the opportunity to question, to test, and to provide alternatives to the entrenched educational values of their day. Before we sell them on the validity of competency models, we have to respond to their ambivalent view of the school as an iatrogenic agent: We must face the fact that many of our brightest students come to see the school as a stigmatized symbol of their deepest sense of powerlessness, futility, and failure. They see the school also as the single greatest resistant force to significant social change. Paradoxically, they come into teacher education with a profound sense that education is where the final beachhead is going to be established against the insanity of a world bent on self-destruction. They demand a professional training which confronts the reality of values, attitudes, and social crises, as well as training which provides them with the basic skills they will need in the classroom.

The first step in revitalizing teacher education is to understand, as did John Dewey, that the primary responsibility of an educator is to begin with what troubles the student most deeply, and then proceed in such a way as to enable the student to gain rational insight into these concerns. C. Wright Mills always maintained that such an education must be carried one step further. Each professional educator has the additional responsibility of helping the student continually to translate his personal problems into public issues. That is, students must be given the training to understand that personal crises are inseparable from public or social crises, and that resolution comes only when the personal-social dialectic is clarified.[8] This is what Mills called the cultivation of "the sociological imagination," and it underscores the startling lack of this kind of imagination in teacher education.

I am proposing that the teacher education model balance its commitment to performative training with a sense of reformist zeal. In addition to becoming learning strategists, we might help students to become reform strategists. I am proposing that we ask four questions whenever we sit down to examine our curricula—four questions which will assess the degree to which we have fetishized the skills dimension of teacher training.

1. To what extent is the curriculum confronting the education student with the realities of the school and the society in which he will be spending his professional and personal lifetime? The older sentimentalist-progressivist model for teacher education has its modern analogue for irrelevance in the competency model which effectively insures that teachers never ask meaningful, disturbing questions about education, schools, and the social order. Until we sensitize students to the value dimension of human behavior, and to the resolute stubborn-

ness of people and institutions to change; and until we help them to
understand the complex interplay of personal, institutional and social
forces, we are only deluding students when we claim that competency
training will enable them to face their professional careers realistically. Also, at least one contemporary critic of education has warned us
that we must train teachers to be "futurologists." We must teach
students not only to identify and to understand data, but to manipulate and to discard data. Likewise students must know when and how
to discard old ideas and values, and how and when to replace them.
Our students must be trained in learning how to learn. Such training
realistically prepares teachers for several possible futures.[9]

*2. To what extent are we including educational experiences which
help students to get from the realities of the school to what they would
like the school to be?* Currently there are very few courses in under-
graduate colleges of education which could aid the prospective teacher
in moving from the "is" situation in the school to the "ought" desire
for school reform. We offer no definitive work in tactical or strategic
measures which a beginning teacher might employ in making his classroom a more "open" one, or in accomplishing substantial educational
reform without alienating colleagues, supervisors, parents, or students.
Current neoromantic notions of reform in education are doomed to
failure, in part, because students are not being prepared to be change
strategists. Similarly, competency-based models are failing because
their notion of educational change is fixed on the micro-level of individual behavioral modification. Such micro-change strategies often
miss the point because they ignore Mills' admonition that effective and
enduring change occurs only when individualized behavioral modification is systematically related to the personal and social worlds.

*3. To what extent are we preparing the student to take his place in the
classroom, the administrative office, or the counseling situation as a
critic of the educational status quo, rather than as a conformist in the
name of "professionalism"?* There ought to be opportunities for
students in teacher education to examine those assumptions about
education which educators themselves manage to conceal. Students
should be given intense training in exposing the fallacious logic,
spurious analogies, deceptive sloganeering, and superficial band-
wagoneering which characterize the pronouncements of so many educational professionals.[10] So, too, students need extensive background
work in being able to identify those forces in the school and community who will react most harshly and disproportionately to those criticisms. The most effective critic of education is one who has identified
the problems, who is aware of the most resilient and sympathetic

pockets of concern in the community, and who then proceeds toward a program of reform with a sense of resoluteness, reasonableness, and responsiveness to the feelings of those less committed to change than he. Students have to understand that they can be responsible critics of the educational status quo without having to resort to the self-defeating demagoguery of those who cry for change at any cost.[11]

4. Finally, we must ask, *To what extent are we as teacher educators becoming models for educational and social change?* Are we overly cautious about revealing our own deepest value assumptions about education, or our most visionary dreams for educational and social reform? Have we become apopletic apologists for a do-nothing professionalism? Or are we initiators of change in our committee work, our curriculum revision, our daily teaching, and in our frequent interpersonal relationships with colleagues and students? Do we raise issues over grading, arbitrary entrance and exit requirements, more pertinent course experiences for students, greater community involvement on the part of faculty and students, and a hundred other concerns which signify our personal interests in educational and social reform? Have we resisted the tendency among academicians to align with one or another school in psychology or philosophy? Or are we continuing to perpetuate the artificial divisiveness which is present in so many colleges of education in the name of behaviorism, or humanism? Such categorical enclaving precludes any consensual commitment among a faculty to educational reform, because faculty members begin to think in terms of positions consistent with their categories, rather than taking direct action on a number of specific issues which require ad hoc reform.

What can be said of teacher education at its worst is that it is bland, normatively obtuse, esthetically archaic, and intellectually insipid. At its best, teacher education can touch those hidden, unrealized potentialities in each of us so that we can create better lives for ourselves and others. It is my feeling that if we continue on an exclusive path toward performative competency in our curricula, we will be increasingly vulnerable to those who charge us with trivial, fetishistic thinking. We are capable of a great deal more.

FOOTNOTES

1. Kevin A. Ryan, "A Plan for a New Type of Professional Training for a New Type of Teaching Staff," National Commission on Teacher Education. Occasional Paper No. 2, February, 1968.

2. Fred M. Hechinger, "A Program to Upgrade Schools for the Deprived," *Sunday New York Times Week in Review,* July 26, 1970.

3. See news items, *New York Times,* July 26, 1970, pp. 52, 56.

4. For a stinging review of operant conditioning and its terminology see Alfred A.

Baumeister, "More Ado about Operant Conditioning—or Nothing?," *Mental Retardation,* October, 1969, pp. 49–51.

5. For a philosophical analysis of positivism and education see Michael B. McMahon, "Positivism and the Public Schools," *Phi Delta Kappan,* June, 1970, pp. 515–17.

6. For a review of the recent research on college students and values see Nevitt Sanford, "The College Student of 1980," in *Campus 1980,* Alvin C. Eurich, ed. New York: Dell, 1968, pp. 176–99 (paper).

7. Theodore Roszak, *The Making of a Counter Culture.* New York: Doubleday, 1969 (paper).

8. C. Wright Mills, *The Sociological Imagination.* New York: Grove Press, 1959, pp. 186–88 (paper).

9. Alvin Toffler, *Future Shock.* New York: Random House, 1970, pp. 353–78.

10. A similar training is advocated for liberal arts students by a historian. See Howard Zinn, *The Politics of History.* Boston: Beacon Press, 1970, pp. 5–34.

11. A hopeful example of responsible criticism is that made by a group of elementary principals in their journal, *The National Elementary Principal,* June, 1970. The entire issue was devoted to the theme: "Dehumanizing our society through education and with the active support of the public."

For Further Reading

PART I

"Accountability for Whom? For What?" *Phi Delta Kappan,* 52:193, December 1970.

"Accountability in Elementary and Secondary Education." *Compact,* 4:19–23, October 1970.

"Accountability in Higher Education." *Compact,* 4:24–27, October 1970.

"Accountability Method Makes Failure the Teacher's Fault." *College and University Business,* 49:451, July 1970.

Advisory Council of State Departments of Education, *Federal State Partnership for Education: Fifth Annual Report.* U.S. Office of Education Publication, OE-23050-70, 1970, 182 pp.

Allen, J. E., Jr. "Competence for All as the Goal for Secondary Education." *National Association of Secondary School Principals Bulletin,* 54:9–17, May 1970.

"American Public Ill-Informed about Education." *Nation's Schools,* 84:16, October 1969.

Austin, G. R. "Educational Acountability: Hallmark of the 1970's." *Science Teacher,* 38:26–128, April 1971.

Bain, H. "Self-Government Must Come First, Then Accountability." *Phi Delta Kappan,* 51:413, April 1970.

Bair, Medill. "Developing Accountability in Urban Schools: A Call for State Leadership." *Educational Technology,* 11:38–40, January 1971.

"Balanced Presentation of Accountability." *American Vocational Journal,* 46:88–90, February 1971.

Barber, W. R. "Accountability, Bane or Boon?" *School and Community,* 57:14–15, April 1971.

Barnes, C. S. "Who Cares About Education?" *Compact,* 5:3–4, April 1971.

Bell, Terrel H. "New Federal-State Relationships." *Compact,* 4:68, October 1970.

Benne, K. D. "Authority in Education." Bibliography, *Harvard Educational Review,* 40:385–410, August 1970.

Berdie, F. S. "To Rile Your Community, Ask Questions Like These." *American School Board Journal,* 157:28, June 1970.

"Boardmen Can't Think of One Good Thing To Say about Voucher Plans." *American School Board Journal,* 158:33–37, October 1970.

Brick, M. "Support for Public Education? Who's Kidding Who?" *National Elementary Principal,* 49:64–66, May 1970.

Brown, S. B. "Accountability." *Reading Newsreport,* 4:2–3, April 1970.

Bureau of Educational Personnel Development. "Do Teachers Make a Difference? A Report on Recent Research on Pupil Achievement." U.S. Department of Health, Education and Welfare, Office of Education, Washington, D.C.: Government Printing Office, 1970.

Campbell, Roald L., Lucy Ann Marx, and Raphael O. Nystrand. *Education and Urban Renaissance.* New York: John Wiley & Sons, Inc., 1969.

Carline, D. E. "Why Do You Teach? Or How Accountable Are You?" *Journal of Reading,* 14:385–386, March 1971.

Cass, J. "Accountable to Whom? For What?" *Saturday Review,* 54:41, March 20, 1970.

Cook, Constance. "Sharing the Duty To Account." *Compact,* 4:24–25, October 1970.

Coolidge, R. A. "Values in American Education." *Music Journal,* 28:324, November 1970.

Darman, R., and G. Thompson (eds.) "An Interview with James Allen." *Harvard Educational Review,* 40:533–546, November 1970.

Davies, Don. "The Relevance of Accountability." *Journal of Teacher Education,* 21:127–133, Spring 1970.

Domyahn, R. A. "Annotated Bibliography on Accountability." Compiled by *AV Instruction,* 16:93–101, May 1971.

Durost, W. N. "Accountability: The Task, the Tools, and the Pitfalls." *Reading Teacher,* 24:291–304ff, January 1971.

Elam, S. "Age of Accountability Dawns in Texarkana." *Phi Delta Kappan,* 51:509ff, June 1970.

English, F., and J. Zaharis. "Are Accountability and Governance Compatible?" *Phi Delta Kappan,* 52:374–375, February 1971.

"Education and Government." Bibliography, *Yearbook School Law,* 1970: 1–21.

Gillis, James. "Performance Contracting for Public Schools." *Educational Technology,* 9:17–20, May 1969.

Goldstein, W. "On Seeing Through the Academic Looking Glass." *Clearing House,* 45:131–134, November 1970.

Goodman, K. S. "Promises, Promises." *Reading Teacher,* 24:365–367, January 1971.

Green, Edith. "The Business of Education." *Nation's Schools,* 86:40–45, December 1970.

Grieder, C. "Educators Should Welcome Pressure for Accountability." *Nation's Schools,* 85:14, May 1970.

Harlacher, E. L., and E. Roberts. "Accountability for Student Learning." *Junior College Journal,* 41:26–30, March 1971.

Harrison, C. H. "How To Respond to Public Demands for Accountability." *Nation's Schools,* 86:32–34, November 1970.

Hitchens, H., Jr. "Accountability." *AV Instruction,* 16:116, May 1971.

Idstein, P. "Count Ability and the Draggin." *Phi Delta Kappan,* 52:508–509, April 1971.

Jordan, B. "Educational Accountability: A Crucial Question." *Junior College Journal,* 41:23–25, March 1971.

Kirkpatrick, D. W. "Agony of Relevance." Bibliography, *Pennsylvania School Journal,* 119:71–74, September 1970.

Lanham, W. M. "What's Wrong with Education in America?" *School and Community,* 57:75, November 1970.

Lessinger, Leon M. "Accountability and Curriculum Reform." *Educational Technology,* 10:56–57, May 1970.

————. "Accountability for Results: A Basic Challenge for America's Schools." *American Education,* 5:2–4, June 1969.

————. "Accountability in Public Education." *Today's Education,* 59:52–53, May 1970.

————. "Focus on the Learner: Central Concern of Accountability in Education." *AV Instruction,* 15:42–44, June 1970.

————. "Powerful Notion of Accountability in Education." *Journal of Secondary Education,* 45:339–347, December 1970.

————. "Accountability: What's It Mean?" *Educate,* 3:38–39ff, March 1970.

———— (ed.) "Accountability in Education." *Educational Technology,* 11:11–31ff, January 1971.

———— (ed.) "Symposium on Accountability." *Journal of Secondary Education,* 45:339–380, December 1970.

Lieberman, M. "An Overview of Accountability." *Phi Delta Kappan,* 52:194–195, December 1970.

———— (ed.) "Overview of Accountability: Symposium." *Phi Delta Kappan,* 52:194–239, December 1970.

Lippincott, W. T. "Accountability and Change." *Journal of Chemical Education,* 48:211, April 1971.

McCall, T. "States and the Schools: Last-Chance Alliance." *American School Board Journal,* 158:14–16, July 1970.

McLenon, T. B., M. Caperton, and F. G. Nilson, Jr. "Can Parents Demand Accountability?" *Instructor,* 80:47, August 1970.

McMahon, M. B. "Positivism and the Public Schools." *Phi Delta Kappan,* 51:515–517, June 1970.

Milstein, M. M. "Roles of the States and the Federal Government in Metropolitan Education Organization." Bibliography, *Urban Education,* 5:179–198, July 1970.

Motzkus, J. E. "Accountability and the Reverend Dogood." *Today's Education*, 60:57, March 1971.

Nelson, F. B. "Some Reflections on Quality Education and Responsibility." *Education Horizons*, Special Issue, 9–14, June 1970.

Nyquist, Ewald B. "Measuring Purposes and Effectiveness." *Compact*, 4:21–22, October 1970.

"OEO's Voucher Plan Opposed by NEA, ISTA." *The Indiana Teacher*, 115: 147–150, Spring 1971.

Opinion Poll. "How Education Groups View Contracting." *Nation's Schools*, 85:31–33, June 1970.

Opinion Poll. "Large Majority Favors Teacher Accountability." *Nation's Schools*, 86:33, December 1970.

Ott, Jack M. "Taxonomy of Administrative Information Needs: An Aid to Educational Planning and Evaluation." *ERIC Document* ED-044-423, Ontario Institute for Studies in Education, Toronto, Canada, March 1970, 17 pp.

Pharis, William L., *et al.* "Decision Making and Schools for the 70's." *Research in Education, ERIC Document* ED-041-732, N.E.A., Center for the Study of Instruction, January 1971, 81 pp.

"Pump Those Federal Funds into Local Schools: Resolutions Adopted at 39th Annual Convention of NSBA." *American School Board Journal*, 157:33–35, June 1970.

Rajpal, P. L. "Relationship Between Expenditures and Quality Characteristics of Education in Public Schools." *Journal of Educational Research*, 63:57–59, October 1969.

Ramo, Simon, and Leo E. Persselin. "Changing Functions of Urban Schools: The Role of Industry." *Educational Technology*, 10:58–60, September 1970.

Randall, R. K. "Toward a Better Mix of Teaching Resources." *AV Instruction*, 16:15, May 1971.

Ratliff, F. E. "Accountability at What Cost?" *English Journal*, 60:485–490, April 1971.

Rice, A. H. "Good Teachers Stand To Benefit from Accountability." *Nation's Schools*, 86:16, November 1970.

Roaden, Arliss. *Citizen Participation and the Need for Public Accountability.* Columbus, Ohio: Assessment Task Force, Urban Education Coalition, 1969.

Roche, John P. "A Vacation from Responsibility." *The New York Times Magazine*, July 20, 1969, p. 26.

Rogers, David. "The Failure of Inner City Schools: A Crisis of Management and Service Delivery." *Educational Technology*, 10:27–32, September 1970.

Schwartz, R. "Accountability." *Nation's Schools*, 85:31–32, June 1970.

Seltz, Judith. "A Teacher's Guide to Performance Contracting." *Grade Teacher*, 88:32–35ff, April 1971.

Smith, B. L. "Educational Trends and the Seventies." *American Association of University Professors Bulletin*, 56:130–136, June 1970.

Smith, H. "In Education, Are Publishers Accountable?" *Publishers Weekly,* 199:39, January 18, 1971.

Southern Association of Colleges and Schools. "Evaluating the Elementary School: A Guide for Cooperative Study." *ERIC Document* ED-044-440, Atlanta, Georgia, 1964, 63 pp.

Stenner, J. "Accountability by Public Demand." *American Vocational Journal,* 46:33–37, February 1971.

Stocker, J., and D. F. Wilson. "Accountability and the Classroom Teacher." *Today's Education,* 60:41–56, March 1971.

Timpane, P. M. "Educational Experimentation in National Social Policy." *Harvard Educational Review,* 40:547–566, November 1970.

Voegel, George H. "A Suggested Schema for Faculty Commission Pay in Performance Contracting." *Educational Technology,* 57–59, January 1971.

Wagoner, D. "Do You Know Anything at All about How Well or How Much Your Teachers Teach?" *American School Board Journal,* 158:21–22, August 1970.

"What the Public Thinks about the Public Schools: Results of the 1970 Survey." *Education Digest,* 36:1–4, December 1970.

"What's Right with American Education?" Papers from the 54th Annual Convention, Washington, D.C., National Association of Secondary School Principals: Bibliography. *National Association of Secondary School Principals Bulletin,* 54:iii–181, May 1970.

White, F. J., Jr. "Autonomy and Accountability." *New York State Education,* 58:48, January 1971.

Williams, L. "Governance Is Integral to Accountability." *Today's Education,* 60:59–60, April 1971.

Part II

The Initial Response
to Accountability

Accountability, for the most part, is a simple concept which becomes complex only when applied. It has developed mostly through trial-and-error procedures, and as yet, no one form of accountability appears to have satisfied the concerns of fairness and effectiveness as examined by the various authors in Part I.

It might be tempting, indeed, for school systems to do nothing and to hope the specter of accountability disappears so that schools can "get on with the business of education." The spiraling costs of education, the surplus of teachers, and the state of the nation's economy conspire to induce greater public demand for accountability.

Additionally, the cult of efficiency is making increasing demands on all of society's institutions. Such groups as Nader's Raiders and the Welfare Rights Organization, for example, have gained prominence because they provide organized consumer protection while demanding accountability and adequate performance from bureaucratic organizations. Never before have social institutions been pressed for effectiveness by the clients they serve to such an extent.

Some view accountability as a potential vehicle for consumer protection against those who take shelter in the bureaucratic woodwork of educational institutions, perpetuating tradition and serving as effective barriers to progress. With the emphasis on demonstrated performance, as required by accountability, the stress in education is no longer one of utilization of certain procedures, approaches, methods, rituals, or material usage.

Several writers have dubbed accountability the watchword of the 1970s. Jonathan Spivak of the *Wall Street Journal* calls it "the coming revolution in American education." School systems which seek to ignore accountability may, like the citizens of Lilliput, awake one day to find themselves with a sleeping giant in their midst and few viable solutions for the confrontation.

As Pharis and his group explain:[1]

> Whether or not one agrees that more pressure ought to be put on educators to produce objective evidence about the results of instructional programs, such pressure will be a fact of life in the 70's. Though the United States has great wealth, there will never be sufficient economic or human resources to meet all the demands of the many interest groups that make up society. Choices must and will be made. Therefore, there will be increasing pressures on educators to present concrete evidence that demands for more resources will result in specific gains.

The failure of America's schools to educate *all* students, as well as the massive educational retardation which exists especially among minority-group students, has caused a number of influential organizations to espouse accountability as a catalyst for educational reform.

In the late 1960s, Nathan Glazer interpreted the new demands of minority groups in education:[2]

> The demand for economic equality is now not the demand for equal opportunities of the equally qualified. It is now the demand for equality of economic results. . . . The demand for quality in education . . . has also become a demand for equality of results, of outcomes.

The concept of accountability carries with it the promise for "quality in education," but which of its many forms is the most effective one? Once the decision has been made as to who shall be accountable for a student's progress, three key requirements must be met. First, the parties involved need an effective student information system in order to establish a basis for evaluating the quality of education. Second, a prescribed method for measuring student information is needed. Third, goals of achievement must be set before pupil progress can be measured.

Gathering information so that student learning progress can be measured objectively and attributed honestly to the efforts of one particular teacher, one particular program, or one particular school, presents problems of great magnitude. Variables such as a student's health, his home environment, socioeconomic circumstances, previous education, already learned skills, self-concept, and motivational index will have to be considered.

Added to the tasks of testing and measuring knowledge, prescribing goals, and measuring student progress towards such goals are the determination of rewards and punishments and, most importantly, determination of who is to be responsible for making all these decisions. Setting up a system of accountability that is fair to all levels of educators appears to be the greatest problem to be overcome.

As if the complexity of the task of applying the accountability were not a sufficient obstacle, battle lines are being drawn in influential groups declaring support for certain forms of accountability while condemning others.

The National Association for the Advancement of Colored People (NAACP), in their 1971 annual convention, demanded that schools be both integrated and accountable for providing effective, quality instruction: "There is no choice between the urgency of ending all forms of segregation and the urgency of providing high educational standards and accountability of schools for effectively teaching Negro children." Performance contracting as a guarantee of accountability was endorsed, while any kind of voucher payment plan was rejected. The delegates felt that educational vouchers could serve to promote segregation by permitting white parents to use public funds to send their children to all-white private schools.

At the 1971 annual convention of the National School Boards Association (NSBA), a resolution was passed to "strongly oppose" the education voucher plan. The NSBA said vouchers could "encourage the proliferation and growth of nonpublic schools and cause a corresponding erosion of the American public school system." Education vouchers could lead to segregation of many children according to race, religious denomination, ability, or educational philosophy, the resolution said.

Performance contracting and differentiated staffing, as forms of accountability, were more favorably received by the NSBA. Not only did they pass a resolution on accountability, noting that school boards "must devise measurable relationships between dollars spent and educational results obtained," but recommended that local school boards set aside at least 2 percent of their budgets for research and evaluation programs. Furthermore, they urged adoption of differentiated staffing to allow recognition for excellence in teaching. NSBA's endorsement of performance contracting states that such programs should be "limited to those areas where objectives can be determined and criteria agreed upon."

Although a number of performance contracts were operative in America's schools in early 1970, the first school to operate completely under a guaranteed performance contract was the Banneker Elementary School in Gary, Indiana, operated by the Behavioral Research Laboratories (BRL) of Palo Alto, California. BRL reports some early success after overcoming overwhelming problems. Such problems included:

a threatened teacher strike by the teachers union over the selection of teachers for Banneker by BRL;

threatened removal of state department of education accreditation and $200,000 in state aid because it taught nothing but reading in the morning and math in the afternoon;

concern from the state department of education over non-use of state-approved textbooks;

community pressure applied after the removal of supportive school personnel, such as the nurse, speech therapist, psychologist, and social worker;

another furor over the revelation that the pupil-teacher ratio was 38 to 1 and that some classes had over 50 pupils;

frequent clashes between the school system's educational policies and BRL's systems-oriented policies.

All these problems posed serious threats to the Banneker Elementary School project and were resolved during the first five months of the school year.

It becomes apparent that forms of applied accountability rise and fall according to the support or opposition they encounter from various concerned groups, and because of the effectiveness inherent in that particular form of accountability application. Although all forms of accountability have had to overcome some resistance from organized groups, those which have met the most opposition appear to be forms which pose the greatest threat to the present order of public education. Education vouchers and performance contracts would head this list.

Articles in Part II identify a number of approaches to application of accountability, as well as reports of accountability attempts or plans in specific cities and states. The following questions are pursued in this section:

What is performance contracting and what are some precautions to be taken?

Under what conditions could education vouchers be realistically utilized?

What are some of the problems and promises of education vouchers?

Which approaches provide for other levels of accountability than just the teacher?

How are educational evaluators best utilized in moving a school system towards accountability?

How can the school budget be regulated so that sufficient funds are allocated to practices or components with the greatest output?

In which system of applied accountability are teachers best motivated?
What are the strengths of each system of applied accountability as well
   as the weaknesses?
Where have accountability projects been attempted?

Pressing problems in education—such as the large numbers of
students lacking basic education skills, the failure of compensatory
education in urban schools, and the unprecedented rate of taxpayer
rejection of school tax issues—cry for solution. Accountability is no
panacea for the ills of education, but it does offer the potential for
triggering important educational reform. Declaration of educational
priorities will become necessary in order to develop objective criteria
for professional accountability. The need to develop performance
criteria will necessitate a changed emphasis from how teaching proceeds to how learning occurs. Efforts to accomplish this goal signal the
necessity for expanding our limited knowledge of the human learning
process. The drive to obtain a qualitative measure of educational
effort will undoubtedly lead educators to the task of developing more
adequate diagnostic tools.

Accountability, as it becomes more widespread, carries with it the
seeds of promise for energizing needed changes in American education.
It could also become the new battleground for old problems in education as well. The resolution of these potentials will come only through
the passage of time—possibly during this, the decade of the 1970s.

REFERENCES

1. William L. Pharis, and others, "Decision Making and Schools for the 70's,"
(Washington, D.C.: National Education Association, Center for the Study of Instruction, 1970), p. 64.

2. Lee Rainwater and William L. Yancy, *The Moynihan Report and the Politics
of Controversy* (Cambridge: Massachusetts Institute of Technology Press, 1967),
p. 49.

CHAPTER 3.
PRACTICAL APPROACHES
TO ACCOUNTABILITY

Performance Contracting for Instruction

ALBERT V. MAYRHOFER

A statement of position of the Bureau of Elementary and Secondary Education, U.S. Office of Education, views performance contracting as a tool in the educational process with the potential for good or evil. Important areas covered by the author here are elements to consider in entering into performance contract agreements, the function of the management support group (MSG), and a list of steps toward employment of educational technology to meet the needs of children and society.

A contract is a legal agreement in which one party promises to deliver goods or services to another party for a consideration of value. Fulfillment of a promise is the essence of the agreement. Specification of redress for non-fulfillment is usually included in the agreement. Education has long used contracts for the delivery of goods and services.

The term performance contracting is used only because it more clearly describes the intent of the agreement—increased student achievement as measured by specified performances. Performance contracts accentuate output rather than input as the criterion of fulfillment. Performance contracts include provision for redress for non-fulfillment.

Because of the stress on output with redress, the performance contract has the potential for being a valuable tool which schools might use to improve their accountability in the use of public resources.

Since the Bureau of Elementary and Secondary Education, Office of Education, regards the performance contract as a tool, we neither approve nor disapprove its use.

Albert V. Mayrhofer, "Performance Contracting for Instruction." Unpublished, 19 pp. Used by permission of the author.

An analogy may prove helpful. A tool can be used in many ways. A hammer, for instance, can be used to pound nails into wood and some people might enjoy this activity. It can also be used to drive nails into wood for the purpose of constructing something useful. This would require non-random pounding of nails into non-randomly chosen construction material. I will freely admit that randomly pounding nails into randomly chosen materials might produce what someone might consider an art object. The possibility of producing a product having general social utility is impossibly slight.

We believe that the random use of the performance contract has not only less possibility of social utility but may have counter productive social consequences. One must not forget that a hammer can be used in criminal pursuits.

Experience has taught us that the hammer, skillfully orchestrated with the use of other tools and materials by skilled people following a well conceived planned display can and has achieved structures of great social utility, homes, for instance. And the social utility of the home will be only as great as the matching of that home with the needs of the family which is to use it.

The performance contract has all of the promise and problem of any potentially useful tool of man. The socially productive use of this tool requires much more care, study, work and sensitivity than would the *analogous* hammer, partially because education had had little experience in its use.

But we are not without any heritage from which to seek guidance.

The Bureau of Elementary and Secondary Education, Office of Education, will support, with what limited technical assistance we have available, those who seek to responsibly use performance contracts as an accountability tool. We can do no less. Accountability for results is one of the objectives in the Office of Education management by objectives plan.

The heritage I referred to a moment ago, is one developed over the past decade. Many people in the local, State, federal and private sector, have contributed their insights and energies. Its history is speckled, as you might imagine, with limited successes and failures. But it is maturing. We are beginning to achieve a technology of instruction and methods for more reliable replication of success. The concept is educational technology as a humanistic process rather than a bunch of materialistic things. The history is sprinkled with names: Cooke, Kaufman, Trivett, Lessinger, Johnson, Esbensen, Schure, Mager, and Brown, to mention but a few.

These, and others, the educational architects, engineers or craftsmen, have helped to produce the tools and practices which hold promise for greater cost effective learning gains by children. Forum

Nine of the recent White House Conference on Children recommended that educational technology, as a process, be used in all educational efforts.

This will, in my judgment, be difficult to achieve quickly for two main reasons. First, there is a limited pool of skilled personnel upon which to draw. Second, educators being people will, I assume, act like people. Some will resist changing their perceptions and practices. Neither of these problems is insurmountable. America has enough talented and willing people who can quickly acquire the requisite skills if given the opportunity. And the broad history of evolution, suggest the survival consequences for those who would resist appropriate change when competing in environmental stress conditions.

What is this process called educational technology? It is nothing more than the *distilled* and *organized* practice of successful practices. It is the skilled use of appropriate tools and strategies in the cost effective, socially responsible execution of a plan to meet documented needs of children and society.

Conceptually, the process has six components:

The first component requires identification of the problem, using documented needs as criteria. A need is simply the discrepancy between what is and what should be. The statement of the problem also requires the specification of requirement for problem resolution or a definition of terminal product or behavior. This is the component which documents that for which we will be held accountable. For this reason, statement of the problem must also identify conditions such as time, materials, personnel, and funds.

The second component involves the determination of solution requirements and solution alternatives. An analysis is performed which determines the detailed requirements for proceeding from the current condition to the required condition, or what should be. These requirements must be stated in measurable performance terms. Possible solution strategies and tools are identified to meet the requirements. Their advantages and disadvantages relative to producing the required outcomes are documented.

The third component involves the *selection* of strategies and tools from among the documented alternatives. Criteria for selection should certainly contain cost *effectiveness* indicators. All too often cost efficiency is used in its stead. Basing "how to do it" decisions on what will do the best job for the least expenditure of time, resources, and effort of both learner and educator *makes good sense*.

The fourth component involves implementation. Based on needs, solution requirements and the selected tools and strategies, a plan is designed and followed. The tools and strategies are obtained and utilized. This is the "doing" component in which the tools and strategies are utilized and performance data is collected.

The fifth component involves the determination of performance effectiveness. The application of the implementation plan to the solution of the problem is evaluated to determine the extent to which results are achieved. Data on interim and terminal performance, and process utility are collected, analyzed, compared to requirements and used to determine *revision* requirements.

The sixth component involves *revision as required. Any time* a performance requirement is not met, either *during* or *at the end* of an educational technology application, revision is required. If this is not accomplished, the planned relationships among and between the tools and strategies will be changed and the program will be limited to a greater or lesser extent in achieving the resolution of the problem. This component applies to all of the other components, individually and as a group.

Since most people conceptualize what they practice rather than practice concepts, one must expect that many people will attempt educational change by starting with the third component, selection of strategies and tools. They will do this because they are *good* people. Their experience will lead them to feel a need through their perception of the children for whom they feel responsible. Much investment in educational reform has been dashed against the rocks in the past because of this practice. Dewey expanded Chen Fu's *"I hear; I forget; I see; I remember; I do; I understand to a "learn by doing literature."* We claim to be humanistic. Let us apply this to those of our colleagues who need time and opportunity to learn by doing.

The process of educational technology must include humaness to function. Those who are practitioners know that the sum of the parts is greater than the whole; that the straight line of the physical engineer is rarely the shortest or best distance between two points.

The performance contract, as a tool for increasing the capability of our schools to meet their burdens, has great potential. It *might* be an option one would select in the third component. It might not. Its social utility will depend on the criteria for its selection as a tool, from among other options, and how skillfully it is orchestrated within the educational technology process. This is what we mean when we ask: Was this a responsible selection of a tool?

Some Advantages of Performance Contracting

The advantages of performance contracting are inherent in the nature of the serious problems that confront education today.

First, it facilitates the targeting and evaluation of educational programs. Many good instructional programs have not been given the opportunity to demonstrate their potential due to the lack of an effective delivery system at the school level. The recent evaluation of Title I of ESEA notes not only this operational inadequacy, but also the inability of educational organizations to evaluate the effectiveness of most instructional programs. Although the principle of educational accountability has been implemented in the Bilingual and Dropout Prevention Programs, the lack of *an adequate means to evaluate makes accountability an academic issue. The performance contract approach, which utilizes a separately managed and operated center with separate accounting procedures, fosters the objective evaluation of educational results and also the managerial processes by which these results were achieved.*

Second, performance contracting for instructional services could introduce greater resources and variability into the public school sector. Right now, new programs are being offered to the public outside the school system; the process of fragmentation and competition has begun. Several large corporations are establishing franchise learning centers across this country. One company has at least forty centers operational in the major cities of this country; ten others are establishing centers in other cities. Performance-type contracts to improve student achievement in deficient areas are usually enacted between the parents and the franchise. The dollars parents spend with the contractor are over and above the property taxes which they pay for schools' operations. As these franchised centers expand, it is conceivable that parents will begin to refuse to pay property taxes through continuing to defeat tax and bond issues. The performance contact approach, on the other hand, would allow the school system to utilize the services and products of a particular firm so that the public schools can be renewed through a "turnkey" process. *Performance contracting could be looked upon as a means to foster and catalyze institutional reform within a school system, allowing school systems to continue operations and to become competitive with private schools and franchised learning centers.*

Third, the performance contract approach allows a school system to experiment in a responsible manner with low costs and low political and social risks. Both school officials and critics have expressed the need to determine the relative cost effectiveness of various instructional methods in contractor-operated centers, as well as upon incorporation into the particular schools. The performance contract approach not only allows for determination of these costs and benefits but also provides the basis for projecting initial adoption costs as well as operating cost when the system is implemented into the schools. *In this sense, the approach allows lay board members to make rational choices when choosing new credible techniques for extension into the classroom.*

Fourth, the new "Bill of Rights in Education," the right of every child to read at his grade level, will undoubtedly place great burdens upon the schools' limited resources. If the Nation's schools are to make this principle a reality, they might want to consider using performance contracting for the development and validation of new reading programs. Upon successful demonstration, the school can then adopt the program or programs thereof. The success of these programs, that is, the child's ability to read, will in large part depend upon the ability of the school skillfully to design and execute performance contracts and then effectively incorporate the project into its normal operation.

Fifth, according to the most recent decision rendered by the Supreme Court, school systems across this country will be required to develop effective desegregation plans which will provide not only equal opportunities, but also equity of educational results. One of the major fears of the white community is that "black" or "brown" children, upon integration, will hold back the progress of their children. *Through the use of the performance contract approach, many of the previously segregated children will have their academic deficiencies removed on a guaranteed achievement basis while they are attending the newly integrated schools. Performance contracting would allow communities to desegregate in the most nondisruptive, educationally effective, and politically palatable manner.*

Finally, the approach creates dynamic tension and responsible institutional change within the public school system through competition. Leaders will now have alternatives to the traditional instructional methods when negotiating salary increases; performance contracting and its variant, performance budgeting, permit the authorities to base salary increases on increases in effectiveness. As the *Dallas Morning News* has stated: "Taxpayers can now tie results to tax dollars expended." *Boards of education can finally establish policy and choose among alternative instructional programs.*

PROBABLE TRENDS

After the Texarkana breakthrough, the response by public school systems to performance contracting has been great, and a sense of immediacy has been created. Well over 250 school systems have inquired about the concept of performance contracting and the procedures for its use. At the state level, at least three states are drafting legislation to permit performance contracting at the elementary and secondary levels, as well as the junior and community levels. Some consortia of states, local education agencies, and the U.S. Office of Education are exploring the possibility of utilizing ESEA Title I and Title III funds under the performance contract approach.

Proper guidance, in the form of descriptive material as well as guidelines for implementing performance contracting and/or performance budgeting within school systems should be made available to avoid the potential for a backfire to occur. For example, certain firms which develop tests and sell curriculum might bid on performance contracts; other firms might develop specific reading and math curricula around specific tests. Franchise learning centers are bidding on performance contracts with schools in order to force state agencies to accredit their programs. Certain schools facing desegregation problems are considering very seriously the establishment of performance contract projects without a capability or an in-depth knowledge of the concept.

Performance Contract Elements to Consider

"A Catalyst and Buffer Mechanism," first introduced in Texarkana, was the concept of the management support group (MSG), something new to education. Its precedent was established in the defense-aerospace area when, in the mid-50's, the Aerospace Corporation was created to act as a buffer and technical assistance team between the Air Force and weapons systems suppliers for the Air Force. The Aerospace Corporation's major functions were to develop programs, design requests for proposals based on performance specifications, assist in evaluating proposals, and provide management services to contractors. The major functions of the management support group (MSG) in education under the concept of educational technology would be in the following areas:

A. FUNCTIONS PROVIDED BY MSG

1. Program planning and development assistance. School systems generally lack such a management capability, or, if such is available, "day to day" operations prevent effective utilization of that resource. Moreover, an outside group provides new insights and a different perspective in analyzing educational and other problems and in developing alternative solutions. For these and other reasons, it is advantageous for the school to have an MSG develop the RFP. The MSG could assist in the following ways during program development and planning:

a. Analyze and determine the community's educational needs and the desired levels of student performance.
b. Conduct program definition phase studies and determine sources of funding.

c. Develop the RFP and experimental design to be used for "turn-key" purposes as well as national dissemination.
d. Develop and recommend "program change proposals" on a continuing basis during the initial stages.
e. Develop means for gathering and maintaining political and community support for the program during all phases.
f. Contact potential bidders in the education industry and R&D laboratories to ensure that the latest innovative techniques are considered and are encouraged for application by the direction and flexibility allowed in the RFP.
g. Determine the qualified bidders and send the RFP to them.

1. Project management assistance. Too often, proposals are developed by outside groups who curtail relationships with the school once the contract has been awarded. The management support group has to provide extended and sustained services in the areas ranging from establishing the project management office to the development of evaluation techniques. The project management services would be in the following areas:

a. Develop a multi-year management plan for the conduct of the demonstration and "turnkey" effort including an administrative system for the LEA's project management office.
b. Conduct, when appropriate, pre-proposal development and bidders' conferences with all interested parties.
c. Establish a proposal evaluation procedure and assist in the evaluation by presenting strengths and weaknesses to the LEA.
d. Continually evaluate the contractor's progress and assist in contract negotiations as required.
e. Manage pilot programs when specifically requested to do so by the LEA.
f. Analyze the administrative and managerial changes required when the techniques proven in pilot programs are integrated into the school system. This "turnkey" phase is critical to overall success and requires careful analysis *and* program planning and budgeting.

3. Linages for communications and coordination. As an unofficial advocate of change and ombudsman for the public interest, the MSG can provide an effective, disinterested, and politically palatable linkage between federal, state and local agencies so that priorities and program directions are coordinated. Because many firms of unknown or questionable reliability will be entering this newly created multi-billion dollar market, the MSG is a necessary mediator and honest broker between the firms and the school systems. At the community

level, the vested interests of powerful groups and important decision-makers must be determined. Here, the MSG, acting as a buffer between the LEA and these interest groups, both within and outside the school system, can obtain such information in an effective and politically advantageous manner (e.g., the superintendent could point to the MSG as a scapegoat if specific ideas or recommendations are not accepted by the Board). The MSG can provide an on-call manpower pool curing planning and implementation. It can hire potential school employees in order to allow officials to see them in action. Moreover, the MSG has access to consultants around the country, and on short notice it can provide their service without having to go through cumbersome bureaucratic procedures.

In short, the politics of experimentation where private industry, local schools, and the Federal Government are all involved creates the need for unofficial "advocates" and "buffer mechanisms" to protect politically all parties concerned, while ensuring that the project does in fact become a reality. Note the success thus far in the Texarkana, Dallas, and Jacksonville projects:

a. A radically innovative concept acceptable to many districts in many States was conceived for multi-year funding and was in operation ahead of schedule.
b. New ventures were initiated with private industry, despite some experts' prediction that no firms would bid.
c. A cost-effective program run by an outside private firm and promising early and effective adoption was accepted by the school systems.
d. Projects are operating which have the support of responsible citizens regardless of their political persuasion and the interest of media ranging from the *Washington Post* to the *Dallas Morning News*.

B. PROBABLE TRENDS

The concept of the management support group was made legitimate by the Title VII and Title VIII, ESEA grant guidelines. Only a few firms have the capability to perform this function on their own although a larger number of individuals do exist and could form a fertile cadre to advise and train others. The concept of catalytic buffers was included in the enabling legislation for ESEA Title III, presented to Congress in 1964–65; however, it was deleted in final legislation. Many people attribute the failures of Title III projects to the lack of a MSG that would have provided the necessary political and technical skills to ensure effective planning and implementation and eventual adoption by LEA's. A strategy for developing this capability within education across the country would reap enormous cost savings, reduce time wastage, and effect early adoption of new programs.

Independent Educational Accomplishment Audit Group

"Closing the Loop." Similar to the earlier demand for fiscal audits, the public is now demanding an account of student accomplishment. Just as the independent fiscal audit of schools had eliminated most fiscal illegality and has forced fiscal management changes, the IEAA group can also be used to create the demand for the necessary instructional reforms. The concern for results in education among the electorate is a recent development, but it is gaining momentum. "Equal opportunity" in education no longer mollifies the majority; "equity of results is demanded. This is especially true of the educational benefits conventionally called the "basic skills." Even though Title I language reflects a traditional concern over inputs such as equipment, teachers, space, and books, the subsequent questions raised by the Congress have moved beyond *how* the money was spent to whether the students are learning, securing jobs, or falling behind. This is the political soil from which the independent accomplishment audit has grown.

A. PROCESS

The Independent Educational Accomplishment Audit is a process similar to that used in a fiscal audit. The emphasis, however, is on student performance as a result of financial outlays. The Independent Educational Accomplishment Audit (IEAA) relys upon outside independent judgement and has six essential parts: the pre-audit; the translation of local goals into demonstrable data; the adoption or creation of instrumentation and methodology; the establishment of a review calendar; the assessment process; and the public report.

1. *The Pre-Audit.* The auditor selected by the school system starts the IEAA process by discussing with the staff, students, and community the objectives and plans of the particular program to be reviewed. This phase produces a list of local objectives and a clear description of the programs in some order of priority. In performance contracts, he reviews the project's "procedures" manual.

2. *The Translation.* In concert with local people, the auditor determines a clear formulation of the evidence indicating that the objectives have been met and the methods that will be used to gather the evidence. This phase produces a set of specifications revealing what the student will be able to do as a result of the educational experience,

the manner in which the evidence will be secured, and the standards which will be applied in interpreting the success of the program in bringing the students to the objectives.

3. *Instrumentation.* Along with the translation, the auditor, working with the LEA, determines the audit instruments, such as tests, questionnaires, interview protocols, and unobtrusive measures which will be used to gather the evidence. The product of this activity is a set of defined techniques and procedures for data gathering.

4. *Review Calendar.* An agreement is secured in writing which indicates the nature of the reviews, where they will be held, how they will take, when they will occur, and who is responsible for arrangements, the nature of the arrangements, and other logistical considerations. It is essential that the calendar be determined in advance and that all concerned be a party to the agreement and have the authority to honor the agreement.

5. *The Audit Process.* This is a responsibility of the auditor. In this phase, the auditor carries out the procedures agreed upon in the pre-audit, translation, and instrumentation phase as codified in the review calendar.

6. *The Public Report.* The auditor files a report at a public meeting, giving commendations and recommendations as they relate to the local objectives. The report is designed to indicate in specific terms both accomplishments and ways in which the programs may be made more effective.

B. ADVANTAGES

The IEAA is a new technique designed to put local school personnel and the clients they serve in a problem-solving mode of thinking. It is built around a financial core since money is a common denominator for the heterogeneous elements of inputs, but its focus is upon student attitudes, skills, and knowledge. Out of the IEAA, a whole range of useful by-products are anticipated. First, it may lead to a knowledge of optimum relationships between outputs and inputs, i.e., the "critical mass" in funding different types of compensatory programs. Second, it can form a basis for the discovery and improvement of good practice in education. Third, the IEAA creates the need for performance-type contracting and/or budgeting in the basic academic and vocational skill areas. Finally, it can renew credibility in the educational process, effect more responsiveness to the needs of children, and supply the understanding necessary to produce change. The power of the electorate over public education must be politically, not administratively, derived. If techniques can be developed to convince the community of the benefits of responsible leadership through accountability for results, those interested in furthering education can better support the educational enterprise. If a school district responsibly selects the performance contract as a tool with which to solve their problem, we will try to help with what little technical assistance we have available. We know that you want to operate the most socially constructive and cost-effective programs possible for your children and community.

And so, the position of the Bureau of Elementary and Secondary Education, U.S. Office of Education, has not changed. We encourage the responsible and discourage the irresponsible use of tools.

Performance Contracting: Making It Legal

REED MARTIN

Basic considerations needed to satisfy the legal requirements for entering into a performance contract agreement by a school district are covered by Reed Martin. He cautions against the use of sole-source contracts and stands as an advocate of request for proposals (RFP), which encourages competitive bidding and establishes a set of educational specifications to be contracted for, allowing the school district to retain control over policy matters. The two most controversial areas of the performance contract—testing and payment—are discussed also.

The history of performance contracting in education has shown that, when this process is planned and executed carefully, it can show positive results, but when improperly planned, it can be a terrible mistake. A large part of the planning of a performance contract involves legal considerations.

Authority to contract: The first consideration is the ability of a local school district to contract with private organizations to perform instructional tasks. Local education agencies, as creations of the state, are given very limited powers to contract, and any contract in excess of that power is void, even though both parties agree to it.

Most schools may contract with outside parties to provide certain services, but those are generally services not imposed upon the school by constitutional declaration or by state delegation. Where the school is under a duty to perform a task, then an outside contract for its performance may be null.

Although there are as yet no judicial decisions directly on educa-

Reed Martin, "Performance Contracting: Making It Legal," *Nation's Schools*, 86: 62–63, January 1971. Reprinted by permission.

tional performance contracting, cases on the general problem indicate that a controlling factor may be that a school cannot contract to employ private individuals when public employes have been retained to perform a comparable job.

Thus, having a private company take over the full operation of a school, even with the purpose of doing a "better" job than an employe already retained on the public payroll, may raise a legal barrier. A contract for more limited services which the school cannot provide may come closer to meeting legal requirements.

Delegation of powers: Assume that a school has the authority to contract for the type of services it desires. A second legal obstacle may then arise: improper delegation of powers. States delegate certain educational policy-making functions to the local school and these powers cannot be delegated to a private group. That would be an abdication of responsibility on the part of the local school.

Cases seem to indicate that courts will examine a school's policy-making role even more closely than its authority to contract. It is not clear where a court might draw the line in regard to the various educational tasks a school might ask a company to perform, but policy roles *must* be controlled by the school.

Three factors are important in determining whether a school is retaining control under a performance contract. First, properly drafted program specifications, contained in a Request for Proposals, can indicate the school's intent to remain in charge. If the specifications are incomplete or vague, and subject to the bidder's own interpretation, then the school may be delegating too much authority to the bidder. The outside agency might thus be making decisions tantamount to policy-making.

A second area is staff expertise. The school must provide a monitoring function during the program in order to retain authority and protect policy-making prerogatives. If staff does not have the expertise to do this, the company will in reality be in control and the school would have abdicated its responsibility. Many schools secure outside management support not only to increase their capability in planning but also to assure their ability to retain control over the program.

The third area for consideration is the basic purpose of the contract. Some schools unfortunately perceive performance contracting as a way to contract out their problem students, foisting responsibility for failure onto an outside party that guarantees success. One cannot really blame overburdened schools for finding such a notion so attractive, but contracting out as an end in itself may be a delegation of too much authority. If a program were to be conducted for a specified period of time, evaluated and then either abandoned or absorbed by the school, the school would obviously be retaining full authority. If a program might be extended indefinitely, always under contract to an outside agency, then effective control of decisions with policy implications may have passed to the contractor.

The state commissioner of education in Texas, which has four performance projects underway, drew that line clearly in posing this question recently to the state's attorney general: May a school district enter into performance contracts with private corporations where the program is primarily proposed for a study of the capability of the private sector to facilitate desirable educational reforms, as distinguished from any general plan or movement to contract with private corporations for actual instructional services? The attorney general answered in the affirmative.

One may assume that a school is on safest legal ground when it specifies in the original contract the procedures for taking over the operation of a successfully demonstrated instructional program. This process has come to be called the *turnkey* phase—when the contractor turns the "keys" over to the school so the school can run the program thereafter. Where the purpose of the contract is not "to facilitate desirable educational reforms," and the contractor insists on keeping the keys rather than turning them over, the state may insist that the school change its lock.

Assuming that the school has the legal authority to contract for instructional services, and that it is clearly retaining its policy-making role, the next step is developing the contract. (The delegation question, however, must constantly be kept in mind.) At this point, the school may choose one of two courses of action: 1) it may develop a Request for Proposals (RFP), a set of educational specifications to be contracted for, which is the subject of open competitive bids, or 2) it may skip this step and contract with a company on a "sole source" basis. Most schools choose competitive bidding.

Developing the RFP: Assuming that the school will seek open bids, the RFP becomes important because it will be the basis of all that follows. It specifies the type of programs the school wants proposed in terms of time, cost, levels of performance, guarantees and conditions, such as training local personnel.

Consistent with the turnkey process, the RFP should ensure that the program being developed specifically for that school, if successfully demonstrated, would be a program that could be expanded throughout the entire school system and acceptable to all parties concerned.

The major legal consideration should be the conduct of the bidding process, according to cases involving housing turnkey problems. The delegation problem inherent in program specificity has already been noted. In addition, the proposals must be evaluated in a way that is fair to bidders and serves the public interest in selecting the best proposal. Evaluation standards and procedures should be stated in the RFP and scrupulously followed by the school decision-makers. Unless the RFP requires bidders to supply all the information needed for evaluation, in a consistent format that allows proposals to be contrasted, then the award of a contract may be susceptible to challenge.

"Sole source" contracts: The school may choose to award the contract on a sole source basis. In this type of contract, there is usually no public goal setting, no community participation in decison-making, and no accountability for the decision-making process. Experience of several school systems in recent months has shown that the cost of these contracts is usually higher, the performance guarantee lower, and the public interest less likely to be served.

This last consideration raises a possible legal problem. A court might find it strange that the purchase of many goods and services by schools is required to be on open bid but the service most related to the constitutionally mandated educational function can be purchased behind closed doors. Such a practice might be found not to be in the public interest.

A sole source arrangement raises the further legal problem of how much authority is being given to the company. Where a company initiates the contract with the school (rather than the school seeking out companies), proposes an approach which includes curricular contents and the scope of the program, and the school signs the contract, the company may have in fact assumed too much responsibility in the area of educational policy formulation. Courts might feel that program specifications (the RFP) initiated by the school, with the school choosing among competing bidders, better demonstrates the school's control over policy questions.

Drafting the contract: A contract can be drawn up which incorporates the necessary terms and conditions of the RFP and the successful bidder's response. Two areas that are the most difficult, and also the most controversial, are testing and payment.

The whole question of testing is one of the most complicated in developing a workable contract. Testing instruments must be specified in the contract, and the responsibilities for administering and scoring tests should be stipulated. Procedures for testing students before and after the program, testing replacement students when they enter the program, and testing students who are dropping out of the program should all be considered. The school should be protected against the contractor's including test items in his curriculum. Testing instruments should also be developed to measure interim as well as final performance. As an indication of the complexity of these provisions, they require about ten pages in most performance contracts currently in use in the education field.

The next most difficult area in the contract is spelling out the payment provisions. Payment schedules should reward performance above the minimum guaranteed level and penalize the failure to perform. In addition to final payment, the school will probably want a schedule of payment for meeting interim performance objectives. There will have to be a different schedule of payment for students, depending on when they entered and when they left the program and whether they were pretested or post-tested adequately. There may be a dollar ceiling on the total contract so the payment schedule must reflect a graduated scale which cannot exceed a certain amount. And of course the contract must stipulate the conditions under which no payment will be made to the contractor.

It is vital that payment schedules provide real incentives for the contractor to maximize the performance of each child and to continue the program at a full level of effort all year long. Some "performance" contracts allow a contractor to ignore slower students or push them out of school, maximize the performance of a few individuals, and cut back the level of effort as maximums are achieved. Other contracts provide little or no penalty for failure.

Virtually all of the legal questions raised by the involvement of the private sector in public education revolve around the public interest. That interest cannot be served by schools' seeking easy solutions to educational problems, or companies' seeking quick profits. The public interest will best be served if performance contracting is used as a legal tool for institutional reform so that schools can increase their ability to meet their responsibilities to their state, their students, and themselves.

Testing for Accountability

RALPH W. TYLER

Norm-referenced tests, which measure the relative standing of one student with others, are not adequate for use as accountability measures. The small samples of knowledge assessed by these tests are poor indicators of the skills a student has learned. Changes in student scores from one testing to another may be due to chance variations. Ralph W.

Ralph W. Tyler, "Testing for Accountability," *Nation's Schools,* 86:37–39, December 1970. Reprinted by permission.

Tyler urges the use of criterion-referenced tests, and an 85 percent mastery of the items as reliable indicators of achievement.

The growing concern about accountability has put new emphasis on measuring what and how much a student has learned in a short period of time. To measure educational outcomes in such a period requires tests designed for this purpose—and the problem for administrators is that most tests currently available are not very suitable.

A good example of the problem is in the area of performance contracting, where schools contract for instruction with private companies on a fee arrangement based on student performance. Since it appears that performance contracts will generally be let to cover students considered to be low achievers from disadvantaged environments, the standard achievement tests in common use do not furnish a dependable measure of how much these children have learned during one school year or less.

They were not constructed to do so.

A typical achievement test is explicitly designed to furnish scores that will arrange the pupils on a line from those most proficient in the subject to those least proficient. The final test questions have been selected from a much larger initial number on the basis of tryouts and are the ones which most sharply distinguished pupils in the tryouts who made high scores on the total test from those who made low scores. Test questions were eliminated if most pupils could answer them or if few pupils could answer them, since these did not give much discrimination.

As a result, a large part of the questions retained for the final form of a standard test are those that 40 to 60 percent of the children were able to answer. There are very few questions that represent the things being learned either by the slower learners or the more advanced ones. If a less advanced student is actually making progress in his learning, the typical standard test furnishes so few questions that represent what he has been learning that it will not afford a dependable measure for him. The same holds true for advanced learners.

This is not a weakness in the test in serving the purpose for which it was designed. The children who made lower scores had generally learned fewer things in this subject than those who made higher scores and could, therefore, be dependably identified as less proficient. Furthermore, a good standard test has been administered to one or more carefully selected samples, usually national, regional or urban samples, of children in the grade for which the test was designed. The scores obtained from these samples provide norms for the test against which a child's score can be related.

These tests—called *norm-referenced tests*—thus provide dependable information about where the child stands in his total test performance in relation to the norm group. But when one seeks to find out whether a student who made a low score has learned certain things during the year, the test does not include enough questions covering the material on which he was working to furnish a dependable answer to that question.

This leads to another problem encountered when one attempts to measure what a child learns in a school year or less. In the primary grades, particularly, each child's learning is dependent on what he had already learned before the year began and what sequence he follows. For example, in reading, some children enter the first grade already able to read simple children's stories and newspaper paragraphs. Measures of what they learn during the first year should be based on samples of reading performance that go beyond this entry level.

On the other extreme, some children enter the first grade with a limited oral vocabulary and without having distinguished the shapes of letters or noted differences in their sounds. Measures of what such a child learns during the first year must take off from his entering performance and be based on the learning sequence used in his school to help him acquire the vocabulary and language skills that are involved in the later stages of reading instruction.

A standardized test, however, is designed to be used in schools throughout the nation, despite the different learning sequences they have and with children coming from a variety of backgrounds and at various stages of learning in the field covered by the test. For this reason, it cannot include enough questions appropriate to each child's stage of development to measure reliably what he has learned during a single school year.

Recognizing the norm-referenced tests can provide dependable information on the relative standing of children, but cannot reliably measure what a child has learned or how much he has learned in a year or less, efforts are now under way to construct and utilize tests that are designed to sample specified knowledge, skills and abilities and to report what the child knows and can do of those matters specified. Since the criterion for a performance contract is that each child will learn specified things, a test that samples them is called a *criterion-referenced* test.

For example, in primary reading, the children who enter without having learned to distinguish letters and sounds might be tested by the end of the year on letter recognition, association of letters with sounds, and word-recognition of 100 most common words. For each of these specified "things to be learned," the child would be presented with a large enough sample of examples to furnish reliable evidence that he could recognize the letters of the alphabet, he could associate the appropriate sounds with each letter, alone and in words, and he could recognize the 100 most common words. A child has demonstrated mastery of specified knowledge, ability or skill when he performs correctly 85 percent of the time. (Some small allowance, like 15 percent, is needed for lapses common to all people.)

At a higher level of initial performance, a group of children may be expected to read and comprehend typical newspaper paragraphs, simple directions for making or doing something, etc. Similar specifications are made in arithmetic and in writing. Science and the social studies represent greater problems because of the variations in content and the lack of agreement on essential objectives.

The National Assessment of Educational Progress utilizes criterion-referenced tests and reports to the public about the performance of various categories of children and youth rather than individuals. The public is given the percentage of each group—9 year olds, 13 year olds, 17 year olds, and young adults—who know certain facts, can use certain principles in explaining phenomena, are able to do certain things. The reports reveal the exercises that were used and give the percent of each group who answered the question correctly or who demonstrated the ability or skill involved. The public can get a better grasp of what children and youth are learning by these reports than by trying to interpret abstract scores.

The need for criterion-referenced tests is particularly acute when a contractor undertakes to aid the education of disadvantaged children. Currently used standard tests are not satisfactory tools to appraise the learning of disadvantaged children that can be expected in a single school year. Because most of the disadvantaged begin the year at much earlier stages than a majority of pupils, the standard tests developed for that grade include very few questions that represent what these children are learning.

For this reason, when such a test is given at the beginning of the year and a second test at the end of the year, the changes in score for an individual child may largely be chance variations, since both scores are based on very small samples of knowledge, abilities or skills to which these children could respond. Furthermore, since the number of questions on which the initial score is based is small, coaching for these particular items can give a large relative gain. For example, if a child answered four questions correctly in the initial test, being able to answer four more in the final test will place him very much higher on the relative score of a standard test than would a gain of four points when his initial score was 40.

This fact increases the temptation for coaching in the case of contracts involving disadvantaged children. Criterion-referenced tests constructed for the learning sequences actually being followed will include a much larger sample of appropriate questions.

Although there are few criterion-referenced tests presently available, if performance contracting continues to expand rapidly, both schools and contractors will soon recognize that they do not have the tests they need to furnish dependable measures of performance. Publishers may well respond by a crash program of criterion-referenced test development.

How OEO will test

The Office of Economic Opportunity's $6.5 million experiment with performance contracting to teach reading and math in Grades 1 to 3 and 7 to 9 could act as a catalyst in the development of new testing technics. OEO officials are watching to see how highly individualized criterion-referenced tests will be developed for and administered to nearly 11,000 students under learning programs with six education companies.

This type of test has never been given before on such a large scale, according to OEO officials. OEO Project Director Jeffry Schiller feels that at least 500 separate criterion-referenced tests will have to be developed for the 10,800 pupils in the project's so-called "experimental groups."

These tests will be used in determining up to 25 percent of the payments for student performance to the companies. Scores on *standardized* tests will determine payments on the other 75 percent. In three school districts involving performance contracts with teachers' groups (see page 83), all of the payments will be determined by standardized tests.

The testing is being handled by the Battelle Memorial Institute of Columbus, Ohio, under a two-year $614,000 contract with OEO. The first year of testing will determine payments and evaluate the progress of the students in the experiment. The second year of testing will help determine skill retention.

Under the criterion-referenced tests, also called by OEO "interim performance objective tests," a student must reach a certain level of proficiency in the reading or math program he is using in order for the company to receive maximum payment. These tests will be administered five times during the school year at about six-week intervals.

The curriculum objectives around which these tests are developed, as well as the items which constitute each of the five tests, were submitted by each of the teaching companies to Battelle on the opening day of school. Each education company also had to provide a written justification explaining the relationship between the individual items and the curriculums. This data arrived at Battelle "literally in crates," according to Schiller.

Ultimately, each company, Battelle and OEO must agree on what individual items reflect a fair and relevant test of the specified curriculums. The company then puts together a test for each child from these test items.

Scoring of the criterion-referenced tests will be done by hand, since individualized tests do not lend themselves to the scanning possible in marking standardized achievement tests.

Battelle must provide each school with a listing of each child and the differences between pre and post performance on both the criterion-referenced tests and the standardized tests. Progress on standardized tests will be translated into grade-level increases, as measured by national norms.

To avoid "teaching to the test," OEO has developed an elaborate procedure for giving *standardized* tests. Each of the contractors submitted three such tests. At the beginning of the school year, Battelle assigned these tests among three groups of students in each class. These three pretests were given at least ten days after schools opened.

Different forms of the same standardized tests will be given at the end of the school year to the same student groups. When the standardized tests are given, all identifying information on the tests themselves will be blanked out.

Also, Battelle will carry out evaluations of the program not translatable into contractor payments. These include an opinion survey among parents on perception of the school. Battelle will also interview some 50 ninth-graders in the experimental group, 50 in the control, and 50 in the comparison groups at all 21 sites. These surveys, at the end of the year, are designed to assess attitudes toward school and feelings toward the experimental program.

Performance Objectives:
Foundation for Evaluation

FLOYD L. McKINNEY and ALFRED J. MANNEBACH

The authors here discuss development of performance objectives as a necessary requisite for accountability. Although the article applies to vocational agriculture, the strategy of development is such that it could be readily transferred to other areas of the curriculum. In addi-

Floyd L. McKinney and Alfred J. Mannebach, "Performance Objectives: Foundations for Evaluation," *Agricultural Education Magazine*, 42:301–302, June 1970. Reprinted by permission.

tion to suggestions for clearly stating performance objectives, the authors discuss sources of objectives, the need to define levels of performance, and the assessment of the worth or value of an objective.

As the public depends increasingly on education to solve its social and technical problems, it also increases its expectation of the quality of educational product which is to be produced. Today, there is an increasing emphasis on accountability. More frequently we are seeing the public demand performance and refusing to accept promises. Agricultural education is not and should not be excluded from the increasing public interest in accountability.

Most teachers of vocational agriculture have a high interest in program evaluation. But faced with a toughening public attitude toward educational accountability and with what many of those outside of agriculture describe as a rapidly deteriorating industry, our tools for evaluation may need some sharpening and refining.

BASIS FOR EVALUATION

Upon what basis can we determine student progress and the success of the local program of vocational agriculture? What are the criteria against which evaluations should be made? How can the teacher of agriculture insure that he is meeting the needs of students and the community?

Educators are placing more and more stress on the importance of evaluating student progress and programs on the basis of explicitly defined objectives. If objectives are stated in measurable performance terms, it is much easier to determine the degree of attainment of the behavior specified.

The development of well defined, measurable objectives is a crucial aspect of evaluation. Evaluation should be conducted in light of stated objectives rather than solely on the basis of outside criterion such as other programs of agriculture or the opinion of an "outside expert." Using objectives as a basis for evaluation, however, precludes that the objectives developed are relevant, explicit, measurable, and well defined.

PERFORMANCE OBJECTIVES

What is a performance objective and how can the development of performance objectives help the teacher of agriculture in the classroom? A performance objective is an objective which uses an action verb and specifies the conditions and standards of performance associated with the behavior of the student. It is a statement which specifies what the student is to do, how he will do it, under what circumstances, and to what level of proficiency.

A performance objective must be both measurable and observable. Performance objectives are of benefit to teachers because they define the level of performance which the student is to perform during the process and at the termination of the course, unit, lesson, or task. They also are stated to provide a measure of attainment of the objective. Thus the teacher will have the performance criteria to be attained by his students defined explicitly and will have a basis for measuring the degree of attainment of the objective.

Objectives are frequently confused with purposes and functions. If we state that the agricultural education program is to provide education in leadership development, we have stated a purpose of the agricultural education program. To state that the vocational agriculture department should provide a FFA chapter to enable students to practice leadership abilities is to designate a function which should be performed in school.

A performance objective related to leadership development might be stated as follows: Students will be able to conduct a fifteen minute meeting during the vocational agriculture class according to Robert's Rules of Order. This objective specifies the performance desired (conduct a meeting according to Robert's Rule of Order) within a specified time element (fifteen minutes).

An example of a poor objective might be to "know about fertilizers." What does this objective tell us? How will we measure whether or not the student "knows" about fertilizers? A more appropriately stated objective is: Given the soil test results for a ten-acre field, the crop to be produced, the yield and profit desired, calculate within the next fifteen minutes the amount and kind of fertilizer needed. In this example the behavior expected is stated in performance terms, a realistic situation is assumed, and the teacher could logically determine whether or not the objective was attained. Evaluation, then, can be based upon the attainment or degree of attainment of the objective.

LEVELS OF OBJECTIVES

Objectives in agricultural education can be found at many levels. Important to the teacher are objectives at the national, state, and local levels. As one moves from the local to the national level, objectives by necessity become more general. Teachers of agriculture also have less influence on objectives at the state and national levels. The broad objectives of the agricultural education program with further delineation in course objectives, unit objectives, and daily lesson objectives should receive major consideration and attention of the teacher of vocational agriculture.

Regardless of the hierarchical stage of objectives with which one is concerned, it is well to remember that we should attempt to state the objective so that it reflects a level of proficiency which will be required of the student for effective use later in life. Frequently, objectives are stated which lead students to believe that it is important only to perform well on the quarterly or course examination. Today's students are interested, and agricultural educators proclaim to be interested, in the development of skills that will contribute to the full realization of an individual's potential as a citizen and wage earner. Follow-up studies of former students and employer surveys will need to be used more frequently to account for the long-range performance of former students.

DEVELOPING OBJECTIVES

Objectives are derived from many sources. Objectives emerge from the needs of individuals and the needs of society. The teacher's experiences and the statements of authoritative individuals, societies, and agencies will influence the objectives. If we were to consider a unit regarding agricultural sales and service, our first task might be to determine the competencies needed by a prospective employee and the present level of knowledge of the individual. In our hypothetical situation, it is feasible to speculate that the individual will need to know how to complete a bill of sale. This, then, becomes the basis for stating a performance objective.

Once the objective has been derived, the specifications for the objective must be developed. Remember, we should know what the student is to do, how he will do it, under what circumstances, and to what level of proficiency.

What is the student to do? The student should be able to write a bill of sale.

How will the student perform this activity? The student will use a pencil and regular commercial bills of sale.

Under what circumstances will the students perform? He will perform the activity in a store, under normal sales conditions with a minimum of wasted time.

What level of proficiency will the student achieve? The student will complete the bill of sale so that it is legible and free of errors.

The performance objective might now be stated: Given a situation where a customer has purchased six items, write a bill of sale in five minutes which is free of errors and legible.

Writing a bill of sale represents a very small portion of the total part of an agricultural sales and services unit. There will be many other objectives to determine and specify. Once all possible objectives have been determined the teacher will be confronted with selecting the most important objectives. There will not be time to teach every-thing. Students, citizens, and the teacher should decide jointly the most important objectives.

Once the objective has been derived, specified, and selected, it must be implemented. The activities and functions necessary to accomplish the performance specified in the objective must be identified and put into action. It is the responsibility of the teacher to provide the optimum learning environment to implement the objective.

ASSESSMENT

Our final consideration is assessment or evaluation. In evaluation the teacher should be concerned about the worth or value of the objective. Is the performance or behavior specified in the objective valid and realistic? An evaluation procedure should be developed that will provide feedback on the attainment of the objective. Evaluation may take place at many stages of the learner's career. It is important to have feedback at the time of teaching and follow-up information regarding the value of the performance specified in the objective after the student is employed.

The success of programs of agricultural education depends upon the success of the enrollees attaining the desired outcomes of the program. It is essential that the outcomes desired be specified in performance terms. Only when agricultural educators and others evaluate agricul-tural education programs on the basis of student's performance in relation to valid and realistic performance objectives will progress be made in educational program improvement.

Performance Contracting Is a Hoax!

GIRARD D. HOTTLEMAN

Girard D. Hottleman is opposed to the entire concept of educational accountability on terms imposed by groups other than teachers. He makes his case for opposing performance contracts, calling them ma-chinations of the new "industrial-education" complex established by accountability panderers practicing the new black art of profit con-tracting. His revelations of the relationships between former U.S. Office of Education employees and private learning corporations lend substance to his point of view.

Girard D. Hottleman, "Performance Contracting Is a Hoax!" *The Massachusetts Teacher*, pp. 4–10, April 1971. Reprinted by permission.

I'm just a meanderin', panderin' mandarin
And a helluva engineer" . . . old drinking song from Georgia

"I'm a messenger
From Leon Lessinger
Proclaiming the accountability news.
I'm just a meanderin', panderin' mandarin
And you'll pay, pay, pay for my views." . . . new song from Georgia,
   guaranteed to drive you to drink.

Leon M. Lessinger, former associate commissioner of education, United States Office of Education, and now Callaway Professor of Education at Georgia State University, has been variously described as the founder, father, or midwife of the concept of educational accountability. He is also a leading advocate of performance contracting as one means of gaining accountability in education.[1]

Dr. Lessinger contends that taxpayers are greatly concerned, even more so than usual, about whether or not they are getting the maximum value for their dollars. He quotes President Nixon to buttress his point:

> . . . From these considerations we derive another new concept: accountability. School administrators and school teachers alike are responsible for their performance, and it is in their interest as well as in the interests of their pupils that they be held accountable.[2]

Incidentally, the President in his message on education also called for an end to increasing education expenditures until we can be assured that we are getting maximum value for those expenditures.

Dr. Lessinger and President Nixon share several things in common besides their years of government service, but their major common belief seems to be that the best method of improving the value of the educational dollar is to reduce the amount actually spent on educating children. For example, the President this year has appropriated $6.5 million to private profit-making industries from his budget in the Office of Economic Opportunity (administered directly from the White House Budget) for the purpose of performance contracting. (A performance contract is an agreement between a school governing body and a contractor in which the contractor agrees to produce specified rates of learning for specified rates of pay. Any residue of payment above cost is profit.)

Lessinger's plan for greater economy is as follows: He says the LEA should hire an MSG to produce a RFP with a performance contract, and this should be evaluated by an IEAA.

Baffled? Don't be. Remember, Dr. L. worked at O.E. at H.E.W. in

Wash., D.C. One hesitates to conjecture, but apparently, that, combined with the rarefied atmosphere of Academia in Georgia, tends to produce this kind of Scrabblese. Let me walk you through again:

Dr. Lessinger says that the Local Education Agency (LEA) should hire a Management Support Group (MSG) who would produce a request for a proposal (RFP) with a Performance Contractor (PC?), and that the whole operation should be evaluated by an Independent Education Accomplishment Audit (IEAA).[3] That's how we save money in education and produce results.

Let me review:

1. We pay a new group (MSG) to produce a proposal.
2. We pay a new group, a profit-making corporation to carry out the proposal.
3. We pay a new group (IEAA) to evaluate the proposal.

Shazam! Reduced costs.

Even with five years of Jesuit logic behind me, I still don't understand it, but there it is. We add a group of university or private business consultants to our payroll to help us hire a group of university or private business implements, and we hire a group of university or private business consultants to evaluate what the previous consultants have done, and we reduce our costs.

A WORLD OF FICTION

Compared to Dr. Lessinger, Isaac Asimov and Rod Serling are rank amateurs in the world of imaginative fiction.

Since both the NEA and the AFT have taken strong positions against performance contracting as it is currently being implemented,[4] we can assume that teachers everywhere will be faced with the usual accusation of "logjamming" that we encounter every time we oppose the most recent pontification that issues from the latest version of Mt. Olympus.* The arguments this time, however, will be much stronger

---

* For example, Donald Rumsfeld, formerly with OEO and now a White House assistant in responding to NEA and AFT's attacks on Lessinger's new pet theory, said, "A major effort has been mounted by a handful of self-appointed education spokesmen to halt any inquiry into the possibility of educational reform. I doubt that these people speak for most teachers."

In a recent speech in San Francisco (See Boston Globe, Feb. 28, 1971) speaking further of professional organizations of teachers, he said, "They reject the idea of accountability and want to ensure that their paychecks . . . are maintained regardless of what is achieved in the classroom." Although Mr. Rumsfeld is not an enthusiastic teacher advocate, he does have some accurate insights. For example, in that same San Francisco speech, speaking of his disappointment with the results of five years of federal funding, he said, "The poor have grown cynical. They are fed

than before and they will be framed by more sophisticated propagandists than ever before, because a lot of people stand to make a lot of money if this particular pontification is sold.[5] Also, the credentials of the new pontificators will be, in many cases, "impeccable." Consider for example the significant increase in income that will become immediately available to university consultants if Lessinger's concept of a M.S.G. and an I.E.A.A. were to be adopted on a wholesale basis. For example, Dr. Lessinger himself is currently being sought by several school boards who desire his services as a consultant to help them prepare performance contracts.[6] Also, he is a consultant to a firm established to audit the production quality of public schools, the Education Audit Institute, Washington, D.C.[7] I am by no means attempting to impugn the personal motives of Dr. Lessinger, but it is true that he is the major spokesman for the "accountability movement" and it is also true that if the movement moves according to his design, he will probably benefit significantly. Based on this knowledge, I merely allude to an old principle in Rhetoric I—"Consider the source."

The accountability and performance contracting movements are literally littered with mutual backslapping by those within the business. For example: "He (Leon Lessinger) wishes to acknowledge Charles Blaschke of Educational Turnkey Systems . . . for (his) valuable insights and assistance."[8]

"Blaschke gives much of the credit to Dr. Leon Lessinger, former associate commissioner of education, for beginning the Texarkana project . . ."[9]

"Texarkana is the most successful dropout prevention program in history,"[10] said Lessinger. (The Texarkana project was designed by Blaschke.)

Blaschke (who now holds a $600,000 contract from OEO as the overall consultant to the OEO performance contracting experiments) and Lessinger are both alumni from the federal agencies which are now funding performance contracts. Blaschke's route was Pentagon to OEO to founder of Education Turnkey Systems, which now holds the $600,000 contract with OEO. Lessinger's route was superintendent of schools to HEW (OE) to Georgia State and consultant to Education Audit Institute. When Lessinger took over as Associate Commissioner

---

up with promises not kept . . ." Rumsfeld's answer to the cynicism of the poor is, of course, to transfer O.E.O. and O.E. money to Westinghouse and Thiokol Chemical. This magic plan will no doubt produce the same level of reduced cynicism that occurred when former U.S. Commissioner Allen announced the "Right to Read" campaign only to find that Nixon insiders refused to appropriate any money to fund it. The "Right to Read" campaign was to be the keystone of the Nixon thrust at H.E.W. When is the last time you heard that slogan?

for Elementary and Secondary Education, "he vowed to bring accountability to federal aid programs administered by his bureau."[11] Like Blaschke, he spent his term of office promoting his philosophy and imbuing his government agency with his own personal stamp. And like Blaschke, he left after a short stay only to become immersed in the contracting business recently adopted at his insistence.

THIOKOL AND SULLIVAN

Another Damon and Pythias team has turned up in Massachusetts Commissioner of Education Dr. Neil V. Sullivan and the Thiokol Chemical Corporation. Speaking to a joint meeting of the Massachusetts Association of School Committees and the Massachusetts Association of School Superintendents on Oct. 14, 1970, Sullivan said,

> Industry has finally gotten its feet wet in the billion dollar enterprise called education. I not only applaud this involvement, but I urge each and every one of you here this evening to do all you can to sustain this partnership.[12]

Thiokol holds a $208,000 contract in the Dallas schools. On Tuesday, Dec. 8, 1970, Dr. Sullivan spent the morning visiting the Thiokol program at James Madison High School in Dallas. On Tuesday afternoon at a press conference, Dr. Sullivan said, "It is an exciting innovation and I'm very enthused by the student reaction. I like it very much."[13] Dr. Sullivan omitted revealing that he was a paid consultant of Thiokol until after the admission was brought about by questions from the Dallas Times Herald. "I'm a Thiokol consultant and have been for many years," he conceded.[14] Superintendent Nolan Estes withdrew tapes of the news interview when the discovery was made that Sullivan was on Thiokol's payroll. Dr. Estes had "become suspicious" of Dr. Sullivan "when he (Sullivan) saw everything good and nothing bad."[15] "It just puts a shadow over everything,"[16] Estes said.*

Another shadow loomed large in the precedent-setting Texarkana performance contract. Designed by Blaschke, praised by Lessinger, and run by Dorsett Educational Systems of Norman, Okla., the Texarkana project made national headlines when it was disclosed by evaluator Dean C. Andrew that there had been direct teaching of test items to

---

* A telephone call by MTA to the *Dallas Times-Herald* revealed that Sullivan's appearance in Dallas had been preceded by a telephone call, a letter, and a telegram from the New York–based public relations firm of Zobel & Jacobs. None of the three releases mentioned Sullivan's relation with Thiokol. Zobel & Jacobs later revealed that they were acting as the public relations firm for Thiokol. Similarly, the Dallas paper discovered that School Superintendent Estes (also a former associate commissioner of education at HEW and a strong advocate of performance contracting, by the way) had no knowledge of Sullivan's relationship with Thiokol.

such an extent that the test results could not be used as a valid measure of achievement.[17] Further investigation revealed that the programmer, Rosella Scott, who resigned in April, 1970, to found her own company, was the sister of President Lloyd G. Dorsett.[18] "I did everything I could to see that company made money on the project,"[19] she said. She readily admitted that "teaching to the test" occurred. But, she said, this was largely to compensate for some low I.Q. students enrolled despite prior agreement that Dorsett would be working with normal I.Q. youngsters.[20]

A GROWING PRACTICE

Despite the resistance by experienced teachers and despite the widespread knowledge of the highly questionable practices of the advocates, performance contracting threatens to grow in leaps and bounds. One sure indicator is the recent announcement by OE official Albert Mayrhofer that, "Expenditures for management support, outside evaluation, outside audits and performance contracts are legitimate under Titles I and III of ESEA."[21]

Another significant omen can be seen through analysis of the background of the 16 newly-appointed top aides to Commissioner of Education Sidney P. Marland Jr. Not one is a teacher and four of the top aides are not educators at all, but systems analysts hired out of such places as the Rand Corporation. Interestingly enough, with the accountability panderers calling for outside audits, OEO chose the Rand Corporation (at a cost of $300,000) to evaluate the 18 projects currently let out to other corporations, despite the widescale availability of qualified educational research units from the non-industrial sector. Rand is a well-known systems management firm whose executives are already publishing articles publicizing performance contracting.[22]

In case you've forgotten, all this money that is going to Rand and Westinghouse and Thiokol and Singer-Graflex is out of the "poverty" budget at OEO. Now that Mayrhofer has opened up the Title I money, the corporations will also have access to the billion-dollar appropriation for disadvantaged students. Oh, the burden that the poor place on our society!

THE REAL ISSUES

The real issues in the "accountability movement" are far more significant than the wholesale emergence of the new educational profiteers, and far more important than any question of the respectability of the methods by which the advocates of the "movement" attempt to make it popular. As teachers, we ask only one question—will the accountability-performance contracting movement improve the education of children?

It is this author's contention that it will not. As a matter of fact it is most obviously apparent from an examination of the literature that the performance contracting industry will prove to be harmful to children.

One of the major reasons for this conclusion is the obvious lack of understanding of the education establishment by the practitioners of this new black art. For example, Lessinger asserts, "Professionalism . . . goes hand in hand with accountability; with clear-cut proof of performance. And in education we have time and again refused to produce that proof."[23]

Another advocate, J. D. Comas, dean, College of Education, University of Tennessee, Knoxville,* pronounces: "Public institutions always have had a moral obligation to be accountable. However, an examination of practices in public education often reveals that educators have hidden schools from the public by a selective system of communication and public relations."[24]

This kind of criticism, often stated by the performance contract advocates, that the teaching profession has refused to be accountable, is nothing more than pious, pompous pap. It is inaccurate. It is the pandering of the new self-appointed, would-be educational mandarins. Since teachers have been systematically and deliberately denied any meaningful role in the decision-making apparatus of public education, they are obviously not accountable for the mess we're in.

At this writing, the New York City School Board has just announced its intention to lay off 6500 city school teachers. Who's accountable for that move? And who will be accountable for the subsequent drop in educational quality?

School boards deal with money. Superintendents deal with money. The Federal Government deals with money. Thiokol Chemical Corporation deals with money. But teachers deal with children. It may warm the hackles of an assembled group of tax guardians to hear Commissioner Sullivan refer to education as "a billion dollar enterprise." It may be very reassuring to the hundreds of panting corporations to hear Lessinger calling for "educational engineering." But all the new jargon in the new lexicon will not resolve the basic issue that the new

---

* Readers who are as interested in moral obligations and public relations as Dr. Comas purports to be also might be interested in the September issue of *Esquire* magazine. (Wills, G., *How Nixon Used the Media, Billy Graham, and the Good Lord to Rap with Students at Tennessee University*, p. 119–122.) This carefully documents the cooperation of the University of Tennessee in engineering the Nixon-Billy Graham public relations charade to convince America that college youth still loves the Nixon administration despite the then recent Kent State shootings.

mandarins are trying to avoid—education is woefully underfunded. More money is needed, much more money, and so is a substantially more powerful place for teachers in the school hierarchy. What is not needed are new ways to excuse the refusal of a society with inverted values to avoid its responsibility to school children.

THE POLLUTED CHILD

Another reason to fear the performance contracting menace is because of the ultimately harmful effects of the usual process of education that is employed by most of the projects. It becomes obvious that it is not performance contracting at all, but profit contracting—and the kids are the waste products.

We have finally reached the age where we are about to sanction the wholesale production of the polluted child. The approach is almost universally mechanistic, automated, programmed, and built on extrinsic rewards. The Bronx project is typical. If a student learns at a predetermined accelerated rate (and by the way, what is being "taught" there are narrowly defined skills) he may earn enough green stamps to get a toy gun. "Why do you learn, Johnny?" "To get a gun, of course." When measurement becomes king and profit the motive, reading, for example, does not become "reading for pleasure" or "reading for appreciation" or "reading for leisure" or "understanding," but straight de-coding or "reading for profit."

Consider the obvious conditioning of a child caught up in the grip of a profit contractor. "If I can learn this thing called 'Hamlet' well enough and fast enough, I might double my green stamp reward." Many well-qualified educators have expressed themselves on this in an effort to prevent too many children from being crushed by the new runaway juggernaut.

Herbert M. Kliebard, professor at the University of Wisconsin, describes how the schools have taken on the principles of scientific management and have become "dominated by the criterion of social utility"[25] which results in channeling students into predetermined slots in the social order:

> "Modern curriculum theory, currently being influenced by systems analysis, tends to regard the child simply as input inserted into one end of a great machine, from which he eventually emerges at the other end as output replete with all the behaviors, the 'competencies,' and the skills for which he has been programmed." Says Kliebard, "Even when the output is differentiated, such a mechanistic conception of education contributes only to man's regimentation and dehumanization, rather than to his autonomy."

The problem lies not so much in ferreting out the details of this new movement toward wholesale charlatanism, since many competent educators will be doing that, but in finding effective weapons to combat it.

Teachers are always at a disadvantage in the war of propaganda vs. truth because schools represent, generally, more than half of the tax rate of any local municipality. The politically ambitious and the special interest representatives who frequently populate school boards recognize this, and pander to the taxpayers' fiscal pains at every opportunity. Personal short-term gains are made at the considerable sacrifice of the quality of the future lives of succeeding generations. Only teachers can thwart this continuous long-standing lack of accountability displayed by those who have so long reserved power over schools for their own ends. It is time to hold them accountable.

Lessinger, for example, points with horror at the school's record: "Today, about one of every four American children drops out of school . . . hundreds of thousands of parents . . . have decided that their children are *not* stupid—that either some educators are incompetent, or that methods they are using are inadequate."[26]

This kind of statement is typical of the leaders of the new industrial-education complex. Tell the parents that teachers have cheated their children. Get the community angry enough and they'll beg for industry to solve their problems.

THE MYTH OF INDUSTRIAL SANCTITY

Before parents dial the hot line to industrial headquarters, perhaps we had better remind ourselves again about the humanitarian track record that profit-making corporations have compiled in their race to make America more productive: Lake Erie is dead; food companies are now selling their cyclamate reserves to overseas markets; the major car companies recall thousands of defective cars each year; no one eats fish any more without feeling anxious. Despite all this, a wholesale indictment of industry in America would not only be unfair, it would be inaccurate. Yet the fact remains that industry makes mistakes and industry has done extensive damage to our public good. Industry is no panacea. Furthermore the industrial mind-set (profit first/humanity second) has led to some appalling behavior that is totally unacceptable to experienced educators:

> *Item:* In Hartford, Conn., where Alpha Systems, Inc. holds the contract, a serious proposal (rejected by the teachers) was made that pinball machines and slot machine pool tables be installed in the schools. Children would be permitted access to these recreational outlets as a

reward for learning, with a portion of the money in the till to go to the school system and a portion to the performance contractor.

Item: In the Bronx, where Learning Foundations (one of Fran Tankerton's major economic interests) holds the contract, children were pre-tested in one large group in an assembly hall at 95 degrees temperature for five hours in one day. Learning Foundations' rate of payment depends upon the difference between the initial pre-test score and later scores computed from tests conducted under much more favorable circumstances. Also, the Bronx project incorporates a reward system of green stamps for learning (a common practice among performance contractors). Children are given a cheaply-printed company catalog displaying toy guns and other merchandise which is used to motivate achievement.

In addition to these bizarre practices, in almost all performance contracting experiments, the pupil-teacher ratio has been drastically increased by adding low paid para-professionals and reducing the number of professional teachers. (Now do you understand the school board's interest?) The money saved goes to the high-priced consultants that Lessinger advocates (10 to 15 percent of the total cost of a contract) and to the hoped-for profit margin. The major ingredients of most contracted experiments are machine-oriented programmed materials, and extrinsic reward systems (tokens, recreation time, green stamps, color TV sets, The American Way.)

WHERE TEACHERS STAND

Despite the pious pandering of the educational critics, these facts remain: Schools have been controlled not by teachers, but by school boards. Curriculum decisions, pupil-teacher ratios, availability of special services, availability of adequate text-books, materials, equipment, etc., have always been touted as "management prerogatives." The shallow thinking that historically created the image of the teacher as a public servant, directed by the whim of elected laymen, has led to the wholesale abuse of talent that has created the horrendous statistics of failure which any cavalier critic of education can easily cite. These statistics are the product of irresponsible school boards who have always had the power to enact change and who, in fact, have not. There can be no accountability without power. School boards have had the power; they are accountable when teachers gain power over professional practices they will be accountable. But that time has not arrived—yet.

The time has arrived to end the unfair exposure that teachers have been subject to because they have been forced to teach under intolerable conditions.

The time has also arrived to end the drastically inferior conditions of education that have frustrated and cheated so many children. We must tell our school boards forcefully and, if need be, dramatically that we will not permit them to hide their irresponsibility behind the comfortable and deceiving illusion which the new catchwords, "accountability," and "performance contracting," really are.

We have for years been our own most active critics. We have been very deeply aware of the shortcomings of public education. We have repeatedly suggested what is needed to improve education, and our suggestions have been rejected. What is needed is not Lessinger's managerial triple play or Rumsfeld's double talk or Thiokol Chemical Corporation or green stamps, but the implementation of the suggestions of experienced teachers.

Since school boards won't listen, let us, as the critics have done, go to the community. We must fully inform the local communities, in paid advertisements if necessary, of the needs of children. We must also inform them that it is their elected representatives who are responsible for the failure of children, not us. When we request additional specialists, reduced class size, time for curriculum revision, opportunity for individualizing instruction, improved diagnostic and placement services, and money in the budget for curriculum experimentation or instructional improvement, and we are refused, we must notify the community at large that we have offered to be accountable and our offer has been refused.

When the day finally arrives when school boards become accountable to their public trust by permitting the conditions necessary for any real degree of teacher accountability to exist, the problems so glibly catalogued by the critics will begin to be solved. But in the meantime, let the pandering mandarins go peddle their green stamps elsewhere.

FOOTNOTES

1. Lessinger, Leon, "Engineering Accountability for Results in Public Education." *Phi Delta Kappan,* December, 1970, pp. 217–225.

2. President Richard M. Nixon, Education Message of 1970. As cited by Lessinger, Leon, "Robbing Peter to Pay Paul": Accounting for Our Stewardship of Public Education, *Educational Technology,* January, 1971.

3. Op. cit.

4. See *Policy Statement by the NEA Executive Committee on Performance Contracting,* Dec. 5, 1970, and the *American Teacher,* Jan. 1971, pp. 20, 21.

5. For example, a spokesman for the Wall Street firm of Dominick & Dominick told a recent conference called to promote private investment in pre-school day care centers that "the education area is the last remaining capital investment industry" with "significant long term thrust." (See the *American Teacher,* Sept. 1970.)

6. Report of NEA Resource Committee on Performance Contracts, an unpublished paper, p. 7.

7. Sigel, E. and Sobel, Myra, *Accountability and the Controversial Role of the Performance Contractor*, Knowledge Industry Publications, Tiffany Towers, White Plains, N.Y. 10602, p. 39.

8. Editor's note prefacing Lessinger, Leon, "Engineering Accountability for Results in Public Education," *Phi Delta Kappan*, Dec. 1970, p. 217.

9. *The Sunday Star*, Washington, D.C., July 19, 1970, Mathews, John "Contracting to Teach Opens Education Era."

10. Sigel, op. cit., p. 11.

11. Sigel, op. cit., p. 1.

12. Sullivan, Neil V., *MASC Journal*, "Survive—or Thrive?" December, 1970, p. 5.

13. *Dallas Times Herald*, Wednesday, Dec. 9, 1970.

14. Ibid.

15. Ibid.

16. Ibid.

17. *The Washington Post*, Sept. 20, 1970, Wentworth, Eric, "Teaching Experiment Is Dropped."

18. *Washington Post*, op. cit.

19. Ibid.

20. Ibid.

21. Sigel, op. cit., p. 48.

22. See Barrio, Stephen (an economist with the Rand Corporation), "An Approach to Developing Accountability Measures for the Public Schools," *Phi Delta Kappan*, Dec. 1970, p. 196–205.

23. *Educational Technology*, op. cit., p. 13.

24. Op. cit. p. 31.

25. See Haubrich, Vernon F., ed., "Fredom, Bureaucracy and Schooling," *A.S.C.D.*, *Yearbook*, 1971, NEA, Washington D.C.

26. *Educational Technology*, op. cit., p. 13.

ADDENDUM: Portrait of a Steamroller about To Go into Third Gear

As we are about to go to press, we have received the most recent report from the highly influential Committee for Economic Development entitled *Education for the Urban Disadvantaged*.

CED is composed of 200 leading businessmen and educators who cite as one of their basic objectives "to develop through *objective* research . . . for private and public policy (to achieve) steady economic growth at high employment and reasonably stable prices . . . providing greater and more equal opportunity for every citizen, and improving the quality of life for all."

The Board of Trustees of CED consists of 90 chairmen of the boards of directors of the largest corporations in America, 20 Vice-chairmen, 56 Board presidents, five partners, five board members, 14 educators, and 22 others, not identified by position.

Corporations included are: S&H Green Stamps, Westinghouse, Xerox, General Motors, Ford, Standard Oil, and numerous other giants. Their latest objective report (which lists Leon Lessinger as an advisor[1]) says: "Educators too often have rationalized poor school performance by labeling students 'slow,' 'unmotivated,' or 'retarded.' They have convinced themselves that the fault is not theirs. . . ."[2]

The report then calls for education to be held accountable and urges that financial support be tied to actual productivity. It then continues: "To illustrate a few possible modes, we call attention to the proposals of a leading advocate of accountability, Leon M. Lessinger . . ."[3]

Then the report details Lessinger's scheme for performance contracting and the I.E.A.A.

FOOTNOTES

1. C.E.D., *Education for the Urban Disadvantaged*, 477 Madison Avenue, New York, N.Y. 10022, March 1971, p. 6.
2. Ibid., p. 60.
3. Ibid., p. 61.

How To Be Accountable

A FOUR-POINT PLAN FOR ACCOUNTABILITY

1. Survey the learning needs of the children in your school system.

A few appropriate questions are: Are the diagnostic systems adequate? Is there enough staff? Are there enough specialists and special programs? In the event of difficulty or failure on the part of a child, are there sufficient remediating programs available? Do teachers have adequate time to plan, think, consult, evaluate, experiment? Are adequate opportunities provided to teachers for self improvement? Are programs adequately funded? Is the system for curriculum improvement functional? Is the school system flexible enough to adapt to individual needs or changing problems quickly and effectively?

2. Based on your survey, present suggested changes in current practices to the school committee and attempt to negotiate improvements.

3. In the event of favorable results in negotiations, monitor the results closely in order to continue to improve the educational process.

4. In the event of unfavorable results in negotiations, publicize to the community your efforts to act in behalf of their children. Warn them of the impending consequences to their children brought on by the refusal of the school committee to accommodate the changes suggested by competent, professional opinion.

Education Vouchers

PETER A. JANSSEN

Arguments that favor the use of education vouchers, as well as those opposed to such a move, are presented in this article. Those favoring education vouchers believe that vouchers can break the monopoly of public elementary schools—making them more competitive, more responsive to the needs of children and the wishes of parents. The past use of vouchers in some Southern states to avoid integration while using public funds has led several civil rights groups beyond the point of rejection to condemnation of the principles underlying the voucher plan.

A student attends the elementary school nearest his home in most U.S. public school systems. The elementary school feeds into a junior high school where students come from a slightly wider area, and the junior high school, in turn, sends its graduates on to a high school which pulls students from a still larger area. There are exceptions—due to perseverance or luck—but in general, the school a student attends is determined by where he lives.

The system offers few alternatives, and most students are stuck with it. If the local school does not respond to the student's needs, or if his needs differ from his neighbor's, he can leave the system, either by moving to another school district or by enrolling in a private school. For years middle income parents have exercised exactly those options. Lower income parents, of course, can do neither. They are forced to accept the local public school as it is, and then hope—if conditions are right and their patience holds—to work for reform from within. More often, they and their children give up.

Soon, however, the range of alternatives may be broadened considerably. This would happen under a voucher system, a revolutionary concept in American public education that would allow parents to use public money to buy an education for their children at any school they choose, public, private, or parochial. Under the system, the parents of all school-age children in a community would be given a voucher roughly representing their child's share of the public school budget. The student would turn in the voucher at the school he wanted to attend; the school then would turn it in to a government agency to collect its money.

Peter A. Janssen, "Education Vouchers," *American Education*, 6: 9–11, December 1970. Reprinted by permission.

One study of the voucher concept has been developed at the Center for the Study of Public Policy in Cambridge, Mass., under two grants from the Office of Economic Opportunity. The first, in December 1969, was for $196,000; the second, in June 1970, was for $325,000.

Christopher Jencks, director of the center, says that the main argument in favor of the voucher system is that public schools are unresponsive today because they are monopolies; they have no competition. There is no place else for most urban children to go to learn how to function positively in society.

The vouchers, however, would give students a choice; if the closest school did not offer what they needed, they could go someplace else. The schools then would have to be good enough to attract students; the bad schools would be driven out of business. The proposal also has some major side effects. It would give parents a major responsibility in their children's education, and it would overcome the racial and economic limitations of the neighborhood school—unless the neighborhood school was a very good school.

The voucher system is supported by liberals and conservatives alike, ranging from psychologist Kenneth Clark and critic Paul Goodman to conservative economist Milton Friedman. Friedman, a professor of economics at the University of Chicago, says he first proposed a voucher idea in 1953 and has been pushing it ever since, because "I think parents should be free to send their children to any kind of school they want." The schools of the poor, he adds, have to improve or lose their customers the same way other schools have been losing the children of the middle class. Friedman supports vouchers because they would lead to an open market for elementary education, a competitive school economy.

Actually, proposals for some type of voucher system far predate Friedman. In 1776, Adam Smith suggested that the master of a public school should receive only part of his salary from the government. "If he was wholly or even principally paid by it," Smith said, "he would soon learn to neglect his business." A few years later, Thomas Paine proposed that State governments pay poor families a small amount to provide for the education of each child under 14. More recently, the G.I. Bill provided a type of voucher, permitting veterans to select their higher education from the college and university marketplace.

Despite this heritage, the voucher system is not without its potential problems or its powerful opponents. Civil rights organizations clearly remember that some Southern States have used vouchers to avoid integration and to channel public funds to private schools—until the Supreme Court ruled that such machinations were unconstitutional. The NAACP condemned the voucher plan in principle at its convention last July, saying, "The result would be the perpetuation of segregation in schools."

The National Education Association also is against vouchers. At its convention in July the NEA passed a resolution saying that vouchers "could lead to racial, economic, and social isolation of children and weaken or destroy the public school system." The NEA also warned that competition would widen the gap between rich and poor schools since students would desert poor schools to flow into better ones, leaving a dumping ground for students whose parents don't have the sophistication or knowledge to use the system. John M. Lumley, the NEA's assistant executive secretary for government relations and citizenship, further cautioned a Senate subcommittee that even if safeguards were built in to prevent segregation, private schools might try "hucksterism" to induce parents to patronize them.

Responding to these attacks, OEO director Donald Rumsfeld gave a speech in San Francisco charging that the opposition of some teachers' organizations "borders on the irrational" and obstructs reform. Rumsfeld pointed out that the existing public schools were not doing a satisfactory job of educating the poor. In many cities, he said, disadvantaged students score two years below grade level by the sixth grade and three grades below by the ninth grade. Rumsfeld tried to reassure civil rights groups by promising that the OEO "certainly will prohibit racial segregation or racial discrimination." Still, illustrating the intensity of feeling about the voucher proposal, Carl Megel, legislative director of the American Federation of Teachers, charged that Rumsfeld's speech was "another safari into educational fairyland."

For his part, Jencks is not too worried about the criticism. Steps to insure integration, he says, could be written into voucher plans. He also believes that the voucher system can be designed to avoid church-state problems. Several States now provide aid to parochial schools for nonreligious items such as textbooks. And Thomas K. Glennan, Jr., OEO's director of research and evaluation, says simply that OEO "is not wedded" to including parochial schools in all the pilot projects, particularly in a State that has strong requirements for church-state separation. "We would not rule out a city from participating in a voucher plan," Glennan says, "if the parochial schools do not participate."

Glennan is more worried that the system would not help the most disadvantaged students. He fears that children who need the most help are those with parents who are the least likely to hustle out with a voucher to enroll their children in a better school. Jencks responds that policymakers have assumed that middle class parents are capable of making these decisions, and they should assume that, with enough information, poor parents can make them, too.

Many of those in favor of the vouchers say that giving parents more of a sense of control over their environment—and their children's education—is a valid end in itself. The more control parents have over what happens to their children, the more responsible they will feel for the results; they also will tend to hold officials more accountable for the quality of education their children actually are getting in school.

The question of whether low income parents actually will join in selecting a school for their children is central to the success of the voucher plan. "The success of the program," Jencks says, "depends on the effectiveness of the effort to give parents some idea of what constitutes a good school and what constitutes a bad school. Some parents have a straightforward idea of what they want. Some just want to know if a school is integrated or not. Others might want whatever it is that we call quality. I'd say there isn't that much difference right now between the sophistication of most middle class parents and most poor parents. They all want good schools, but most of them aren't sure how to get them. Nobody really knows how to do that; the experts are only right 49 percent of the time."

Jencks also is unsure about how much participation is necessary for the system to work. "If only 15 percent of the parents participate," he asks, "does that justify the system? What makes it a success or a failure? We don't know yet."

The OEO isn't sure what will make the system succeed either, but it is committed to trying to find out. "I believe that there's enough potential so that the vouchers are worth trying," says Glennan. "But we're not sure under what conditions they will work. I think that the system's main advantage is that people can get some accountability. Teachers and principals will have to develop a style of education to attract and keep people in school. That style, of course, will be different in different places, depending on what parents and students want. But the schools will have to react to what people want. If a few people in a school are unhappy, if they don't like sex education or whatever, they can withdraw and go someplace else. If a large group withdraws, however, then the principal will have to react. He'll have to change something."

Glennan also hopes that the ability of a student to attend any school will promote integration. "The great benefit of the voucher system," he says, "is that blacks who are now segregated by the restrictions of housing or school boundaries could choose not to be segregated any more." The proposed OEO experiment would require that each participating school have the same proportion of minority acceptances as it had minority applicants.

The first step of a voucher system would be the creation of an Education Voucher Agency (EVA). It would be controlled locally, like a school board, but it would not operate schools. Local and State education funds, plus an increment from the Federal Government to support "compensatory" vouchers for the children of poor families, would go to the EVA to be distributed in the form of vouchers.

Federal funds would also be available to provide the additional transportation required.

In the spring, each participating school—public, private, parochial —would tell the EVA how many students it could take in the fall. It then would have to take everyone who applied. If it was oversubscribed, half its enrollment would be filled by a lottery. No one would be excluded from the school because his family was not rich enough— or white enough.

The EVA would publicize information about each participating school and would give each parent a voucher equivalent to the average per pupil expenditure in the public schools. Under the plan proposed by Jencks, vouchers actually would be written on a sliding scale, so the voucher for the poorest child would be perhaps twice as much as the basic voucher. The parents would give the voucher to the school of their choice, and the school would cash it in to get a check from the EVA. The EVA would police the system to make sure that disadvantaged children were not discriminated against in admissions.

In its preliminary report to the OEO, the Center for the Study of Public Policy said that the most important priority in American education is to reallocate resources so that disadvantaged children are exposed to their share of talented, sensitive teachers and classmates. "A student's classmates are probably his most important single 'resource.' " the report said, "even though they do not appear in most calculations of per pupil expenditures."

A student's classmates often determine how much instruction he will get from his teachers. "If, for example, a disadvantaged child attends a school in which most children never learn algebra," the report continued, "his teachers will not expect him to learn algebra, even if he is perfectly capable of doing so." A voucher would enable him to transfer to a school where teacher expectations were higher and their performance better.

To be eligible for the voucher system, a school would have to agree to accept a voucher as full tuition payment; to accept any applicant so long as there was room, to agree to abide by uniform standards set by the EVA about the suspension and expulsion of students, and to make public a wide range of information about its facilities, teachers, programs, and students.

Even the proposal's leading advocates acknowledge that a voucher system must contain many built-in safeguards. Jencks believes that the courts, Congress, and State legislatures will come to view schools in a voucher system as instrumentalities of the state and will require them to meet the same responsibilities in desegregation and other public policies as they make public schools face today. "An unregulated voucher system," warns the center's report, "could be the most serious setback for the education of disadvantaged children in the history of the United States. A properly regulated system, on the other hand, could inaugurate a new era of innovation and reform in American schools."

The OEO is talking to several communities about the voucher system for next fall. OEO officials hope to develop a five-year, pilot project costing about $6 million per year. It would operate in a large city with enough of a mix of public and private schools—and disadvantaged and middle class students—to create a valid experiment. The officials are aware of the political pitfalls inherent in such a major departure from the traditions of American public education. They are determined to have the pilot program approved by the teachers' organizations, the school board, the mayor, and anyone else who might be involved.

"We want a number of communities to develop ideas," says Glennan. "We want all the parties involved to understand it better than they do now. This is something that represents a difficult change for a school system."

School systems are not given to making difficult changes overnight, and it may be many years before any of them embark on a voucher program on a large enough scale to reverse the despair that now grips schools in poverty areas. That despair, however, certainly is not going to be lessened by maintaining the status quo. The vouchers, it would seem, may possibly offer a way out.

Options for Students, Parents, and Teachers:
Public Schools of Choice

MARIO FANTINI, DONALD HARRIS and SAMUEL NASH

Consumer choice is presently lacking in today's public schools, giving parents a single option when many are possible. Seven possible types of elementary schools are identified here, as well as seven criteria for quality public education. Although the use of education vouchers is not identified as a vehicle for actualizing the authors' options, the need for a similar consideration is apparent.

The art of governance in a free society rests with citizen decision making. The more informed the citizen, the more capable he is of

Mario Fantini, Donald Harris, and Samuel Nash, "Options for Students, Parents, and Teachers," *Phi Delta Kappan,* 52:541–543, May 1971. Reprinted by permission.

making decisions. The more options he has, the more chance he has of making a selection which is self-satisfying.

Transferring this notion to schools, the citizen as consumer should be able to decide on the kind of school his child should attend or the kind of educational environment he would like his children to have. This type of decision making would be school governance in its purest form. Making every parent the decision maker for his family's education is a significant stage beyond electing representatives to decide what kind of education makes the most sense for the majority in the locality. This is what we now have through our representative form of school governance, that is, through electing local school boards. In any majority-rule approach, significant numbers of citizens must accept majority rule in the kind of education their children receive. Therefore, diversity in education is severely restricted. Public schools then become social institutions which foster uniformity rather than diversity. Citizens who want other options must turn to private schools, if they can afford them. The private-school option is not available to many low-income citizens.

The trick is to get the *public schools* to respond to both diversity and individual rights in school decision making. However, in addition to governance, both *substance* and *personnel* are essential pillars which must be altered if genuine reform is to take place in American education. We therefore need to examine the implications of these two areas in a pattern which maximizes choice for the consumer.

A system of choice maximizes variation in both the substance and personnel of education. For example, consumers who select a school program based on a Montessori model will have important substantive differences from those who select a classical school. Choice does legitimize new programs, each of which carries with it new curriculum and new personnel.

Certainly, professionals who are attracted to a Summerhill-like school are different from those who prefer a classical school environment.

The point is that a public school system that maximizes consumer choice legitimizes new as well as old educational approaches to common objectives. The new educational approach will be made operational by public consent. Moreover, *educators* will also be able to choose from among these educational alternatives, possibly enhancing their sense of professional satisfaction.

This choice model, therefore, tends to minimize conflict among interest groups because *each* individual is making *direct* decisions in educational affairs. Furthermore, as a supply and demand model, the choice system has a self-revitalizing capability. As the options prove successful, they will increase in popularity, thereby increasing the flow of successful programs into the public schools and generating a renewal process for public education.

Under the present system, new programs are introduced into the public schools largely through professional channels, with parents, students, and teachers having little say. However, parents, students, and teachers can actually veto any new program. Some programs, such as sex education, become controversial, especially if they are superimposed by the administration.

School systems are currently structured to present only one model or pattern of education to a student and his parents. If economic factors or religious beliefs preclude nonpublic schools as an alternative, the parent and student have no choice but to submit to the kind and quality of public education in their community. With the exception that one or two schools may be viewed as "better" or "worse" by parents and students (generally because of "better teachers" or because "more" graduates go to college or because the school is in a "good neighborhood"), the way materials are presented and "school work" is done is essentially the same in all schools on the same level. It should be possible to develop within one school or cluster of schools within a neighborhood, district, or system several different models that would offer real choices to all those involved in the educative process.

A school district might offer seven different options in its elementary schools:

Option one: The concept and programs of the school are traditional. The school is graded and emphasizes the learning of basic skills—reading, writing, numbers, etc.—by cognition. The basic learning unit is the classroom, which functions with one or two teachers instructing and directing students at their various learning tasks. Students are encouraged to adjust to the school and its operational style rather than vice versa. Students with recognized learning problems are referred to a variety of remedial and school-support programs. The educational and fiscal policy for this school is determined entirely by the central board of education.

Option two: This school is nontraditional and nongraded. In many ways it is very much like the British primary schools and the Leicestershire system. There are many constructional and manipulative materials in each area where students work and learn. The teacher acts as a facilitator—one who assists and guides rather than directs or instructs. Most student activity is in the form of different specialized learning projects done individually and in small groups rather than in the traditional form where all students do the same thing at the same time. Many of the learning experiences and activities take place outside of the school building.

Option three: This school emphasizes learning by the vocational processes—doing and experiencing. The school defines its role as diagnostic and prescriptive. When the learner's talents are identified, the school prescribes whatever experiences are necessary to develop and enhance them. This school encourages many styles of learning and teaching. Students may achieve through demonstration and manipulation of real objects, as well as through verbal, written, or abstractive performances. All activity is specifically related to the work world.

Option four: This school is more technically oriented than the others in the district. It utilizes computers to help diagnose individual needs and abilities. Computer-assisted instruction based on the diagnosis is subsequently provided both individually and in groups. The library is stocked with tape-recording banks and "talking," "listening," and manipulative carrels that students can operate on their own. In addition, there are Nova-type video-retrieval systems in which students and teachers can concentrate on specific problem areas. This school also has closed-circuit television facilities.

Option five: This school is a total community school. It operates on a 12- to 14-hour basis at least six days a week throughout the year. It provides educational and other services for children as well as adults. Late afternoon activities are provided for children from the neighborhood, and evening classes and activities are provided for adults. Services such as health care, legal aid, and employment are available within the school facility. Paraprofessionals or community teachers are used in every phase of the regular school program. This school is governed by a community board which approves or hires the two chief administrators and is in charge of all other activities in the building. The school functions as a center for the educational needs of all people in the neighborhood and community.

Option six: This school is in fact a Montessori school. Students move at their own pace and are largely self-directed. The learning areas are rich with materials and specialized learning instruments from which the students can select and choose as they wish. Although the teacher operates within a specific and defined methodology, he remains very much in the background, guiding students rather than directing them. Special emphasis is placed on the development of the five senses.

Option seven: The seventh is a multicultural school that has four or five ethnic groups equally represented in the student body. Students spend part of each day in racially heterogeneous learning groups. In another part of the day, all students and teachers of the same ethnic background meet together. In these classes they learn their own culture, language, customs, history, and heritage. Several times each week one ethnic group shares with the others some event or aspect of its cultural heritage that is important and educational. This school views diversity as a value. Its curriculum combines the affective and cognitive domains and is humanistically oriented. Much time is spent on questions of identity, connectedness, powerlessness, and interpersonal relationships. The school is run by a policy board made up of equal numbers of parents and teachers and is only tangentially responsible to a central board of education.

Distinctive educational options can exist within any single neighborhood or regional public school. The principle of providing parents, teachers, and students with a choice from among various educational alternatives is feasible at the individual school. In fact, this may be the most realistic and pervasive approach, at first. For example, in early childhood a single school might offer as options: 1) a Montessori program, 2) an established kindergarten program, 3) a British infant school program, and 4) a Bereiter-Engleman program. Again, parents, teachers, and students will have to "understand fully" each program and be free to choose from among them.

Some may ask whether a Nazi school or a school for blacks that advanced the notion that all white people were blonde-haired, blue-eyed devils and pigs could exist within the framework of a public system of choice. Plainly, no. Our concept speaks to openness; it values diversity; it is nonexclusive; it embraces human growth and development and is unswerving in its recognition of individual worth. Within these bounds, however, is an infinite spectrum of alternative possibilities in creating new educational and learning forms.

Although we have suggested several different ways in which schools might be structured under a public schools of choice system, it should be clear that there are many other possibilities. The flexibility of the concept lends itself to a whole range of options without forcing people to accept any one option they are not attracted to. The choice educational system starts where the public school system and the clients are and develops from that point. For example, we have described above what could be developed within a school district. The same variety of offerings, teaching styles, and learning environments could be presented within *one* school facility. This would permit the bulk of parents and students in our hypothetical district to continue with educational programs and activities just as they have been, but those who wanted to try different options could do so. There could be six or seven choices in the educational supply of options from which parents and students could choose.

Another application of the public schools of choice system could be implemented on the high school level in a moderate-size city.

Distinctive high school models could be integrated into the public system, providing parents and students with choices about learning style, environment, and orientation that best met the individual needs of the learner and teacher. For example, there could be a standard or traditional high school; a university experimental high school that is a learning center for students, teachers, and those who train teachers; a classical school that emphasizes languages, learning, and rigid disciplines (Boys Latin in Boston is an example) ; a vocational-technical complex; a high school that emphasizes independent work and personal development, where students and teachers share a joint responsibility for the program; a high school (or student-run high school supplementary program) that in some way addresses itself to the special concerns of particular students—where perhaps black students could work out questions of identity, power, and self-determination on their own terms in their own style; and, finally, a high-school-without-walls concept, such as in Philadelphia, where students utilize the resources and institutions of the city and community as learning environments.

These alternatives, and others, are not unrealistic or significantly beyond the reach of a city school system that is concerned with the quality of its public education. Although many of these ideas have been tried in isolation, they have not been incorporated into a public education system. When they are, we will have entered a new era of public education.

We have learned from our early experience with participation that the mood among the major parties of interest is tense. The lessons from our experiences with reform can be summarized as follows. A good reform proposal:

1) demonstrates adherence to a comprehensive set of educational objectives—not just particular ones. Proposals cannot, for example, emphasize only emotional growth at the expense of intellectual development. The converse is also true. Comprehensive educational objectives deal with careers, citizenship, talent development, intellectual and emotional growth, problem solving, critical thinking, and the like.
2) does not substantially increase the per student expenditure from that of established programs. To advance an idea which doubles or triples the budget will at best place the proposal in the ideal-but-not-practical category. Further, an important factor for reformers to bear in mind is that the new arena will deal with wiser use of *old* money, not the quest for more money.
3) does not advocate any form of exclusivity—racial, religious, or economic. Solutions cannot deny equal access to any particular individual or groups.
4) is not superimposed by a small group which is trying to do something *for* or *to* others.

5) respects the rights of all concerned parties and must apply to everyone—it cannot appear to serve the interests of one group only. Thus, for instance, if decentralization plans of urban school systems are interpreted to serve only minority communities, then the majority community may very well oppose such efforts. Similarly, if plans appear to favor professionals, then the community may be in opposition.

6) does not claim a single, across-the-board, model answer—is not a blanket panacea to the educational problems. Attempts at *uniform* solutions are almost never successful.

7) advocates a process of change which is democratic and maximizes *individual* decision making. Participation by the individual in the decisions which affect his life is basic to comprehensive support.

These seven ground rules should be borne in mind, whatever options we offer, but, above all, we must offer options, through public schools of choice.

The Voucher Plan: Is It Worth the Investment?

RUDOLPH J. FOBERT

The author states his case against education vouchers primarily on the grounds that such a procedure would fail to realize the dream of parental self-determination in educational policies. School policy is set not by individual parents but by powerful organized groups. Vouchers open the door to a "take-over" of schools by extremist groups, posing a real threat to the maintenance of a stable society, according to the author.

The voucher plan proposed by the Office of Economic Opportunity has created a spectrum of reactions among educators and the general public. Proponents of the plan claim it to be the elixir that will treat a variety of problems in public education. A partial list of its remedies follows:

Rudolph J. Fobert, "The Voucher Plan: Is It Worth the Investment?" *The School Administrator*, published by the American Association of School Administrators, May 1971. Reprinted by permission.

- It will improve the quality of education for ghetto children (both poor blacks and whites).
- It will redistribute decision-making power.
- It will help solve the nonpublic school financial dilemma.
- It will give parents and special interest groups control over the education of children.
- It will lead to the closing down of those public schools that are ineffective.
- It will create competition among schools, thereby leading to more innovative schools and an improvement of existing school systems.
- It will enable educators to establish their own schools based on their own philosophy and to offer these schools to parents.

In summary, you name the problem, the voucher plan will help to solve it.

One can understand the need for appealing to as many vested interest groups and publics as possible to gain support for the idea. However, educators and others who have wrestled with the complex problems of public education know that there are no simple light-switch solutions to problems that require fundamental changes in man's attitudes, values and behavior.

In perspective, the voucher plan will offer parents an opportunity to select the schools of their choice. Their degree of influence or control over what should or does happen in a school is still dependent upon the power base that controls the school. No individual parent can require a classroom teacher to personalize the program for his child according to the parent's prescription. In reality, each parent has to accommodate his prescription to the teacher's objectives and activities, which are usually geared to the whole class or some subdivision of it.

The overriding inherent principle of the voucher plan is *self-determination*. I need not recite the litany which supports the notion that self-determination is one of the strongest and most appealing principles in our country at this time. To oppose it completely is not only unpopular but also heretical. However, I remember Paul Mort's comments on the need to set opposing principles against each other to achieve the balanced judgment required in an orderly society. To carry one principle to its logical end without consideration of others leads to chaos and anarchy.

A competing principle of self-determination is social responsibility, or the accommodation of one's own needs and goals to the more general ones of other groups or society as a whole. The Friedman plan does not balance these two principles of self-determination and social responsibility. Carried to its logical end without limits the plan could lead to a proliferation of self-serving schools organized by vested interest groups (including the more extreme ones like the Black Panthers and the KKK). Each would organize its school to indoctrinate children for its own purposes. The notion of free exchange of ideas and opinions would be generally nonexistent. The concept of public education as we know it now would be replaced by a plethora of conflicting, self-serving groups which would make it extremely difficult, if not impossible, to maintain a stable society.

Does the principle of self-determination have so high a valence that one accepts all its consequences, including segregated schools? I think not. The Jencks plan is supposedly designed to prevent segregated schools. However, it has to be sold in the political arena and given this reality. What it would look like after the vested interest groups finished with it is anyone's guess. One would have to be unbelievably naive to underestimate the extent to which each special interest group would adapt and manipulate the plan to achieve its own ends.

Given the inherent problems of the plan and the stated opposition of the AASA, NEA, AFT and others, and also recognizing the long list of critical needs wrenching our schools and this society, is the voucher plan worth the investment of 30 to 48 million dollars over the next five to eight years?

I believe that it should not be funded and that there are more appropriate uses for this money. If it *is* funded, there must be controls to prevent it from damaging and possibly destroying the imperfect but functional public school system that now exists.

In essence, the voucher plan strikes directly at the fundamental purpose of free public schools. Although these schools have not fully realized their goals, they represent a better vehicle for achieving a viable democratic society than voucher schools, which would move us in the opposite direction.

Education Vouchers

CHRISTOPHER JENCKS

A strong advocate of education vouchers and one of the pioneers of this approach, Christopher Jencks attempts to answer some of the most common objections voiced by opposers. The establishment and functions of a regulatory watchdog, the Education Voucher Agency (EVA),

Christopher Jencks, "Education Vouchers." Reprinted by permission of *The New Republic,* © 1970, Harrison-Blaine of New Jersey, Inc.

is discussed. Jencks sees education vouchers as a vehicle for giving parents a choice in the schooling of their children and an approach for making schools accountable to the needs and desires of the clientele they serve.

The Office of Economic Opportunity announced last May that it hopes to fund an experiment which would provide parents with vouchers to cover the cost of educating their children at the school of their choice. This news has provoked considerable liberal opposition, including charges that the equipment is unconstitutional, that it is part of a Nixon plot to perpetuate segregation, and that it would "destroy the public school system." What, then, does OEO really have in mind?

If state and local cooperation is forthcoming, the first step will be the establishment of an Educational Voucher Agency (EVA) in some community. This EVA will resemble a traditional board of education in that it will be locally controlled and will receive federal, state, and local funds for financing the education of all local children. But it will differ from a traditional board in that it will not operate any schools of its own. That responsibility will remain with existing school boards, both public and private. The EVA will simply issue vouchers to all parents of elementary school children in its area. The parents will take these vouchers to a school in which they want to enroll their child. This may either be an existing public school, a new school opened by the public school board to attract families who would otherwise withdraw their children from the public system, an existing private school, or a new private school opened especially to cater to children with vouchers. If the school meets the basic eligibility requirements laid down by the EVA, it will be able to convert its vouchers into cash, which will cover both its operating expenses and the amortization of capital costs. Such a system would enable anyone starting a school to get public subsidies, so long as he followed the basic rules laid down by the EVA and could persuade enough parents to enroll their children in his school. It would also give low-income parents the same choice about where they sent their children that upper-income parents now have. This would include all the public and private schools participating in the system.

The effect of these changes on the quality of education would depend on how effectively the EVA regulated the newly created marketplace, and especially on the rules it laid down for determining which schools could cash vouchers and which schools could not. Since the EVA would presumably be controlled by the same political forces that now dominate local school boards, some prophets anticipate that it would soon develop a regulatory system as complex and detailed as that now governing the public schools. If this happened, both publicly and privately managed voucher schools would soon be entangled in the usual bureaucratic and political jungle, in which everything is either required or forbidden. They would probably end up indistinguishable from existing public schools. Nothing would have changed, either for better or for worse.

This vision may, however, be unnecessarily gloomy. Today's public school has a captive clientele. As a result, it in turn becomes the captive of a political process designed to protect the interests of its clientele. The state, the local board, and the school administration establish regulations to ensure that no school will do anything to offend anyone of political consequence. By trying to please everyone, however, the schools often end up pleasing no one. The voucher system seeks to free schools from these managerial constraints by eliminating their monopolistic privileges. Under a voucher system, parents who do not like what a school is doing can simply send their children elsewhere. Schools which attract no applicants go out of business. But those which survive have a much greater claim to run their own affairs in their own way.

Most opponents of the voucher system worry more about the possibility that the EVA would establish too few regulations than about the possibility that it would establish too many. They particularly fear the development of a system in which schools would compete with one another in terms of social and/or academic exclusiveness, much as colleges now do. Left to their own devices, many schools would restrict admission to the brightest and most easily educated youngsters, leaving the more difficult children to somebody else. Many would also try to increase their operating budgets by charging supplemental tuition. This would have the not-always-accidental effect of limiting the number of low-income children in the more expensive schools.

An unregulated system of this kind would have all the drawbacks of other unregulated markets. It would produce even more racial and economic segregation than the existing neighborhood school system. It would also widen the expenditure gap between rich and poor children, giving the children of the middle classes an even larger share of the nation's educational resources than they now get, while reducing the relative share going to the children of the poor.

Fortunately, OEO has shown no signs of funding a completely unregulated voucher system. Rather, OEO is contemplating an experiment in which extremely stringent controls are placed on participating schools' admissions policies, and also on their tuition charges. At the same time, it is hoping for an experiment which places minimal restraint on schools' staffing practices and programs.

In order to cash vouchers, a school would have to offer every applicant a roughly equal chance of admission. To ensure this, the school would have to declare each spring how many children it could take the following year. Parents would apply to schools each spring, and unless a school had more applicants than places, it would have to take everyone who had applied. If there were more applicants than places, the school would have to fill at least half its places by a lottery among applicants. It would also have to show that it had accepted at least as high a proportion of minority group students as had applied. Thus no school would be able to cream off the most easily educated children or dump all the problem children elsewhere.

The redemption value of a middle- or upper-income family's voucher would approximate what the local public schools are currently spending on upper-income children. Vouchers for children from low-income families would have a somewhat higher redemption value. This reflects the fact that schools with high concentrations of low-income children also tend to have more than their share of educational problems. It should also help discourage schools from trying to attract exclusively middle-class applicants. Participating schools would have to accept every child's voucher as full payment for his education, regardless of its value. Otherwise, parents who could afford to supplement their children's vouchers would inevitably have a better chance of getting their children into high-cost schools than parents who could not supplement the voucher.

These regulations would not result in as much racial or economic integration as massive compulsory busing. But that is hardly a likely alternative. The real alternative is the continuation of the neighborhood school, whose racial and economic composition inevitably and deliberately reflects the racial and economic exclusiveness of the private housing market. Under a voucher system, no child could be excluded from any participating school simply because his family was not rich enough or white enough to buy a house near the school. Furthermore, the EVA would pay transportation costs, so that every family would have genuinely equal access to every participating school. Most families, both black and white, would doubtless continue to prefer schools near their homes. But at least no family would be legally or financially required to choose such a school if they thought it was educationally inadequate. Those black parents who wanted their children to attend integrated schools would be in an excellent position to ensure that they did so.

If all goes according to plan, the OEO experiment would be far more permissive with regard to schools' staffing and curricular policies than with regard to admissions. Schools would have to conform to existing state and local regulations governing private schools, but these are relatively lenient in most states. Experience suggests that while such leniency results in some abuses, the results over the long run seem to be better than the results of detailed legal and administrative regulations of the kind that shape the public schools. While these regulations often seem rational on their face (as in the case of teacher certification requirements), they generally create more problems than they solve. Teaching and learning are subtle processes, and they seem to resist all attempts at improvement by formal regulation. Rule books are seldom subtle enough to prevent the bad things that can happen in schools, and are seldom flexible enough to allow the best things.

So instead of telling schools whom to hire, what to teach, or how to teach it, the EVA will confine itself to collecting and disseminating information about what each school is doing. Every family will be given extensive information about every participating school. This should ensure that families are aware of all the choices open to them. It should also help discourage misleading advertising, or at least partially offset the effects of such advertising.

One common objection to a voucher system of this kind is that many parents are too ignorant to make intelligent choices among schools. Giving parents a choice will, according to this argument, simply set in motion an educational equivalent of Gresham's Law, in which hucksterism and mediocre schooling drive out high quality institutions. This argument seems especially plausible to those who envisage the entry of large numbers of profit-oriented firms into the educational marketplace. The argument is not, however, supported by much evidence. Existing private schools are sometimes mere diploma mills, but on the average their claims about themselves seem no more misleading, and the quality of the services they offer no lower, than in the public schools. And while some private schools are run for little but profit, this is the exception rather than the rule. There is no obvious reason to suppose that vouchers would change all this.

A second common objection to vouchers is that they would "destroy the public schools." Again, this seems farfetched. If you look at the educational choices made by wealthy parents who can already afford whatever schooling they want for their children, you find that many still prefer their local public schools if these are at all adequate. Furthermore, most of those who now leave the public system do so in order to attend high-cost, exclusive private schools. While some parents would doubtless continue to patronize such schools, they would receive no subsidy under the proposed OEO system.

Nonetheless, if you are willing to call every school "public" that is ultimately responsible to a public board of education, then there is little doubt that a voucher system would result in some shrinkage of the "public" sector and some growth of the "private" sector. If, on the other hand, you confine the label "public" to schools which are really equally open to everyone within commuting distance, you discover that the so-called public sector includes relatively few public schools. Instead, racially exclusive surburbs and economically exclusive neighborhoods serve to ration access to good "public" schools in precisely the same way that admissions committees and tuition charges ration access to good "private" schools. If you begin to look at the distinction between public and private schooling in these terms, emphasizing accessibility rather than control, you are likely to conclude that a voucher system, far from destroying the public sector, would greatly expand it, since it would force large numbers of schools, public and private, to open their doors to outsiders.

A third objection to vouchers is that they would be available to children attending Catholic schools. This is not, of course, a necessary feature of a voucher system. An EVA could perfectly easily restrict participation to nonsectarian schools. Indeed, some state constitutions clearly require that this be done. The federal Constitution may also require such a restriction, but neither the language of the First Amendment nor the legal precedents are clear on this issue. The First Amendment's prohibition against an "establishment of religion" can be construed as barring payments to church schools, but the "free exercise of religion" clause can also be construed as requiring the state to treat church schools in precisely the same way as other private schools. The Supreme Court has never ruled on a case of this type (e.g., GI Bill payments to Catholic colleges or Medicare payments to Catholic hospitals). Until it does, the issue ought to be resolved on policy grounds. And since the available evidence indicates that Catholic schools have served their children no worse than public schools, and perhaps slightly better, there seems no compelling reason to deny them the same financial support as other schools.

The most common and most worrisome objection to a voucher system, in my view, is that its results depend on the EVA's willingness to regulate the marketplace vigorously. If vouchers were used on a large scale, state and local regulatory efforts might be uneven or even nonexistent. The regulations designed to prevent racial and economic segregation seem especially likely to get watered down at the state and local level, or else to remain unenforced. This argument applies, however, to *any* educational reform, and it also applies to the existing system. If you assume that any given EVA will be controlled by overt or covert segregationists, you must also assume that this will be true of the local board of education. A board of education that wants to keep racist parents happy hardly needs vouchers to do so. It only needs to maintain the neighborhood school system. White parents who want their children to attend white schools will then find it quite simple to move to a white neighborhood where their children will be suitably segregated. Except perhaps in the South, neither the federal government, the state government, nor the judiciary is likely to prevent this traditional practice.

If, on the other hand, you assume a board which is anxious to eliminate segregation, either for legal, financial, or political reasons, you must also assume that the EVA would be subject to the same pressures. And if an EVA is anxious to eliminate segregation, it will have no difficulty devising regulations to achieve this end. Furthermore, the legal precedents to date suggest that the federal courts will be more stringent in applying the Fourteenth Amendment to voucher systems than to neighborhood school systems. The courts have repeatedly thrown out voucher systems designed to maintain segregation, whereas they have shown no such general willingness to ban the neighborhood school. Outside the South, then, those who believe in integration may actually have an easier time achieving this goal than they will with the existing public school system.

National Assessment of Educational Progress

WILLIAM A. MEHRENS

A rather concise description of the philosophy, goals, and methods used in the National Assessment Program are found in this article. The overview of National Assessment identified this movement as a form of educational accountability with a well designed approach for establishing an educational index of American schools. The knowledge, skills, and attitudes of four different age groups are measured in ten subject matter areas. William A. Mehrens explains the carefully selected sampling plan and the unique features of the testing devices and their uses.

The National Assessment of Educational Progress (NAEP) is the most extensive assessment project ever initiated in the United States. Originated in 1964 under the auspices of the Committee on Assessing the Progress of Education (CAPE), since July of 1969 it has been a project of the Education Commission of the States (ECS). Here is a brief overview of NAEP—its purposes, goals and methodology.

"National Assessment of Educational Progress," by William A. Mehrens. From *Childhood Education*, May 1970, vol. 46, no. 8. Reprinted by permission of William A. Mehrens and the Association for Childhood Education International, 3615 Wisconsin Avenue, N.W., Washington, D.C. Copyright © 1970 by the Association.

Purpose of National Assessment

A popular term these days is accountability—used typically in education to justify costs by presenting the positive effects derived from expenditures. Presently little is known about the effectiveness of the billions of dollars the nation spends each year for education. As a recent NAEP brochure points out: "The purpose of National Assessment is to gather data which will help answer the question, how much good is the expenditure of so much money doing, in terms of what Americans know and can do?[1]

Logically one could argue that the public has a *right* to know what it is getting for its money and that educators have an *ethical obligation* to present such information. But historically this argument has not been very persuasive for, if educators have recognized such an ethical obligation, they certainly haven't been very energetic about fulfilling it. A more persuasive argument might be to remind educators of the number of taxpayers' revolts at the local level, where many bond issues and increased-millage requests have recently failed. If the state and federal governments assume greater financial support of education, taxpayer revolts may well manifest themselves at those levels also.

National Assessment data will be amenable to methods of reporting that give an accounting to the public. But, perhaps even more importantly for the educator, assessment is essential to sound educational decision-making and aids in professional planning.

With the increased demand on the education dollar we must move, and rather quickly, from implicit to explicit cost effectiveness models.[2] Although advocates of the National Assessment recognize that the outcome data they are gathering will not in itself be sufficient to determine the cost effectiveness of our educational expenditures, they rightfully maintain that such data will form a necessary part of any models to be developed.

The stated goals of National Assessment, then, are to make available baseline census-like data on the educational attainments of young Americans in view of certain objectives and periodically to obtain evidence concerning progress in meeting those objectives. How are these goals being accomplished?

Methodology of National Assessment

AREAS TO BE ASSESSED

Knowledge, skills and attitudes are to be assessed in ten subject matter areas, for four age groups. Not all of the ten subjects, which include Art, Career and Occupational Development (COD), Citizenship,

Literature, Mathematics, Music, Reading, Science, Social Studies, and Writing,[3] will be assessed each year (during 1969–70, only Citizenship, Science, and Writing). The current cycling plan for the assessment is as follows:

CYCLE 1		CYCLE 2	
Year	Areas	Year	Areas
1969–70	Citizenship, Science, Writing	1975–76	Math, Science
1970–71	Literature, Reading	1976–77	Literature, Reading
1971–72	Music, Social Studies	1977–78	Music, Social Studies
1972–73	COD, Math, Science	1978–79	COD, Math, Science
1973–74	Reading, Writing	1979–80	Reading, Writing
1974–75	Art, Citizenship	1980–81	Art, Citizenship

Plans call for subsequent cycles to be the same as Cycle 2. Notice that Math, Reading, and Science are to be assessed twice in each cycle, reflecting the importance accorded these areas. By using approximately 60 percent of the same exercises the second time an area is assessed as were used the first time, change can be measured (about 40 percent of the exercises in each area will be made public after the first assessment and accordingly they cannot be reused).

About 480 minutes of exercises will be used each year for each age group, with each subject matter area receiving approximately equal time. So that no student will have to spend more than about 40 minutes in the assessment, the exercises are divided into about 12 different packages, with each student taking only one package (the time and number of packages will vary somewhat from age to age and year to year). With the exception of the Reading exercises, all group-administered exercises are presented on tape to standardize procedures and to facilitate understanding for youngsters with poor reading ability. Some packages at each age level are individually administered.

THE SAMPLING PLAN

The four age groups in the assessment are: 9, 13, 17, and young adults (ages 26–35). Approximately 32,000 individuals at each of the younger ages and 20,000 young adults will be assessed each year. Samples for all the 9's and 13's and for approximately 75 percent of the 17-year-olds are being obtained through the schools. For the 17-year-old graduates or dropouts and for the young adults, household sampling procedures are used.

In 1964 and 1965 many educators expressed concern that the NAEP might involve invidious comparisons between states, school districts, etc. To meet these objections, the sampling procedure has been done by geographic region (northeast, southwest, central, and west), type of community (large, city, suburban fringe, middle-sized city, and rural-small town) , and socioeducational status—so that state, school, teacher or individual comparisons *cannot* be made.

Now, in 1970, many educators are wishing that results were available by states. As the public, somehwat belatedly, clamors for accountability data and as educators, very belatedly, begin to recognize not only their responsibilities in accounting but also the positive role of assessment in educational decision-making, more and more states are setting up their own assessment programs, a duplication that could have been avoided if irrational fears had not been so prevalent earlier.

FIELD WORK, REPORTING, AND ANALYSIS

The Research Triangle Institute (RTI) , which administers the exercises, has subcontracted a portion of the work to the Measurement Research Center (MRC) . With excellent cooperation from the schools, the first year of the assessment has been completed. The sample is being redrawn so that schools participating in the first-year assessment will be unlikely to participate in the second, which will begin in October 1970.

Reporting will be by separate exercises, as well as by small subsets that measure the same objectives and/or produce similar results. National P-values (percentages) will be reported, making comparisons across reporting categories where relevant (age, geographic region, type of community, sex, socioeducational status and race) . It is expected that at least some of the results of the first year of assessment will be available in the summer or fall of 1970, with release of complete technical reports for each subject area as well as reports for the general public.

Unique Features of National Assessments

Some people who are quite in favor of assessment ask if the *particular* National Assessment Project we are discussing is necessary, in view of similar data already available from existing standardized testing programs. Similarities certainly can be seen in the data obtained from standardized tests and that from National Assessment. But also evident are some very important differences, which to my mind make the National Assessment data much the more useful, both for accountability and educational decision-making.

Sampling, objective formulation, exercise development, administration and reporting procedures of the National Assessment project have all been planned with the *specific goal* in mind of assessing progress. To assume that other assessment programs can measure progress as well as one specifically designed for that purpose requires a great faith in serendipity.

The objective formulation and exercise construction stages of the assessment did have much in common with exercise construction for standardized tests, but again important differences exist.

First, National Assessment involved more lay people and paid more attention to validity by appearance. Eleven different lay panels reviewed the objectives for each subject-matter area—an important consideration if one is concerned with accountability to the public. *Second,* a conscious effort was made to devise exercises requiring a variety of formats. Essay, open end, and multiple choice are the most frequently used formats, but structured interviews and group discussion exercises are also included. *Third,* by not being dependent on exercise amenable to machine scoring, a larger variety of objectives can be assessed. *Fourth,* a related point: an effort was made to assess attitudes as well as knowledges and skill. A *fifth* difference in the exercises relates to the difficulty levels. Standardized tests, being devised for the purpose of differentiating between individuals, have used, for sound psychometric reasons, exercises of around 50 percent difficulty. These exercises are not efficient in assessing what the very poorest or very best students can do. The National Assessment program, on the other hand, intentionally includes some exercises that are so easy almost everyone can get them right and some exercises so difficult that they challenge the very best students. This is more acceptable when, as in the National Assessment, there is both person and exercise sampling and no intent to obtain scores on individual pupils.

The method of administrating the National Assessment exercises has been carefully planned to hold measurement error to a minimum. Such procedures as playing a tape to equate for reading abilities, assessing in small groups, and using professional administrators assure a high degree of precision in the measurement process. Also, keeping exercises confidential until they are administered rules out direct teaching for the exercises.

The method of reporting, however, constitutes the most important difference between standardized tests and the National Assessment project. It costs a lot to construct a good set of exercises and, as is done with standardized tests, to norm the results. Publishers are quite naturally opposed to releasing the actual exercises to the public. Reporting is limited to releasing how a student, or sometimes a school, scored in comparison to the norm group but the public is never actually told what the exercises are. In National Assessment the exercises themselves as well as the results are reported. Without such reporting we have really communicated very little to the public.

CONCLUSION

I have suggested in this paper that educators should assess not only to account to the public but also to improve their decision-making capabilities. National Assessment type data are necessary prerequisites for both these goals.

FOOTNOTES

1. National Assessment of Educational Progress, *Questions & Answers About National Assessment of Educational Progress,* December 1969, p. 1.
2. See Marvin C. Alkin, *Evaluating the Cost-Effectiveness of Instructional Programs.* CSEIP Report No. 25. Los Angeles: University of California, Center for the Study of Instructional Programs (offset).
3. The procedures for developing the objectives and actual exercises have been written up elsewhere. See, for example, Jack C. Merwin and Frank B. Womer's "Evaluation in Assessing the Progress of Education To Provide Bases of Public Policy," in *Educational Evaluation: New Roles, New Means,* NSSE Yearbook (Washington, D.C.: NEA, 1968), pp. 305–34. A complete statement of the major objectives for all 10 areas and of the detailed objectives in Citizenship, Literature, Math, Music, Reading, Science and Writing may be obtained from the National Assessment Office.

Using PPBS To Overcome Taxpayers' Resistance

ROBERT F. ALIOTO and J. A. JUNGHERR

The rising rate of educational costs has brought with it a correspondingly high rejection of school budgets by the voting public. Program-planning-budgeting system (PPBS) is described as an accountability approach which was utilized in the Pearl River School District of New York. The authors claim that PPBS has the potential for greater community involvement, better explanation of services, and more relevant information for decision making regarding the school budget.

Spiraling costs of public education have heightened taxpayer resistance to a level unprecedented in the history of American public education. School districts throughout the country have faced voter rejection

Robert F. Alioto, and J. A. Jungherr, "Using PPBS To Overcome Taxpayers' Resistance," *Phi Delta Kappan,* 51:138–141, November 1969. Reprinted by permission.

of budgets and bond issues. This resistance has not been limited to the public sector. Parochial and private schools also experience considerable difficulty in obtaining adequate financial support.

The defeat of 135 school budgets in New York State this year established a new record.[1] This compares with 76 budget defeats for the 1968–69 school year.[2] Several districts failed to achieve approval of their 1968–69 budgets and were placed on an austerity budget in accordance with New York State education law.

Inflation and teacher militancy are the chief causes of the accelerating rate of education costs. For instance, in the past year consumer prices have increased 6.7 percent.[3] On September 1, 1967, the Taylor Law became effective in New York State, giving a new dimension to educational decision making.[4] This law mandated, for the first time, formal bargaining between representatives of the employee organizations and boards of education. The attainment of legal bargaining power by the employee has resulted in a sharp escalation of demands. Many boards have been forced into settlements much more costly than the old unilaterally determined contracts.

The Pearl River School District was among those districts whose budgets were defeated in 1968. Pearl River is a fairly typical suburban community located in Rockland County approximately 20 miles outside of New York City. In May, 1968, a budget in the amount of $5.088 million was defeated by a 58 percent majority. It would have required a 21 percent increase over the previous year's budget.

This $5.088 million budget was subsequently reduced by $91,700 and resubmitted to the voters in June, 1968. The new budget was defeated by essentially the same margin. Finally, after a still further reduction ($9,225), a budget representing an 18 percent increase over the 1967–68 budget was passed by a 55 percent majority the day after school opened in September, 1968.

These budget defeats created an atmosphere of hostility, negativism, and suspicion between school officials and the public. Many acrimonious statements were made at public meetings. Staff morale was affected. Students began attending board meetings to protest the community's vote on the budget. The administration and Board of Education, working under severe time restrictions, had to rework budgets that normally take six months of preparation. Therefore the full implications of some cuts were not given serious consideration.

In response to the turmoil created by the budget defeats, the board and administrative staff analyzed a number of alternative actions in an attempt to insure that such a situation would not recur. Following this analysis, it was agreed that at least three critical requirements had to be met in order to increase the probability of passage of the 1969–70 budget:

1. Greater community involvement in the budget process.
2. Better explanation of the services to be provided by the tax dollars.
3. More relevant information of decision making on the budget.

The vehicle selected to accommodate these critical requirements was the Planning Programming Budgeting System, which was at that point being examined in the district.

The essence of PPBS is the development and presentation of relevant information on certain implications (the cost and benefits) of major alternative courses of action.[5] The system is aimed at assisting management to make better decisions on the allocation of resources to attain organizational objectives. The primary characteristics of PPBS are: 1) identification of the fundamental objectives of the school, 2) establishment of relationships of activities to objectives, 3) consideration of long-range aspects of programs, 4) consideration of all related costs, and 5) systematic analysis of alternatives.[6]

PPBS has the following major phases: 1) *planning,* which is concerned with generating educational goals and objectives; 2) *programming,* which is concerned with the preparation of alternative sets of activities and services to achieve program objectives; 3) *budgeting,* which is involved with the formulation of detailed plans, accounting, and reporting; and 4) *evaluating,* which is concerned with progress outputs and effectiveness of programs.[7]

Development of the major components of a PPBS design for Pearl River was a complex process involving the consideration of many alternatives. For the purposes of this article only major components of the system developed will be outlined, including the program structure, program analysis memorandum, and program accounting system.[8]

Program Structure—The program structure provides the framework within which program analysis is conducted and decisions are made. In Pearl River, due to the recognized fragmentation of educational programs, it was decided to organize the program structure on a K-12 basis. This was done specifically to provide for the articulation and continuity of subject area content. The K-12 subject area structure included all subject areas, with the exception of those which are initiated in the upper grade levels, such as business and foreign language. Twenty separate programs were identified and grouped as follows:

Basic Instructional Services

Program Code	Program Description
60	Language arts, including English and reading
61	Science and health
62	Mathematics
63	Social studies

64	Physical education, intramural and interscholastic athletics
65	Business
66	Foreign language
67	Unified arts, including industrial arts, homemaking, driver education, and mechanical drawing
68	Art
69	Music
70	Special and vocational education

Supporting Educational Services

Program Code

71	Library services
72	Guidance and psychological services
73	Medical services
74	Adult education and summer school

Other Supporting Services

Program Code

80	Pupil transportation
81	Operation and maintenance of plant
82	District management
83	Debt service
84	School lunch

Program Analysis Memorandum—The purpose of the program analysis memorandum was to organize in a uniform manner for management review certain information and data on each program, including a statement of objectives, a description of the existing program, an explanation of major deficiencies, and a multi-year budget plan. A separate memorandum for each subject area was prepared by program specialists.

Program Accounting System—A twelve-digit coding system was developed to provide financial accounting on a program basis. This coding system, which was computer processed, utilized a format illustrated thus:

Fund	*Program*	*Location*
A0 General Fund	62 Mathematics Grade K-12	02 Evans Park Elementary School

Function	*Object*
220 Teaching	200 Equipment

The coding system adopted provided a number of alternative combinations for presenting financial data. In order to meet the reporting requirements for expenditures to the State Department of Education, traditional function-object data was provided. Total costs were produced on a district-wide basis. The same data were also displayed by building location and subject area in order to provide for a comparison of expenditures.

PPBS had been under study in the Pearl River School District for the past several years and a pilot study had been completed in the area of physical education. In the process, several staff members became familiar with the basic concepts of this new management system. These key staff members were utilized to familiarize the administrative staff with PPBS. Following several meetings it was decided to adopt the system. Department chairmen assumed responsibility for developing the program analysis memoranda for their respective subject areas. Building administrators reviewed the program memoranda and made an addendum to each report giving their assessment and recommendations for revision. The role of the central office staff during this period was to facilitate agreement between department chairmen and building administrators. Where differences of opinion could not be accommodated, it was noted in the report. Program memoranda were submitted for review to the Budget Advisory Committee and then presented to the Board of Education for final action.

During the period when the program memoranda were being prepared, the Board appointed 25 citizens to serve on a Budget Advisory Committee. The committee consisted of a cross section of the community and included some of the most outspoken critics of past budgets. Unlike previous citizen advisory committees, this committee began during the initial stages of budget preparation. During their review of prior years' budgets, the committee repeatedly expressed frustration over the lack of relevance of expenditures to the educational program. It was at this point that PPBS was presented to the Budget Advisory Committee. Initially, there was some apprehension by the committee that the adoption of a new budgeting system might further confuse an already complex area. But there was agreement that PPBS promised more relevant and detailed data. Therefore, the Budget Advisory Committee endorsed the PPBS concept and immediately began developing its plan of action.

Language arts, science, mathematics, physical education, and social studies—representing the largest portion of the budget—were reviewed by the entire committee. Three subcommittees were formed to review the remaining 15 program memoranda. A time schedule was established. Ground rules included the submission of the written program memoranda in advance of oral presentations by department chairmen and building administrators. Each department chairman was responsible for providing the oral presentation for his respective subject area. There was a considerable amount of discussion and debate on the professional staff's analysis of program deficiencies and alternative solutions.

Following a review of all program memoranda, the subcommittees submitted written reports to the entire committee, which in turn began the delicate job of synthesizing the recommendations for a final report. The committee as well as the administration experienced difficulty in comparing prior years' budgets to the PPBS. However, attempts were made to convert prior year budget data to the K-12 program structure in order to provide some comparable data. It should be noted that the framework within which the Budget Advisory Committee operated was determined by the program structure. Materials were presented to the committee by subject area; oral presentations were made for each subject area; and the committee's final report presented recommendations on a K-12 program basis.

The Board of Education received separate written recommendations from both the administration and the Budget Advisory Committee. Both reports, with very few minor exceptions, were comparable, and the board adopted a final budget for presentation to the public. During subsequent public hearings on the budget, the fund of information which had been compiled under the PPBS was utilized in explaining the proposed expenditures. A coalition was formed among members of the staff, the Board of Education, and the Budget Advisory Commiteee to present the budget to the community. Members of the committee were able to articulate and describe in considerable detail the proposed expenditures in relation to the educational objectives.

The budget vote held on May 7, 1969, resulted in a 67 percent vote in favor of the proposed budget. This represented the greatest margin of "yes" votes in the recent history of school budget elections. This budget represented the first attempt by the Pearl River School District to utilize PPBS. There is considerable need for improvement. The objectives in some cases were not stated in concrete terms. Additional alternatives for achieving program objectives need to be developed. It is evident that more emphasis needs to be placed on long-range planning and the development of evaluative criteria. However, in the minds of the Board of Education and the staff, PPBS proved to be a valuable vehicle in achieving greater community participation and understanding of the budget and provided more relevant data for allocating resources.

It was recognized that PPBS was not the sole factor in securing voter approval of the 1969–70 budget. The fact that the budget was only increased by five percent over last year's budget certainly contributed to its passage. In addition, some voters expressed a willingness to pass any budget in order to avoid a recurrence of the previous year's turmoil. Notwithstanding these factors, the board and administrative staff were convinced that the movement to PPBS was a major factor in obtaining a favorable vote on the budget for the following reasons:

1. Information about specific subject areas and special services was organized and presented in an understandable manner.
2. The objectives of each program were clearly identified.
3. The staff, in setting its priorities, considered the entire program, K-12. They also considered the relationship between subject areas. This resulted in the allocation of resources in line with the agreed-upon district-wide priorities.
4. The services received by the taxpayers were related to specific dollar amounts. The attempt to integrate the financial plan fully with the educational program was recognized by the community.

Harry J. Hartley has stated that "once the public is forced to think in program terms, they will be more reluctant to cut the budget."[9] The experience in Pearl River tends to bear out his hypothesis. In the past the public in Pearl River has been willing to request lump sum or "across the board" reductions. The PPBS approach has provided information that allows for the identification of the specific services which would be curtailed or lost as a result of reductions in the budget. The public is unwilling to support most reductions once they recognize the specific services to be reduced. The integration of the fiscal plan with the educational program allowed the board and administration to go to the taxpayers with a budget that they felt was educationally defensible as well as fiscally responsible.

As the staff of the Pearl River School District sharpens its capability in the utilization of PPBS, the benefits will increase. More specifically, it is anticipated that once long-range objectives and priorities have been established under PPBS, the district will be able to relate its collective negotiations to the stated organizational objectives. Teacher demands, for example, can be related to the objectives of the school district and this will facilitate the achievement of these objectives. Another dimension of the future utilization of PPBS is management by objectives. This could include some plan to reward staff for the achievement of stated goals. There are many additional uses of PPBS, such as in the area of capital outlay, unification of school districts, reorganization of specialized educational services, and intergovernmental relationships.

As more school districts adopt PPBS, the previously suggested uses will be greatly expanded, for it is a viable system of management. Of all the possible applications of PPBS, one of the most significant is its utilization as a vehicle for organizing and displaying data to overcome taxpayer resistance to school budgets.

NOTES

1. *New York State School Board Association Newsletter,* Vol. XI, No. 8, August, 1969.
2. *School Business Management News* (State Education Department, Albany, N.Y.) , August, 1968, line 17.
3. *U.S. News and World Report,* August 25, 1969, p. 76.
4. Public Employees Fair Employment Act, Chap. 392, Laws of New York State of 1967.
5. "What Is PPB?," State Local Finances Project, George Washington University, p. 1.
6. *Ibid.,* p. 2.
7. Association of School Business Officials, draft of *Educational Resource Management Design* presented at June, 1969, meeting in Denver, Colorado, Fig. 2.
8. For additional information on PPBS, see Harry J. Hartley, *Educational Planning-Programming-Budgeting: A Systems Approach.* N.Y.: Prentice-Hall, 1968; David Novick (ed) , *Program Budgeting,* Cambridge, Mass.: Harvard University Press, 1965; "Planning-Programming-Budgeting System: A Symposium," *Public Administration Review,* December, 1966; and "Planning-Programming-Budgeting System Reexamined: Development, Analysis and Criticism," *Public Administration Review,* March/April, 1969.
9. Harry J. Hartley, speech on "The Mounting Crime in Financing Public Education," March 17, 1969, Nyack, New York.

A System Approach to Accountability in Education

ROGER A. KAUFMAN

Identifying the primary task of educators as that of learning management, the author presents a systematic approach through a generic model for education management. The integration of some newer educational tools with the stated purpose of achieving an accountability for educational results removes the author's process model from the theoretical to the practical level. Improving education through the

"A System Approach to Accountability in Education" by Roger A. Kaufman, Ph.D., Professor of Education and Communication, Graduate School of Human Behavior, U.S. International University, San Diego, California. Prepared under contract with the U.S. Office of Education, Department of Health, Education and Welfare. Based in part upon an article in *Educational Technology Magazine,* Issue on "Accountability," 1971. Reprinted by permission.

systems approach probes the variables of time, materials, resource personnel, and funds with a number of alternatives for this solution of identified educational problems.

At this time a crisis is upon us—a crisis of demands for predictable learning in a context of decreasing funds, increasing teacher demands, and an unwillingness if not fear of using more effective and efficient means for reaching required goals.

In an era where "performance counts," education is faced with achieving success, and being accountable for success. Should we expect any less?

If Lessinger is not the father of educational accountability then he must be at least the midwife. During his tenure at the Office of Education and following, he has assisted in the birth of not only accountability, but has assisted in providing the neonate with tools for achieving a realistic accountability (21, 22, 23). These tools include (but are not limited to): Auditing, System Analysis, System Approach, Performance Contracting.

Other tools also exist, and are useful to those concerned with the quantitative improvement of education. These additional tools include Needs Assessment, Measurable Performance Objectives, Planning-Programming-Budgeting System (PPBS), Systems Analysis, Methods-Means Selection techniques, PERT (Program Evaluation Review Technique), and other related network-based management tools, testing and assessment, and summative and formative evaluation techniques.

The material following intends to suggest an integration of these thrust tools for the measurable improvement of education, an accountability which is realistic and achievable, and the attainment of professional role and responsibility for educators.

Accountability in education is a concept that is *here*. Accountability for what is important to determine lest we are held accountable for variables for which we have little or no input or control. Accountability has been defined by Lessinger as " . . . a policy declaration adopted by a legal body such as a board of education or a state legislature requiring outside reports of dollars spent to achieve results. The concept rests on three fundamental bases. Student accomplishment, independent review of student accomplishment and a public report relating dollars spent to student accomplishment" (22). Accountability, then, includes the demonstration of accomplishing what you have said you would accomplish.

If we educators, then, are going to be accountable, it would be well if we had tools by which we could (1) determine what we will be accountable for accomplishing, (2) determine methods for achieving predictable results, including the effectiveness and efficiency of each, (3) determine methods for deciding among alternatives, (4) determine methods for the management and control of educational operations, and (5) determine methods for ascertaining the extent to which needs and associated objectives have been met.

Following is an attempt to identify various available tools for achieving a "just" accountability, with the proper perspective of values and valuing (28) and to suggest a relationship between these tools so that educators and partners in the educational process may determine the utility of each for his own program of accountability.

The primary function of education is to bring about relevant learning, and the primary task of educators is learning management (16, 18). The learning management job could be conceived of as being the planning, organizing, designing, implementing and evaluating of learning situations and outcomes, and making required continuing revisions to assure ongoing relevancy and practicality. It *is* an accountability process.

If the above is valid, then the way in which salient variables and required resources are identified and utilized becomes the critical question for achieving relevant and practical learning outcomes.,

It is not uncommon for managers to erroneously start to determine *HOW* something should be accomplished before *WHAT* is to be accomplished has been adequately identified and defined—perhaps due to a lack of a reasonable, cohesive model for valid educational change. Following is a possible *process* model for education based upon a problem-solving referent, and suggests some alternatives for identifying and possibly integrating current thrusts towards the systematic and valid improvement of education.

A Possible Educational Process Model

Process may be defined as the steps or manner in which an outcome is achieved. A product is an outcome. In the case of education it may be identified with observed learner skills, knowledges, and attitudes which are identified and measured at a specific time.

Education may be viewed as a process, a process to provide learners with the required skills, knowledges and attitudes to be able to survive and contribute in the world to which they are to go when they legally leave the educational agency (19). In keeping with this process analogy, education may be viewed as the identification and resolution of problems—what should learners know and be able to do when they graduate (or legally leave), and what should be done to provide them with the requisite skills, attitudes and knowledges.

A number of models, not too dissimilar, have been proposed for both education and problem solving (4,9,10,15) . One model, known to some as the "scientific method" basically consists of the steps of problem identification, setting goals or hypotheses, selecting solution strategies, hypothesis testing, evaluation and revision. John Dewey's suggested problem-solving process was not unlike this generic process model.

Dorrigan and Kaufman (4,9,10) have suggested a six-step problem solving model that seems applicable to the management of learning. The six steps are shown in Figure 1.

		(Revise as Required)		
1.0	2.0	3.0	4.0	5.0
Identify	Determine	Select	Implement	Determine
Problem	Solution	Solution		Performance
	Requirements	Strategies		Effectiveness
	and	and		
(From Needs)	Alternatives	Tools		

Figure 1. A six-step problem solving model for application to education. The six steps are identified, five within the boxes, and the sixth represented by the broken line which indicates revision as required by performance.

This model has been frequently called a "System Approach" to education, representing a closed-loop, self-correcting process for proceeding from identified needs to predictable outcomes. It represents a suggested process model for defining educational accountability and for being accountable.

Other models have been suggested for "systems" approaches (8) , varying from Lehmann's seven-step model (20) to other models which frequently start the educational process from varying points of departure (5,11,29,33) .

It is suggested that the above six-step "system" process model is appropriate for describing the educational management process, and that it may be used for a preliminary referent for identifying and integrating current useful thrusts and tools for the quantitative improvement of education. Such thrusts include Needs Assessment; System Analysis; Behavioral (Performance) Objectives; Planning-Programming-Budgeting Systems (PPBS); Systems Analysis; Methods-Means Selections; Performance Contracting; Testing; Assessment and Auditing.

Description of the System Process

The above identified process model for education indicates six functions, or parts:*

* This process was recently recommended by The Forum on Educational Technology at the 1970 White House Conference on Children.

1. Identify problem (based upon documented needs).
2. Determine solution requirements and solution alternatives.
3. Select strategies and tools (from among the alternatives).
4. Implement.
5. Determine performance effectiveness.
6. Revise as required.

Identify problem: The first step in the suggested process model is to identify the problem(s) based upon documented needs. A need may be defined as the discrepancy between "what is" and "what should be" (15). A problem is identified when a particular discrepancy or set of discrepancies have been selected for resolution (15). The identification of a problem includes the specific delineation of requirements for problem resolution—a definition of required terminal product (or outcome). This step identifies and documents that for which we are to be accountable.

Included in this step is the identification of current and predictable conditions and resources, including (but not limited to) time, materials, resources, personnel and funds. Thus, current and/or anticipated scarcities and surpluses are identified to help serve as a basis for functional planning and success achievement.

Determine solution requirements and solution alternatives: After the problem has been identified, an analysis is undertaken to determine the detailed requirements (or specifications) for proceeding from the current condition (what is) to the required condition (what should be). These consist of delineation of overall objectives and sub-objectives (products and sub-products) stated in measurable, performance terms. Additionally, while detailed requirements are being analyzed and identified, *possible* solution strategies and tools (such as performance contracting) are identified (but not selected) for accomplishing the requirements, including a determination of the advantages and disadvantages of each relative to producing the required outcome (s).

Select strategies and tools from among alternatives: From the alternatives identified in the previous step, criteria for selection are determined, and the actual selection of appropriate tools and strategies is accomplished. Frequently selection criteria include cost-benefit or other effectiveness-efficiency indicators.

All too frequently cost-efficiency is used, not including any consideration of effectiveness (or achievement of relevant product, or outcomes). There is a difference between economy and economics. In relevant and practical education it makes sense to make decisions on "how-to-do-it" on the basis of what will do the *best* job for the least expenditure of time, resources and effort of both learner and implementer.

A case in point could well be the increasing labor-intensivity of education. Each time a new requirement for learning is mandated we seem *automatically* to increase professional staff to meet the requirement. If we were to begin to make cost-effectiveness decisions we would probably start utilizing more and more learning aids and equipment to do those portions of the required tasks which actually can do parts of the job better, more accurately, more quickly, and more reliably. (Think of what the average household would be like if we were to fail to take advantage of recent advances in labor-saving hardware.) Our selection process should revolve around determining what will do the best job for learners, and do this job for the least cost.

Implement: Based upon the needs, the detailed requirements, the alternative ways of getting the outcomes accomplished, the selected tools and strategies (the ways and means of getting from "what is" to "what should be") are designed, purchased, or obtained, and utilized. This is the "doing" phase, where the actual solution strategies and tools are utilized and appropriate performance data collected. If for example, performance contracting was selected "method-means," the development of an "RFP" would begin, a contractor would be selected, and implementation begun.

Determine performance effectiveness: Based upon the needs and the requirements, the outcomes of the application of a problem-solving process to this point are evaluated to determine the extent to which required results have been achieved. Here the data for terminal achievement (summative evaluation) and for process utility are collected, analyzed, compared to requirements and used to determine revision requirements.

Revise as required: Anytime a performance requirement is not met (either *during* a program or at the end), necessary revision is required. This critical step assures that a self-correcting process is utilized, and increases the probability of effective and efficient outcomes being obtained. It should be noted that in the suggested model, revision may be required at any step, or point, in problem resolution —it is not necessary to commit to a "disaster plan" and have to wait until the plan has been fully implemented to institute required changes.

It is suggested that this process model may have basic utility for the design and accomplishment of effective and efficient education—the first two steps identify the "whats" of problem solution, the remaining steps identify and define the "hows."

Current Thrusts for Measurable Improvement of Education

Springing from a number of philosophical and operational sources, several tools have come to the attention of educators as providing rational and realistic ways of improving the educational product. These include:

1. Needs Assessment (9, 15, 30, 31)
2. System Analysis (4, 9, 10, 15, 16, 17, 18)
3. Performance Objectives (24, 26, 30)
4. Planning-Programming-Budgeting System (3, 14, 25, 27, 34, 35, 36)
5. Methods-Means Selection Process (1, 8, 10)
6. Systems Analysis (5)
7. Network-based Management Tools (6, 7)
8. Performance Contracting (24a)
9. Auditing (21)
10. Testing, National Assessment, Summative and Formative Evaluation (2, 12, 0)

Rather than indicating that any of the above tools are better than others, or even requiring a selection of one, each individually and collectively seem to hold promise to educators for the measurable improvement of educational activities and outcomes, and for defining and achieving a realistic educational accountability.

Needs Assessment: Many educators have become concerned with not only learning, but the determination of WHAT should be learned as a necessary prerequisite to achieving relevant learning outcomes. Needs assessments are formal attempts at determining what should be done and learned in schools. First attempts in California, for instance, were made by many of the ESEA Title III PACE Centers, and the results of these are well covered by Sweigert (31, 32). Several school districts and State educational agencies have or are implementing needs assessments.

Needs Assessment procedures seem to be keyed to the concept that relevancy of education must be empirically determined from the outset by a formal procedure which precedes educational planning, design, and implementation (often starting from the identification of symptoms). In most forms, needs assessment identifies and documents the discrepancies (or gaps) between "what is" and "what should be" and provides a valid starting point for education. By involving the partners in education, the questions of (1) accountability for what and (2) how and who will determine successful accomplishment may be derived and agreed upon. As part of the analysis of "what is" current and future resources and conditions are identified and documented. This serves as the basis for further analysis and decision making.

System Analysis: System analysis is a process for determining the requirements for getting from "what is" to "what should be." As conceived by Kaufmann and Corrigan (9, 10, 15), it consists of analysis, in levels or layers, of requirements for problem solution. They identify the analytical steps of (a) mission analysis, (b) function anlaysis, (c) task analysis, and (d) methods-means analysis. The outcome of a system analysis is a delineation of feasible "whats" for problems solution, and a listing of possible strategies and tools for achieving each "what."

Performance Objectives: A number of usable presentations have been made on behavioral (or performance) objectives (24, 26, 39), all agreeing on the desirability of stating learning outcomes in measurable, performance terms. Usually included in an objective is the statement of (a) what is to be done, (b) by whom is it to be done, (c) under what conditions is it to be done, and (d) what criteria will be used to determine its accomplishment. While most discussions of performance objectives are related to the instructional process directly, the same criteria may be applied to other educational activities as well.

Planning-Programming-Budgeting System (PPBS): Perhaps first formally applied to the context of national defense, PPBS represents an extremely powerful tool for educators. In the main, it provides a means for answering questions of education relative to "what do I give" and "what do I get." PPBS deals with these questions. It identifies the relationships between product outcomes and costs for achieving the outcomes for various alternative methods and means. Many discussions of PPBS indicate that it starts with a "systems" analysis (or work breakdown structure or program structure) in order that viable alternatives may be considered, projected and evaluated. A number of good, detailed references are available (3, 14, 25, 27, 34, 35, 36). Frequently, PPBS efforts inappropriately focus on budget and ignore the critical "PP" elements.

Methods-Means Selection Processes: Closely related to PPBS are procedures for deciding among alternative methods and means (or media) (strategies and tools) for achieving required outcomes. Briggs, et al. (1), offers a test on methods-media selection, and Corrigan has developed procedures for making effective and efficient media decisions. These methods-means selection procedures are generally based upon the specification of the nature of the learner and the characteristics of available tools and strategies, and the specifications for the learning to be accomplished. Cost-effectiveness is a key criterion.

Systems Analysis: Frequently, techniques for selecting among alternative solutions those which will provide the greatest cost-benefit are called "systems" analysis (5). Perhaps the plural form of the word "system" indicates the close lineage with the word used in conjunction with computers and hardware (solutions) (18).

Performance Contracting: A relatively new procedure in education, this tool provides a possible alternative to the overly labor-intensive educational system. Here, ideally, a contract is let to existing personnel or private sect or agencies for the achievement of specific learning outcomes.

If handled correctly and in a responsible manner, this procedure may increase the overall cost-effectiveness of education. The goals and measurable objectives should be criterion-referenced (derived from the Needs Assessment and further detailed by the System Analysis). Its selection as an alternative method-means should be on the basis that it is the most viable alternative—not because it is a new or flashy "gimmick" for education!

Mayrhofer (24a) discusses some critical considerations for implementing performance contracting efforts.

Network-Based Management Tools: Cook and others have introduced the concepts of PERT (Program Evaluation Review Technique) and CPM (Critical Path Method) to educators in order for them to better manage and control the educational implementation process (6, 7). It is suggested that these tools are best applied when all requirements are delineated and the methods and procedures are selected, and the job is to maintain control over the "doing" process.

Testing, National Assessment, and Summative and Formative Evaluation: Testing, of course, is not new to education—in fact most of the major testing tools have been developed by or for educators. Testing provides an understood manner for determining the effectiveness of any treatment, and new tests are being developed constantly. There appear to be, however, some developments in testing which seem to offer promise for educators interested in planned change. One of these developments which relate to measurable performance objectives is "Criterion-Reference" testing (13) which provides an alternative to norm-referenced tests. Some major testing concerns are, it is understood, developing criterion-referenced testing instruments.

Summative and Formative Evaluation (0) form a pair of related procedures. Summative Evaluation (Step 5 in the System Approach Model) is a familiar procedure. Coupled with an on-going evaluation of progress and the opportunity to make relevant modifications during program operation (the sixth step shown as a dotted line in the model) offers great power for designing and implementing successful educational programs.

Educational Auditing: This concept which has been best explained by Lessinger (21) is analogous to the Certified Public Accountant who reviews the accomplishments of industrial firms and businesses in terms of expenditures and outcomes. The audit is different from but related to "classical" evaluation in that it is oriented towards the statement of accomplishments and does not intend to provide suggestions for revision—it is status and accomplishment oriented only. National assessment is now underway, and will provide empirical data relative to how well and how much education is teaching our youngsters (2).

Testing is an evaluation tool for determining the extent to which we have achieved that which we set out to achieve.

These tools, described all too briefly above, are of interest for a number of reasons: (1) they are empirically grounded, and attempt to quantify that which should or that which is being accomplished in education, and (2) they are being considered and in some cases being used by educators, and (3) in some cases they are mandated.

These tools are not unrelated, and following is a suggested manner in which these tools may be related each to the others and to an overall model for the educational process.

An Attempt at an Integration of Educational Tools

If logical problem solving may be said to follow the above six-step model, then it would seem to be critical to start the process with the advantage of having empirical data to document the problem and its characteristics. Such a beginning referent may be accomplished by an *Educational Needs Assessment.* Such an assessment of needs might well tell us (perhaps only *minimally*) the discrepancies between "what is" and "what should be" so that a valid starting point may be identified.

After a Needs Assessment has been accomplished, and the specification of the two dimensions of problem solving stated (what is and what should be), further delineation of requirements should be made to determine the sub-objectives and requirements for getting from where we are to where we are to be. This analysis may be accomplished by the process tool described earlier as System Analysis. The system analysis will provide detailed information relative to solution requirements, and will indicate possible alternative methods and means for accomplishing each requirement. Where instructional programs are being considered, the requirements may be stated in terms of Behavioral Objectives—learning specifications in measurable performance terms. (For management programs the requirements would be also stated in performance terms.)

The third function identified in the Problem Solving Process Model is to select solution strategies from alternatives. Here, the basic intent and tools of PPBS and/or Systems Analysis seem appropriate. Based upon the data obtained ffrom the Needs Assessment, the System Analysis (and possible statement of Performance Objectives), alternative outcomes and tools may be considered, compared each to the others, projected and selected. In the case of media, Methods-Means selection procedures may offer a usable tool for selection of appropriate tools and strategies.

Implementation, the fourth function is the "meat" of the process which is familiar to most educators, and certainly to educational administrators. This how-to-do-it portion is not formally considered here, primarily because it is covered in great detail in texts for schools of administration and management. Now, powerful tools such as performance contracting offer great potential promise. Tools such as PERT/CPM and other network-based techniques have much to offer the implementer.

The fifth step is "Determined Performance Effectiveness." Here testing and assessment procedures provide a natural tool for determining how well or how poorly we have achieved our objectives and reduced or eliminated the delineated needs. Evaluation based upon the determined requirements will tend to improve the validity of the testing/assessment procedure especially if both summative and formative evaluation modes are exercised. The independent educational accomplishment audit will provide status and outcome data.

By following the functions described in Figure 1, there seems to appear a natural relationship between extant tools for the improvement of education, and for each tool with the overall problem-solving process—a process for defining and achieving educational accountability—Figure 2 presents a graphic of this suggested relationship.

FORMATIVE EVALUATION
(Revise as Required)

1.0 Identify Problem (From Needs)	2.0 Determine Solution Requirements and Solution Alternatives	3.0 Select Solution Strategies and Tools	4.0 Implement	5.0 Determine Performance Effectiveness
Needs Assessment	System Analysis, Behavioral	PPBS, Methods-Means Selection, Systems Analysis	Network-Based Management Tools, Performance Contracting	Testing Assessment, Audit, Summative Evaluation

Figure 2. The relationship between current tools for the improvement of education and their relationship with a problem-solving process and a possible model for educational management, and defining and achieving educational accountability.

It should be noted that not all of the above tools are completely independent—for instance, PPBS should be preceded by a Needs Assessment System Analysis; and frequently, discussion of objectives include the requirement for a System Analysis and/or a Needs Assessment. Use of performance contracting should be based upon a needs assessment, a system analysis, and a cost-benefit analysis.

It would seem to suggest, however, that greater utility may be obtained from current local, state-wide, and national efforts if each of the "thrust" tools could be defined, and each group working on the improvement of education could work together from a common referent of what is to be done, and how to do it. Perhaps cooperative efforts could reduce or eliminate redundancy of efforts, and provide a single, understandable referent to educational practitioners. Much confusion exists today concerning what are the "tools" and how and where they should be used. (As an example, many educators and concerned citizens incorrectly equate accountability, performance contracting and auditing—a confusion between means and ends!)

Summary

The preceding presentation was intended to set a rationale for cooperation and interdependence between professional educational practitioners who are working to measurably improve the products and processes of education and define and achieve a functional accountability. An overall, or possible generic model for educational management was presented, identifying six steps for problem solving. Additionally, tools currently being used for the quantifiable improvement of education were briefly presented, discussed and an attempt was made to relate these tools for the improvement of education with a suggested process model of education, and also relating the tools, each with the others. It is hoped that an integration of tools and purposes may be achieved so that education may be aided, in processes and outcomes, by a cooperative, systematic, empirical, evaluatable attack on current and future problems—to achieve and assume an accountability for educational success.

REFERENCES

0. Bloom, B. *Summative and Formative Evaluation.* McGraw-Hill, New York, in press.
1. Briggs, L. J., et al. *Methods–media, Selection in Education,* American Institutes for Research, 1967, Pittsburgh, Pa.
2. Brain, G. B. "What's the Score on National Assessment?" *CTA Journal,* May 1969.
3. Carpenter, M. B. *Program Budgeting as a Way To Clarify Issues in Education.* RAND Corporation, July 1968.

4. Carter, L. F. *The Systems Approach to Education—The Mystique and the Reality.* System Development Corporation, SP-3291, Jan. 1969.

5. Cleland, D. I., and King, W. R. *Systems Analysis and Project Management.* McGraw-Hill Book Company, N.Y. 1968.

6. Cook, D. L. "PERT: Applications in Education," Cooperative Research Monograph Number 17, OE-12124, 1966, U.S. Government Printing Office.

7. Cook, D. L. "Better Project Planning and Control Techniques through the Use of System Analysis and Management Techniques." A paper presented at the Symposium on Operations Analysis in Education, sponsored by the National Center for Educational Statistics, U.S. Office of Education, November, 1967.

8. Corrigan, R. E. "Method-Media Selection" Operation PEP, 1965.

9. Corrigan, R. E., and Kaufman, R. A. "The Steps and Tools of the System Approach to Education." Operation PEP, Tulare County Department of Education, Visalia, California, 1966. (A number of documents were produced for operation PEP and the Chapman College Experienced Teacher Fellowship Program in the area of a System Approach by R. E. Corrigan, Betty O. Corrigan, D. Goodwin, and R. A. Kaufman during the period 1965–68.)

10. Corrigan, R. E., Corrigan, Betty O., Goodwin, O., and Kaufman, R. A. *System Approach for Education (SAFE)*. R. E. Corrigan Associates, Garden Grove, California, 1969.

11. Gibson, L. "Instructional Systems Design Through In-Service Education." *Audiovisual Instruction,* Sept. 1968.

12. Ellam, S.—Accountability-roasting article reference.

13. Glaser, R. "Psychological Bases for Instructional Design." *AV Communication Review,* Winter 1966.

14. Katzenbach, E. L. *Planning, Programming Budgeting Systems: PPBS and Education.* The New England School Development Council, March 1968.

15. Kaufman, R. A. "A System Approach to Education: Derivation and Definition." *AV Communication Review,* Winter 1968.

16. Kaufman, R. A. "A Management Model." A paper presented to Nova University Conference on Innovations in Educational Management, April 1969.

17. Kaufman, R. A. "A Possible Integrative Model for the Systematic and Quantitative Improvement of Education." *American Psychologist,* in press.

18. Kaufman, R. A. "System Approaches to Education: Discussion and Attempted Integration." ERIC/CEA Monograph, University of Oregon, 1970.

19. Kaufman, R. A., Corrigan, R. E., and Johnson, D. W. "Toward Educational Responsiveness to Society's Needs: A Tentative Model." Accepted for Publication, *Journal of Socio-Economic Planning Sciences.*

20. Lehmann, H. "The Systems Approach to Education." *Audiovisual Instruction,* Feb. 1968.

21. Lessinger, L. M.—educational auditing reference.

22. Lessinger, L. M. "The Powerful Notion of Accountability in Education." Paper presented at the Academy on Educational Engineering, Oregon State Department of Public Instruction, Werme, Oregon, August 10–14, 1970.

23. Lessinger, L. M. "Evaluation and Accountability in Educational Management—Robbing Dr. Peter to 'Pay Paul.'" Paper presented at the Academy on Educational Engineering, Oregon State Department of Public Instruction, Werme, Oregon, August 10–14, 1970.

24. Mager, R. F. "Preparing Instructional Objectives." Fearon Publishers, 1962.

24a. Mayrhofer, A. V. "Performance Contracting for Instruction." U.S. Office of Education, BESE, undated.

Accountability in Education

FELIX M. LOPEZ

Felix Lopez probes reasons for the failure of accountability systems to gain acceptance and suggests an approach for overcoming this problem. The charter of accountability advocated is a modified version of "Management by Objectives," also known as planning-programming-budgeting system (PPBS). Use of the charter approach provides for goal-setting at all levels of the educational ladder—top, middle, and base. An approach which establishes accountability measures for superintendents, principals, and supervisors, as well as teachers, appears to be a primary step in minimizing opposition to accountability from various groups.

Accountability refers to the process of expecting each member of an organization to answer to someone for doing specific things according to specific plans and against certain timetables to accomplish tangible performance results. It assumes that everyone who joins an organization does so presumably to help in the achievment of its purposes; it assumes that individual behavior which contributes to these purposes is functional and that which does not is dysfunctional. Accountability is intended, therefore, to insure that the behavior of every member of an organization is largely functional.

Accountability is to be distinguished from responsibility by the fact that the latter is an essential component of authority which cannot be delegated. It is the responsiblity of a board of education to insure the effective education of the children in its community. Board members cannot pass this responsibility on to principals and to teachers. But they can hold teachers and principals accountable for the achievement of tangible educational effects *provided* they define clearly what effects they expect and furnish the resources needed to achieve them.

REASONS FOR FAILURE

A review of accountability programs underlines its uneven, trial-and-error progress and its current inadequacies. Initiated when psychometric theory was largely underdeveloped, embedded early in unrealistic management and legislative mandates, imposed usually from above on an unwilling and uncomprehending supervisor, the program has struggled with the common conception that it is an end rather

Felix M. Lopez, and associates, "Accountability in Education," *Phi Delta Kappan,* 52:231–235, December 1970. Reprinted by permission.

than a means and with an administrative naiveté that treats it as a student's report card. Personnel textbooks have stressed the idea that an accountability plan must be characterized by simplicity, flexibility, and economy. Ignoring the fact that these qualities are not wholly compatible, administrators have attempted to develop programs along these lines. Their inevitable failures have led to the current disillusionment and distrust and, in some quarters, to the belief that the establishment of an effective program is impossible. Nevertheless, a careful examination of efforts to establish accountability programs suggests some underlying misconceptions that explain the many failures.

1. Most accountability programs have been installed in organizational settings that lack the necessary background and organizational traditions to assimilate them. Insufficient emphasis has been placed on the development of an organizational philosophy and on the determination of accountability policies before the implementation of the program.

2. The administrative procedures governing the program have not been attuned to its purposes. There has been a tendency to make the program accomplish a great deal with an oversimplified procedure. The evidence strongly suggests that despite the ardent wish for economy and simplicity, only a program designed for a specific purpose or involving a multimethod approach is likely to succeed.

3. Accountability systems have not been designed to gain acceptance by those who are covered by them nor by those who have to implement them. For the most part, they have been designed by specialists, approved at the highest levels, and imposed without explanation on those who have to implement them. This occurs because the problem is approached from an organizational rather than an individual perspective.

4. The measures of accountability so far developed have not met even minimum standards of reliability and relevancy. This failure is known as the "criterion problem" and can be summarized briefly as follows:

a) Criteria of effectiveness in a position generally lack clear specifications.
b) Objective measures, when examined closely, are usually found to be either nonobjective or irrelevant.
c) Subjective measures, when examined closely, are usually found to be biased or unreliable.
d) Seemingly adequate criteria can vary over time.
e) Position effectiveness is really multidimensional. Effectiveness in

one aspect of a position does not necessarily mean effectiveness in others.

f) When effectiveness in different aspects of a position is measured, there is no sure way to combine these measures into a single index of effectiveness.

g) Different performance patterns achieve the same degree of effectiveness in the same job.

To be successful, therefore, the accountability program must meet the following requirements:

1. It must be an important communications medium in a responsive environment through which members are informed of what is to be accomplished, by whom, and how; wide participation in the obtainment of organization goals must be invited; and the attention of top management must be focused on the accomplishment of individual employees' personal goals.

2. It must reflect an organizational philosophy that inspires confidence and trust in all the members.

3. It must be based on ethical principles and sound policies that can be implemented by a set of dynamic, flexible, and realistic standards, procedures, and practices.

4. It must clearly specify its purposes so that standards, procedures, and practices can be conformed to them.

5. It must be designed primarily to improve the performance of each member in his current job duties. Other effects, such as the acquisition of information on which to base salary and promotion decisions and the personal development of the employees' capacities, may accompany the main effect of improved job performance, but these must be considered merely by-products of the main process.

6. The manner in which the supervisor discusses his evaluation with the subordinate constitutes the core of the process. If this is handled poorly, the program, no matter how well designed and implemented, will fail.

7. To be effective and accepted, both those who use it and those who will be judged by it must participate in the design, installation, administration, and review of the total accountability system.

These principles, then, outline the dimensions of an approach to the establishment of accountability in education. The approach encompasses three broad interventions into the current system, each aimed initially at a distinct level of the organization structure: the top, the middle, and the base, the last named being the teachers themselves. Ultimately, however, all three levels will be involved in all three phases of the accountability program.

Intervention at the Top

Basically, intervention at the top consists of the establishment of organizational goals by the use of a technique referred to in private industry as "Management by Objectives" (MBO) and in government as the "Planning, Programming, and Budgeting System" (PPBS). Since there are many excellent books describing these techniques in detail, we shall confine ourselves here to a brief summary of the method.[1]

GOAL SETTING

The underlying concept of the goal-setting approach is simple: The clearer the idea you have of what you want to accomplish, the greater your chance of accomplishing it. Goal setting, therefore, represents an effort on the part of the management to inhibit the natural tendency of organizational procedures to obscure organizational purposes in the utilization of resources. The central idea is to establish a set of goals for the organization, to integrate individual performance with them, and to relate the rewards system to their accomplishment.

While there is general agreement that this method represents the surest approach to effective management, there is no primrose path to its practical implementation.

In its most commonly accepted form, MBO constitutes an orderly way of goal setting at the top, communication of these goals to lower-unit managers, the development of lower-unit goals that are phased into those set by the higher levels, and comparison of results in terms of goals. The program operates within a network of consultative interviews between supervisor and subordinate in which the subordinate receives ample opportunity to participate in the establishment of his own performance objectives. Thus, the whole concept is oriented to a value system based upon the results achieved; and the results must be concrete and measurable.

When properly administered, Management by Objectives has much to recommend it:

1. It involves the whole organization in the common purpose.
2. It forces top management to think through its purposes, to review them constantly, to relate the responsibilities of individual units to pre-set goals, and to determine their relative importance.
3. It sets practical work tasks for each individual, holds him accountable for their attainment, and demonstrates clearly how his performance fits into the overall effort.
4. It provides a means of assuring that organization goals are even-

tually translated into specific work tasks for the individual employee.

It is, therefore, virtually impossible to conceive of an effective accountability program that does not operate within the umbrella of the goal-setting process. When properly designed and implemented, goal setting becomes an ideal basis for other forms of performance evaluation. It insures that subordinate goals and role performances are in support of the goals of the higher levels of the organization and that ultimately the institutional purposes will be achieved.

THE CHARTER OF ACCOUNTABILITY

One way of implementing the goal-setting process that has been found useful in education is through the development of a charter of accountability. This approach was originally developed by the Ground Systems Group of the Hughes Aircraft Company.[2] The charter is agreed to by two individuals or groups—one in a superordinate and the other in a subordinate capacity—after consultation, discussion, and negotiation. Ultimately, the entire organization is covered by the series of charters beginning at the top with a major organization unit, say, the English department in a local high school. Each teacher's goals are shaped by his unit's charter of accountability. Each unit head is held accountable for the results specified in his charter, which he draws up and which he and his superiors sign. Ultimately, all charters are combined into a system-wide charter that provides the basis of accountability for the board of education and the superintendent of schools.

A charter contains a statement of purposes, goals, and objectives. *Purpose* constitutes the organization's reason for existence and gives meaning and direction to all its activities. Purposes, therefore, are usually stated in broad inspirational terms.

Goals and *objectives* are the tangible expressions of the organization's purposes. Goals are long-range, concrete, end results specified in measurable terms. Objectives are short-range, specific targets to be reached in a period of one year, also specified in measurable terms.

Specifically, a charter of accountability contains the following features:

1. A statement of system-wide purposes or areas of concern and the purposes of the next level above the unit completing the charter of accountability.
2. A statement of the specific purposes of the unit completing the charter.

3. A description of the functional, administrative, and financial accountability necessary to accomplish the unit's purposes.
4. A set of basic assumptions about the future economic, sociopolitical, professional, and technological developments likely to affect the attainment of goals but which are beyond the control of the accountability unit.
5. A listing of the major goals of the unit to be aimed at for the immediate five-year period.
6. A subseries of performance tasks that provide unit supervisors with definitive targets toward which to orient their specialized efforts and with which to define the resources necessary to accomplish them.
7. Statements of the authority and responsibility necessary to complete these tasks.

Space does not permit the full exposition of the process of establishing a charter of accountability. Very broadly, and quite superficially, it would follow this pattern:

1. A central committee or council composed of representatives of key members of the system—school board, local school boards, union, teachers, parent and community groups—would convene to define the broad purposes of the school system. Putting it simply, their job would be to answer these questions: "What is the business of the school system?" "What are we trying to accomplish?" While the answers to these questions may seem obvious, in practice they are difficult to articulate. Answering them serves the larger purpose of clarifying thinking about the realistic aims of a school system. In business, the definition of purpose has led to dramatic changes in organization structure, business policies, product mix, and, ultimately, in return on investment.

The purposes delineated by this council are then discussed widely in the community. In particular, they serve to determine the major areas of concern of the school system that have been assigned to it by the community. Both the purposes and the areas of concern, however, must be considered at this point to be tentative and subject to modification by lower levels of the system. They will provide, however, the necessary guidelines for the goal-setting process and the development of charters of accountability by the school districts and other lower level units.

2. Each major subunit—school district, division, or department—meets to define its goals and objectives and to prepare its charter of accountability. Since these goals and objectives can differ substantially according to the needs of specific localities, the criteria of accountability will also differ. This is the important, even crucial point that constitutes the major advantage of the goal-setting process. It provides

for multiplicity of measures of accountability that are tailored to the needs and hence the goals of specific operating units. The objectives of a principal of an inner city-school will differ from those of a principal of a surburban school, and so must the measures of accountability. Reading grade equivalents may be an appropriate measure of teacher effectiveness in one school and not in the other.

3. The charters of all units are collated and reviewed by the central council or school board with the advice and assistance of the planning and budgeting unit of the office of the superintendent of schools. Appropriate approvals are granted in accordance with existing policy and legislation. Thus, the combined charters constitute *the* charter of accountability for the board of education and the entire school system. While there will be some uniformity to this charter, it is apparent that it will resemble more a patchwork quilt than a seamless cloak and will, therefore, adhere more closely to the reality it attempts to reflect.

4. As each charter is approved, subcharters are developed in the same way for individual units in each district. Obviously, the heads of these units will have had a voice in the formulation of the district charter so that this will not be a new task for them. But in developing the subunit charters in the schools themselves, all the members of the system will ultimately have a voice.

5. Once the charters have been adopted, they are implemented. In some cases, new inputs will eliminate or change previously stated objectives. In others, objectives will be found to be quite unrealistic. Provisions must be made, therefore, to amend the charters of accountability as experience dictates. In most cases, however, it is advisable to stick with the original charter until the year-end review and appraisal of results.

6. The evaluation of the achievement of the period's objectives is made as plans for the next charter are formulated. This is the essence of accountability: results compared to objectives. It is important to note, however, that this evaluation is made not in a punitive, policing climate to check up on people, but rather in a supportive, constructive atmosphere to find out how objectives were achieved and, if they were not, why not. Both parties to this process assume the responsibility for the results and approach the task with the idea of exploring what happened for purposes of problem solving and resetting goals and objectives.

Intervention in the Middle

The implementation of an accountability program depends, to a large extent, on the attitudes and the skills of the supervisory force. If it is skeptical, anxious, or hostile to the plan, it will fail no matter how well it is conceived. This has been the bitter experience of many firms that have attempted to install goal-setting and performance-evaluation programs without first preparing their managers and supervisors to implement them.

Thus, a second essential step in introducing accountability into a school system is the establishment of a massive supervisory development program. Such a program must be practical, intensive, and primarily participative in nature. Its purpose is not merely to disseminate information but rather to change attitudes and to impart specific skills, particularly the skill of conducting accountability interviews with subordinates.

This will not be easy. Most supervisors, principles, and teachers have had no experience with such a program to prepare them for the tasks involved. A development program must be tailor made to meet their needs.

The development program must also begin at the top with the superintendent and the assistant superintendents. There is a practical reason for this. When presenting this subject matter to middle managers in other organizations, an almost universal response from them is, "Why can't our bosses take this course? They need it more than we do." Since the program content is likely to be quite strange, even revolutionary, to many of the lower middle-management participants, its credibility can be insured only by its being accepted at the highest levels and applied there first.

The program must enable the top-level people to examine the basic assumptions on which they operate and give them as much time as possible to get these assumptions out in the open. The specific objectives of the program would be:

1. To emphasize the influence process in handling subordinates, managers, and supervisors, as well as teachers, and to de-emphasize the formal authority-power-coercion approach to supervision and administration.
2. To provide a deeper understanding of the communications process itself. Such a program must heighten the awareness of the supervisor as to how he comes across best to others and develop his flexibility in dealing with the broad spectrum of personalities encountered in the fulfillment of his responsibilities. Each supervisor should be given an opportunity to prepare a plan for his self-growth and development.
3. To consider ways of dealing with the more routine aspects of teaching by considering job enrichment techniques.
4. To emphasize the sociopsychological realities that education faces today. The program should make supervisors aware that they simply cannot rely on authoritarianism alone to get results with people.

The format of the program should be primarily participative in nature, that is, it should consist of learning experiences and exercises which require the supervisors to participate actively in the training sessions. Frequent use should be made of audiovisual displays, role playing, conference discussions, and case study techniques. Theoretical ideas and concepts that help develop new ways of thinking and approaching problems can be introduced and amplified through specifically designed case studies. The solutions which result from the systematic examination of these case studies should be applied directly to specific school system problems. And finally, attention must be given to problem areas that may be unique to an individual supervisor.

Intervention at the Base

The third phase of the accountability system, and the most pertinent, is the development of specific instruments and techniques to evaluate how individual members of the school system are performing their assigned roles. Since this phase touches the teachers directly, it is the most difficult and also the most delicate. If it is handled properly, it can accelerate the educational development of the community's children. If it is handled poorly, or indifferently, or as just another routine task (as it so often has been in other public agencies), problems of academic retardation will persist.

Description and discussion of the design, development, and installation of individual performance standards and measures for teachers is beyond the scope of this paper.[3] There are a number of approaches to this effort utilizing both objective and subjective measures. But regardless of the measures and procedures employed, there are some general principles that warrant mention here.

REQUIREMENTS OF A TEACHER ACCOUNTABILITY PROGRAM

First, an individual teacher accountability program can function effectively only within the context of a goal-setting program, such as the charter of accountability previously described, and a program of continuous supervisory development in coaching and evaluation interviewing.

Second, it must be quite clear from the outset that the purpose of the accountability program is improvement of present role performance. If the measurements and standards developed are used for other purposes, such as discipline, promotion, and salary increases—the program will fail, positively and absolutely. Of course there must be a relationship between the measures of accountability and these other personnel actions, but the relationship must be indirect and antecedent rather than direct and casual.

Third, the immediate intentions of the instruments developed as part of the accountability program should be to provide the teacher (or other professional worker) with feedback on his efforts and to provide him and his supervisor with material for discussions of ways to strengthen his professional performance.

INSTRUMENTS OF ACCOUNTABILITY

The instruments or standards of measurement of performance must be designed to fulfill two purposes:

1. They must be meaningful and acceptable to the person who is evaluated by them.
2. They must permit quantitative consolidation in the form of means, standard scores, and percentiles to serve as criteria with which to evaluate the department, school, and district achievement of objectives.

Such instruments can be of two basic types:

1. *Results-oriented data.* These are hard data geared to the effects of the teacher's performance—attendance, standarized achievement test scores, grade point averages, etc.
2. *Person-oriented data.* These consist of ratings completed by peers, superiors, and subordinates describing the *style* of the teacher's performance—that is, his initiative, technical competence, interpersonal competence, etc. It is possible to design the instrument so that the person completing it cannot consciously control the outcome.

None of the information obtained at this level should go beyond the school principal except in a consolidated and hence anonymous form.

To insure the acceptance of these instruments, it is necessary that the teachers themselves and their supervisors actively participate in this research, design, and implementation. This is done in two ways. First, in the initial development of the program, teachers and supervisors should actively assist the professional researchers at every stage.[4] Second, and even more important, in the accountability interview, the teacher takes an active role in what is essentially a problem-solving process.

THE ACCOUNTABILITY INTERVIEW

The entire program described in this paper pivots around the accountability interview betwen supervisor and teacher. If it is conducted well throughout the school system, then the educational process in that community will thrive. If it is done poorly, the whole accountability program will fail and the school system will be in trouble. Therefore, this encounter is crucial.

To make the interview effective, a number of conditions must exist before, during, and afterward. First, the supervisor must have discussed his own performance with his superior—the principal or the superintendent. He must also have participated in the development of his charter of accountability and that of his school or district. Both the teacher and the supervisor must be familiar with these documents.

They must also be aware of the department's and the school's goals and objectives. The supervisor must have adequate preparation in coaching and interviewing skills. Both the supervisor and the teacher must have met earlier to agree on the dimensions of the teacher's role and on acceptable standards of performance. The teacher must be given adequate time for self-evaluation, and both must have reviewed the data resulting from the accountability instruments referred to above.

During the interview, both discuss the material collected on the teacher's performance. They analyze the teacher's strengths and explore ways of capitalizing on them. They identify areas for improvement, develop an improvement plan, and choose the resources to implement it. The teacher also discusses his professional problems with his supervisor and ways in which the latter can be of greater assistance to him. They establish follow-up schedules with milestones to determine progress. And they put all of this—the plan, the schedule, and the milestones—in writing for subsequent review and follow-up.

This accountability program, sincerely pursued at all these levels, is guaranteed to achieve positive results. There will remain, however, one major obstacle—time. It is obvious that the program will make major demands on a supervisor's time. Consequently, most supervisors will assert that they do not have the time for such a meticulous and detailed approach. In part they will be wrong, and in part they will be right.

They will be wrong, first, because they are not really using the time they now have to maximum advantage. If they are like most managers, they waste a good deal of time in superfluous activities. Secondly, they will be wrong because they are mistaken in their notions of the proper functions of their job. They tend to overemphasize the professional and functional aspects of their responsibilities and to underemphasize the managerial and supervisory concerns that are of paramount importance in the organizational system.

But they will be right because their present school system, like nearly every other organizational system in the United States, requires them to perform many functions that interfere with their basic duties of manager and supervisor.[5]

The answer to this problem, which is one of the chief stumbling blocks to the implementation of an accountability program, seems to lie in a searching examination of the functions performed at each level of supervision. Many of these, upon closer examination, will be found to be delegatable, thus enriching the jobs of their subordinates and freeing them for their real responsibilities of managing one of the most vital enterprises in society—the school system.

NOTES

1. For example, G. S. Odiorne, *Management by Objectives.* New York: Pitman Publishing Co., 1965; and C. L. Hughes, *Goal Setting: Key to Indivdual and Organizational Performance.* New York: American Management Association, 1965.

2. P. N. Scheid, "Charter of Accountability for Executives," *Harvard Business Review,* July–August, 1965, pp. 88–98.

3. Felix M. Lopez, *Evaluating Employee Performance.* Chicago: Public Personnel Association, 1968.

4. For an expansion of this principle, see Lopez, *op. cit.,* pp. 68–69.

5. See, for example, F. M. Lopez, *The Making of a Manager: Guidelines to His Selection and Promotion.* New York: American Management Association, 1970, Chapter 4 ("What Does a Manager Do?") .

Educational Evaluators—A Model for Task Oriented Position Development

DAVID RICE, ROBERT BUSER

and JOE ELLIS

A conceptual model for task-oriented development of evaluators is described by the authors along with forty-four explicated tasks. Implications for development of evaluator tasks, training, and positions are suggested by the project model. Prospective application of the model and the identified tasks include evaluator job descriptions, analysis of evaluation needs within an institution, determining the effectiveness of evaluation in specific institutions, and development of training programs for evaluators.

David Rice, Robert Buser, and Joe Ellis, "Educational Evaluation—A Model for Task Oriented Position Development," *Contemporary Education,* 41:115–118, January 1970. Reprinted with the permission of the authors and Indiana State University.

It appears that a new position is rapidly emerging in education—that of the evaluator. This position seems to be emerging in part from the demands of current educational legislation, particularly the Elementary and Secondary Education Act; in part from an awareness and appreciation for the significance of evaluation as a basic component of the decision making process; in part from the demands of a society that is being asked to expend an ever increasing share of its wealth on education; in part from an appreciation for Program Evaluation and Review Techniques (PERT) by policy makers; and finally by the measurement-evaluation specialists. Certainly this movement to employ "evaluators" in educational institutions is most desirable.

However, a number of practical questions related to institutionalization of evaluator positions in school settings exist, not the least of which is where would even a small percentage of the 25,983 school districts[1] in the United States turn to employ "evaluators"? Two equally significant question areas are discussed below:

(1) What specific functions should evaluators be expected to perform? What are the available position models or job descriptions for evaluators? Will evaluators be mainly processors of evaluative data or will they themselves be the ultimate judges?

(2) How will these "evaluators" be trained? Who will train them? Will we rely upon traditional graduate programs with advanced graduate work in statistics, measurement, and evaluation? If so, how realistic is it to expect significant changes in the implementation of the elements of evaluation? Or, can functional training programs for evaluators be designed systematically to prepare candidates for evaluative tasks of the sort they can be expected to perform in real school settings?

Task-Oriented Position Development

The writers of this article propose a functional approach to evaluator position and training development based upon the Evaluator Development Program of the Cooperative Educational Research Laboratory, Inc.[2] Even though this program is incomplete, the Buser-Bates-Rice-Ellis Model for Task-Oriented Position Development outlined therein offers a viable approach to both position development and training. The sequential steps delineated in the model include:

1. *Task identification.* The tasks essential to the implementation of sound evaluation procedures in selected settings were derived from a review of literature, confrontations with measurement-evaluation theorists, administrators, teachers, specialists, and an occupational sociologist.

2. *Task explication.* Each of the identified tasks is described and the terms employed within the description are defined. The task is elaborated through the identification of the main acts or behaviors essential to the successful execution of the task. Finally, the main outcomes expected from the implementation of each task within an institutional setting are described.

3. *Task skill-competency analysis.* The skills and competencies necessary in the effective performance of the task are identified and described.

4. *Treatment prescription.* Treatments in the form of materials and instructional processes are selected and/or designed to produce the skills and competencies identified for each specific task.

5. *Treatment application.* The specified treatments are applied in a given instructional setting on a trial basis.

6. *Treatment modification.* The treatments are systematically observed to determine effectiveness and to prescribe modifications in instruction.

7. *Task development.* The task is developed when it has been explicated, skills and competencies identified, and treatments prescribed and tested to cause effective skill-competency development. A developed task is capable of replication.

8. *Position development.* Position development is the final phase of this program. It consists essentially of the clustering of tasks for position implementation within particular school settings. These tasks can be grouped in different ways for different purposes. They can be clustered according to training needs, the functional relatedness of the tasks, and the institutional or organizational needs of the institution employing the evaluator.

The Model

Thus, the conceptual model for task-oriented development for evaluators is as follows:

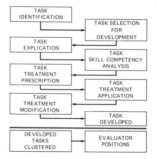

Figure 1. Buser-Bates-Rice-Ellis model for task-oriented position development

The implementation of this model in the development of training for and positions of evaluators should provide prospective developers with answers to the questions raised earlier in this paper: i.e., what functions might evaluators be expected to perform? How might training programs be designed and implemented? And, concurrently, the individual elements for evaluator position descriptions are identified. Thus, it merely remains for administrators, institutional governors, prospective evaluators, etc., to install positions, and ultimately new rols, through the clustering of tasks and the assignment (or reassignment) of consequent responsibilities to personnel.

Explicated Tasks

Forty-four evaluator tasks were explicated in the first stage of the Evaluator Development Program of the Cooperative Educational Research Laboratory, Inc. Additional tasks were identified for explication and two tasks were developed through the treatment prescription stage of the project model. The forty-four explicated tasks are listed below.[3]

1. To identify the broad objectives of the institution.
2. To identify and select criteria upon which judgments about institutional objectives may be made.
3. To identify procedures and processes for the evaluation of professional personnel of the institution.
4. To identify the outcomes which are contingent upon particular antecedent conditions or strategies.
5. To identify the consequent side effects of the strategies or practices in a program implementation.
6. To develop valid and reliable measurement instruments and techniques.
7. To design procedures and processes for the evaluation of professional personnel of the institution.
8. To design field testing procedures.
9. To prepare project or program proposals.
10. To design studies for given institutional purposes.
11. To assist curriculum specialists, supervisors, and teachers in the development of materials and practices that can be evaluated in terms of specific objectives.
12. To develop descriptive information about programs.
13. To develop generalizations about the program and its practices.
14. To develop practitioner readiness for evaluation.
15. To judge the relative merits of each of the broad purposes of the institution.

16. To assess the consequences of educational practices.
17. To assess the consequences of educational programs.
18. To evaluate programs or practices developed, tested, or adopted in other settings.
19. To make judgments about programs or practices developed, tested, or adopted in other settings.
20. To assess the congruence between what the program does and intends to do.
21. To translate the broad purposes of the institution into forms suitable for treatment and application.
22. To report the results of the evaluations of programs and practices in terms of given criteria.
23. To interpret the results of the evaluations of programs and practices in terms of given criteria.
24. To aid in the interpretation of the results of the evaluation of programs and practices.
25. To encourage the adoption of innovative programs and practices.
26. To interpret for the public (s) the results of the evaluation of programs and practices as they relate to objectives and outcomes.
27. To explicate the rationale for developmental programs.
28. To translate program objectives into behavioral or operational terms.
29. To feedback the data relating to the congruence of the outcomes and intents resulting from the program.
30. To present generalizations and data to the decision-makers in a form that will enable them to identify gains and losses from a particular program.
31. To determine the nature of the decision-making process in the institution.
32. To apply valid and reliable measurement instruments and techniques.
33. To direct field testing procedures.
34. To analyze the findings of the evaluations of programs and practices in terms of given criteria.
35. To accumulate project or program information about similar programs in other settings.
36. To implement and maintain a data bank.
37. To implement and maintain a feedback system for a data bank.
38. To implement procedures and processes for the evaluation of professional personnel of the institution.
39. To advise users in the selection, construction, and use of measurement instruments.
40. To provide counsel with teachers about the problems and procedures of individual pupil evaluation.

41. To provide counsel for educational practitioners in the process of self-evaluation.
42. To provide measurement and evaluation services.
43. To aid in the process of training users in the utilization of the results of evaluation.
44. To assist curriculum specialists, supervisors, and teachers in the adoption of materials and practices that can be evaluated in terms of specific objectives.

It should be pointed out that the tasks might be grouped according to evaluation needs related to a) the implementation of continuous institutional responsibilities, b) personnel needs of the institution, and c) program or project needs of the institution. Or they might be clustered according to existing organization and/or personnel assignments.

Prospective Application

The prospective application of the model, the tasks, and the concepts described in this presentation are as follows:

(1) a content base for developing evaluator job descriptions;
(2) a criteria base for analyzing evaluation needs within particular institutions;
(3) a base from which to pursue the future identification of evaluative tasks;
(4) potential criteria for judging the effectiveness of the evaluation function as implemented in specific institutions;
(5) a model for developing training programs for evaluators; and/or
(6) a model for position development in educational settings.

Summary

This paper has described the Buser-Bates-Rice-Ellis Model for Task-Oriented Position Development. The forty plus tasks explicated in the Evaluator Development Program of the Cooperative Educational Research Laboratory, Inc. were outlined. Although the development work described is not yet completed, significant implications for the subsequent development of evaluator tasks, training, and positions are suggested by the project model and its prospective application. In addition, the model is appropriate for application in the development and modification of educational positions other than evaluators.

FOOTNOTES

1. Source: U.S. Office of Education Digest of Educational Statistics 1966, reported in the Standard Education Almanac, Academic Media, Los Angeles, California, 1968, p. 185.
2. The Evaluator Development Program, Working Paper No. 10, Cooperative Educational Research Laboratory, Inc., June 15, 1967.
3. Op. cit., pp. 24–27.

Outlook for Teacher Incentives

NATION'S SCHOOLS

Reports of attempts to utilize teacher incentive contracts based on pupil achievement as measured by standardized tests in three different cities bring different reactions from the teachers themselves and their organizations. On one hand, the ability of teachers to produce higher student achievement is demonstrated, while revealing the deep opposition of teachers to such a movement on the other hand.

Almost as controversial as the performance contracting movement has been an adjunct to it involving the use of teacher incentive contracts. These are agreements between school systems and teachers which offer teachers the opportunity to earn bonus pay, contingent upon academic improvement by their students on standardized achievement tests.

Purpose of the incentive arrangements, like performance contracts with outside firms, is to promote educational accountability by giving instructors direct stake in the scholastic successes and failures of their students.

While some educators have pointed to internal incentive contracts as an alternative to contracting with private firms, teachers have resisted the idea to date.

In fact, although incentive contracts have been tried or suggested to faculties at only a handful of schools around the country, the concept has already aroused bitter opposition from teacher groups that view it as a setup for merit pay and a powerful threat to teacher solidarity. But the merit pay argument is only one of a host of objections teachers have mustered. Several key questions have emerged in the debate over incentives and the answers will undoubtedly have an important bearing on the future of educational accountability.

"Outlook for Teacher Incentives," *Nation's Schools,* 86:51–55, November 1970. Reprinted by permission.

The following examination of three districts which have had some experience with incentive agreements or with plans for teacher accountability offers some basis for understanding the problems and issues involved.

PORTLAND, OREGON

In addition to contracting with a private firm during the second half of the 1969–70 school year, to provide a reading lab for 130 seventh and eighth graders, Portland left the door open to teachers to develop new methods for reading instruction and come up with performance proposals of their own.

Three incentive contracts were developed as a result. But despite the district's effort to make the incentives as lucrative as possible—in one case offering a guaranteed bonus of $200 just for participating— only 11 teachers were involved.

What the contracts lack in numbers they make up in variety.

In the first contract, a team of five teachers agreed to try to match the contract terms under which the private firm was already operating in the schools. The firm had agreed to double the reading rate advancements of the students or forfeit a part of their fee. Based on results from standardized tests, student reading rates advanced as much in 4.5 months as they had in the previous nine months, and the firm received the full contract price. The team of five teachers, however, had equally successful results.

Unlike the private firm, the teachers' contract was not on a "no learn—no pay" basis. Instead, their agreement was to work for their regular pay on a guaranteed basis, with only the bonus contingent on student performance. Significantly, the teachers also stated that they would not divide any bonus money among themselves but would put it into additional reading materials.

In the second incentive agreement, covering fifth and sixth grade summer school reading instruction, one teacher proved herself a gambler at heart when she decided to work on an all or nothing basis. The teacher's total salary for the summer was based on gains made by her students. Since students gained twice the amount expected, the gamble paid off with the teacher doubling her regular summer earnings.

Under the terms of the third agreement, also involving summer school reading, the Portland administrator in charge of the incentive experiment, James Holmes, contracted with five teachers on a no-learn no-pay basis, while the teachers subcontracted with a private firm to guarantee their basic income. The firm agreed to furnish reading materials and to take all the financial loss if the summer school students failed to double their normal reading achievement. Under the terms of the agreement, the firm was to get 80 per cent of any earned bonus, while the teachers would split the remaining 20 per cent. The project was successful in that the gains made by the total group exceeded the school board's expectations, but the results failed to match the company's goals. The company lost money, but the teachers came out ahead, with their guaranteed salary plus the bonuses they earned for participating.

Although school officials in Portland are cautious about playing up what they consider to be minor successes in incentive experiments, there is some feeling among them that the positive results achieved by the teachers may encourage some others to measure their skills on a performance yardstick.

Why were so few of Portland's teachers willing to participate in the experiments?

For several reasons: "The majority of Portland's teachers are married women, earning supplemental incomes, and, frankly, they feel they have a pretty good situation as it is," explained one school official. "For the most part they aren't interested in the competitive aspect of incentive agreements or in putting their salaries on the line."

Offering additional explanations, several schoolmen felt that teachers have been influenced by opposition from the national teacher organizations, with pro-union teachers tending to view incentive contracts as a threat to their across-the-board bargaining position.

So far, Portland schoolmen are undecided about how they'll go about extending incentive experiments, if they decide to extend them at all. One certainty, according to Holmes, is that any extension will generate more opposition.

DALLAS, TEXAS

Teachers in Dallas, like their colleagues in Portland, have for the most part reacted negatively to feelers about incentive contracts. According to teacher spokesmen, the group regards incentive agreements with as much hostility as they do performance contracts with private firms.

Their objections are similar to those offered in a recent resolution by the American Federation of Teachers calling for the abolition of contracts with private firms or any similar plan which: 1) "threatens to dehumanize the learning process," or 2) "would sow distrust among teachers through a structured incentive program."

Dallas has two outside performance contracting programs underway this fall—one Office of Economic Opportunity funded program with the firm of Quality Education Development, covering math instruction for 300 students, and the city's own program for approximately

775 students in five inner-city schools involving contracts with two other firms.

To encourage teachers to enter the performance contracting race, the district has set aside minigrants to provide incentive bonuses and full funding for teacher-developed programs.

According to Donald Waldrip, the assistant superintendent in charge of accountability, a guarantee from teachers that instructional objectives would be met would give them a far more effective bargaining position, too— ". . . much more effective," he claims, "than going to a board and saying that, compared to cities X, Y, and Z, we should be receiving this much more money and benefits.' " But spokesmen for the Dallas Classroom Teachers Association (DC-TA) disagree. They feel that incentive contracts would weaken their bargaining strength by fostering divisiveness and competition among teachers.

Furthermore, they object strenuously to the use of achievement test scores as a basis for evaluation of teacher performance and subsequent bonus pay. "It's impossible to judge what effect an individual teacher has on a student . . . by looking at a few test scores," contends Herb Cook, executive director of the DCTA. There are too many other factors related to the way students test, he believes, many of them, like an empty stomach, beyond a teacher's control.

Other comments from the Dallas group suggest more than a little rivalry between teachers working in regular instruction programs and those involved in private performance contracting experiments.

Cook claims, for example, that if the non-contract group had class sizes conducive to dealing individually with each student, if they had proper equipment and supplies, if they weren't saddled with clerical and babysitting duties, they could show results as impressive as contract teachers. "The trouble is," he adds, "that we're caught up in a system that's been largely organized for the administration, not in the best interests of the students and learning situation."

DCTA President Jewel Howard questions the reward system used in performance contract experiments, feeling that teachers under incentive contracts might have to adopt similar motivational technics because Dallas youngsters would have come to expect them.

"Teachers in the performance contract experiments are free to give the students radios and green stamps, while we've never been allowed to give them even a piece of bubble gum or candy," says Mrs. Howard. "What we're more concerned about though is whether these rewards are a lasting kind of incentive, or if the reward system is really the right kind of motivation for children."

Though a DCTA task force is studying the incentive offers, the teachers' initial reaction suggests that they may turn down the district's proposal, unless they can agree upon what they would consider to be more equitable terms—in particular, a system other than stand-ardized testing for measuring teacher performance.

WASHINGTON, D.C.

The strongest and most articulate resistance to an incentive system has emanated from the powerful Washington local of the American Fed-eration of Teachers, which recently threatened both strike and sabo-tage if a proposal prepared by psychologist Kenneth Clark was effected in D.C. schools.

While the Clark proposal rejects "performance contracting to out-side firms as an abdication of the responsibility for educational leadership," it insists upon teacher accountability, and outlines a system of differentiated staffing and rewards for teachers based on training, evaluations and the performance of their students on stand-ardized tests.

Specifically, Clark suggests that teachers be classified and salaried on a four-track system: (a) beginners, just out of college, who would serve three to five years as resident teachers before they are certified; (b) staff or certified teachers; (c) senior teachers, paid as much as assistant principals; and (d) master teachers, paid as much as prin-cipals.

Promotion from one category to another would depend in large part on student advancement on achievement tests in reading and math which would be administered three times a year.

While the plan involves a number of other controversial points, such as the dismissal of some of the popular environmental theories used to explain low achievement by minority group pupils, the pro-posal teachers appeared to single out as most intolerable was the one regarding the use of test scores as a basis for ranking, pay and promotion.

Washington Teachers Union President William H. Simons objected strenuously to the use of tests "designed for white middle-class chil-dren" in a system where the pupil population is 94 per cent black, and threatened that teachers could sabotage the plan by giving students test answers. He also opposed the hierarchical staffing plan, saying the emphasis on competition and merit pay would create a hostile climate and keep teachers from sharing successful ideas. While Simons agreed that there is a need for some new system of teacher evaluation, the differentiated staffing plan isn't the way, he contends.

In a recent interview, Clark countered that schools do want the competition: "Tell me, how else does one evaluate a teacher? I'm a teacher and how else can I evaluate myself except in terms of the progress of my students? The funtion of a teacher is to teach. And you make your judgment as to the quality of a teacher by the results of that. It may be a serious limitation on my part, but I do not see that the teaching profession can have a unique set of criteria for evaluating . . . teachers that does not apply to other professions."

While the debate over the Clark plan has calmed down somewhat in recent weeks, the issues are far from resolved. The D.C. local won an initial victory—a pledge by the board that achievement test results would not be used to evalutate teachers. The teachers agreed to get some joint committees of union members and administrators to recommend sometime this month how the tests would be used and to settle other differences. But at this writing it was unclear what would happen if the committees failed to agree.

THE FUTURE

At this point, it seems logical to assume that any major plan for teacher accountability and evaluation will take some time to bring into being. That teachers have raised valid objections to current incentive plans is unquestionable—and their objections point to a critical need for devising new methods for evaluation which teachers, administrators and the public can agree upon as both equitable and effective.

At the same time, teachers who reject accountability demands by hiding behind the union door may be out of touch with the realities in schools today.

The kind of argument which teachers may find themselves confronting increasingly in the near future was crystallized by an editorial in the *Washington Star* during the Clark controversy: "The ideology of unionism which clings to the old ideas of a uniform up-grading of worker pay might be perfectly all right for assembly-line laborers. But it seems to us a rotten way to evaluate school teachers—or to upgrade the profession in these times of so many demonstrated failures of the traditional educational patterns."

Three Districts Will Get OEO Funding for Incentive Experiments

As part of its $6.5 million experiment to test the validity of performance contracting, the Office of Economic Opportunity has selected three districts—Mesa, Ariz., Stockton, Calif., and an unidentified Michigan district—to operate on an incentives only basis with teachers.

OEO's contract with the Michigan district is still awaiting approval at the local level.

The OEO experiment is also testing the role private industry can play teaching under a performance guarantee. In July, OEO matched up 18 school districts with six private firms.

The three incentives districts will operate this year under contracts similar to those in the other 18, except that district teachers, not corporations, will receive payment for student achievement. OEO contracted with the three school districts which, in turn, subcontracted with the local teacher organizations.

Teachers will be paid their regular salary plus a bonus of up to 20 per cent of their salary pro-rated according to achievement gains.

OEO officials conceded that teacher opposition to performance contracting, based largely on the fear that it was another form of merit pay, did delay the lining up of the three districts. "When we announced we were going to get private contractors to come into 18 school districts, our doors were being knocked down," said one OEO official. "When we announced we were going into these three districts with incentive plans, there was dead silence." Both the Stockton and Mesa teacher organizations are affiliated with the National Education Association, which opposes OEO's experiment.

CHAPTER 4.
APPLIED ACCOUNTABILITY

The Performance Contract in Gary

JAMES MECKLENBURGER and JOHN WILSON

Banneker Elementary School in Gary, Indiana, received much publicity as the first school to have its entire program managed by a private business corporation. Opposition to this performance contract stemmed from many sources, including the Gary Teachers Union and the Indiana State Department of Public Instruction. The authors identify some major issues that have developed out of this conflict and describe major operations of the program.

Never before, anywhere, has a private corporation contracted with a city school board to manage the entire program of one school—as Behavioral Research Laboratories, of Palo Alto, California, have done this year with the School City of Gary, Indiana. (Gary's public schools are called "School City.")

BRL, as consultant to School City, manages Banneker Elementary School, an inner-city school of 850 students. Gary has pledged its average cost per student to BRL; no federal money is involved. BRL guarantees to raise the achievement of Banneker's students; the guarantee states that BRL will return its fee for any child who fails.

In 1971 jargon, BRL is "accountable" for results. This "performance contract" involves more money (over $2,000,000), more responsibility (an entire school), and a longer period of time (four years) than any performance contract yet written in education.

Three Partisans

Gordon McAndrew, Gary's superintendent, once called this project a trial balloon at which every one can shoot. "It has lost air, but not as much as I thought it would—and the best evidence is that the balloon is still up there," he told us early in January. He predicted that the

James Mecklenburger and John Wilson, "The Performance Contract in Gary," *Phi Delta Kappan*, 52:406–11, March 1971. Reprinted by permission.

project will work the kinks out of itself within this first year and operate smoothly thereafter.

"I think it's a badly administered and badly run school," Charles Smith, president of the Gary Teachers Union, states. "If I had to make a prediction right now," he told us in December, "I would predict BRL would not be here for the duration of their contract unless they change the system and they change the administration of the school."

"Banneker School is not being operated in accordance with the State Board of Education rules and regulations," State Superintendent Richard D. Wells stated at the conclusion of several months of investigation. At the January 19 meeting of the state board, a resolution called for Gary to comply with all rules and regulations by February 18, or the Banneker School would automatically be decommissioned.

A Brief History

BRL's *Project Read*—a sequence of programmed textbooks developed by M. W. Sullivan—has been used in Gary in recent years and has shown promise, first in summer remedial programs, then in six schools. Friendship developed over time between BRL and Gary.

"George and I got to talking once," McAndrew told us, referring to George Stern, BRL's president. "This must have been a year ago, and somehow we got to talking about what we thought about this whole 'accountability' notion. I said, kind of facetiously at the beginning, 'Tell you what. We'll contract with you to do this on a school-wide basis, not just reading but the whole shebang. Two conditions: One, it can't cost any more money than we're now spending, and two, you have to take a school as it now exists.' Out of that came a proposal." That was April. By August, in-service training of staff had begun.

Most performance contracts begin, unlike Gary's, with elaborate preparation. A school board prepares a "request for proposals" (RFP) which specifies the board's purposes, standards, funds available, constraints, and preferences for entering, then evaluating, then terminating a contract. Frequently a management consultant assists in the preparation; often teachers, parents, and community leaders assist also. Finally, the RFP is published, requesting potential bidders to submit proposals; bids are received and bidders chosen to receive contracts. (BRL was among 10 bidders on the Texarkana RFP, for example.) This procedure is commonplace in the defense industry, new to education.

None of these steps occurred in Gary. Despite national efforts to establish RFP's as preconditions for performance contracts,* only one school board member in Gary even questioned that no bids except BRL's had been sought.

"Why no RFP in Gary?" we asked McAndrew. "I don't know that there were any hard and fast reasons," he said. "I suppose one could argue we should have done that. I knew something about the BRL program, I had some indication of it; I think also in talking with Stern and some of his people, I felt they kind of grabbed the concept as well as I did. For those kinds of reasons, we went that route."

Charles Smith attributes the lack of bids to BRL's merchandising expertise. We surmise deeper reasons also. One can ask, What was the hurry to begin this project? Why not wait a year, plan the project thoroughly?

Impatience to innovate. Impatience, we sensed in Gary, permeates the city's large minority-group populations and its school board, which has only recently become minority-group dominated. Moreover, desperation characterizes many parents and schoolmen over the failure of many students, particularly nonwhite students, to acquire adequate basic skills. Banneker School, for example, ranked twenty-seventh among 29 elementary schools in achievement test scores by one reckoning; it had only one student in four reaching national norms for reading and mathematics. School City administrators tell us that the school board and the community are zealous believers in test scores, and such scores are hard to swallow.

Impatience and desperation prompted a declaration by the school board in 1970 of a "right to learn" philosophy, which calls for innovative attempts at teaching basic skills. Gary is studded with experiments to achieve better learning of basic skills, including experiments with BRL's *Project Read*. In this setting of impatience and experimentation, the nationwide emphasis on accountability made performance contracting seem irresistible.

Moreover, some insiders judged that if Gary had waited, union and Indiana state education policies would likely have scuttled such a project politically. BRL may be scuttled yet.

McAndrew himself embodies Gary's impatience. "Let's get the bugs and work them out by experience, rather than on paper," he said. "I wasn't interested in developing all kinds of fancy objectives; what I want to know is, can we teach the kids to read and add? And here's a school where 75% of them can't. That's the objective."

---

* See issues of *Education Turnkey News*, published monthly by Education Turnkey Systems, Inc., Washington, D.C.; or *Every Kid a Winner*, by Leon Lessinger, Simon and Schuster, 1971.

The Grand Design

McAndrew's "trial balloon" may not survive the slings and arrows the Gary Teachers Union, the state of Indiana, some parents, some teachers, and others are hurling. Or it may spring its own leaks and collapse. Survive or not, the grand design of the program—as revealed in BRL's proposal, the contract, press statements by BRL and School City, and in interviews—will remain tantalizing.

To orchestrate its systems approach to schooling, BRL provides a center manager, a "systems man," so to speak. Gary provides a learning director, responsible for supervising the academic portion of the system. Five curriculum managers bear responsibility for each of the five curriculum areas. These are language arts, mathematics, science, social studies and foreign language, and enrichment—"enrichment" being arts and crafts, music, drama, and physical education. Seventeen assistant curriculum managers perform the major instruction; 27 learning supervisors recruited from among the parents of Banneker students round out this differentiated staff.

In keeping with Gary's "right to learn" philosophy, the project began with heavy concentration on reading and mathematics, and as performance at Banneker improves, BRL will phase in the other areas.

BRL's *Project Read, Project Math,* and *Project Learn* serve as the cornerstone of teaching materials; BRL has chosen Allyn and Bacon's social studies materials and AAAS science. Inservice training prepares the staff to teach each of these materials.

BRL liberally employs consultants from outside Gary to aid whenever necessary; in fact, several consultants serve full time. As many as 15 consultants at once were present during the two weeks of in-service staff training in August.

Day-to-day evaluation of student progress is built into the teaching materials; frequent evaluation will also be provided by the staff. A "profile" on each student's mastery of a host of skills in reading, mathematics, and other areas is to be updated by the staff monthly and supplied to the child and his parents.

Moreover, two independent firms provide long-range evaluation of each child's progress. One firm, Bernard Donovan's Center for Urban Redevelopment and Education (CURE) from New York, periodically administers the Metropolitan Achievement Test. CURE also monitors the program monthly to see that BRL and Gary both adhere to the terms of the contract. The second firm will audit CURE's findings.

Banneker is designed to be a truly nongraded school, for each child begins at a point where his own knowledge ends and proceeds at his own pace. "Classes" as such disappear in these circumstances, and classrooms become "learning centers." In each center, games and activities daily supplement and reinforce book learning. In practice, children of varied ages share one learning center based on their level of skills; over time children move from center to center as they learn.

An extensive community relations program and an advisory council of famed educators and local persons are promised by BRL.

Some Leaks in the Balloon

The letter of the Gary-BRL contract sometimes lacks the grandeur of the design.

For example, advocates say the program "costs no more," but analysis shows that—if successful—it will cost more, for two reasons.

First, roughly $34,000 per year accrues to BRL as "extra" income; this is so because Indiana schools determine cost per pupil based on "average daily *attendance*" while BRL is paid based on "active *enrollment*." If enrollment is 850 students, and daily attendance averages 95% of enrollment, BRL receives 5% more than a Gary school would; 5% means 43 students BRL is paid for that a Gary school would not be.

Second, BRL is paid the average annual cost per pupil in grades one through 12, which is roughly $800. However, in Gary, the average elementary school cost per pupil is less. McAndrew estimated for us that K-6 expenditures average $700; the union says $696. This means Gary pays BRL approximately $85,000 per year more than it would spend in an average elementary school.

Based on these estimates, the program could cost Gary nearly 20% more than it spends for an average elementary school.

Three qualifications modify this analysis. First, if BRL were only 80% successful at raising achievement of every child, BRL would return to Gary roughly 20% of its fee. That is, at 80% success, it is true that the Banneker program would cost no more. In fact, if BRL were less successful than 80%, Gary would save on Banneker School. Second, because salaries differ among schools, based on the staff's experience, some elementary schools in Gary may cost $800. Some also may cost less than $700. (McAndrew did not know the cost per pupil at Banneker last year.) Third, this analysis does not criticize School City for deciding to commit more money to one school, which is its prerogative; it only questions the many public assertions that this program costs no more.

When one estimates BRL's costs at Banneker, he begins to doubt that BRL is motivated by profits to be made there, even at $800 per pupil per year. Every observer we interviewed concurred with the conclusion of Otha Porter, Gary's assistant to the superintendent, that "I don't see BRL carrying dollars away from Gary." However, BRL does profit in Gary from the visibility BRL receives nationally (such as from this article), from whatever increased sales this visibility brings to BRL's publications, and—if the Banneker project succeeds—from the subsequent prestige for BRL.

In the January *American School Board Journal,* BRL's president, George Stern, reveals that BRL can afford not to make a profit. If one considers the large profit margin that business usually requires in a high-risk enterprise, and if one suspects that BRL may not even recoup costs in Gary, he begins to wonder what it would really cost to contract with a corporation that had to make its profit on site. It seems that Gary has gotten a bargain rate; one may look askance at the publicity that says this project can be endlessly duplicated at the Gary price. It might better be thought of as a "loss leader" aimed at the education market.

While BRL is nominally "accountable" for every student, the contract reveals a substantial minority of students for whom no guarantee applies. The annual turnover of students in Banneker School is reported at 5% to 7%. Because a student must be in the program a full year for either portion of the guarantee to apply, as many as 15% of the students at Banneker, over three years, will not qualify. Moreover, even at Banneker some students are already at grade level or about and should remain so without BRL. If these number 25%, as is said, then BRL has no effective accountability under the contract for this one-fourth of the school's students.

Most intriguing, there will be a number of students for whom an overwhelming effort would have to be mounted to raise them to grade level—special education students, for example, or simply children years below grade level who do not work well in programmed texts—much more than $800 worth of effort. Would a corporation make this effort, or instead concentrate on the vast majority most likely to succeed? That is, if one is motivated by profit, are there some students too expensive to teach?

School City's contract with BRL makes an intriguing contrast to School City's agreement with the Gary Teachers Union. The latter is precision honed to cover every contingency, while the BRL contract is often sketchy, even incomplete. It reads as if the two parties had agreed more to each other's good intentions than to a program. One wonders how CURE can monitor such a contract.

For example, the "differentiated" staff, from center manager to learning supervisors, consists mostly of the titles of positions; the contract says little about their functions or responsibilities. There shall be teaching in all curriculum areas; but there is no statement of how much instruction, its substance, or how anything but reading and math will be evaluated by School City. Who holds proprietary rights to materials developed at Banneker? What will the advisory council do? What might happen in the fourth year? When is payment refunded for any sixth graders who fail this year? For all these there are no provisions. Subject to School City's final authority, the contract provides BRL tremendous latitude with few guidelines.

The powerful 120-day withdrawal clause provides that either party may withdraw at will on written notice to the other. If either party withdraws, what happens to the guarantee? No answer. It appears to be a contract based more on good faith than on good business sense.

Slings and Arrows

One criticism during the first semester was that several provisions of the contract had not been implemented fully, some not at all. Despite the provision for monthly student evaluation on a profile of basic skills, the profile has yet to be issued. One "mini-report" was released in December. That report prompted some adverse community reaction, for some parents realized for the first time that their children had studied only reading and math; they feared their children might be getting shortchanged. Apparently, the promised extensive community relations program had not been extensive enough to reach many parents.

Even Superintendent McAndrew became critical of the slow pace with which the three other curriculum areas had been phased into the school; meetings over Christmas vacation resulted in a promise that by second semester these areas would all have begun. In mid-January, Mrs. Sandra Irons, vice-president of the Gary Teachers Union, reported that BRL was still teaching "only reading and math, *all day long!*"

The second evaluator, the so-called auditor, was to be selected by BRL, according to the contract, in September, 1970. It has not yet been named. There never has been an advisory council.

In addition, the Gary Teachers Union (GTU) which represents virtually every teacher in Gary, has some specific grievances. A strike vote, called in September, was rescinded in the face of a threatened court order, and at mid-winter, the issues remained in advisory arbitration.

GTU objected to what it saw as three violations of its agreement with School City. One related to class size—the pupil-teacher ratio was said to be greater than 40–1 (850 students, 22 teachers). School City responded first that there are no "classes" as that word is used in the union agreement, and second, that the many paraprofessionals create a ratio of pupils to adults more nearly 20–1.

A second grievance related to a clause in the BRL guarantee;

School City agrees to transfer any staff person within 15 days of written notice from BRL; otherwise the guarantee will not be valid. School City responded to the union that certainly the union has no grievance until such a transfer occurs.

The third grievance related to the summary transfer of 14 teachers from Banneker in August. In Gary, teachers are virtually secure within their buildings unless they request transfer, and several provisions of the agreement prescribe procedures for involuntary transfer; these were violated, according to GTU. School City points out that none of the teachers involved filed a grievance, which indicates that the transfers were not involuntary, and that the experimental nature of the program necessitated the transfers.

Fundamental Issues

Performance contracting in schools, like a crystal dropped into a stream of light, acts as a prism, displaying a colorful spectrum of fundamental educational issues and requiring they be examined anew.

Advocates of the RFP procedure state that fundamental issues are best met in the planning stage—there conflicts can be anticipated and resolved before they disrupt a program. In Gary, where much planning was postponed until the program began, only now have major issues surfaced. And they may indeed disrupt the program.

Of what importance are teachers? for example. The emphasis on "performance," "guarantee," and "evaluation"; teachers "replaced" by paraprofessionals, reliance on "teacher-proof" materials; the denial to teachers of "professional" decisions traditionally made by teachers, such as pupil placement, or curriculum decisions—these have prompted many in Gary, not only teachers, to wonder what respect BRL and School City have for teachers. Charles Smith, of the union, echoes a frequently heard sentiment in Gary that BRL would rather have hired "technicians" than teachers.

By some reports, teacher morale throughout Gary has been affected. Rumblings were reported in the *Gary Post-Tribune* of December 20 that half the teachers in Banneker are considering or requesting transfer; Smith affirmed this for us in mid-January. Some observers charge that teachers are being made scapegoats for School City's financial inability to pay for needed new programs.

Who determines what schools shall be like? This question lurks behind a standing offer to the union by Gary's school board and superintendent. They propose for the union a project like the one with BRL, "under the same arrangements we've made with the contractor. We'll give them the same fees, the same help, the same control, if they'll agree to the same terms," in the words of Gary school board president Alphonso Holliday. The union is very much interested in implementing better schools, the union will tell you. But not being in the business of publishing and selling materials, the union cannot afford to compete on the same terms as BRL offers. Besides, says Smith, just sit and watch one or two classrooms at Banneker for a few hours, and you won't be so excited about trying to compete with BRL on BRL's terms. Smith deems the board offer not worthy of formal reply.

How shall we know who has learned what? Testing, an issue educators have slipped under the rug of collective guilt for two decades, emerges with a vengeance in a contract like BRL's. For Gary and BRL have agreed to raise test scores, and it is for test scores that BRL is accountable.

The suggestion, to student and community alike, is that standardized achievement tests provide a precise yardstick against which an individual student's learning can be measured. Educators have sold this notion—or allowed school boards and politicians to sell it—for a long time.

But such tests are not that precise. As measuring devices for individual learning, they have more nearly the precision of a fist than a fine yardstick. While these tests yield "scores" that can be treated as if they are precise data, these numbers are very imprecise data. (See "Testing for Accountability," in the December, 1970, *Nation's Schools*, for a fuller treatment of testing problems.) Moreover, many factors besides learning—such as maturation, testing conditions, the timing of the tests, and student attitudes toward a test—can cause scores on standardized tests to improve sufficiently to fulfill a contractor's guarantee.

While a contractor could contract on the basis of specific skills taught, most, including BRL, have not yet done so. In this ill use of testing, contractors may undercut their own future.

Raise the testing question among people involved in performance contracts and they get defensive. For example, McAndrew responded, "In fact, for better or worse or right or wrong, that's the way we do it! We let kids into college based on the SAT, and we let them into graduate school based on the Miller Analogy, and we let them into industry based on all kinds of standardized tests."

Who wields authority in education? This issue has been especially virulent in Gary, because BRL, as an interloper, makes public school authorities tense. The contract itself does little to clarify the division of authority between BRL and Gary. Between Superintendent McAndrew and BRL's George Stern, this proved tolerable. But facing this issue at Banneker, the division of authority between learning director and center manager became crucial. The learning director, a former principal, and the center manager, not a professional educator, found themselves sharing the kingpin position that Banneker's principal had for years occupied alone. The contract's only guideline was that the learning director manage academic affairs, the center manager manage nonacademic affairs. By January, sensitive feelings had grown into conflict and a host of BRL and Gary referees belatedly rushed in to straighten out the gnarled problem.

By this time, the Indiana School Board, a more powerful referee, decided that neither the contract split of authority nor the true split (according to some observers, the learning director had unwillingly become a figurehead) was legal. A man who performs the administrative duties listed in state regulations must be certified as an administrator. The question of who wields authority jumped, then, to the state level.

The state investigators identified other violations of state rules and regulations. After a series of summertime events as the contract was being written and signed, and subsequently as Gary and BRL forged ahead on their own, regardless of statutes, they communicated to the state superintendent "an attitude of . . . complete contempt" for the state office. State investigators identified six of Banneker's 22 teachers as improperly certified and found that BRL's materials had never been approved by the State Textbook Adoption Commission (and Gary never asked for a waiver of that regulation), that the teacher-pupil ratio at Banneker exceeded legal limits, and that BRL's heavy dose of reading and mathematics violated regulations about time allocation for a well-rounded curriculum.

So on January 19, the General Commission of the Indiana School Board resolved that Gary would comply with all rules and regulations within a month, or the state would decommission the school, thus withdrawing all state money from the Banneker budget.

In the face of the state's resolution, the arbitration with the Gary Teachers Union, some unrest in the community, and several fundamental issues still unresolved, we hesitate to predict (as we write this article January 20) the health of the BRL project as you read this in March.

Toward Objective Criteria of Professional Accountability in the Schools of New York City

HENRY S. DYER

The author proposes a concept of professional accountability which emphasizes the use of school effectiveness indices (SEIs) and is based upon three general principles involving professional staff and the board of education. Dyer describes SEIs and how they might be used by a school staff to find ways of improving its performance. Both short- and long-range planning must be used to avoid false starts.

I. The Concept of Professional Accountability

The concept of accountability can have many levels of meaning, depending upon where one focuses attention in the structure of the school system. Throughout this paper I shall be using the term in a restricted sense as it applies to the individual school as a unit. At this level I think of the concept as embracing three general principles:

1. The professional staff of a school is to be held collectively responsible for *knowing* as much as it can (a) about the intellectual and personal-social development of the pupils in its charge and (b) about the conditions and educational services that may be facilitating or impeding the pupils' development.
2. The professional staff of a school is to be held collectively responsible for *using* this knowledge as best it can to maximize the development of its pupils toward certain clearly defined and agreed-upon pupil performance objectives.
3. The board of education has a corresponding responsibility to provide the means and technical assistance whereby the staff of each school can acquire, interpret, and use the information necessary for carrying out the two foregoing functions.

I emphasize the notion of *joint accountability* of the entire school staff in the aggregate—principal, teachers, specialists—because it seems

Henry S. Dyer, "Toward Objective Criteria of Professional Accountability in the Schools of New York City," *Phi Delta Kappan,* 52:206–211, December 1970. Reprinted by permission of the author and the *Phi Delta Kappan.*

obvious that what happens to any child in a school is determined by the multitude of transactions he has with many different people on the staff who perform differing roles and presumably have differing impacts on his learning, which cannot readily, if ever, be disentangled. I emphasize the notion that staff members are to be held accountable for keeping themselves informed about the diverse needs of their pupils and for doing the best they can to meet those needs. In light of what we still don't know about the teaching-learning process, this is the most one may reasonably expect. To hold teachers, or anybody else, accountable for delivering some sort of "guaranteed pupil performance" is likely to do more harm than good in the lives of the children. Finally, I emphasize that professional accountability should be seen as a two-way street, wherein a school staff is to be held accountable to higher authority for its own operations while the higher authorities in turn are to be held accountable for supplying the appropriate information and facilities each school staff requires to operate effectively.

An important implication in the three principles set forth above is that there shall be developed a district-wide educational accounting system optimally adaptable to the information needs of each school in the district. Later in this paper I shall describe the salient features of such a system and shall suggest the procedures by which it might be developed and put to use. In this connection it should be noted that the type of *educational* accounting system here contemplated is to be distinguished from a *fiscal* accounting system. The kind of information provided by the former should not be confused with the kind provided by the latter. At all levels, the two types should complement each other in an overall management information system capable of relating benefits to costs. At the individual school level, however, educational accounting per se is of prime importance and is not usefully related to fiscal accounting, since the staff in a single school does not have and, in ordinary circumstances, cannot have much if any latitude in the raising and expending of funds for its local operations.

The next section of this paper outlines what a fully functioning educational accounting system might be like and how it could operate as a means for holding a school staff accountable, within certain constraints, for continually improving the effectiveness of its work. The last section briefly sketches plans by which the system might be brought into being and contains some cautions that should be heeded along the way.

II. *Characteristics of an Educational Accounting System*

A. PUPIL-CHANGE MODEL OF A SCHOOL

The theory behind the first of the three principles stated in the preceding section is that if a school staff is to fulfill its professional obligations it must have extensive knowledge of the pupils it is expected to serve. This theory is based on the notion of a school as a social system that effects changes of various kinds in both the children who pass through it and in the professional personnel responsible for maintaining the school. The school as a social system becomes an educational system when its constituents are trying to ensure that all such changes shall be for the better. That is, the school as a *social* system becomes an *educational* system when its constituents—pupils, teachers, principal—are working toward some clearly defined pupil performance objectives.

There are four groups of variables in the school as a social system that must be recognized and measured if one is to develop acceptable criteria of staff accountability. These four groups of variables I call *input, educational process, surrounding conditions,* and *output.* Taken together, they form the pupil-change model of a school.

The *input* to any school at any given level consists of the characteristics of the pupils as they enter that level of their schooling: their health and physical condition, their skill in the three R's, their feelings about themselves and others, their aspirations, and so on.* The *output* of any school consists of the same characteristics of the pupils as they emerge from that particular phase of their schooling some years later.

According to this conception, the input to any school consists of the output from the next lower level. Thus, the output of an elementary school becomes the input for junior high, and the output of junior high becomes the input for senior high. It is important to note that the staff of an individual school which is not in a position to select the pupils who come to it has no control over the level or quality of its input. In such a case, the pupil input represents as *fixed condition* with which the school staff must cope. The pupil output, however, is a variable that depends to some extent on the quality of service the school provides.

The third group of variables in the pupil-change model consists of the *surrounding conditions* within which the school operates. These are the factors in the school environment that may influence for better or for worse how teachers teach and pupils learn. The surrounding

---

* Note the restriction of meaning of the term *input* as used here. It does *not* include such variables as per pupil expenditure, institutional effort, facilities, and the like.

conditions fall into three categories: home conditions, community conditions, and school conditions. Home conditions include such matters as the level of education of the pupils' parents, the level of family income, the family pressures, and the physical condition of the home. Community conditions include the density of population in the enrollment area, the ethnic character of the population, the number and quality of available social agencies, the degree of industrialization, and so on. School conditions include the quality of the school plant, pupil-teacher ratio, classroom and playground footage per pupil, the esprit de corps of the staff, and the like.

In respect to all three types of surrounding conditions, one can distinguish those that the staff of a school finds easy to change from those that it finds hard to change. For example, in respect to home conditions, the school staff is hardly in a position to change the socio-economic level of pupils' parents, but it may well be in a position to change the parents' attitudes toward education through programs that involve them in the work of the school. Similarly, in respect to school conditions, it might not be able to effect much change in the classroom footage per pupil, but it could probably develop programs that might influence the esprit de corps of the staff through in-service training. The identification of hard-to-change as contrasted with easy-to-change surrounding conditions is of the utmost importance in working toward objective criteria of professional accountability, since the staff of a school can hardly be held accountable for changing those factors in its situation over which it has little or no control.

The final set of variables in the pupil-change model are those that make up the *educational process;* that is, all the activities in the school expressly designed to bring about changes for the better in pupils: lessons in arithmetic, recreational activities, consultation with parents, vocational counseling, etc. Three principal questions are to be asked about the educational processes in any school: 1) Are they adapted to the individual needs of the children in the school? 2) Do they work, that is, do they tend to change pupils in *desirable* ways? and 3) What, if any, negative side effects may they be having on the growth of the children?

The four sets of variables just described—input, output, surrounding conditions, and educational process—interact with one another in complex ways. That is, the pupil output variables are affected by all the other variables. Similarly, the educational process variables are influenced by both the pupil input and the surrounding conditions. And certain of the surrounding conditions may be influenced by certain of the educational processes. This last could happen, for instance, if a school embarked on a cooperative work-study program with businesses in its enrollment area.

From the foregoing considerations, it is clear that if a school staff is to maximize pupil output in any particular way, it must be aware of the nature of the interactions among the variables in the system and be given sufficient information to cope with them in its work. This in turn means that, insofar as possible, all variables in the system must be measured and appropriately interrelated and combined to produce readily interpretable indices by which the staff can know how much its own efforts are producing hoped-for changes in pupils, after making due allowance for those variables over which it has little or no control. I call such indices *school effectiveness indices* (SEI's). They are the means whereby a school staff may be held responsible for *knowing* how well it is doing.

B. NATURE OF THE SEI

The functioning of a school can be described by a profile of school effectiveness indices, so that each school staff can readily locate the points at which its educational program is strong or weak. Such a profile is fundamentally different from the traditional test-score profile, which is ordinarily generated from the grade equivalencies attached to the general run of standardized achievement tests. The underlying rationale of an SEI profile rejects grade equivalencies as essentially meaningless numbers that tend to be grossly misleading as indicators of a school's effectiveness. Appropriate indices in the SEI profile of any given school at any given level can be derived only through a procedure involving *all* the schools at the same level in the district. The procedure consists of a series of regression analyses which I shall touch upon presently.

Two features of an SEI profile differentiate it from the usual test-score profile. First, each index summarizes how effective the school has been in promoting one type of pupil development over a definite span of years; for example, the three years from the beginning of grade four to the end of grade six. Second, the profile has two dimensions: a pupil development dimension comprehending different areas of pupil growth (e.g., growth in self-esteem, growth in the basic skills, growth in social behavior) and a level-of-pupil-input dimension which might encompass three categories of children in accordance with their varying levels of development in any area at the time they entered grade four.

With this sort of profile it should be possible to discern in which areas of pupil development a school is more or less effective with different groups of pupils. Thus, an SEI profile for a grade four to six school should be capable of answering questions like the following: In its teaching of reading over the three-year period, has the school done a better or worse job with pupils who entered grade four with a low level of reading performance as compared with those who entered with a high level of reading performance? During the three-year period, has the school been more or less effective in developing children's number skills than in developing their sense of self-esteem, or their social behavior, or their health habits?

The areas of pupil development to be incorporated in the educational accounting system for any district must grow out of an earnest effort to reach agreement among all the parties involved (teachers, administrators, board members, parents, pupils) concerning the pupil performance objectives that are to be sought. Such objectives will vary for schools encompassing different grade levels, and they will also vary, in accordance with local needs, among schools serving any given grade levels.

Securing agreement on the objectives is no mean enterprise, but it is obviously fundamental to a meaningful approach to the establishment of any basis for holding professional educators accountable for their own performance in the schools.

C. DERIVATION OF THE SEI

One important point to keep in mind about any school effectiveness index is that it is a measure that must be *derived* from a large number of more fundamental measures. These more fundamental measures consist of three of the sets of variables suggested earlier in the discussion of the pupil-change model of a school as a social system, namely, 1) the pupil input variables, 2) the *hard-to-change* surrounding conditions, and 3) the pupil output variables. Measures of *easy-to-change* surrounding condition variables and of the educational process variables do not enter into the derivation of SEI's. They become of central importance subsequently in identifying the specific actions a school staff should take to improve the effectiveness of its operations.

The fundamental measures from which the indices are to be derived can take many different forms: academic achievement tests; questionnaires to get at matters like pupil self-esteem; physical examinations to assess health and health habits; a wide range of sociological measures to assess community conditions; and measures of various aspects of the school plant, equipment, and personnel. Techniques for securing many of these measures are already available, but new and more refined ones will be required before a reasonably equitable educational accounting system can be fully operable.

Given the total array of measures required for the derivation of the SEI's, the first step in the derivation will be to apply such measures in all schools in the system at any given level—e.g., all the elementary

schools, all the senior high schools—to secure the necessary information on pupil input and on the hard-to-change surrounding conditions.

The second step, to be taken perhaps two or three years later, will be
to obtain output measures on the same pupils, i.e., those pupils who
have remained in the same schools during the period in question.*

The third step will be to distribute the pupils within each school
into three groups—high, middle, and low—on each of the input
measures. Two points are to be especially noted about this step. First,
the distribution of input measures must be "within school" distributions, with the consequence that the pupils constituting the "high"
group in one school could conceivably be in the "low" group at
another school where the input levels run higher with respect to any
particular "area of development." Secondly, within any school, a
pupil's input level could be high in one area of development (e.g.,
basic skills) and middle or low in another area of development (e.g.,
health).

The fourth step in deriving the SEI's is to compute, for each school,
the averages of the hard-to-change condition variables that characterize the environment within which the school has had to operate.

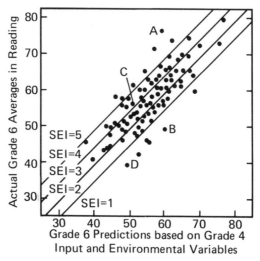

Figure 1. Illustration of method of deriving school effectiveness indices in the
teaching of reading

* The problem presented by the movement of pupils from school to school is
one that can be handled in various ways at the district level, but not at the level
of the individual school. Therefore, it will not be discussed here. Under the present
conception of staff accountability, it appears reasonable to assume that the only
fair index of school effectiveness is one that rests on input-output data obtained
only on those pupils with whom the school staff has been in *continuous* contact
over a specified period of months or years.

The fifth step is to get, again for each school, the average values of all the output measures for each of the three groups of pupils as identified by the input measures.

When all these data are in hand it becomes possible, by means of a series of regression analyses, to compute the SEI's that form the profile of each school.

A rough impression of how this process works may be obtained from an examination of the chart in Figure 1, which was developed from reading test scores obtained on pupils in 91 schools.** The measures of input in reading were taken at the beginning of grade four, and the measures of output at the end of grade six. The numbers along the horizontal axis of the chart summarize the level of grade four reading input and hard-to-change conditions with which each school has had to contend. This summarization is expressed in terms of the grade six predicted average reading levels as determined by the regression analysis.

The numbers along the vertical axis show the *actual* average reading levels for each school at the end of grade six. For each school, the discrepancy between its *predicted* grade six reading level and its *actual* grade six average reading level is used as the measure of the effectiveness with which it has been teaching reading over the three-year period. It is the discrepancy between predicted and actual level of performance that is used to determine the SEI in reading for any school. In this case the SEI's have been assigned arbitrary values ranging from a low of one to a high of five.

Consider the two schools A and B. They both have predicted grade six reading averages of about 60. This indicates that they can be deemed to have been operating in situations that are equivalent in respect to their levels of input at grade four and the hard-to-change conditions that have obtained over the three-year period during which their pupils have gone from grades four through six.

The actual reading output levels are grade six for schools A and B are considerably different. A's actual level is about 73; B's actual level is about 48. As a consequence, school A gets an effectiveness index for the teaching of reading of five, while school B gets an effectiveness index of only one.

Schools C and D present a similar picture, but at a lower level of pupil input and hard-to-change conditions. Both have predicted averages of about 50, but C's actual average is about 56, while D's is only 38. Therefore C gets an SEI of four, and D gets an SEI of only one.

From these two pairs of illustrations, it should be noted that the

** It should be noted that this example does not include the important refinement that calls for assessing the schools' effectiveness for each of three levels of pupil input in reading.

proposed method of computing school effectiveness indices *automatically* adjust for the differing circumstances in which schools must operate. This feature of the index is a sine qua non of any system by which school staffs are to be held professionally accountable.

D. USES OF THE SEI

It was suggested at the beginning of this paper that one of the general principles underlying the concept of professional accountability is that the staff of a school is to be held responsible for *using* its knowledge of where the school stands with respect to the intellectual and personal-social development of its pupils. This is to say that it is not sufficient for a school to "render an accounting" of its educational effectiveness. If the accounting is to have any educational payoff for the pupils whom the school is supposed to serve, the indices should point to some specific corrective actions designed to increase the school's effectiveness.

Many of such actions will perforce be outside the scope of the school itself, and responsibility for taking them must rest with the central administration. In most cases, however, a considerable number of such corrective actions should be well within the competence of the professional staff of the individual school. Responsibility for carrying them out can and should rest with that staff.

The function of school effectiveness indices in this connection is to indicate where a school staff might turn to find ways of improving its performance.

To illustrate how the SEI's might serve this purpose, let us speculate further about the relative positions of schools A and B in Figure 1. Since both schools show the same *predicted* output in reading for such pupils, it can be presumed that both schools are operating under equivalent advantages and handicaps in respect to the conditions that affect the reading ability of those pupils. Therefore, it is entirely legitimate to raise the questions: Why is school A doing so much better than school B in the teaching of reading? and What specifically is school A doing for its pupils that school B is not now doing, but presumably *could* be doing and *ought* to be doing to close the gap?

The reasons for the discrepancy between the two schools on this particular SEI are to be sought among the two sets of variables that did not enter into the derivation of the SEI's: namely, those variables that were designated "educational process" and those designated "easy-to-change surrounding conditions." A systematic comparison of how the two schools stand with respect to these variables should provide the professional staff of school B with useful clues for actions that might be taken to increase its effectiveness in the teaching of reading.

The outcome of this exercise might turn up something like this:

1. School A conducts an intensive summer program in reading; school B does not.
2. School A has a tutorial program conducted by high school students for any pupil who wishes to improve his reading; school B has no such program.
3. School A conducts parent-teacher study groups to stimulate more reading in the home; school B has little contact of any kind with the parents of its pupils.

There is, of course, no absolute guarantee that if school B were to initiate such programs it would automatically raise its SEI in reading from one to five. The factors involved in the life and workings of a school are not all that certain and clear-cut. Nevertheless, there should be a plain obligation on the staff of school B to at least *try* the procedures that appear to be working for school A and to monitor such efforts over a sufficient period to see whether they are having the desired effects. This particularization of staff effort contains the essence of what must be involved in any attempt to guarantee the professional accountability of a school staff.

The approach to accountability through a system of SEI's, if it is well understood and accepted throughout the schools of the district, should provide a mechanism for stimulating directed professional efforts toward the continuous improvement of educational practice on many fronts in all the schools.

III. Plans and Cautions

A. SHORT-RANGE AND LONG-RANGE PLANS

Clearly a full-scale educational accounting system of the sort here envisaged is hardly one that can be designed and installed full-blown in a year or two. It is one that would have to be worked out, piece by piece, over a considerable period of years. It contains technical problems many of which cannot be foreseen in advance and can only be tackled as the accounting system comes into actual operation. More importantly, it would require a massive effort to secure the necessary understanding and cooperation from all the professional and community groups to be affected by it.

Nevertheless, because of the urgency of the situation in urban education and because no adequate and equitable educational accounting system can ever eventuate until some practical action is taken to get it under way, it is strongly suggested that a beginning should be made forthwith by means of a two-pronged approach. One approach would look to the carrying out of a *partial* short-range plan over the next two years; the other to the laying out of a long-range plan for the fullscale operation of the system to be achieved in, say, six years.

The *short-range plan* could begin with the reasonable assumption that there are two areas of pupil development that are of universal concern, especially as they touch the lives of minority group children in the early years of their schooling. These areas are reading and health. Acting on this assumption, one might, from currently available data, obtain input measures of these two variables on all children entering grades one and three with a view to getting output measures on the same children two years later. During the two intervening years a number of the more readily available measures of the hard-to-change conditions affecting each of the elementary schools in the system could conceivably be obtained—e.g., socioeconomic status of pupils' parents, population density and ethnicity of each enrollment area, pupil-teacher ratio, classroom and playground footage per pupil, rate of pupil mobility, and the like. Thus, by the end of the second year, one would be in a position to compute tentative school effectiveness indices and prepare two SEI profiles for each elementary school in the system—one covering grades one and two, the other covering grades three and four. These profiles could then be used as bases for local discussions concerning their meaning and utility as measures of professional accountability.*

The purpose of a short-range program of this sort would be two-fold: 1) to provide a first approximation of two important and practically useful objective criteria of professional accountability, and 2) to provide a concrete basis for bringing about a genuine understanding of what an educational accounting system is and how it can work for the benefit of the schools and the children who attend them.

Concurrently with the foregoing short-range effort, the development of a *long-range plan* should get under way. The first step in this planning process would be to initiate parent-teacher discussions to try 1) to reach a consensus on educational objectives in terms of the areas of pupil development that should be involved in an overall annual system for professional accounting, and 2) to agree on the priorities among such objectives as they might most appropriately apply to the educational needs of the pupils in each school. The second step in the long-range plan would be to assemble instruments for measuring input and output which would be appropriate and compatible with the objectives for each level of schooling. The third step would be to work

---

* As rapidly as community acceptance was achieved, the system could be put on an annual basis and enlarged year by year to include more grades and more areas of pupil development.

out the means for collecting and analyzing the necessary data for measuring the conditions within which each school is operating and the specific processes that characterize its operations.

B. AVOIDING FALSE STARTS

One reason for initiating long-range planning concurrently with working through a partial short-range program is to try to ensure that the ultimate goal of the full-scale system will not be lost from sight while major attention is necessarily focused on the detailed problems of getting a partial operating system under way quickly. In the search for ways around the short-range problems, it is altogether probable that a number of compromises will have to be made. The danger is that, unless the final end is kept in full view, some of these compromises will be such as to preclude attainment of a variable total system.

One mistake, for instance, that could be made at the outset of the short-range program would be to yield to demands to use the input or output measures as if they were themselves measures of school effectiveness. The whole point of this paper is that a meaningful and equitable accounting of school effectiveness is possible *only* under two stringent conditions: 1) it must rest on at least two measures of pupil performance with a sufficient interval between them—probably not less than two years—to permit the school to have an effect on pupil learning which is large enough to be observable; and 2) any output measure of pupil performance must be read in light of the level of pupil input and also in light of the conditions in which the school has been forced to operate during the period for which its effectiveness in the several areas of pupil development is being indexed. This point cannot be too strongly stressed. To compromise with this basic principle would wreck the entire enterprise.

A second mistake that could seriously damage the development of the system would be to introduce into it measures of I.Q. as though they were measures of pupil input available simultaneously with measures of pupil output. This type of misuse of test scores has had a disastrous effect on the interpretation of educational measurements for at least 50 years. It should not be prolonged.

A third type of mistake to be avoided is that of concentrating the effort to develop SEI's on a certain *selected* group of schools (e.g., those in poverty areas) but not on others. If this is done the SEI's simply will not mean anything. A basic requirement in their derivation and use is that the essential measures must be obtained on *all* schools in the system so as to determine which schools are indeed comparable.

One other type of mistake that could be made in embarking on the short-range project would be to concentrate all the effort on a single area of pupil development, namely, the "basic skills." The danger here—and it is one by which schools have all too frequently been trapped—is threefold. First, it encourages the notion that, as far as the school is concerned, training in the basic skills is all that matters in a society where so many other human characteristics also matter. Secondly, it tends toward neglect of the fact that if a school gives exclusive attention to this one area of pupil development, it may purchase success in this area at the expense of failure in other areas—social behavior, for instance. Thirdly, it tends to blind people to the interrelatedness of educational objectives, that is, to the fact that pupil development in one area may be heavily dependent on development in other areas. Learning to read, for example, may be dependent on the pupil's maintaining good health. And the pupil's sense of his worth as a human being may be dependent on his ability to read. It is for these reasons that the short-range program suggested above includes at a minimum two widely different areas of pupil development.

C. AVOIDING FALSE ANALOGIES

The term educational accountability, as used most recently by certain economists, systems analysts, and the like, has frequently been based on a conceptualization that tends, by analogy, to equate the educational process with the type of engineering process that applies to industrial production. It is this sort of analogy, for instance, that appears to underlie proposals for "guaranteed performance contracting" as exemplified in the much-publicized Texarkana project. The analogy is useful to a point. But there is also a point beyond which it can be so seriously misleading as to undermine any sensible efforts to develop objective criteria of professional accountability.

It must be constantly kept in mind that the educational process is *not* on all fours with an industrial process; it is a social process in which human beings are continually interacting with other human beings in ways that are imperfectly measurable or predictable. Education does not deal with inert raw materials, but with living minds that are instinctively concerned first with preserving their own integrity and second with reaching a meaningful accommodation with the world around them. The output of the educational process is never a "finished product" whose characteristics can be rigorously specified in advance; it is an individual who is sufficiently aware of his own incompleteness to make him want to keep on growing and learning and trying to solve the riddle of his own existence in a world that neither he nor anyone else can fully understand or predict.

It is for this reason that the problems involved in developing objective criteria of professional accountability will always be hard problems. They are problems, however, that must be tackled with all the human insight and goodwill that can be mustered if the schools of this urban society are to meet the large challenges that now confront them.

Texarkana: The Second Year Around

NATION'S SCHOOLS

There has been a lot of controversy over education's first performance contract awarded in October 1969 to the town of Texarkana. However, charges of "teaching for the test" have not kept the school system from continuing performance contracting for a second year. In this article, some of the strengths and weaknesses of the first year's contract are analyzed by the local officials.

Texarkana, Ark.—When the U.S. Office of Education funded education's first performance contract in October 1969, attention immediately focused on this small town straddling the Texas-Arkansas border. More than a year later, after some widespread publicity, local officials here commented on what was learned during their initial experience and on how the performance contract for the second year of the experiment reflects this experience.

Their comments and conclusions:

"Of all the weaknesses we had last year, testing was the most glaring," says Martin J. Filogamo, director of the Texarkana project. Aside from the fact that "teaching to the test" had tainted some results of the project, another fault Filogamo points to was the heavy reliance on standardized tests. "Last year we had 100 per cent standardized tests. This year it's 25 per cent criterion-referenced tests (based on skills taught to an individual student) and 75 per cent standardized. If this year is a success, we might go 50-50 next year. And then, someday, we'll use all criterion-referenced tests."

Management support: "We probably had some failure built in from the beginning," admits Thomas C. McRae, Model Cities Director for Texarkana. In the $250,000 grant from USOE, two key components established in the planning phase of the contract had been deleted: management support and additional testing.

"Texarkana: The Second Year Around," *Nation's Schools*, 87:32–33, March 1971. Reprinted by permission.

"One of the things that was cut out was management support and expertise to work with the schools . . . that is, integrating successful portions of the program into the regular school system and monitoring the program from outside the system to prevent some of the things which perhaps happened [teaching to the test]" says McRae. "OE cut out additional tests that would have eliminated the possibility of teaching to a test, because there would not have been a single test you could have taught to. Also, they cut out provisions for retesting after a delayed length of time to see whether students had retained learning."

The need for the services of a management support group "to get you going at the very beginning," was underscored by E. D. Trice, superintendent of the Texarkana, Ark., school district and fiscal agent for the OE grant. (A management consultant helps the district obtain funding for the project, draw up a request for proposal, select the company, and monitor the program during its operation.) "No small or medium-sized town is going to have that kind of capability by itself," McRae declares.

There can also be problems in persuading a school board which has used little outside help to hire a consultant, he adds. "People accept the fact that you have to hire a lawyer, but it's hard to accept the fact that you have to buy a consultant to do a specialized job. It's very difficult for any elected body . . . to believe that any human being is worth $100 a day."

Texarkana did have management support from a Washington-based consultant; but the contract was severed once the project got underway, leaving only an internal evaluator.

RFPs: The request for proposals should outline succinctly the characteristics of the target population and the requirements of the program. According to Filogamo, the first year's RFP was confusing to some of the education companies, requiring them to keep in close contact with school officials in drawing up their proposals. The second year's RFP was a "little clearer," he says. "But some companies will still come in with irrelevant proposals. Some people just don't follow an RFP, because they give you what they want. . . ."

The introduction to the RFP for the second year of Texarkana's experiment was worded, in part:

"Approximately 300 students deficient by two or more grade levels in reading and/or mathematics will participate in the programs to be offered during the school year 1970–71. The contractor will be required to maximize student performance in the areas of mathematics and/or reading achievement within time and cost constraints. A fixed price plus incentive and penalty fee or modified performance incentive contract will be specified" (by the contractor).

Material backing up the RFP's introduction outlines the evaluation design, including dates of testing, plus the guarantees of performance and penalty the company must be willing to give the schools. The RFP, however, permits the company to propose its own formula for payment, providing it can be started on a per-student basis.

Selection of the company: "You should not always look for the lowest bidder," advises Superintendent Trice, ". . . but at what each company proposes to do." Filogamo concedes that this year's contract with Educational Developmental Laboratories, Inc., carried a higher cost per grade level increase than last year's with Dorsett Educational Systems, Inc. But in the final analysis, he points out, the costs will not be that much different since a purchase requirement with Dorsett for equipment boosted the contract higher than the payment rate of $80 per grade level increase per student.

"It takes about $125 to $150 to get a grade level increase in reading or math—and there are no short cuts to it," says Filogamo.

Staffing: Texarkana officials agree that for the "turnkey" (the process by which the experiment is turned over by the contractor to the school district) phase of a performance contract to be successful, school administrators and teachers must participate in the planning and operation of the project from the beginning. In Texarkana, 20 local teachers worked after hours as "consultants" to the contractor, helping to refine the program in the first year.

One of the problems with in-house staffing is that experience is usually gained on the job through a process of trial and error. "The first year was very disconcerting to me, because I didn't know very much about performance contracting or technical management. I had been an elementary principal (in the Texarkana schools)," says Filogamo.

Attitude—the greatest problem: A performance contract cannot be grafted onto a school system unless traditional attitudes on the part of local officials and teachers undergo a metamorphosis. Trice himself admits he was reluctant at the beginning to welcome industry into the school system.

"It may have been the fact that, as a professional educator, I had the feeling 'I'm trained to do this job. I know how to do it better than industry.' I think this is a natural reaction for an educator."

The local board of education also had to be sold on the idea. Mrs. Vera Kilpatrick, board president at the time the first year's contract was under consideration, was an early convert and had the job of convincing other board members to approve the contract. She created a committee of three board members to study the contract and report back to the board.

"I tried to select people for the committee who needed to be sold on the idea," she says. These members would be the "most influential" members on the full board. The tactic, of course, worked.

Contract Teaching—A Reality

LLOYD HENDRICKSON

One of the byproducts of the accountability movement is a renewed emphasis on individualized instruction. One method of accomplishing this is through contract teaching. Lloyd Hendrickson identifies three essential and unique characteristics of a typical contract teaching plan, and he outlines the major structural components of most contracts. The use of contracts in some North Dakota high schools is one way accountability is being applied at the local level.

Teachers have almost always recognized that children have different abilities, learn in different ways, and learn at different rates; but it has always been a struggle to find a way to take this into consideration in the typical classroom.

Today, fortunately, the individualization of instruction is becoming more of a reality than it ever has in the past. Increasingly larger numbers of innovative educators are seeking new ways, as well as exploring more fully the methods used in the past, to individualize instruction.

Several North Dakota high schools have introduced contract teaching as a means of individualizing instruction. The writer surveyed several high school teachers in these schools to secure first-hand information about the contracts. The North Dakota high schools currently using contracts in one or more classes include: Buxton, Central Valley; Cooperstown; Drake, Drayton; Edmore; Grand Forks, Central and Red River; Lakota; Litchville; Maddock; Northwood and West Fargo.

The contracts are being used in high schools using the conventional class schedule as well as flexible schedules. In some schools they are used for short periods of time, while in others they may be used the entire school system.

Opinions on their effectiveness varies, as with any teaching method.

Lloyd Hendrickson, "Contract Teaching—A Reality," *North Dakota Journal of Education*, 50:26–27, October 1970. Reprinted by permission.

Many teachers are very enthusiastic about the results they are getting, while others expressed some doubt. Contracts can hardly be classified as a panacea for all the ills of the teaching-learning situation in a particular school. When used by an enthusiastic, skillful teacher with adequate teaching-learning resources, they can provide an excellent means of individualizing instruction on either a small or large-scale basis.

A typical contract teaching plan has three essential and unique characteristics. First, the teacher is a very integral and indispensable part of each contract. He fills the role of guidance person, human relations person, confidant, and to a lesser degree, a dispenser of information and evaluator. Second, there must be built-in opportunities for the student to make choices. He must be able to choose from a variety of learning activities to reach a specific objective. He should also have the opportunity to explore the topic in greater depth if he so chooses. Third, clear instructional objectives or goals to tell the student exactly what it is that he is to do.

The Contract

A student contract contains a common core of knowledge and skills that all students are expected to master. Students who have completed the core may pursue related areas of interest if they so desire.

Structurally, most contracts are made up of the following components:

1. Title or Content Classification: Simply a heading to facilitate identification. May or may not include a numerical identification.

2. Rationale or Purpose: An explanation of what, why and where this contract fits in the total subject picture. It may include a motivational rationale or justification to enhance its attractiveness to the student. This rationale may be written in the language of the learner.

3. Instructional or Behavioral Objectives: The purpose of an instructional objective is to make clear to teachers, students and other interested persons what it is that needs to be taught—or what it is that has been taught. The basic intent is to write instructional objectives that will communicate without misunderstanding.

4. Pre-Test: Here the student is asked to determine the extent to which he has already achieved the instructional objectives as a result of earlier learning experiences. The pre-test serves two purposes. It points out areas of weakness to give the student direction to the areas of study and activities that will help him overcome this weakness. It also permits a student who is already familiar with much of the material to complete the contract in a minimum amount of time or select areas of the topic for in-depth or quest study if he wishes.

5. *Resources or Activities:* In preparing this list, the teacher should use a multi-mode and multi-media approach to teaching-learning. Large group instruction, small group work, independent study and lab work are provided. Student conferences with the teacher may also be written into this section. The utilization of many different textbooks on the same subject allows the student to have the material presented to him in a variety of written forms.

Audio and video tapes, movies, slides, magazines, filmstrips, programmed materials, education games, written assignments, physical activities and teaching machines are included in the multi-media approach. Within this variety of activities and materials, the student is free to select the ones which he feels will best aid him in meeting the instructional objectives. Without this freedom to choose, the contract may become nothing more than a written worksheet. This variety of activities is also an important motivational factor in maintaining high student interest in contracts.

6. *Self-test:* The self-test, based on the instructional objectives, may be taken by the student at any time he feels he is ready and able to pass. The test is self-administered and self-corrected. If the student fails to pass the self-test, it provides the necessary feedback he needs as he goes back to his list of resources to complete additional work that will enable him to achieve the necessary competency. The student may then retake the self-test or take the final evaluation.

7. *Post-test:* The final evaluation, which is graded by the teacher, is designed to measure the instructional objectives as stated in the contract. If the student passes this test, he is directed to the next contract in the series or allowed to select a contract of his own preference depending upon the school's policy. If he fails, he is directed to the resources section of the contract to complete additional activities.

8. *Quest:* Provisions for optional work on the topic in the form of in-depth or quest activities may be included in this section of the contract. They should permit the student to apply the new knowledge, develop additional competencies in this area, or permit the development of an activity of his own choice.

A student progresses through each contract at a pace unique to him and at a degree of sophistication that is appropriate to his level of ability. The slower student is expected neither to keep up or to fail. The better student will not have to slacken his efforts while the remainder of the class is catching up. Students absent from school are able to make up the work and need not fall behind. Each student has the opportunity to continually progress through the contract, literally picking up each day where he left off previously.

Educators wishing to further explore the use of contracts might begin by reading the following books: *Working with Individualized Instruction* by Thorwald Esbensen and *Preparing Instructional Ob-*

jectives by Robert Mager. The writer does not wish to imply that this will prepare you to design and use contracts but it should provide a foundation on which to build. With additional reading, discussion and visits to schools using contracts; you are on your way to individualizing instruction through contract teaching.

Three Reports of Performance Contracting Now in Action

THE INSTRUCTOR

Project IMPACT in Duval County, Florida, emphasizes learning by discovery and is developmental in nature rather than remedial. The Incentives Only Project in Mesa, Arizona, is based on the use of teacher and pupil incentives to increase reading and math skills of selected disadvantaged students. The Program for Reaching Potential Dropouts Early in Dallas, Texas, uses Accelerated Learning Achievement Centers to aid in meeting its objectives.

Project IMPACT, Duval County, Florida

Major features: IMPACT (Instruction and Management Practices to Aid Classroom Teaching) ; funded by Duval County School Board and Title I; involves 300 first graders in three Jacksonville schools; excluded were students with an IQ below 75; participants attend "Maximum Achievement Centers" during the day; teachers come from existing faculties, selected for willingness to participate and capacity for innovation; proposal written by school system, private contractors bid on basis of that proposal; program emphasizes learning by discovery and is developmental rather than remedial; Phase I began February 1, ends in June, Phase II will run from September 1971 to June 1972, Phase III from September 1972 to June 1973; no incentives being used.

Contractor: Learning Research Associates.

Contract objectives: Raise IQs of elementary pupils and increase thinking, reading, writing, math, social studies, and science skills; determine cost/effectiveness of such instruction; improve teaching skills and use of professional resources.

"Three Reports of Performance Contracting Now in Action." Reprinted from *Instructor* © June/July 1971, The Instructor Publications, Inc., Dansville, NY 14437.

Auditor: Educational Testing Service.

Anita Garner, principal of Jacksonville Beach Elementary, one project school, says the classroom teacher is the key to this program.

Pam Riechmann is a first-year teacher who agreed to sign a three-year contract in order to take part in the program at Jacksonville Beach. She's very optimistic about what can be achieved during the next two years.

"Perhaps this program runs smoothly for me because this is the first year I've taught—I didn't have any patterns established or habits to break. Teaching on such an individualized basis seems natural to me because I've never had to teach thirty children at once."

Are incentives to motivate children a part of IMPACT?

"Teachers involved in IMPACT are enthusiastic because care was taken to select those whose approach to teaching was compatible with the open education techniques we wanted to employ.

"At the beginning of the program we 'discarded' all of our textbook series and began to use *Words in Color, Algebricks, The Taba Social Studies Curriculum,* and *Science: A Process Approach.* For three weeks immediately preceding February 1, project teachers were engaged in full-time in-service training with consultants. For each subject area, they examined the inquiry process and learned how to apply it in the classroom. They also became familiar with the materials I mentioned and observed classroom demonstrations. They worked long hours during those three weeks preparing themselves for a new kind of teaching."

We asked IMPACT teacher Sarah Thomas, Garden City Elementary, how she and her students adjusted to the program that began at midyear.

"After a couple of weeks I think we began to feel quite comfortable with the inquiry approach. It took time for the students to adjust to asking, probing, and discovering instead of our telling them what is to be learned. They used to rely on us for praise or verbal reinforcement—now they are beginning to realize that the self-satisfaction that comes from grasping a concept is the real reward in learning.

"Using this very individualized approach, I find I'm a more patient and understanding teacher. I feel I've been able to develop closer relationships with my students."

"No—we don't give the kids candy, toys, and rewards if that's what you mean. You see, our classroom is such a fantastic place to be that it's incentive enough just being there. The worst punishment you can give a child is to make him leave. Our room is a warm, congenial learning environment. We already have a variety of wonderful materials and anything else we need is furnished by the company. All we have to do is ask."

Bernice Scott, who is director of the program's planning and design, talked about how student progress will be evaluated.

"We'll measure pupil performance with standardized achievement tests and criterion-referenced tests which are specifically constructed to measure a student's mastery of the program's objectives."

At the end of Phase I, judgment of LRA's success will be based on a variety of criteria, and payment made according to prearranged percentages. Fifty percent is based on the reading and math performance of project pupils as compared with a random sample of other Title I pupils. Thus, unless the IMPACT pupils do at least as well as the random sample, the contractor will be denied half of the payment.

Twenty-five percent is based on IMPACT pupils' performance on criterion-referenced tests. Based on individual pupil performance, the amount paid to LRA will be prorated so that achievement of less than 40 percent will result in no payment at all.

Twenty percent of LRA's earnings is based on performance in reading, math, social studies, and science over and above normal expectations. This 20 percent is broken down further as follows: 40 percent for reading, with a gain of .5 grade level, as measured by the SAT, required for payment to begin, 40 percent for math under the same conditions as for reading, and 20 percent for social studies and science with evaluation based on scores on Part I of the Stanford Early School Achievement Test. The remaining 5 percent of the contract price will be paid to LRA based on gains in IQ scores.

How does the community feel about Project IMPACT?

Mrs. Garner says articles and features which appeared in the local press, and TV specials, did a lot to tell the public what IMPACT was all about. "From the beginning of the project, we've involved the community—we've held several informational meetings and open houses. Some parents have even been able to sit in on the teacher-training sessions. We send home a newsletter once a month which keeps them up-to-date. We also encourage them to visit the classroom. Parents who think that this type of learning atmosphere is too unstructured or too permissive begin to understand the inquiry method when they see it in action."

Incentives Only, Mesa, Arizona

Major features: OEO-funded; involves one junior high and three elementary schools and an equal number of control schools; offers remedial work in math and reading for 100 students per grade in grades one through three and seven through nine; involves use of incentives to increase reading and math skills of selected disadvantaged students who show low achievement; no outside private contractor; carried out by regular teachers, using regular methods of instruction in their own classrooms; project participants selected on basis of low income and low achievement; students not aware of experimental grouping; began in November, ends in May; incentives for both students and teachers; all students in project classes receive incentives even though not all are part of testing group.

Contractor: Mesa School District and Mesa Education Association.

Contract objective: To determine if the use of student and teacher incentives can accelerate mastery of basic skills by disadvantaged students.

Evaluator: Battelle Memorial Institute.

Doug Barnard, director of the "Incentives Only" program, explains the way it works, as follows.

"We began this project with the assumption that, for the average child, a report card and teacher praise is all that is needed for incentive. We believe that the economically deprived child must be rewarded more frequently and in different ways."

Designated experimental schools were presented with an overview of the project task. Each faculty voted to be a part of the project or to be excluded. No students were transferred, bussed, or homogeneously grouped for the study. In all schools, normal classroom teaching methods and materials are being utilized. Project classes remain basically as they were when the school year began—the addition of incentives is the only differences. Some classrooms of thirty students may contain only seven or eight designated as project students, but in such cases, all students receive incentives.

Don Blair, principal of Lehi Elementary, one of the participating schools, says:

"Our teachers establish with each student a set of goals to be achieved. When students reach the goals, they are rewarded. Our incentives program corresponds with the student's level of achievement. It consists of immediate rewards, such as candy and small toys, and delayed rewards, such as time to use educational games, watch movies, and go on field trips. Each teacher tailors a reward system to fit the personality of the child involved."

Lois Williams, who teaches a first-grade class at Lehi School, is happy to be involved in the project.

"It requires a very individualized approach which is very different from the traditional teaching methods you learn in college—it's challenging but gratifying when you see the results."

How does she feel about the reward system?

"I use the incentives in two ways: to reward scholastic achievement and to modify behavior. Because of the rewards I think the students are more motivated, and I've noticed fewer discipline problems. Let's face it, children will clean up their desks faster if they know they'll get a piece of candy when the job is done. Giving little but meaningful rewards seems to make the school day go along much more smoothly now."

How lasting are the effects of the incentives?

"This is a question parents ask—we began with small material rewards which we are slowly replacing with social incentives such as group activities. Of course, our ultimate objective is to make gaining knowledge the incentive for learning."

Mrs. Audrey Young, a second-grade teacher at Jefferson School, was opposed to the program at first.

"I didn't like the idea of giving tangible rewards—it seemed that praise and the satisfaction of understanding should provide enough incentive for achievement. Now I view the program more objectively—it works very well for some children. For others, I've had to find different ways of 'turning them on' to learning. The teacher must be very perceptive—he must sense what will motivate a child and how much pressure he can take. Rewards must be given for real mastery of a skill, real accomplishment of a goal—not just the appearance of having accomplished it."

Do students get used to being rewarded for what they do?

"One of my little boys took a story home to read. His mother said she'd love to hear it. The little boy replied 'OK, but what are you going to give me for it?'

"We try to explain to children that receiving rewards for achievement is a little arrangement we've made just to use in school—most children understand this."

How have parents reacted to the Mesa project?

"Favorably, for the most part," says Mr. Blair. "The Mesa School District has always made it a point to work closely with the community and this project is no exception. We held briefings, wrote newsletters, and had extensive coverage in local newspapers and on television. No parents have requested that their child be removed from the project thus far. Many have been impressed with the results they see—kids actually say they like school and attendance has improved."

The program's teacher incentives are given in June if project students gain more than one grade level over their pretested achievement. Incentives are of four types: a cash salary supplement, cash for hiring aides, cash for purchasing additional materials, and released time for planning. At this writing, each school would decide what to do with the money it receives.

Teachers at Jefferson School are thinking about using the money to buy materials for the school but the Lehi School faculty favors giving each teacher a salary bonus for each project student who shows a grade-level gain.

What will happen next year when the funds are gone? Mrs. Williams feels no teacher could afford to personally sponsor a program of this nature, but she's convinced rewards work and she plans to purchase small items with her own money and make use of intangible incentives such as free time for games and play.

Dr. Barnard says that the results in June will determine whether a similar program will continue.

"We're simply asking ourselves, 'Will a child who knows he'll receive candy or a toy for a successfully completed task work harder than a student rewarded only by praise and a good grade?' The incentives approach may not work for all students, but if it proves to be a way of reaching some, then educators should consider it."

Reaching Potential Dropouts Early, Dallas, Texas

Major features: OEO-funded; remedial education experiment in raising achievement levels of disadvantaged children in math and reading; involves six hundred students from grades one through three in one elementary school, and seven through nine in one junior high; an equal number of schools and students in control group; contract held with private firm but local teachers are used; contractor, not teacher, held accountable for student achievement; released-time incentives for students, cash-bonus incentive for teachers; teaching done in ALACs (Accelerated Learning Achievement Centers), made from regular classrooms which were air-conditioned, carpeted, and redecorated; began August 1970.

Objectives: To identify potential dropouts at an early stage of academic development and design an academic program that will interest them in academic achievement and improve their basic math and reading skills.

Contractor: Quality Education Development, Inc., taking educational responsibility; Education Turnkey Systems, Inc., providing management support.

Evaluator: Battelle Memorial Institute.

"With the exception of first graders, participating students were recommended by former teachers as being students lacking the desire or the ability to achieve," explains Donald Waldrip, Assistant Superintendent of the Dallas Independent School District. "Their measured IQs had to be 70 or over and they had to be at least two years below their appropriate grade level in reading. This data was provided by standardized tests. All project students also had to be from the group classed as 'disadvantaged' by Title I guidelines.

"First-grade participants were selected differently. Forty-six of the total one hundred students were designated on the basis of readiness tests obtained at the kindergarten level, and the remaining fifty-four students were chosen at random from entering first-grade students. All first graders would have been chosen on the basis of kindergarten data, had enough of them been able to attend kindergarten.

"Low-achieving, disadvantaged children make up the control group and one hundred similarly selected students serve as replacements for project students.

"Pre- and postachievement tests and interim performance criterion-referenced tests, supplied and administered to both control and experimental groups, will serve as data sources for comparative analyses."

Each ALAC houses one teacher, one aide, and twenty-five students per hour. A recent visitor to the ALACs in the H. S. Thompson Elementary School described them this way.

"Four classrooms open to a hall which is separated from the rest of the school by colorful dividers. The walls of the ALAC are brightly painted—several gaily colored designs hang from the ceiling and delightful student art is displayed on both sides of the hall. Going from a regular classroom into the ALAC hall may startle the casual passerby. The contrast shows the effect a bit of paint, a little money, and some rearranging can have on the educational environment of an old building."

The program is totally individualized. Teachers stress letting every student progress at his own rate. In reading, students begin with i/t/a and change to traditional orthography when they are ready. In arithmetic, unit tests provide the information on which teachers base individual prescriptions. Small-group instruction, one-to-one tutoring, and individual work with both hardware and software are common sights in the ALACs.

Lois Palfrey, a reading teacher at Anderson Junior High, feels that students who haven't learned to read before are doing so now because in the individualized program they aren't experiencing failure.

"I have some of the students who were doing poorly in my language arts class last year—their progress is amazing. Since the materials match their level, they don't become frustrated and quit."

The Dallas project offers no tangible incentives to students for academic achievement as several other projects do. Instead, successful completion of work is rewarded with time to spend in a special area stocked with records, tapes, books, and educational games.

Teachers involved in the program receive a salary bonus 14 percent above the regular salary schedule. The bonus is not tied to pupil gains. Instead, it is paid for the extra duty involved (work at night and an occasional weekend).

For the contractor, however, payment is received on a different basis.

"Unless the students, achieve at least a 1.4 grade-level increase, we do not give the companies one cent," says Mr. Waldrip. "The company absorbs the cost of teacher salaries and equipment."

When the project began it had both supporters and opponents. A member of the Classroom Teachers of Dallas questions using business methods in teaching. "Business has a materialistic approach," he said. "The contracts are a new scheme by businessmen to sell more of their products—a way to market more machines and prepackaged materials."

A committee of classroom teachers is studying the present program, and the local administrators' organization has recently contracted with the school district to manage their own guaranteed performance program. It's still too early to draw definite conclusions about what's going on in Dallas, but school authorities describe themselves as "cautiously optimistic."

EPIC: Educational Auditor in Arizona

ARIZONA TEACHER

Evaluation and feedback are essential components of any accountability system. To meet the need for evaluation, private firms are now contracting to provide the necessary expertise in educational program auditing. Dr. Robert E. Kraner is president of one of these firms. In this interview, he describes the role of EPIC in evaluating Title III and Title VII programs in Arizona. He discusses the functions of educational auditors and the need for behavioral objectives in evaluation.

The term "accountability" loomed not so long ago on the educational horizon and refuses to go away. Those educators concerned with the concept look for answers to the questions: "What quality of education are we providing" and "How effective are we as providers?" According to Robert E. Kraner, president of EPIC and subject of this interview,

"EPIC: Educational Auditor in Arizona," An Interview with Dr. Robert E. Kraner, *Arizona Teacher*, 59:10+, May 1971. Reprinted by permission. Dr. Robert E. Kraner is President, EPIC Diversified Systems Corporation, Tucson, Arizona.

accountability means simply that learning should count for more than teaching. Schools and educators are being held responsible for the learning of students and for the quality of the learning.

W. Stanley Kruger writing in "American Education," for March, 1970, commented that rising teacher salaries, mushrooming taxes, and deteriorating social conditions are causing more and more Americans to feel that education should be accountable for the use of society's resources. One measure of current dissatisfaction with the way education is meeting its responsibilities might be the fact, announced by Leon Lessinger, that 85 per cent of all school bond elections were defeated last year.

A new technique for satisfying the demand for accountability in education is educational program auditing. One of the most important of the new educational auditing firms is EPIC Diversified Systems Corporation, in Tucson. (The acronym stands for Evaluative Programs for Innovative Curriculums.)

With a staff of seven professionals and nine supportive personnel, Tucson EPIC (which opened a four-man branch office in Cherry Hills, New Jersey, on March 15 in order to be near east coast projects), has worked as auditor or evaluator for approximately seventy-five school districts. The probings and reports of EPIC staffers have directly affected the daily work of some 300,000 teachers.

According to Kraner, "The educational consultant is becoming an integral part of the educational scene as the demand for technical skills increases. Local school districts do not have the requisite expertise on their staff, nor can they afford to hire a person full time, even if personnel were available. An educational consulting firm that can provide the necessary expertise is extremely valuable to a school district."

One EPIC Project in Arizona

Hoping to help students develop self-respect and self-direction, and feeling a need for feedback to determine the degree to which they were successful in inculcating these values, the teachers and principal of Holmes Elementary School, Mesa, worked last year with EPIC. EPIC staffers and Holmes teachers created an affective behavior checklist designed to identify the measure of self-respect and self-direction demonstrated by students.

The Holmes teachers involved in the EPIC program closely observed the behavior of each child in their respective classrooms. At one week intervals for the first four weeks of school, and every other week for the next six months, each teacher observed students and marked the checklist.

One behavior listed, which is indicative of a child possessing self-direction, was: "Follows daily schedule without teacher solicitation." If the student did follow that schedule during the week, the appropriate space was checked. If the teacher had not observed the behavior, the space was not marked. An item in the self-respect section was: "Keeps self well groomed." If the teacher noticed that the child had been tidy and neat that week, the space beside the item was marked. If the child had not been well groomed, the space was left blank.

At the end of four weeks, or when four checklists had been marked for every child, EPIC provided a cumulative profile of each child's scores. These profiles were utilized by the Holmes School teachers to evaluate pupil progress in developing self-respect and self-direction.

EPIC worked to discover the number of students evidencing each behavior specified on the checklist, so that progress in the development of each attitude could be determined for the total student population. Their analysis of the data indicated that eighty per cent of the classrooms involved in the project made significant gains (.05) in both self-direction and self-respect.

With this feedback, the teachers evaluated the effectiveness of their instructional and classroom techniques in helping each child develop the two major goals.

—Larry Frase
(based on material first appearing in "Mesa Public Schools Today")

How did EPIC begin? EPIC began as a Title III Project in 1967 to provide for continuous evaluation of instructional programs in education. Under a grant from the U.S. Office of Education (USOE), eight faculty members of the College of Education, University of Arizona, planned a three year program for EPIC. Representatives from fifteen school districts in southern Arizona served as a board of directors as we began operations.

During our first year, we worked with educational programs in southern Arizona. The second year we expanded to include the entire state, and the third year, the USOE permitted us to contract with out of state sources. In May, 1970, four of us left the University of Arizona to continue full time in an area which we feel holds great promise for educators.

Currently, EPIC conducts evaluations and audits in forty-two states. We also have contracted with Guam schools to do an evaluation.

What, more specifically, are the services performed by EPIC? We develop and implement approaches to instructional program evaluation, educational program auditing, performance based instruction, needs assessment program, program planning, and management support systems at all educational levels. I'll explain more about some of these later.

One of our programs at Weber State College, Ogden, Utah, in performance based instruction, was just voted the outstanding innovative project in the nation by the American Association of Teacher Training in Higher Education.

Why do you believe educators need an organization like EPIC? To help them assess their efforts in meaningful fashion. Too often, education practices, teaching techniques, organizational patterns, instructional materials, and other educational activities are primarily "an affair of the heart." We feel that educators, as professionals, want to offer more than this. Thus, we train local school personnel in gathering information which they may use to make rational, pertinent decisions.

What do you mean by "an affair of the heart?" As you will recall, several years ago the innovation pendulum was swinging in education. Many new ideas were being adapted and instructional techniques modified. Nobody asked: "Is this better than we were doing before?" or "What do we expect from our new program?" Schools with large classrooms were constructing small cubicles, and schools with small cubicles were tearing down walls to provide large classrooms—both schools "feeling" they had improved their instructional program.

One school district had attempted to introduce modern math into its curriculum. When scores on standardized tests plummeted, the program was about to be discarded. A systematic evaluation showed that the modern math program was producing results on the higher cognitive levels of application and analysis; whereas the traditional math was producing results on levels of knowledge and comprehension. By combining both instructional approaches the school district met its objectives.

There is an old saying that a teacher has a choice of either teaching twenty years or teaching one year twenty times. The latter usually results from an "affair of the heart," where little or no effort is made to modify teaching techniques based on student performance. Developing good teaching skills and techniques requires that a teacher be able to gauge his or her work in terms of student learning.

What can you do with such an obvious conflict of approaches? Frankly, both approaches may be effective or both may be ineffective, depending upon the goals of the instructional program. Once the school personnel phrase their expectations in behavioral terms, they are ready to evaluate both approaches.

I like the excerpt from *Alice in Wonderland,* where Alice comes to a fork in the road and asks the Cheshire Cat, "Which road should I take?" "Where are you going?" asks the Cheshire Cat. "I don't know," replied Alice. "Then," responded the Cheshire Cat, "it really doesn't matter which road you take."

Fortunately, educators realize the importance of knowing where they want to go before deciding which road to take. Most instructional programs are now designed to produce certain behavioral objectives.

Are behavioral objectives a new approach in education? No. Any education textbook from the early 1900's discusses behavioral objectives somewhere between its covers. "Behavioral objectives" simply refers to learner responses which are measurable and define a more abstract phenomena.

What do you mean by "abstract phenomena"? We talk about many things as though we actually see them—electricity, the wind, love, achievement, and so forth. We never do see these phenomena but we do witness behavior associated with them. You have never seen electricity, but you have seen behavior associated with it—a light bulb burning, for instance. As we are able to quantify and describe the behavior associated with electricity, we can use, control, and predict this phenomenon for the good of mankind.

In education, we never see student learning. Rather, we observe and work with, behavior associated with learning—solving a math problem or spelling a word. The better able we are to describe and quantify behavior associated with learning, the more effectively educators will be able to use, control, and predict this behavior for the good of education.

How can behavior objectives solve conflicts? Let's go back to the two math programs—traditional and modern math. Suppose you asked, "Which is the better program?" Without knowing the desired learning outcomes, I could not answer that question.

But suppose the behavioral objectives in math *are* known. This would enable me to answer your question and, most important, the knowledge would assist the teacher in modifying or developing an effective program. Harkening back to Alice, when we know where we want to go, it is much easier to select the road.

Can all the outcomes of education be written in terms of behavior objectives? Naturally not, but this is evading the issue. Educators can describe and measure certain basic objectives and begin work with these.

How does EPIC work with behavioral objectives? They are essential to every project we work with. If none exist, we help the school write them. If the school has stated objectives, we help organize them.

Basically, we work with two types of objectives—performance and process. Performance objectives not only state what the learner is expected to accomplish, they indicate time limitations or the prerequisites necessary for the desired student performance to take place.

Performance goals call for procedures to be established for monitoring and auditing of student behavior.

Process objectives state what is expected of the individuals and groups involved. If the program is to be in such a form that it can be monitored or audited, process objectives must be specified.

What individuals or groups are covered by process objectives? Students, of course, teachers, administrators, specialists, families, and community groups.

So, if a school superintendent can write behavioral objectives, his evaluation problem is solved? No. A behavioral objective must be meaningful or it has little value. We have found some schools writing objectives simply because it is the "in" thing to do. This "inservice busywork" results in a whole lot of very little. Better to have two or three meaningful behavioral objectives operating in a systematic evaluation program than two to three thousand stored in a closet.

What do you mean by systematic evaluation? A systematic evaluation might take the following steps:

1. an assessment to identify existing educational needs
2. the development of behavioral objectives to meet these needs
3. selection of the most appropriate instructional procedure to meet the objectives
4. an evaluation of the procedure in terms of meeting stated objectives or fulfilling the needs

At EPIC, we believe we have developed a system that teaches educators to develop and write behavioral objectives. They must answer four crucial questions: who is going to perform the specified behavior; what behavior is expected or desired; how and under what circumstances is the behavior to be observed; and how will it be measured?

Where does standardized testing fit into this? Everywhere—if the objectives to be measured by the test are the same as those developed in step 2.

Nowhere—if the objectives measured by the test are different from those developed in step 2.

Is all of this testing really essential? As essential as feedback is to learning. Educators must have feedback concerning the results of their efforts. Without independent feedback, we are back to an affair of the heart.

What does EPIC actually do to help? Some evaluations people must do for themselves, but some activities require technical assistance. For these, EPIC is available.

Basically, when we enter into a working relationship with an agency, our purpose is to make them independent as soon as possible. If we succeed, we work ourselves out of a job. Our approaches, materials, and techniques have been tested; they are not mere drawing board dreams.

We are especially interested in current projects in the state of Arizona for which EPIC serves as evaluator or auditor. Can you describe some of these? We have critiqued and developed all Title III proposal evaluation designs for the state.

We have audited the implementation of evaluation designs in all Title III programs in Arizona.

We have conducted evaluation workshops for Title III staff in Arizona State Department of Education.

We have served as evaluators or auditors for four Title VII bilingual programs in Arizona. Two of these are in the Phoenix area, one is in Tucson, and one in Nogales.

An educational auditor has been compared to a school's fiscal auditor. Do you care to comment on this? The roles are similar; however, differences exist. The educational auditor verifies the result of the evaluation, and assesses evaluation techniques.

In fiscal matters, procedures are established and accepted; whereas in education, much of the planning and development is highly individualized by project. Thus, the auditor has some responsibility for development as well as for verification. I feel the audit should be conducted so as to add credibility to local project findings.

You played a key role in the much ballyhooed Texarkana project, in which the firm that had been awarded the performance contract, Dorsett, was suspected of "teaching to the test." (Ed. Note: This was discussed in the January, 1971, Arizona Teacher.) Would you tell us your own response to the Texarkana venture and your opinion of performance contracting in general? I would change your statement: "teaching to the test" to "teaching the test." This was a grave concern; and EPIC's audit report, now a public domain document in the

USOE, states that as the educational auditors, we felt the achievement grade level data were invalid. Unfortunately, most people feel this means that performance contracting is invalid.

Let me ask you: "If a test is misused, who is to blame? The test? Or the user?" Performance contracting is one of several ways of implementing accountability. Just because it might have been misused does this mean the concept of performance contracting is a bad technique?

Personally, I feel the concept of performance contracting is stronger than ever. With evaluating and auditing required as an integral part of the project, you can place a great deal more confidence in performance contract results than in the list of standardized test scores released annually by school district.

In the Texarkana Project, the dropout rate was lowered significantly, the students were enthusiastic, and the local school personnel were quite positive about their program. Other than questions about the test data, it was a successful project.

How do you advise a school district to select an auditing service? You have heard the statement that "anyone over one hundred miles away from home with a new suit is an expert." This presents problems to educators in selecting a consultant. A school district should check very carefully the experience of the firm and know its own needs thoroughly. USOE criteria suggest that the auditor should be independent from the program. His proximity to site, qualifications and record of acceptable past performance, organizational capability, and his attendance at USOE training institutes—all these should be considered.

One final question. How does EPIC fit into the new concept of "accountability"? Evaluation is accountability in a sense. When educators can make decisions about their objectives and results based on reliable information, when they can relate these to tangible performance objectives, then they are accountable.

Florida's Accountability Plan Focuses on the Nation's Principals

NATION'S SCHOOLS

While many programs of accountability offer incentives to students, parents, and teachers, a county in Florida has a plan which provides for accountability pay for principals and other administrative personnel. Included in the article is an outline of a proposal that won bonus pay for one of the district principals. This is one district's response to the demand for accountability by the taxpaying public.

While Florida Supt. Clyde E. Stevens supports the concept of holding teachers responsible for the performance of their students, the first place to start promoting accountability, as he sees it, is at the top of the school hierarchy.

Accordingly, Stevens' district, Lake County, Fla., is working with what may be the first experiment in the country involving accountability pay for principals and other administrative personnel. Salary schedules have been devised which offer yearly bonuses up to $1,000 to those administrators who meet the requirements.

Stevens introduced the bonus plan this fall because: "There's no question in my mind that the biggest incentive for change in education has to come from the principal, since he hands out the rewards and punishments in every school. Teachers are willing to change to update instruction, but they need leadership. If the principal doesn't provide the leadership, teachers can find it almost impossible to carry through with their ideas for change."

Also, like many schoolmen, Stevens says he's gotten the message that "all of a sudden the public has wised up and realized the public schools aren't as good as they should be." The public is demanding results, he stresses, "hopefully, this plan will give us the opportunity to deliver them."

To qualify for accountability pay in Lake County, a principal or county staff member must assess his area of responsibility, determine a specific educational need within that area, and submit a written plan to the superintendent, stating what he intends to do and how he plans to do it.

In a directive to the principals and staff, Stevens outlined the

"Florida's Accountability Plan Focuses on the Nation's Principals," *Nation's Schools,* 86:54–55, November 1970. Reprinted by permission.

format for preparing the plans, putting the accent on simple, specific proposals which emphasized continuity and compatability to the objectives of the system. The staff was also asked to write the proposals in such a way that they could be easily comprehended by laymen, and to avoid all "empty cliches and educational jargon."

If the plan is accepted by Stevens, he works with the administrator to determine a method of evaluation, and the administrator then goes about his task.

Areas which qualify for accountability pay were delimited by Stevens in advance and distributed with the first directive. The areas included: individualization of instruction; teaming of teachers; differentiated staffing; nongrading; inservice training; performance contracting; public relations—stressing effective interpretation of any new educational policies and programs under the accountability plan to the school board and community; and remodeling and renovating for flexible scheduling.

According to Stevens, the response from administrators has been highly encouraging and a half dozen proposals have already been approved for implementation this year. A sample plan with which one administrator qualified for accountability pay is shown below.

To put the plan into effect this year, the 1969–70 salary schedules for administrators were computed partly on the basis of accountability pay. Each schedule provides for a regular annual salary, plus a bonus supplement. The regular annual principal's salary, for example, is based on educational qualifications, experience, and school size, and, under the new plan, a $980 supplement is available for each base salary. When the administrator submits a subsequently approved accountability proposal, he receives half the supplement, or $490, in a lump sum before Christmas, and the additional $490 after he submits his report on the results of his plan, including his recommendations for further efforts. Accountability pay for other administrative staff members is figured on the same basis.

This Proposal Won Bonus Pay for One Administrator

The following proposal, regarding a middle school program in Lake County, Fla., was submitted to the superintendent by one district principal, and met the requirements for bonus pay under the district's accountability plan.

OVERVIEW AND RATIONALE OF THE MOUNT DORA MIDDLE SCHOOL

The middle school movement in the United States, as supported by research in this area, began as a reaction to essentially two factors: 1) failure of existing elementary and junior high programs to meet the needs of students ages 10–14, and 2) the need to recognize, by school organization, another stage of human growth and development, *i.e.* the pre-adolescent.

Educational research and the written works of authorities in the middle school movement have pointed out the following weaknesses in most existing programs:

1. Instructional programs are too subject-matter oriented.
2. Earlier maturation needs of children in the age group 10–14 are not being met.
3. Failure of instructional programs to move toward individualization of instruction.
4. Too rigid time schedules which do not recognize modern research concerning the manner in which the pre-adolescent learns.
5. Failure to provide an instructional program to meet the needs of the pre-adolescent.
6. Lack of involvement of teachers with the motivational needs of the pre-adolescent.
7. Lack of concern for the personal development of the individual child.

PROBLEM

To implement a middle school program in the Mount Dora area for those students in Grades 5, 6, and 7.

LIMIT OF PROBLEM

1970–71 school year at Mount Dora Middle School with existing physical facilities and personnel.

SPECIFIC OBJECTIVES

1. To use test data and teacher evaluation to group students for instructional purposes. Evaluate by observation and schedules.

2. To institute a two-phase faculty inservice training program to gain acceptance by teachers of the established tenets of the middle school concept. Phases of inservice training: (a) rationale of the middle school; (b) methods of improving instructional presentations. Evaluate by the change in teacher behavior of these teachers in working with students, by observation and organizational pattern.

3. To meet individual needs and interests of students by means of:

a. A comprehensive guidance program geared to help the pre-adolescent develop a positive self-concept and find solutions to individual problems. Utilize the services of a full-time guidance counselor.
b. Providing opportunity for independent study commensurate with ability and maturity.
c. Offering an enrichment program which will provide exploratory experiences in a variety of areas; *i.e.,* conservation, music, science investigation, etc. Evaluate by observation.

4. To institute instructional programs which will accommodate any student at any point on a skills continuum. Evaluate by observation.

5. To provide a flexible time schedule independent of disruptive bells and/or required class changes to facilitate organizing around needs and/or interests (ex.: large and small group activities). Evaluate by observation.

6. To communicate to middle school parents the goals and philosophy of the Mount Dora Middle School by: (a) written communication with parents, (b) programs and visitations for parents. Evaluate by observation and survey of parents.

7. To utilize the team approach in solving instructional problems of the middle school as evidenced by: (a) teachers planning cooperatively, (b) a common planning time, (c) more effective grouping for instruction by teachers working cooperatively, (d) more effective use of teachers' instructional efforts. Evaluate by periodical observation.

8. To use effectively the physical plant to implement the establishment of a middle school program. Evaluate by observation and plant utilization charts.

SUMMARY

These eight specific goals to implement a middle school program, among others, will receive my attention and leadership during the 1970–71 school year.

These goals are not all-inclusive, nor do they purport to meet all the needs of the Mount Dora Middle School student body as test data, records and professional observation discern student needs. They are rather, in my opinion, a beginning point to implement a middle school program for Mount Dora.

Purposes of the Michigan Assessment of Education

ROBERT L. CROWSON and THOMAS P. WILBUR

The Michigan Assessment Program was to provide an improved information base for research and planning. Its assumptions were that education is an important investment in human welfare, that both school and nonschool inputs influence educational performance, that educational services are inequitably distributed, and that resources available for education need to be efficiently allocated. The specific assessment in Michigan involved an immediate determination of school performance in the areas of basic skills, then a further determination of educational goals and procedures for assessing them. Descriptions of the level of educational performance and its correlates for the state, for geographic regions and types of communities, and for each of Michigan's local school districts are included. While this assessment procedure will not automatically alleviate educational problems, it can assist state decision-makers in providing equitable education.

Introduction

The Michigan Assessment Program was initially proposed and first designed as a mechanism for an improved information base for research and planning. Statements of the general rationale and "need" for assessment stressed: (a) a lack of reliable statewide data on educational outcomes; (b) a growing public demand for "accountability"; and, (c) the need for a better information base to assist state-level decision-making.

Further explications of the need for an assessment program tied the effort much more specifically to a study of the status and the distribution of educational performance-levels and their correlates. The primary purpose, or focus, of educational assessment thereby became the identification of inequities in both school performances and school resources for the state in order to provide information for those at the state level who make decisions regarding allocations of school resources.

This paper will explore the background of assessment in Michigan in two areas: First, its general rationale and theoretical base; and

Robert L. Crowson and Thomas P. Wilbur, "Purposes of the Michigan Assessment of Education," ERIC Document ED-043-663, March 1970. Reprinted by permission.

second, its specific purposes for the 1969–70 school year. Discussed initially are topics in human capital, in state resource allocation, in school input-output relations, and in equality of educational opportunity. Examined later are the components of the Michigan program, its assumptions and design criteria, and the specific questions it seeks to answer.

Theoretical Background

Educational theory and research suggested four assumptions which are basic to the Michigan assessment program. *First,* investments in education are investments in the capacities and opportunites of human beings. *Second,* the outcomes of schooling are fundamentally influenced by levels of school and non-school "inputs." *Third,* a scarcity of resources for education requires an effort to use each dollar to the best advantage. *Fourth,* it is essential to the welfare of our society that the benefits of education be distributed equitably.

AN INVESTMENT IN HUMAN RESOURCES

In recent years the study of investment in human capital—as expressed in the writings of Schultz,[1] Becker,[2] Miller,[3] and Hansen[4]—has provided evidence of a relationship between economic growth, economic opportunity, and education. Hansen, for example, investigated differential internal rates of return on investment in education, and established profiles of increased returns for increments in years of schooling—concluding on the basis of his findings that:

> . . . the high rates of return to investment in schooling go a long way toward explaining, or justifying, this society's traditional faith in education, as well as the desire of individuals to take advantage of as much schooling as they can.[5]

Evidence from "human capital" studies suggests that investments in education provide substantial payoffs to individuals in terms of enhanced productive capacities, earnings potentials, and occupational alternatives. Similarly, the evidence suggests that under-investments in education, as represented by variations in expenditures for the "rich" and the "poor," represent a substantial economic cost in human productive potential and in individual welfare.[6]

The concept of education as an investment provides direction in state resource allocation. It relates to a consideration of the distribution of available funds among types of programs, levels of education, and groups of students. It relates to the manner in which educational expenditure provides equitable occupational and income opportunities to the entire population—and to the manner in which schools affect the distribution of social and economic advantages among the citizenry.

THE CORRELATES OF SCHOOL PERFORMANCE

A number of important studies, generally utilizing an input-process-output research model, have investigated the question: "What factors are related to student performance in schools?" This research has frequently related *input* variables such as pupil background and school resources to *process* variables, and to *output* or school performance variables such as average student achievement. More specifically, researchers employing this paradigm have: (1) identified a criterion of school performance as a dependent variable, and measures thought to influence performance as independent variables; (2) operationally measured these variables in a sample of educational systems; (3) computed relationships between independent and dependent variables; and (4) drawn inferences from the relationships as to what factors account for variations in school performance.

Research of special significance in the input-process-output area includes Mort's[7] studies of the correlates of educational "adaptability;" the Project Talent[8] studies of the American high school; Benson's[9] investigations of the correlates of educational achievement in California; the Burkhead, Fox, and Holland[10] examinations of input and output in large-city high schools; and the well known, albeit controversial, Coleman[11] report, *Equality of Educational Opportunity*.[12]

Despite some limitations of design, definition, and methodology, we may note at least four contributions to the search for knowledge concerning our educational systems.[13] *First,* much to the chagrin of professional educators, input-process-output research has clearly demonstrated that the independent variables bearing the strongest relationships to pupil performance are of a non-school nature. *Second,* it is also clear that within-school variables are not totally irrelevant to educational success—particularly those variables representing qualities of the instructional staff. *Third,* it may be concluded, at least tentatively, that "money does make a difference"—even if only because the quality of a school system's instructional staff appears to be related to that system's expenditure level.[14] *Fourth,* and perhaps most importantly, the input-process-output paradigm has disabused us of any notions we might have had that the formal and informal educational processes were simple ones. Complex, multicollinear relationships between school and non-school environments offer vexing problems to state decision-makers who seek to distribute equitably and optimally the advantages and opportunities of education.

THE EFFICIENT ALLOCATION OF RESOURCES

As noted, there is good reason to suspect that the outputs of schooling are inputs into the public welfare, and that the "human capital" of a state or nation is a function of its investment in education. There is also good reason to suspect that each individual's opportunities for a satisfying job and for sufficient earnings are generally related to the quality and quantity of his school experiences, and that each individual's educational attainments depend considerably upon the adequacy of expenditure for his instruction.

Arguments may be advanced for the enhanced public support of education, as well as for a re-distribution of education for greater equality. It may be assumed however, that in education as elsewhere some resource allocations are more effective than others. Equity may be served through any number of combinations of human and material inputs. The returns to increased investment in preschool education, for example, may exceed by far the payoff for dropout prevention in later years.[15] The general recruitment of more highly "qualified" teachers may be far more efficient than all other forms of compensatory education.[16]

Resource scarcities, together with increased demands for improved outputs, will require examinations of the costs and benefits associated with alternative allocations. Educational decision-makers at the state level are faced with the problem of how to spend resources in the most effective way possible.

AN EQUALITY OF EDUCATIONAL OPPORTUNITY

The concept of equality and the goal of equal opportunity are well integrated values in the American social order. Although our egalitarian doctrine remains the focus of much debate in attempts to reconcile quality with equality and diversity with conformity, the ideal that every child should have access to the ladder of success is basic to American thought.[17] Educational attainment, as a primary vehicle for mobility, is well recognized. An equal educational opportunity and an equal chance in life are necessarily, if not sufficiently, related.

From the "classic" studies of Hollingshead, Havighurst, and Warner to the present—the evidence is that education and its benefits are unequally distributed. Of major significance to state decision-makers are the findings that: *First,* the benefits of education are closely related to social class background.[18] The lower the status of a child's family the less likely that he will have access to the advantages of education. The lower the socio-economic environment of a child, the less likely that he will attend a school with well-trained and experienced teachers, up-to-date facilities, uncrowded classrooms, and an adequate per-pupil expenditure. *Second,* the benefits of education vary widely among and within states.[19] During 1968–69, nearly three times as much money was spent on the schooling of a child in New York State as in the State of Alabama ($1,159 as compared with $398).[20] During 1968–69 in Michigan, despite a so-called equalizing state aid formula, two-and-a-half times as much money per child was spent by the Detroit suburb of Oak Park as by the rural community of Beaver Island ($1,179 as compared with $445). *Third,* the distribution of educational services by state and local governments as a direct influence upon equities of educational attainment and employment. Both the Coleman Report and two additional studies of inequality in Michigan,[21] suggest that (a) the quality of educational services is distributed inequitably among schools, and (b) the quality of educational services available to an individual does influence his school and post-school performance.

It is the basic assumption of the Michigan assessment program that the most important education-related problem facing the state—and indeed the nation—is the inequitable distribution of school performance levels and their correlates.

Michigan Assessment: Its Specific Purposes

As indicated, the Michigan Assessment of Education was based upon the following propositions: (a) education is an important investment in human welfare; (b) both school and non-school "inputs" influence educational performance; (c) educational services are inequitably distributed; and, (d) resources available for education need to be efficiently allocated in a manner to achieve an equality of opportunity. The principal goal of the assessment effort is to provide reliable and meaningful information on levels of educational performance and their correlates for the public elementary and secondary schools of the state in order to provide a basis for improved state-level decision-making.

During 1969–70, the assessment effort in Michigan involves two complementary and concurrent activities: (1) an immediate determination of school performance in the "basic skill" areas of reading, vocabulary, English expression, and mathematics; and, (2) the further determination of other common goals for Michigan education and of procedures for assessments of these goals.

One major assumption and two criteria have guided the design of Michigan's assessment program. The assumption is that, as indicated earlier, the inequitable distribution of school performance levels and the many factors that influence performance—is the state's foremost educational problem.[22] The criteria are: (1) simplicity, in the formulation of assessment purposes and results for improved state-level decisions, and (2) legitimacy, in the use of input-process-output theory to describe, inter-relatedly, both school system performances and other describable system characteristics.

The Michigan assessment effort has five basic purposes: (1) A description of the level of educational performance and its correlates[23] in (a) the state as a whole and in (b) each of Michigan's geographic regions and "types" of community; (2) A description of how the correlates of education are distributed in terms of educational performance levels in (a) the state and in (b) Michigan's geographic regions and community types;[24] (3) A description of the level of educational performance and its correlates within the state's individual school districts; (4) A description of how the correlates of education are distributed in terms of educational performance within the state's individual school districts; and, (5) A description of Michigan's progress towards, or away from, an equality of educational opportunity over time.

Outlined below, in further detail, are specific questions and procedures for the Michigan assessment of basic skills in 1969–70, and procedures for future years of assessment in other goal areas.

AN ASSESSMENT IN THE "BASIC SKILLS"

The basic skills component of assessment rests firmly on the assumption that at least one common goal area for Michigan education—namely, the acquisition of basic skills in the use of words and numbers—already has been identified and defined, and that techniques are available to begin assessment in that area. Unlike certain outcome areas such as those dealing with interests, values, or the "higher" mental processes, implementation of a program to assess basic skills does not require several months and years of planning—but can be undertaken almost immediately.

The assessment of basic skills in 1969–70 seeks to provide answers to the following specific questions:

1. *For the State of Michigan as a whole, what is the present level of educational achievement and its correlates?* For the 1969–70 basic skills assessment, "educational achievement" includes reading comprehension, English expression, vocabulary, and mathematics. The related "correlates" are of four categories: (1) student socio-economic background; (2) student attitudes and aspirations; (3) school and

school district financial resources; and (4) school and school district human resources. Following analysis of the data, it will be possible to construct a single profile showing educational achievement levels for the state as a whole and the socio-economic status, student attitude and aspiration, school financial resources, and school human resource levels for the state as a whole.

2. *What is the present level of educational achievement and its correlates within Michigan's geographic regions and types of community?* Question 2 differs from question 1 only in that the information gathered will be presented *separately* for the various geographic regions and community types in the state; in question 1 it was presented for the state as a whole. To answer Question 2 Michigan's school districts will be separated into four regions and five community types. The four regions of the state are: (1) the Upper Peninsula; (2) Northern Michigan (the northern half of the lower peninsula); (3) the Detroit SMSA (Wayne, Macomb, and Oakland Counties); and (4) Southern Michigan (the remainder of the lower peninsula). The five "types" of community are: (1) Metropolitan core cities; (2) other cities; (3) towns; (4) the urban fringe; and, (5) rural areas.[25] These divisions will facilitate comparisons between geographic areas and between community types. For example, it will be possible to compare the urban fringe with rural areas, or to compare Northern Michigan with Southern Michigan.

3. *Do schools and school districts that score high (or low or average) on achievement also score high (or low or average) on the correlates of educational performance?* The prime purpose of the first two questions is to explore the status of education in Michigan; it is the purpose of question 3 to describe how the correlates of education are *distributed* in terms of educational performance, and to describe how achievement and its correlates are *related* in the state. How are school district human resources distributed, for example, in comparison with distributions of district scores in mathematics? Or, do schools scoring high on reading comprehension also score high on school financial resources? As was the case with the previous two questions, question 3 will be investigated for the state as a whole and then for each geographic region and community type.

4. *What are the scores of each of Michigan's school districts on achievement and its correlates, and how do these scores compare with state, regional, and community type averages?* Standard score scale "norm" tables for the state, and for region and community categories, provide a basis for comparisons of individual district results with the results of similar and other type districts. Without public identifications or "rankings" of individual district scores, profiles of districts with similar "input" may be compared for "output," the relative

status of "types" of districts may be compared, districts may view their own relations between input and achievement, and individual districts with unusual assessment "profiles" may be identified and investigated.

5. *What is the level and distribution of educational achievement and its correlates within each of the state's school districts?* It is highly likely that within-district scores on achievement and the various input variables may vary greatly by school building. This is particularly likely in the Metropolitan Core and other sizable cities that serve widely divergent student populations.

6. *What changes over time may be noted in the answers to each of the above questions?* Of course, this question cannot be answered in the assessment program's first year. In successive years, however, it will become most important as it will measure: (1) the movement toward or away from equality of educational opportunity—at least insofar as that elusive concept may be measured by the variables here discussed—and (2) the presumed effects of policy changes and/or allocationary decisions at both state and local levels.

THE ASSESSMENT OF OTHER GOAL AREAS

The basic skills assessment program for 1969–70 rests firmly on the assumption that schools exist—in part—to develop skills in reading, English expression, vocabulary, and mathematics. Schools have additional purposes or goals, however, and it is the purpose of the second, concurrent phase of assessment to explore, define, measure, and relate them. Specifically, this phase of assessment in Michigan involves the three interdependent steps of:

1. *Definitions of the goals of Michigan education.* This part of the program involves periodic meetings of representatives of the lay public, scholars, and professional educators as members of a state Task Force on Goals. The purpose is to review, define, and clarify Michigan's common educational objectives.[26]

2. *The development of additional assessment measures.* As added "common" goals are identified, techniques and procedures for an expanded assessment effort are determined, tested, and implemented.

3. *The provision of additional information on the level and distribution of Michigan education.* As additional goal areas are defined and measured, it will be possible to further an understanding of educational achievement and its correlates for the state and for its regions and communities, to more broadly relate an expanded range of educational "outputs" to school and non-school "inputs" and "processes," and to more definitively determine the context of educational opportunity.

Summary

Michigan's assessment of education will generate an impressive amount of data on the state's system of public elementary and secondary education. It is presumed that this data will assist persons at the state level who make decisions regarding the allocation of school resources. It is further presumed that this information will serve the identification of inequities in both school performances and school resources for Michigan, and will thereby assist a more efficient and equitable distribution of educational opportunities.

An assessment of education in Michigan has proceeded from a recognition: (a) that educational investment is an important input into the social and economic advantages of a state's population; (b) that educational performance is variously influenced by both school and non-school "correlates;" (c) that the allocation of school resources importantly affects a state's educational equity and efficiency; and, (d) that the inequitable distribution of school performance and its correlates is a state's major education-related problem.

Michigan's program—including both an immediate determination of "basic skill" achievements and a more comprehensive assessment effort in other goal areas—involves descriptions of the level and the distribution of educational performance and its correlates for the state, for geographic regions and types of communities, and for each of Michigan's local school districts. While an effort to assess a state's educational achievements—to document the status and distribution of school performance and its correlates—will not automatically alleviate pressing educational problems, it can, when designed and used creatively, assist state decision-makers who are concerned with better and with more equitable education.

FOOTNOTES

1. Theodore W. Schultz, "Rise in the Capital Stock Represented by Education in the United States, 1900-57," *Economics of Higher Education*, Selma J. Mushkin, ed. (Washington, D.C.: U.S. Government Printing Office, 1962), 93–101.

2. Gary S. Becker, "Investment in Human Capital: A Theoretical Analysis," *The Journal of Political Economy*, 70 (October, 1962), 9–49.

3. Herman P. Miller, "Annual and Lifetime Income in Relation to Education: 1929–1959." *American Economic Review*, 50 (December, 1960), 962–989.

4. W. Lee Hansen, "Total and Private Rates of Return to Investment in School" in *The Journal of Political Economy*, 71 (April, 1963), 128–141.

5. *Ibid.*, 138.

6. See, for example, Ronald W. Conley, "A Benefit-Cost Analysis of the Vocational Rehabilitation Program," *The Journal of Human Resources*, IV (Spring, 1969) 226–252. Conley demonstrated that from the standpoint of an efficient allocation of resources, vocational rehabilitation programs should concentrate services upon the illiterate, the nonwhite, the middle-aged, and the most severely disabled.

7. See: Donald H. Ross, *Administration for Adaptability* (New York: Metropolitan School Study Council, 1958).

8. John C. Flanagan and others, *A Survey and Follow-up of Educational Plans and Decisions in Relation to Aptitude Patterns: Studies of the American High School* (Pittsburgh: University of Pittsburgh, 1962).

9. Charles S. Benson, *State and Local Fiscal Relationships in Public Education in California* (Sacramento: Senate of the State of California, 1965).

10. Jesse Burkhead, Thomas G. Fox, and John W. Holland, *Input and Output in Large-City High Schools* (Syracuse: Syracuse University Press, 1967).

11. James S. Coleman and others, *Equality of Educational Opportunity* (Washington, D.C.: U.S. Government Printing Office, 1966).

12. For an expanded and more complete summary of input-process-output research see: Thomas P. Wilbur, *Research into the Correlates of School Performance: A Review and Summary of Literature* (Lansing, Michigan: Michigan Department of Education, Research Monograph No. 1, 1970).

13. *Ibid.*, 11–13.

14. See, for example: Henry M. Levin in a letter to the editor, *Saturday Review* LI (February 17, 1969), 50.

15. For a thorough discussion of the cost-benefit approach to an equalization of educational opportunity, see: Thomas I. Ribich, *Education and Poverty,* (Washington, D.C.: The Brookings Institution, 1968).

16. There is, in fact, evidence that recruiting and retaining teachers with higher verbal scores is cost-effective. See: Henry M. Levin, "A Cost-Effectiveness Analysis of Teacher Selection," *The Journal of Human Resources,* V (Winter, 1970), 24–33.

17. Gunnar Myrdal in *An American Dilemma* has, of course, made us well aware of the disparity between American "thought" and American reality.

18. See, for example: Patricia Cayo Sexton, *Education and Income, Inequalities of Opportunity in our Public Schools* (New York: The Viking Press, 1961). Also: James Bryant Conant, *Slums and Suburbs* (New York: McGraw-Hill, Inc., 1961).

19. See, for example: Charles S. Benson, *The Cheerful Prospect* (Boston: Houghton Mifflin Co., 1965) 21–22. Also: J. Alan Thomas, *School Finance and Educational Opportunity in Michigan* (Lansing, Michigan: Michigan State Department of Education, 1968).

20. *Estimates of School Statistics,* 1969–70, Research Report 1969–R15 (Washington, D.C.: National Education Association, 1969), 36.

21. J. Alan Thomas, *op. cit.,* also, James W. Guthrie and others, *Schools and Inequality: A Study of Social Status, School Services, Student Performance, and Post-School Opportunity in Michigan* (no publication place: The Urban Coalition, 1969).

22. Two additional assumptions underlying the state's larger assessment program are: (1) although the purposes and goals of education may differ from district to district, building to building, and child to child, there are also certain common goals and purposes toward which all public schools in Michigan are or should be working; and (2) methodologies are available, or can be developed, which will allow one to determine the progress we are making toward achieving these goals.

23. The term "correlates" is used to describe the input or process factors that bear a strong relation to educational performance. For example, it is known that socio-economic factors bear a strong relation to academic achievement and thus properly are "correlates" of achievement. Additional "correlates" may include school and school system financial resources, school and school system human resources, and pupil attitudes or aspirations.

24. For example, we may ask the question whether school districts that score high on educational performance also score high on student socio-economic background and have greater financial or human resources.

25. *Metropolitan Core:* One or more adjacent cities with a population of 50,000 or more which serve as the economic focal point of their environs. *City:* Community of 10,000 to 50,000 that serves as the economic focal point of its environs.

Town: Community of 2,500 to 10,000 that serves as the economic focal point of its environs. *Urban Fringe:* A Community of any size that has as its economic focal point a metropolitan core or a city. *Rural Community:* A Community of less than 2,500 population.

26. A great deal of work has been done in defining, or attempting to define, the goals of education. Thus, Ammons has written that "Educational objectives have for centuries occupied the attention of educational specialists, of representatives of other areas of study, and of laymen. That they are matters of basic concern is attested to by the amount written about them; both educational and non-educational literature is replete with formal and informal statements of what objectives should be." See: Margaret Ammons, "Objectives and Outcomes," *Encyclopedia of Educational Research,* Robert L. Ebel, editor (Toronto: The Macmillan Co., 1969), 908.

Where the Action Is in Performance Contracting

PHI DELTA KAPPAN

This article describes performance contracting as it is proposed in five different cities. San Diego has negotiated a contract with Educational Development Laboratory to teach reading on a guaranteed basis. Dallas is experimenting with a bilingual dropout prevention program. Detroit intends to embark on an output-oriented program planning and budgeting system. Portland is using the open court guaranteed achievement curriculum materials. Philadelphia is reportedly negotiating a performance-type contract with McGraw-Hill Book Company.

SAN DIEGO has become a hotbed of performance contracting activity. Utilizing $2.4 million in ESEA Title I and III funds, the city schools have entered into a contract with the Educational Development Laboratory, a subsidiary of McGraw-Hill, to teach reading in K-3 on a guaranteed achievement basis for some 9,500 children over the next three years. A cost commitment contract with Science Research Associates is also being negotiated. Both programs were jointly developed and planned by the San Diego schools' research and evaluation staff working with counterparts from each of the participating firms.

EDL guarantees that the students will achieve 25 percent closer to the city norm during the first year, 50 percent closer during the second,

"Where the Action Is in Performance Contracting," *Phi Delta Kappan,* 51:510, June 1970. Condensed from *Education Turnkey News,* April 1970. Reprinted by permission.

and at the same level during the third. The "Listen, Look, Learn system," costing $6,500 to $7,000 per lab, is to be used. EDL will train existing teachers rather than operate a separate center. Total funds budgeted for EDL: $1.4 million.

SRA, using its new Distar Program developed by Siegfried Englemann, is budgeted at $780,000 for 6,000 students, but SRA is not under a performance contract for this project.

Two firms will be competing with an internally developed and administered "maximum effort program," described as an eclectic approach to teaching reading. Competition will exist; however, thus far there has been no indication that a budgeting system will allow the determination of relative cost-effectiveness of the three approaches.

The *DALLAS* Independent School District is embarking upon performance contracting Texas-style. A preliminary proposal submitted to the USOE for funding under Title VIII, ESEA (dropout prevention), indicates that performance contracting will focus on math, reading and communications, achievement motivation, and occupational training. Target population the first year will be grades 9–12.

The preliminary proposal calls for use of bilingual materials, since many potential dropouts are Mexican-Americans.

Requests for proposals were to be sent to some 30 qualified bidders abound May 15, with a pre-bidders' conference scheduled for May 29 in Dallas.

A unique twist: Teachers will be allowed to compete with contractors. Funds are set aside for mini-grants for teachers to develop performance contract projects.

The superintendent of schools in Dallas is Nolan Estes, former associate commissioner for elementary and secondary education, USOE.

As of April, performance contracting in *DETROIT* awaited approval of operational plans submitted to the USOE under Title VIII, ESEA. A request for proposals will be refined and sent to qualified bidders when federal or private funds are available.

Detroit's target population is five inner-city junior highs, with initial concentration on the ninth grade. Math, reading, and achievement motivation components are planned. A primary concern is to have a low operating cost curriculum which can be expanded during later phases throughout schools in the district. An incentive plan is intended to insure that certain achievement levels are reached at lowest cost.

The performance contract approach will be developed concurrently with implementation of a USOE Education Professions Develeopment

Act grant to Detroit. The grant pays for the training of administrators in systems analysis techniques. Detroit intends to embark upon an output-oriented program planning and budgeting system.

Contractual relations based on performance of students has taken a new twist in *PORTLAND,* Oregon. The Martin Luther King Junior High is rewarding teachers on the basis of students' performance. Teams of teachers using Open Court guaranteed achievement curriculum materials are competing with each other in reading programs. Teachers who participate are given stipends of $1,000, with additional bonuses for the most successful teams. Bonuses will be used by teachers to pay teacher aides and procure supplementary materials. This approach has reportedly minimized political conflicts between administrators and teachers, in that team leaders are responsible for team performance, thus reinforcing the existing bonus incentives.

Portland schools also use EDL equipment for about 30 students in the reading area. EDL guarantees a grade level increase every nine months of instruction. The present teaching staff is used, with training assistance from EDL.

PHILADELPHIA is reportedly negotiating a "sole source" performance-type contract with McGraw-Hill.

Performance Contracts Catch On

RONALD SCHWARTZ

Funding for performance contracting has stemmed from several different sources. Grants for experimental programs have been available from the U.S. Office of Economic Opportunity, titled funds from the Elementary-Secondary Education Act, the U.S. Office of Education, and from some private foundations. This article by Ronald Schwartz, which contains additional information from Nation's Schools, *identifies some of the school systems employing performance contracts, agencies that have sponsored these projects, and private educational firms with whom the schools are doing business.*

Business in the education market could be hopping this fall, if a number of school districts follow through with their plans to sign

Ronald Schwartz, "Performance Contracts Catch On," *Nation's Schools,* 86:31–33, August 1970. Reprinted by permission.

performance contracts. At least four states and six cities plan to make the jump with substantial USOE funded programs either this fall or within a year or two. The Office of Economic Opportunity will be getting into the act too, with a $6.5 million contract program involving 21 school districts.

Also, several school districts—such as Portland and Dallas—will inaugurate internal contracts, with teachers receiving "bonuses" as a reward for above average performance by their students.*

Following is a list of those states and cities planning performance contracts with USOE help . . . :

Virginia: Of the three states planning performance contracts, Virginia appears to be providing the strongest thrust from the state house. Gov. Linwood Holton's office had developed a plan by late March. Since then, state school Supt. Woodrow W. Wilkerson has gained the go-ahead from the state board of education, and hopes to have final plans approved by the board this month.

Virginia's plan will be entirely funded by ESEA Title I. State officials say that seven school districts, all rural areas (except for Norfolk), will be selected for pilot projects. The affected districts all have low-achievement problems and some face "resegregation," after integration and a subsequent white movement to private schools.

State officials, by the end of June, were unable to provide a dollar figure on the size of the project, however, they said that about 2,250 students would be involved. Students in Grades 1–9 would be taught reading and mathematics. A unique feature of the Virginia project is that the state will sign performance contracts with two or more companies, thus hoping to introduce competition within the private sector. And, the company (or companies) able to impress state officials the most will more than likely have the inside track on new performance contracts, once the decision is made to include additional districts.

New Jersey: The state is willing to spend up to $10.5 million in Title I money for performance contracts in the 1970–71 school year, although it will probably spend much less, because of lags in starting up individual programs. "We have accepted the basic concept that performance contracting is worth exploring," says Stanley Salette, assistant commissioner for research, planning and evaluation in New Jersey.

Salette added that 35 school districts in the state are "seriously considering" the contracting, but by the end of June, it was too early to name the districts or the size of the programs for this fall. State

---

* Bonuses in Portland will be given to the teachers to pay for teaching aids and supplementary materials.

officials were also waiting for word from the Office of Economic Opportunity, where seven districs had asked to be included in OEO's experimental project: Atlantic City, Trenton, Newark, Hoboken, Plainfield, East Orange, and Paterson.

Michigan: Charles Silas, Title I coordinator for the state department of education in Lansing, says that eight to ten school districts in the state were "doing serious negotiating" with education firms in June. First to sign was the Flint Board of Education. Flint gave the go signal in mid-June to a private business firm to set up multimedia reading labs to serve some 2,000 underachievers this fall—with the expectation that their average reading gains will be doubled. The labs will be installed in each of the city's secondary schools, though the contract only covers ninth and tenth-graders who have been identified as achieving two or more years below grade level.

A major difference between the Flint contract and those entered into by most of the other school systems, according to the district's director of instructional services, John Kouzoujian, "is that the educational prerogatives will remain with the Flint school staff, rather than being contracted completely to the outside firm. There will be much reliance on the expertise of the Flint teachers who will be involved in the program. We expect the existing staff to man the facilities after extensive inservice education."

The Flint contract states that if the students do not make predicted gains, a pro-rated amount of the cost will be returned to the district.

Funding is still in a nebulous state, at present relying primarily on local sources and some NDEA Title III funds, while school officials continue scurrying to piece together a composite of federal, state and private aid.

In other Michigan cities, Detroit was "on the verge" of signing a contract, the final step after it had asked education companies to submit proposals. The city plans a performance contract to improve reading, mathematics and "achievement motivation" of 3,700 inner-city students in Grades 9–12. Funding will be primarily under Title I, since the city has been turned down by USOE for Title VIII funds.

Other cities whose performance-contracting plans are not as far along as Detroit's, but which may be ready this fall, are Lansing, Grand Rapids, and Jackson. All will focus on improving the level of reading and mathematics and are mostly involved with Title I students.

Dallas: This city could have the most intriguing performance contract of all this fall. Funding is a mixed bag of federal (Title I and the Office of Economic Opportunity), city, state (vocational education), and private funds (the Periot Foundation). Dallas also has set aside "mini-grants" for teachers to develop performance contracts and to compete with the contractor.

The project will consist of "Accelerated Achievement Centers," operated by the contractor, located in five inner-city high schools. Students in Grades 9–12 will receive instruction in mathematics, communications, occupational skills and "achievement motivation." Like the Texarkana project, the contractor will "turn-key" (turn over) the project to the school system, if the demonstration is successful, in a year or two.

Under the plan, companies will not get paid if a third-party evaluation finds a student fails to achieve a guaranteed level. For example, a company may guarantee three years' achievement in reading in one year's time. If the company succeeds, the school district would pay the company $213 per child. If the child achieves only 1.5 years, the district would pay only one-half the agreed amount. If there is zero achievement, the company receives nothing.

Payments are to be terminated when a student drops out of school, creating an incentive for the industry involved to aid in dropout prevention.

San Diego: Is it dead? It could be, if federal funds do not come through this summer. The contract had already been signed with the Educational Development Laboratories, a subsidiary of McGraw-Hill, when San Diego found the state had committed all of its Title III funds for the year. But, "we're optimistic," says an aide to Sen. George Murphy (R-Calif.), who has struggled to save the project. The contract with EDL was to teach reading on a guaranteed achievement basis to 9,600, K–3 students. A second contract on a non-performance basis, was to be signed with Science Research Associates, a subsidiary of IBM, for teaching reading, language concepts, and arithmetic.

Jacksonville, Fla.: In mid-June, the Duval County Board of Education gave the green light for a performance contract to teach reading to 400 students in Grades 4–7. Companies submitted bids in July.

Title I: "Where the Money Is"

One of the most significant changes in performance contract projects around the country this year is that many which depend on USOE funds will be getting the money from Title I of ESEA. The famous Texarkana project, which started the performance contract snowball, had been funded under ESEA Title VIII (dropout prevention), and it had been thought that this title would be a prime financial source for additional contracts. However, that has not become the case. "We have no money" for new projects this year, explains Dr. Hyrum M. Smith, chief of the dropout prevention branch at USOE. Title VIII was funded this year at $5 million, the same amount it was last year.

The switch to Title I brought about some hurried action on the part of a number of school systems. Both Detroit and Dallas had submitted requests to USOE under Title VIII, but were informed in April that they could not get the money. Then, they turned to other methods of funding, including Title I. Administrators of this title were receptive to the idea, undoubtedly because they are still smarting from past charges that Title I funds have been used to finance non-educational projects. According to Charles Silas, Title I coordinator for the state department of education in Michigan, "That's where the money is."

Some districts also sought to protect themselves by engineering a mix of funds. When turned down by USOE, Dallas, for example, applied to the Office of Economic Opportunity to be one of the 21 school districts in OEO's $6.5 million performance contracting experiment slated for this fall and was one of the districts finally chosen. (See report on OEO's programs below.)

Dallas also had the advantage of private funds. A $750,000 grant from the Periot Foundation to the school district, for planning and research, enabled it to get an early start on a performance contract project this fall.

Meanwhile, other school systems have launched planning efforts for projects they had hoped to begin this fall, but many of these will probably be delayed because of the time involved in planning, funding and negotiating a contract. Delay could also be caused by the increasing demand for performance contracts and the corresponding inability of the education-industrial complex to respond to this demand all at once.

OEO Announces $6.5 Million Contract Program

With $6.5 million in federal money, the Office of Economic Opportunity has launched a year-long performance contracting experiment which this fall will involve some 28,000 students in 21 school districts in remedial reading and mathematics.

Of the 21 districts chosen from approximately 170 which had asked for funds, OEO will funnel $5.6 million into performance contracts between 18 school districts and six education companies (see table). In the remaining three districts, OEO will sign contracts for programs utilizing a traditional educational framework, with local teacher groups, for example, operating under incentive contracts with OEO.

By employing these two types of contracts—public and private— OEO hopes to learn after a year whether the performance contracting approach should be applied nationwide. Dr. John O. Wilson, assistant director for planning, research and evaluation at OEO, said the experiment would help validate results in the first performance contracting project, in Texarkana, Ark.

Wilson expressed "concern" that the performance contracting approach could lead to "teaching to the test" since payment is geared to achievement scores. In Texarkana, the contracting company, Dorsett Educational Systems, Inc., was reported to be preparing its students for the tests, but the company has denied making a direct coaching effort.

Wilson added that OEO's experiment will contain precautions to guard against the possiblity of teaching to the test. OEO will select three standardized tests, which will be administered on a random basis so that the company will not know ahead of time which test will be given. Also 75 per cent of the payment will be based on the standardized test scores while 25 percent will rest on performance on reading and mathematics tests (criterion reference tests) .

The six private firms were selected on a competitive basis from a group of about 30. OEO said the firms chosen represent a "range of innovative techniques, including: incentives to students, teachers, parents; teaching machines, and programed learning techniques. . . ."

These districts will get OEO funds

School District	Contract Value	Contractor
Portland, Me.	$ 308,184	Singer/Graflex Corp.
Rockland, Me.	299,211	Quality Education Development
Hartford, Conn.	320,573	Alpha Systems, Inc.
Philadelphia, Pa.	296,291	Westinghouse Learning Corp.
McNairy County (Selmer) , Tenn.	286,991	Plan Education Centers, Inc.
McComb, Miss.	263,085	Singer/Graflex Corp.
Duval County (Jacksonville) , Fla.	342,300	Learning Foundations, Inc.
Dallas, Tex.	299,417	Quality Education Development
Taft, Tex.	243,751	Alpha Systems, Inc.
Hammond, Ind.	342,528	Learning Foundations, Inc.
Grand Rapids, Mich.	322,464	Alpha Systems, Inc.
Fresno, Calif.	299,015	Westinghouse Learning Corp.
Seattle, Wash.	343,800	Singer/Graflex Corp.
New York (Bronx) , N.Y.	341,796	Learning Foundations, Inc.
Clarke County (Athens) , Ga.	301,770	Plan Education Centers, Inc.
Las Vegas, Nev.	298,744	Westinghouse Learning Corp.
Wichita, Ks.	294,700	Plan Education Centers, Inc.
Anchorage, Alaska	444,632	Quality Education Development
Total	$5,649,252	

The contracts between the education companies and the 18 school districts will involve about 27,000 under achieving students in Grades 1–3 and 7–9. Approximately 1,000 more students will be involved in the three projects "to assess education incentive system only," OEO said. OEO officials said the performance contract would provide payments of $110 per grade level increase in each of the skills taught, adding that the companies would begin to make a profit at 1.6 grade level increase. The contracts provide a maximum payment ceiling of $220 per child per subject matter, or the fee at 2.3 grade level increase. Disadvantaged students, in the existing educational system progress at a rate of .4 to .5 grade level increases per year, according to OEO.

According to the OEO, the skills of each student will be tested by the contractor at the beginning of the experiment, periodically throughout the school year, and six months after the experiment.

For Further Reading

PART II

Abt, Clark C. "Reforming Urban Education with Cost-Effectiveness Analysis." *Educational Technology,* 10:36–38, September 1970.

"Accountability and the Educational Program Auditor." *Planning and Change,* 1:110–114, October 1970.

"Accountability Through National Assessment." *Compact,* 4:4–12, October 1970.

Alkin, Marvin C. "Objectives and Objective-Based Measures in Evaluation." *ERIC Document* ED-043-666, Center for the Study of Evaluation, University of California at Los Angeles, June 1970, 13 pp.

Andrew, Dean C., and Lawrence H. Roberts. "Final Evaluation Report on the Texarkana Dropout Prevention Program." *ERIC Document* ED-044-466, Education Service Center Region, Magnolia, Arkansas, July 20, 1970, 118 pp.

Bane, Mary Jo. "On Tuition Voucher Proposals." *Harvard Educational Review,* 41:79–87, February 1971.

"Banneker at Bay." *Newsweek,* 77:03ff, March 15, 1971.

Barro, S. M. "An Approach To Developing Accountability Measures for the Public Schools." *Phi Delta Kappan,* 52:196–205, December 1970.

Beagley, Simon. "Evaluating MES: A Survey of Research on the More Effective Schools Plan." *ERIC Document* ED-044-471, American Federation of Teachers, Washington, D.C., April 1969, 7 pp.

Beavan, K. "Accountability Octopus Gains New Territory." *The Times* (London) *Education Supplement,* 2871:11, May 29, 1970.

————. "Rewarded with Transistors, Sweaters, Stamps, and Stock." *The Times* (London) *Education Supplement*, 2857:16, February 20, 1970.

————. "Strike Looms Over Ghetto Merit Pay Plan." *The Times* (London) *Education Supplement*, 2880:11, July 31, 1970.

Berson, M. P. "Texarkana and Gary: A Tale of Two Performance Contracts." Bibliography, *Childhood Education*, 47:339–340ff, March 1971.

Bhaerman, Robert D. "Accountability: The Great Day of Judgment." *Educational Technology*, 11:62–63, January 1971.

Blaschke, Charles, Peter Briggs, and Reed Martin. "The Performance Contract—Turnkey Approach to Urban School System Reform." *Educational Technology*. 10:45–58, September 1970.

Brown, David. "Schema for Measuring Outputs in Higher Education." From *Outputs of Higher Education: Their Identification, Measurement, and Evaluation,* Ben Lawrence (ed.) , *ERIC Document* ED-043-296.

Bratten, Dale. "Performance Contracting: How It Works in Texarkana." *School Management,* 14:8–10, November 1970.

Bumstead, R. "Performance Contracting." *Educate,* 3:15–27, October 1970.

Button, W. "Performance-Contracting: Some Reservations." *Urban Education,* 5:307–308, January 1971.

Cass, J. "Profit and Loss in Education: Texarkana and Gary, Indiana." *Saturday Review,* 53:39–40, August 15, 1970.

Chavez, S. J. "Performance Accountability in Teacher Education." *AV Instruction,* 16:56–57, March 1971.

Chuang, Ying C., and William C. Theimer. "The Philadelphia Model for Title I Evaluation." *ERIC Document* ED-043-654, Philadelphia School District, Pennsylvania, March 1970, 14 pp.

Clark, Richard, and John Rosenback. "Program Evaluations Handbook: Developing Solutions." *ERIC Document* ED-043-672, State University of New York, 1969, 60 pp.

Cleary, Lynn Paul. "The Florida Education Improvement Expense Program." *ERIC Document* ED-043-795, Improving State Leadership in Education, Denver, Colorado, September 1970, 35 pp.

Cox, Richard C., and Carol E. Wildemann. "Taxonomy of Educational Objectives: Cognitive Domain, An Annotated Bibliography." *ERIC Document* ED-043-089, Office of Education (DHEW) , Washington, D.C., March 1970, 54 pp.

Cray, D. W. "What's Happening in Gary?" *School Management,* 15:22–25, May 1971.

Cruse, Keith L. "The Evolution of Planning in the Texas Education Agency." *ERIC Document* ED-043-793, Improving State Leadership in Education, Denver, Colorado, September 1970, 27 pp.

Daniel, Fred K. "Moving Toward Educational Accountability: Florida's Program." *Educational Technology,* 11:41–42, January 1971.

Davis, J. L. "Texarkana Project." *AV Instruction,* 15:97, June 1970.

"D. C. Perspectives on Performance Contracting." *Educational Researcher,* 21:1–3, 1970.

Deterline, William A. "Applied Accountability." *Educational Technology,* 11:15–20, January 1971.

Dochterman, Clifford L. "National Assessment of Educational Progress Summary of Report 1; Science: National Results." *ERIC Document* ED-043-099, Education Commission of the States, Denver, Colorado, July 1970, 24 pp.

_____. "National Assessment of Educational Progress Summary of Report 2; Citizenship: National Results—Partial." *ERIC Document* ED-043-098, Education Commission of the States, Denver, Colorado, July 1970, 16 pp.

"Dropout Prevention Program, Request for Proposal #2." *ERIC Document* ED-043-950, Texarkana School District 7, Arkansas, June 30, 1970, 77 pp.

Durstin, R. M. "An Accountability Information System." *Phi Delta Kappan,* 52:236–239, December 1970.

Dyer, H. S. "Can We Measure the Performance of Educational Systems?" *National Association of Secondary School Principals Bulletin,* 54:96–105, May 1970.

"Education Vouchers: Peril or Panacea?" Symposium. Bibliography. *Teachers College Record,* 72:327–404, February 1971.

"Education Turnkey Systems." *Performance Contracting,* Champaign, Illinois: Research Press, 1970, 122 pp.

Ehrle, Raymond A. "Performance Contracting for Human Services." *Personnel and Guidance Journal,* 49:119–122, October 1970.

English, Fenwick W. "Internal Educational Performance Contracting: A Consortium Thrust at Professional Accountability, Self-Governance and Educational Reform." Paper presented to the National Academy of School Executives, American Association of School Administrators, Dallas, Texas, October 1970, 12 pp.

Esbensen, Thorwald. "Using Performance Objectives: The Inadequacy of Vague Goals." *ERIC Document* ED-043-105, Florida State Department of Education, Tallahassee, April 1970, 42 pp.

"Evaluating the Elementary School." *ERIC Document* ED-043-411, Southern Association of Colleges and Schools, Atlanta, Georgia, May 1963, 98 pp.

Fantini, M. D. "Public Schools of Choice and the Plurality of Publics." *Educational Leadership,* 28:585–591, March 1971.

Filogamo, M. J. "New Angle on Accountability: Rapid Learning Centers." *Today's Education,* 59:53, May 1970.

_____. "Texarkana Battles Drop-out Dilemma: Rapid Learning Centers." *Elementary English,* 47:305–308, February 1970.

Finley, C. J. "National Assessment: Reports and Implications for School Districts." *National Elementary Principal,* 50:25–32, January 1971.

"Gary Gets First OEO Grant To Study Local Voucher Plan." *Report on Education Research,* February 17, 1971, p. 2.

Gillis, James C., Jr. "Performance Contracting for Public Schools." *Educational Technology,* 9:17–20, May 1969.

Grayboff, M. N. "Tool for Building Accountability: The Performance Contract." *Journal of Secondary Education,* 45:355–368, December 1970.

Gronlund, Norman E. *Stating Behavioral Objectives for Classroom Instruction.* ERIC Document ED-043-180. New York: The Macmillan Company, 1970, 58 pp.

Harmes, H. M. "Specifying Objectives for Performance Contracts." *Educational Technology*, 11:52–56, January 1971.

Hempel, M. W. "Accountability and Technology: A Change of Emphasis for Business Education." *AV Instruction*, 16:32ff, May 1971.

Hyer, A. L. "From Gold Stars to Green Stamps." *AV Instruction*, 16:4ff, May 1971.

Jamison, D., P. Suppes, and C. Butler. "Estimated Costs of CAI for Compensatory Education in Urban Areas." *Educational Technology*, 10:49–57, September 1970.

Jencks, C. "Giving Parents Money for Schooling: Education Vouchers." *Phi Delta Kappan*, 52:49–52, September 1970.

Johnson, Frank W. "Performance Contracting with Existing Staff." *Educational Technology*, 11:59–61, January 1971.

Jones, D. M. "PPBS: A Tool for Improving Education." *Educational Leadership*, 28:405–409, January 1971.

Kaufman, Roger A. "Accountability, A Systems Approach and the Quantitative Improvement of Education—An Attempted Integration." *Educational Technology*, 11:21–26, January 1971.

Kowach, R. J. "What Is Performance Contracting?" *Pennsylvania School Journal*, 119:139ff, November 1970.

Krull, R. P., Jr. "Performance Contracting." *Instruction*, 80:22, January 1971.

Lawrence, Ben, *et al.* "Outputs of Higher Education: Their Identification, Measurement, and Evaluation." *ERIC Document* ED-043-296, Bureau of Research (HEW/OE), Washington, D.C., July 1970, 127 pp.

"Legal Questions Raised." *Education Turnkey News*, vol. 1, no. 5, pp. 6–8, August 1970.

Lessinger, Leon. "How Education Audits Measure Performance." *Nation's Schools*, 85:33–34, June 1970.

————. "After Texarkana, What? Accountability and Performance Contracts." *Nation's Schools*, 84:37–40, December 1969.

————. "Engineering Accountability for Results in Public Education." *Phi Delta Kappan*, 52:217–225, December 1970.

Light, R. J., and D. O. Smith. "Choosing a Future: Strategies for Designing and Evaluating New Programs." *Harvard Educational Review*, 40:1–28, February 1970.

Livingston, J. A. "Educational Goals and Program Planning Budgeting System." *Journal of Secondary Education*, 45:305–312, November 1970.

Ludka, Arthur P. "Planning in the Colorado Department of Education To Facilitate Improvements in Education." *ERIC Document* ED-043-794, Improving State Leadership in Education, Denver, Colorado, September 1970, 30 pp.

Manlove, Donald C., and Lyle Mowrey. "Junior High School/Middle School Evaluation Criteria." *ERIC Document* ED-043-671, National Study of School Evaluation, Arlington, Virginia, 1970, 53 pp.

Martin, R., and C. Blaschke. "Contracting for Educational Reform." *Phi Delta Kappan*, 52:403–406, March 1971.

Mayrhofer, Albert V. "Factors To Consider in Preparing Performance Contracts for Instruction." *Educational Technology,* 11:48–51, January 1971.

Mervin, Jack C., and Frank B. Womer. "Evaluation in Assessing the Progress of Education To Provide Bases of Public Understanding and Public Policy." *Educational Evaluation: New Roles, New Means,* Ralph W. Tyler (ed.) Chicago: University of Chicago Press, the 68th Yearbook of the National Society for the Study of Education, 1969, chapter 13.

Miller, Donald R., *et al.* "A Managers Guide to Objectives—Revised Edition." *ERIC Document* ED-043-135, Bureau of Elementary and Secondary Education, (DHEW/OE) Washington, D.C., October 1969, 149 pp.

Morton, J. "Contract Learning in Texarkana." *Educational Screen and Audiovisual Guide,* 49:12–13, February 1970.

Mueller, S. "Interview: M. B. Carus and Theodore B. Dolmatch." *Reading Newsreport,* 4:4–10, April 1970.

Nash, D. "Can We Learn To Govern? Establishing Schools of Choice." *American Journal of Orthopsychiatry,* 40:606–614, July 1970.

"The National Educational Assessment: Initial Report, Reactions, and Benefits." *Education Digest,* 36:1–5, September 1970.

Niblock, J. "Accountability at Work in Two Southern Community Colleges." *College and University Journal,* 10:23–24, January 1971.

"OEO Launches Its Voucher Experiment." *Nation's Schools,* 87:30–31, March 1971.

"OEO Releases Voucher Timetable." *Nation's Schools,* 87:29, April 1971.

"Performance Contracting." *Nation's Schools,* 86:85–86ff, October 1970.

"Performance Contracting as Catalyst for Reform." *Educational Technology,* 9:5–9, August 1969.

"Performance Contracting: Clouds and Controversy Over Texarkana." *Nation's Schools,* 86:85–88, October 1970.

"Performance Contracts Popular But Evaluation Procedures Questionable." *Educational Product Report,* 4:2–4, December 1970.

"Performance Contracting: Why the Gary School Board Bought It." *American School Board Journal,* 158:19–21, January 1971.

"PPBS and Assessment: Where Trouble Could Erupt." *Nation's Schools,* 83:8, June 1969.

Pierce, W. H. "New Directions for Education? Performance Contracting and the Voucher System." Symposium, *Compact,* 5:2–16ff, February 1971.

Ramo, Simon, and Leo E. Persselin. "Changing Functions of Urban Schools: The Role of Industry." *Educational Technology,* 10:58–60, September 1970.

Reynolds, J. D. "Performance Contracting: Proceed with Caution." *English Journal,* 60:102–106ff, January 1971.

"Satisfaction Guaranteed or Money Back." *Saturday Review,* 53:54–55, August 15, 1970.

Schiller, J. "Performance Contracting: Some Questions and Answers." *American Education,* 7:3–5, May 1971.

Schure, A. "Accountability and Evaluation Design for Occupational Education." *Educational Technology,* 11:26–37, March 1971.

Shugrue, M. F. "Educational Accountability and the College English Department." *College Composition and Communication,* 21:250–254, October 1970.

Stenner, J., and M. H. Kean. "Four Approaches to Education Performance Contracting." *Educational Leadership,* 28:721–725, April 1971.

"Subcontracting Teaching 800 Black Pupils in Gary." *Chicago Tribune,* December 20, 1970.

"Technical Report of a Project To Develop Educational Cost-Effectiveness Models for New York State." *ERIC Document* ED-043-097, New York State Education Department, Albany, March 1970, 34 pp.

"Texarkana: The First Accounting." *Educate,* 3:24–37ff, March 1970.

"Two Districts Will Try Teachers' Incentive Contract Plans." *Nation's Schools,* 86:83, December 1970.

Tyler, R. W. "National Assessment—Some Valuable By-Products for Schools." *National Elementary Principal,* 48:42–48, May 1969.

Underwood, Kenneth E. "Before You Decide To Be Accountable, Make Sure You Know For What." *American School Board Journal,* 158:32–33, September 1970.

"The Unknown Good: Educational Vouchers." *Phi Delta Kappan,* 52:52–53, September 1970.

Voegel, G. H. "Accountability and Performance Contracting Implications for the Supportive Staff." *AV Instruction,* 16:16–18, May 1971.

————. "Suggested Schema for Faculty Commission Pay in Performance Contracting." *Educational Technology,* 11:57–59, January 1971.

Wiles, J. W. "Hidden Cost of Performance Contracting." *Educational Leadership,* 28:533ff, February 1971.